2/87

CONSERVATION OF TIDAL MARSHES

Conservation of Tidal Marshes

Franklin C. Daiber
University of Delaware

VNR VAN NOSTRAND REINHOLD COMPANY
———————————————————————— **New York**

Copyright © 1986 by **Van Nostrand Reinhold Company Inc.**
Library of Congress Catalog Card Number: 85-6084
ISBN: 0-442-24873-3

Manufactured in the United States of America.

Published by Van Nostrand Reinhold Company Inc.
115 Fifth Avenue
New York, New York 10003

Van Nostrand Reinhold Company Limited
Molly Millars Lane
Wokingham, Berkshire RG11 2PY, England

Van Nostrand Reinhold
480 Latrobe Street
Melbourne, Victoria 3000, Australia

Macmillan of Canada
Division of Gage Publishing Limited
164 Commander Boulevard
Agincourt, Ontario MIS 3C7, Canada

15 14 13 12 11 10 9 8 7 6 5 4 3 2 1

Library of Congress Cataloging in Publication Data
Daiber, Franklin C.
    Conservation of tidal marshes.
    Includes index.
    1. Wetlands conservation.   2. Marshes, Tide.   I. Title.
QH75.D34   1986   33.91′8   85-6084
ISBN 0-442-24873-3

Contents

Preface / *vii*
Acknowledgments / *ix*

1: **What Is a Tidal Marsh?** / 1

Natural Processes / 1
Human Involvement—Usage and Exploitation / 6

PART I
THE USES AND ABUSES OF TIDAL MARSHES   11

2: **Vegetation Management: Grazing, Fire, Weed Control, and Remote Sensing** / 14

Grazing / 14
Prescribed Burning / 36
Weed Control / 41
Remote Sensing / 47

3: **Water Management: Dikes, Impoundments, Ponds, and Ditches** / 56

Reclaimed Land and Impoundments / 56
Ditching and Ponding for Mosquito Control / 95
Canal Construction / 115

4: **Sewage Disposal and Waste Treatment** / 117

Effects on Vegetation / 118
Pore Water Content / 129

Heavy Metals / 129
Animal Populations / 132
Community Organization / 132
Limitations of Waste-Treatment Application / 133

5: **Dredge Material for Wetland Restoration / 140**

Criteria and Guidelines / 141
Methodology / 147
Results / 151
Synthesis / 176

6: **Insecticides / 178**

7: **Oil Pollution / 190**

Petroleum Hydrocarbon Interactions / 190
Effects of Petroleum Fractions, Season, Age of Oil, and
    Surfactants / 228
Synthesis / 232

**PART II
LEGAL CONCERNS AND MANAGEMENT**

8: **Legal Aspects / 238**

Public Trust Doctrine: Rights and Liabilities / 239
The Boundary Question / 252

9: **Management Concepts and the Future / 261**

Values and Priorities / 263
Management Concepts / 269
A Synthesis with Suggestions for the Future / 281

References / 286
Author Index / 327
Scientific Name Index / 334
Subject Index / 337

Preface

Tidal marshes have been used, manipulated, and exploited for centuries, usually for some economic gain. All too frequently such usages have been for a single purpose with little concern for, or even recognition of, the consequences. Because the marsh, by its nature, is in the intertidal zone, it has been perceived as commons land and part of the public trust— therefore land that anyone could derive benefit from and exploit for a particular purpose. Fortunately, this attitude has begun to change during the past two decades. We now recognize that we must examine the marsh from a holistic point of view, and that there are values other than economic associated with this ecosystem. The managers of our natural resources must strive to find the means to sustain the system as a whole in a viable form and, at the same time, provide the users with what they want from the tidal marsh in the form of economic and cultural benefits.

This book examines the various directions that use and exploitation of this tidal habitat have taken and describes management practices, including the shift from single-usage concerns to the holistic approach. It also points out that much of tidal marsh management is very experimental.

Acknowledgments

I am indebted to many people who over the years have contributed their experience and assistance to this book. While they have been generous with their knowledge, time, and patience, tendering many good suggestions and justifiable criticism, the responsibility for opinions expressed rests entirely with me.

Special thanks are due colleagues who took on the task of reviewing various portions of the manuscript: Drs. W. Meredith and W. Niering, chapter 1; Drs. V. Klemas, W. Meredith, W. Niering and D. Ranwell, chapter 2; Drs. A. Gray, W. Meredith, W. Niering and Mr. A. Smith, chapter 3; Drs. W. Meredith and W. Niering, chapters 4 and 5; Mr. R. Lake and Dr. W. Meredith, chapter 6; Dr. R. Hillman, chapter 7; Mrs. June MacArtor, Dr. W. Meredith, Mr. W. Moyer and Mr. A. Porro, chapter 8; Drs. R. Good, W. Meredith, W. Niering, and R. Reimold, chapter 9.

Thanks are also extended to all my students, who provided the impetus for getting involved in marsh studies over the years.

I am obliged to Dorothy Griffin and especially to Helen Davis for being so patient and gracious in typing the numerous drafts, and for guarding the portal against interruptions.

And finally I must thank my wife, Joanne. Her assistance was no passive encouragement from the sidelines. She became involved directly in the work, going with me on many trips to local and foreign marshes, taking notes, and participating in the interviews with scientists and managers. Not only did she read and edit the manuscript but many of the words and phrases are hers. Her patience and competence frequently rescued and enhanced my efforts and gave them new life.

FRANKLIN C. DAIBER

Chapter 1

What Is a Tidal Marsh?

A tidal marsh is a coastal intertidal terrain with a unique character, including distinctive vegetation, and a variety of functions. Tidal marshes are sometimes freshwater marshes, but they are more often brackish or saline. A salt marsh has been defined as an area of natural or seminatural halophytic grassland and dwarf brushwood on alluvial sediments bordering saline water bodies whose water level fluctuates either tidally or nontidally (Beeftink, 1977*a*). The presence of water is the great stabilizer, whereas salt is the great limiter (Allan, 1950). Tidal marshes are typically associated with the temperate regions of the world but also have a circumpolar arctic distribution. Although they can be found in the tropics, they are singularly located to the landward of mangrove stands (Chapman, 1977).

NATURAL PROCESSES

The tide, of course, is a dominating characteristic of a tidal marsh (Ranwell, 1972; Chapman, 1974, 1977). The configuration of the marsh is largely determined by the vertical range of the tide, which delineates tidal flooding depths and the vertical extent of vegetation; the form of the tidal cycle, which controls the frequency and duration of submergence and emergence; water quality through turbidity, which determines the amount of light available to submerged vegetation, and through salinity, to which plants are exposed; and the frequency and intensity of mechanical disturbance (Ranwell, 1972).

Tidal marshes are sites of sediment accretion where silts and other fine sediments accumulate in the shallow water of sheltered areas of bays, lagoons, and estuaries or behind sand bars (Steers, 1969, p. 516; Niering and Warren, 1980). The process of maturation is promoted if accretion proceeds slowly and gradually (Beeftink, 1977b).

Due to the differential deposition of sediments and the extent of freshwater injections, the tidal marsh can be characterized as a domain of gradients. After the initial stages of marsh formation, the landward edge of the marsh usually has a higher elevation than the seaward edge as a result of differential rates of deposition and removal over each tidal cycle and the accumulation of organic material. This gradient can also be a reflection of a Holocene transgression associated with a rise in mean sea level. Based on the cyclic nature of tidal inundation and exposure, Chapman (1960, 1974) differentiated between lower marshes and higher marshes, placing the line of demarcation at about mean high tide. The lower marsh normally undergoes more than 360 submergences per year; thus the maximum period of continuous exposure never exceeds 9 days and there are more than 1.2 daylight hours of submergence daily. In contrast, upper marshes have fewer than 360 submergences per year, their minimum period of continuous exposure exceeds 10 days, and they are submerged less than 1 hour daily during daylight. While Ranwell (1972) pointed out that Chapman's definitions are not inviolate rules, he did agree with the general thesis. Lower marshes are dominated by factors of submergence, while upper marshes are influenced by factors of emergence. Therefore, Ranwell (1972) characterized lower marshes from about mean high-water neaps to mean high water as *submergence marsh* and upper marshes from mean high water to about mean high-water springs as *emergence marsh*.

A salinity gradient is associated with the vertical transition from the submergence marsh to the emergence marsh. Submergence marshes rarely have salinities higher than those of the tidal waters that regularly and frequently bathe the marsh. The emergence marsh can develop much higher salinities in the soils than in the tidal water due to water evaporation during dry, exposed periods (Ranwell, 1972). This is borne out by Gray and Bunce (1972), who found a gradient in the high saltings (emergence marsh) from low sodium-high calcium with frequent inundation to high sodium-low calcium associated with infrequent submergence. Associated with this sodium-calcium gradient was an increase in nitrogen and organic content from low to higher regions in the intertidal zone. Gray and Bunce attributed these changes to an increase in soil maturity between the pioneer stage of marsh development and the higher intertidal sites. Such a soil-maturity gradient depicts a transition from the physically dominated low submergence marsh to the biologically dominated high emergence marsh.

Salinity not only displays a vertical gradient within a marsh but also depicts a horizontal assymetry in marshes typical of coastal plain estuaries. This is evident not only through the direct measurement of salinity (deWitt and Daiber, 1973, 1974) but in the horizontal distribution of marsh plants (Penfound and Hathaway, 1938; Miller and Egler, 1950; Stewart, 1962) and marsh animals (Dozier, 1947; Stewart, 1962; Miller and Maurer, 1973) in marshes with positive correlations between vertical rise and landward location.

Within a marsh, plant zonation is usually quite evident. Along the Atlantic coast of North America the pioneer plant is Saltmarsh cordgrass, *Spartina alterniflora*, which often appears in pure stands. Higher up the slope Saltmeadow hay, *Spartina patens* becomes dominant, while the upland edges are bordered by Marsh elder, *Iva frutescens* and Groundsell tree, *Baccharis halimifolia* (see Chapman, 1960, 1974). (For additional examples of tidal marsh plant zonation, see Ganong, 1903; Miller and Egler, 1950; Hanson, 1951; Nordhagen, 1954; Steindorsson, 1954; Johnson, 1967; Beeftink, 1977a, 1977b; Niering and Warren, 1980). One of the unique features of these tidal marshes is the circumpolar distribution of many of the plant species (Hulten, 1964, 1971).

The tidal marsh is the border between the land and the sea. Accordingly, two major features of the marine environment—the ebb and flow of tides and salinity—characterize the tidal marsh. On the other hand, the spermatophytes of the marsh had their origins on dry land. Teal (1962), in his examination of a Georgia marsh, characterized the fauna as having three major subdivisions: aquatic, terrestrial, and marsh species. The aquatic species have a center of distribution in the estuary. Some are restricted to the marsh low-water level, some are found only in the stream-side marsh, and others are capable of penetrating well into the marsh. The terrestrial species are invariably air-breathers; they live either on the marsh or at the landward edge and make excursions onto the marsh. As Nicol (1936) pointed out, among those terrestrial invertebrate forms (biting flies) living on the marsh, the adult form has made little adjustment for life on the marsh, while the larva must respond to rather severe osmotic and ionic stresses. The third major group, the marsh species, are unique to this habitat. Most of the invertebrate species are derived from marine ancestors with aquatic larvae. Examples include the salt marsh snail, *Melampus bidentatus* (Russell-Hunter, Apley, and Hunter, 1972); the ribbed mussel, *Geukensia demissa* (Lent, 1969); the Florida clam, *Cyrenoidea floridana* (Kat, 1978); and the fiddler crab *Uca* (Miller, 1961; Crane, 1975). Phleger (1970) considered 11 species of Foraminifera to be endemic to tidal marshes. Among the vertebrates associated with this habitat, the mummichog, *Fundulus heteroclitus* (Hardy, 1978); diamondback terrapin, *Malaclemys terrapin* (Carr, 1952); clapper rail, *Rallus longirostris* (Oney, 1954); willet, *Catoptrophorus semipalmatus* (Bent, 1929); sharp-tailed sparrow, *Ammospiza caudacuta* (Woolfenden, 1956); and seaside sparrow, *A. maritima* (Woolfenden, 1956; Post, 1974), are seldom found elsewhere. In addition, a number of species in the tidal marsh have wider distributions, such as the common oyster *Crassostrea virginica,* anchovy *Anchoa mitchilli,* Atlantic silverside *Menidia menidia,* snowy egret *Egretta thula,* and muskrat *Ondatra zibethica.* In short, the tidal marsh can be considered an ecotonal habitat bounded by two major habitats, displaying features and species characteristic of both yet having its own unique traits and species that will clearly differentiate it from any other habitat.

Among its various attributes, the tidal marsh has been identified as a place of high productivity, a nutrient source, and a sink, as well as a site for nutrient transformations. Odum (1961) was one of the first to call attention to the contribution tidal marshes make to estuarine and coastal productivity. He equated this productivity to that of the best agricultural lands even without any overt acts of fertilization. There has been an abundance of research dealing with marsh productivity and an evaluation of the contribution of such productivity to the estuarine environment (Odum and Smalley, 1959; Morgan, 1961; Teal, 1962; Odum and de la Cruz, 1967; Keefe, 1972; Nixon and Oviatt, 1973; Heinle and Flemer, 1976; Haines, 1976*a*, 1976*b*, 1978; Woodwell and Whitney, 1977; Hatcher, 1977). Morgan (1961) provided an early estimate of *Spartina* productivity during the course of a growing season; Keefe (1972), after a review of the literature, suggested that there might be latitudinal changes in such productivity. Odum and Smalley (1959) called attention to the differential contributions of marsh production to the herbivorous and detrital food chains. Teal (1962) and Nixon and Oviatt (1973) set up an energy flow sheet with a quantitative estimate of this energy flow to the adjoining estuarine system. Odum and de la Cruz (1967) and Day et al. (1973) stressed the significance of detritus generation in the marsh system. Haines (1976*a*, 1976*b*, 1978) argued that estuarine detritus was primarily derived from phytoplankton and upland sources rather than marsh vegetation. Research by Heinle and Flemer (1976), Hatcher (1977), Woodwell and Whitney (1977), and Roman (1981) called attention to the seasonal patterns evident in the flux of various chemical parameters as well as the seeming ambiguity in the direction of net flow of the various forms of such identified nutrients as carbon, nitrogen, and phosphorous. Much attention has been given to the exchanges and transformations that occur within the system that may influence productivity and nutrient exchange (Nixon et al., 1976; Mendelssohn, 1979; Gallagher et al., 1980; Smart and Barko, 1980). It is still not clear whether—and if so, how—the tidal marsh acts as a nutritive source and as a sink. The effects of storm tides and catastrophic floods must also be taken into account in discussions of productivity and nutrient exchange (Pickral and Odum, 1977; Roman, 1981).

The tidal marsh has been recognized as a spawning site and nursery area for fishes (Daiber, 1977; Taylor, Di Michele, and Leach, 1977; Kneib and Stiven, 1978). It is the residence and feeding grounds for the diamond-back terrapin, *Malaclemys terrapin* (Hurd, Smedes, and Dean, 1979). A variety of birds use the tidal marsh for nesting and feeding, while other species find the habitat desirable as a staging area during migrations (Marshall, 1948; Oney, 1954; Stewart, 1962; Kale, 1964; Bongiorno, 1970; Reed and Moisan, 1971; Cadwalladr et al., 1972; Greenhalgh, 1974; Burger, 1977). All these represent the terrestrial-freshwater component in Teal's (1962) characterization of the tidal marsh fauna.

One function of the tidal marsh has received little attention: that of storm buffer and mechanism for flood control. This function was pointed up by Gunter and Eleuterius (1971), Chabreck and Palmisano (1973), Niering (1978), and Reppert et al. (1979). The marshlands bordering the Gulf of Mexico received little impact from two hurricanes because water covered them early and provided protection from the later action of wind and water. Shrubs along the periphery of the marshes acted as baffles protecting trees and homes. Subsequent to the storms, *Spartina alterniflora* bloomed on schedule. One would expect that the dampening effect of the grass would be enhanced where the marshlands were wide in contrast to narrow fringing marshes. At flood time, water rises in a broad sheet flow through the vegetation and the excess water is released slowly, steadily, and evenly. The marsh at this time receives and filters nutrients and sediments; in essence, it acts as a very effective reservoir. Water evaporation is reduced by the thick vegetation, and where the substrate may be somewhat sandy, underground water reservoirs may be recharged (Odum, 1978). This latter activity can be a negative factor because salt-water may intrude.

The production of biting insects is one tidal marsh function that has received a great deal of attention. For pestiferous and public health reasons, there is a voluminous literature focusing on marsh mosquitoes and other biting flies. For a recent review of these bloodsucking and other forms of marine insects, see Cheng (1976). Over the years this particular marsh role has received more attention than any other. Correspondingly, the greatest amount of managerial strategies and manipulative efforts have been directed toward dealing with this production of insects in tidal marshes. The reader should start with Smith (1902, 1904, 1907). Hawkes

(1966) believed that attempts at mass control of these insects probably did more to upset ecological relationships than any other factors short of filling or removing the marsh.

HUMAN INVOLVEMENT— USAGE AND EXPLOITATION

Perhaps the most important function of a tidal marsh is to serve as an energy storage unit for the estuarine ecosystem. Energy can be accumulated in many components of the marsh, such as the fish community, the invertebrates, the organic sediments, or the marsh grass. Storage in plant tissues is especially important because such reserves serve as a buffer against irregular heavy stresses or periods of seasonal shortages. Storage serves as a hedge against fluctuations of abundance and scarcity (Kalber, 1959; Clark, 1974). According to Clark, the following ecologic principle can be applied to tidal marshes: A high capability for energy storage provides for optimum ecosystem function.

Natural ecosystems, including tidal marshes, are of great value to human society and should not be modified without very good reason (Provost, 1977; Darnell, 1978a; Niering, 1978a). Darnell identified four sets of natural values: (1) supportive values through regulation of the hydrological cycle, stabilization of biogeochemical cycles, and purification of the environment; (2) genetic value derived from the gene pool associated with natural diversity; (3) scientific value derived from interpreting and understanding a natural system; and (4) recreational and inspirational values that enrich human life. Odum (1979) established a hierarchical approach to categorizing wetland values and suggested possible methods to quantify such values. Darnell (1978a) went on to say that almost every major activity of human society can be expected to have some impact on wetlands. Through terrestrial modifications there is accelerated natural runoff, reduction of groundwater levels, increased sediment loads, addition of chemical agents, and alteration of thermal regimes. Human intrusion into the aquatic environment has a number of impacts on wetlands: through various kinds of construction activity, lowland filling, drainage, water-table reduction, and construction of dikes or levees.

Darnell (1978a) contended that we are eliminating the diversity of our natural heritage by such rapid environmental modification and habitat homogenization. He also maintained that environmental impacts come in groups. One thing leads to another, producing widening chains of primary, secondary, and tertiary effects. These groups of related impacts tend to follow certain patterns.

Human involvement with tidal marshes can range from visual appreciation of undisturbed marshland to total destruction of the marsh under a garbage dump. Reppert et al. (1979) recognized such involvement as cultural values incorporating socioeconomic and other socially perceived considerations. Beeftink (1977*b*) identified seven types of pressures on tidal marshes resulting from human involvement: agriculture; open cast mining; land reclamation and improvement for agricultural purposes; pollution; recreation; industrial and urban sites; and scientific and field studies. Hawkes (1966) expressed the view that, except for recreation, most human uses of the marsh have involved short-term goals that were obtained at the expense of the longer-run values of the natural marsh. Beeftink (1977*b*) even had some reservations about recreation in European marshes. In the mud-silt salt marshes inshore, fishing and waterfowl shooting would, in his view, have little impact. On the other hand, sandy salt marshes are subjected to a greater impact through camping, trampling, horseback riding, picnics, litter accumulation, and fire. Such activities could disturb waterfowl and lead to erosion by damaging the vegetation.

Pough (1961) has emphasized the muted beauty of tidal marshes and Darnell (1978*a*) has commented on their inspirational value. There are many who seek out the coastal road, pausing at the bridge as it crosses a tidal creek or seeking a vantage point to look out over a tidal marsh. The soft greens of renewed spring growth or the greens and yellows of late summer with splotches of color scattered along the upland borders is a visual treat. Who cannot be stirred by the clattering alarm of the willet as it wheels above the marsh or the pumping notes of the clapper rail during early summer. One is confronted with an ever changing pallet of yellows, golds, and rust hues as one watches a flight of ducks or geese moving above the grasses before a brisk breeze on a clear fall day. A coastal fog has its own innate beauty as it creeps over the still leaves of the marsh grasses. A winter storm lashing the frayed and tattered remains of the brown grasses entrapped in snow and ice has its own harsh attraction. Nothing is taken from the marsh but much can be gained through this uplift to the human psyche. It is unfortunate, however that many people continue to view marshes as desolate wastelands with monotonous vegetation and topography, repugnant smells, too much mud, and too many bugs.

An original use of salt marshes was for animal husbandry, providing pasture and hay for livestock. Acadians, the first French settlers in North America, took advantage of the wild marsh grasses when they first stepped ashore in what is now Nova Scotia (Clark, 1968; Harvey, 1973). Over the centuries they learned to further exploit these lands, manipulating them for livestock, grain, and vegetable production (Wright, 1907; Warren, 1911). While these tidal marshes were the first lands to be used by the French Acadians, they were also the first to be abandoned for upland tracts (Harvey, 1973; Hocking, 1978).

Tidal marshes have provided a source of income other than from agriculture. Muskrats (Dozier, 1953; Errington, 1963) and nutrias (Evans, 1970), turtles, oysters, blue crabs, eels, and other fin fish have provided income to trappers and watermen over the years. These activities have no obvious deleterious impact on the tidal marshes.

At one time the shoreline of Cape Cod Bay, particularly in the area of Dennis, Massachusetts, was devoted to the manufacture of crude sea salt. It is not known to what extent the tidal marshes may have been so involved. Approximately 95% of the marshes of the San Francisco Bay estuary, California, have been leveed or filled. A portion of these leveed marshes have been transformed into salt-evaporation ponds (Atwater et al., 1979). As in the case of the diked Acadian marshes, as long as the levees or dikes and the water-control structures remain intact, these formal tidal marshes have been obliterated and changed to another landform. Marshes have been impacted indirectly and subtly by such manmade changes as causeway construction, which alters normal tidal flushing. The installation of tidal gates across valley marshes to prevent the flooding of residential areas reduces salinity, which, in turn, encourages the common reed, *Phragmites australis* (= *communis*) (Niering and Warren, 1980).

Tidal marshes are also destroyed to provide a source of income when the overlying marsh sediments are removed to gain access to the underlying sand and gravel (Sanders and Ellis, 1961; Ketchum, 1972). Beeftink (1977b) identified another drastic form of mining that is not directly related to income: the removal of clay materials in the low countries of Western Europe to rebuild storm-damaged sea walls. Any excavations such as these have a disastrous effect on the natural geomorphology and vegetation since they leave the sites in complete disarray. A more mild form of mining is turf cutting in England and the Low Countries (Gray, 1970; Beeftink, 1977b). The turf is removed in such a way to encourage regeneration. The effects of such harvesting on the marsh are unclear (Beeftink, 1977b), but it is recognized in England that this slight reduction in marsh elevation encourages another species of grass (*Puccinellia*) to take over the site, replacing the more desirable *Festuca* (Gray, personal communication).

Various construction activities may have profound effects on wetlands. Darnell et al. (1976) have estimated that one-third of the United States' wetlands have been lost through various forms of direct habitat destruction, and well over half of the remainder have been severely modified. They have determined that many aquatic species have been lost or greatly restricted, and other species and habitats are endangered, at least partly because of construction activities.

The primary categories of environmental impacts of construction activities in wetlands include habitat modification and loss; increase in suspended sediments; bottom sedimentation; and modification of water-flow regimes. By modification and loss of habitat through construction, the wetlands are subject to subsidence, reduction of the water table, and salt-water intrusion as well as the physical modification, reduction, and loss of habitat (Darnell, 1978a). Darnell considered sedimentation to be one of the worst impacts we can impose on our aquatic systems through physical and biological impairment of the habitat. Water-flow regimes can be modified by reduced flow, reduced peak loads, reduced flood plain flooding, and modification of seasonal flow patterns.

Darnell (1978b) has categorized the environmental consequences of construction activity into three dimensions. The first dimension is geographic since such impacts occur in specific areas, and the environmental values tend to be clustered in local, site-specific locations. The second dimension is temporal, involving rate, intensity, and duration of impact. All natural systems have the ability to absorb some level of impact, so if it is of low intensity and of short duration, the system will not break down until this threshold is crossed. Darnell believed that a knowledge of this critical level was imperative in minimizing environmental impacts. The time component also determines loss of genetic material through extinction. The third dimension is value. Ecologic values must be identified: what should be protected, and at what level? In the past economics was favored over ecology. While there has been increasing recognition of natural values in the political and legal arenas, there is still much to be done to establish clear, systematic, and quantitative ways of assessing environmental values, prioritizing them, and equating them to economic values. Darnell (1978b) continued by saying that the environmental impacts from construction activities may be minimized by establishing national priorities; passing of appropriate legislation; adopting and implementing managerial guidelines; evaluating preconstruction alternatives, on-site activities, and post construction recovery; and applying the judicial process in the interpretation of environmental policy.

According to Darnell (1979), the values we place on environmental parameters depend on our background, our environmental experience and knowledge, our recognition of alternate environmental uses, and the abundance or scarcity of an environment. Bernstein (1981), in his discussion on values, concluded that "ecological and economic systems are strikingly similar and are connected by important functional links. In spite of this, large-scale economic systems seen invariably to cause environmental degradation and foster behavior that is maladaptive in the long run." Further, "smaller scaled human systems often, but not always, display adaptations to the local environment that foster resilience and long-term persistence."

Tidal marshes have long been used as disposal sites for dredging material, trash, garbage, and sewage. This is the ultimate degradation: the marsh is obliterated forever. Attempts to revitalize such garbage dumps have had varied success. The underlying marsh has been subjected to considerable compaction from overlying refuse. Buildings may rise on dredge material, but the additional weight creates settling problems. Other types of refuse will eventually break down making the stability of the site uncertain.

Odum (1978) has suggested that natural wetlands can develop a modified association of organisms that can process waste materials of human development. Such an interface system, through biological and chemical activity, could break down organic wastes and return these products to their natural form in the ecosystem. He has cautioned, however, against overburdening the system with excessive or highly toxic waste loads. As Darnell (1978b) has pointed out, the receiving capacity of an environmental system cannot be exceeded without penalty.

In short, a tidal marsh is many things. It is a site for a variety of natural environmental processes and has natural values. From the human point of view, it has a number of attributes that, because of the singleness of our intents, fall into conflict. Because the use of these attributes creates some level of disruption, over even obliteration, resource strategies must be developed that permit the natural marsh values to function. As Niering (1978a) has stated so well, wetlands represent a natural heritage that has been unduly exploited without any realization of its highest and best uses for society as a whole. This heritage will be best perpetuated if education, research, recreation, preservation, and sound ecological management are woven together to provide a holistic view of this limited land resource. Many will agree with Niering (1978a) that a national wetlands policy as part of a sound land use plan is long overdue. Niering first advocated this approach in 1970, and Ketchum (1972) later reaffirmed it. Two symposia, on wetlands protection (Montanari and Kusler, 1978) and wetland functions and values (Greeson, Clark, and Clark, 1979), have addressed this need.

The opinions of many may be summed up by the thoughtful perceptions of Friedman and DeWitt (1979). The presence of tidal marshes influences human actions and values, including settlement patterns, transportation, and the definition of worth. On one hand, the awareness of the natural attributes of a marsh may foster concern for its preservation. Conversely, human objection to biting flies may foster the complete obliteration of some tidal wetlands. The natural productivity of a wetland can influence agricultural practices of local farmers, which in turn can affect the economic status of the local community. These perceptions, attitudes, and values become crucial in determining what the community will do. If these result in a decision to modify a tidal marsh, the outcome, which may take only a very few years to accomplish, may initiate a process that could take centuries to bring back under control.

PART I

The Uses and Abuses of Tidal Marshes

Tidal marshes have been manipulated for a variety of purposes for many centuries. Recently Beeftink (1977*b*) analyzed seven pressures induced by human activities:

1. *Animal husbandry*: The most common use, at least in Europe, is for grazing, primarily by sheep but also cattle, and even geese, in northwestern Germany. Grazing involves not only selective cutting and removal of plants but also associated manuring and trampling. With the exception of acquisition of food for human consumption, grazing is the oldest form of marsh use. Damage to the marsh depends on the size of the flock or herd.
2. *Strip or open cast mining*. Turf cutting is a low-impact form of strip mining for the creation of new lawns or the reinforcement of the face of sea walls. Clay or gravel mining is a very drastic process that disrupts the whole habitat for many years, if not permanently.
3. *Land reclamation and improvement for agriculture*. Dikes and embankments have been constructed for centuries. Sedimentation fields on the seaward edge trap silts and clays, which can be planted with *Spartina* to augment the reclamation process further. Drainage behind the dikes lowers the water table and changes the habitat. Tidal exclusion and drainage have very serious impacts on the marsh, which culminate in drying and leaching.

4. *Pollution.* Salt marshes, particularly in industrial estuaries, are being subjected to the influences of manmade detritus, litter, and chemical substances derived from agricultural wastes, fertilizer outwash, urban sewage, and industrial effluents.
5. *Recreation.* Inshore fishing, waterfowl shooting, bird watching, and photography in the mud-silt marshes have little effect. Trampling, litter accumulation, and so forth can have greater impacts where the substrate is firm enough to enable a greater human penetration of the salt marsh.
6. *Establishment of industrial and urban sites.* Salt making and oyster culture are the oldest industrial uses of a salt marsh; both destroy the habitat of the middle and upper marsh. The establishment of modern industrial-urban sites not only destroys the salt marsh but also disturbs the adjoining habitats.
7. *Scientific and field studies.* The fragility of the marsh vegetation cannot easily survive trampling by classes of students or manipulation by investigators.

Several more pressures or objectives can be added to Beeftink's (1977*b*) list:

8. *Insect control.* There have been long-standing attempts at biting fly control in the United States. Initial manipulations took the form of ditching for drainage. Subsequent attempts include the use of pesticides, various forms of impoundments, and a procedure known as open marsh water management (OMWM).
9. *Wildlife management.* Large tracts of marshland are manipulated to attract waterfowl. At first this objective was in direct conflict with insect-control activities in the United States. Subsequent interests have been directed at finding compatible means of achieving both objectives.
10. *Waste disposal.* A number of attempts have been made to take advantage of the energetics and transport mechanisms of the marsh to process sewage effluents to the advantage of the estuarine-coastal ecosystem and at the same time attenuate the massive problem of human waste disposal.
11. *Marsh rehabilitation.* The irrevocable loss of so many acres of tidal marsh habitat has prompted speculation about possibilities of rebuilding them. It might be possible to solve the ever-present problem of dredge spoil disposal by using this material to recreate our usurped marshes.

The use of the word *management* in the context of tidal marshes will be restricted to manipulations that produce a perceived positive ecological, cultural, or economic return from the continued existence of the marsh site as a recognizable wetland. Precluded from consideration will be the irreversible destruction of the site due to construction of industrial or commercial enterprises. Thus, obliterative enterprises such as filling for industrial sites or residential projects, creation of intensive aquaculture facilities, clay or gravel mining, or use of marsh sites as trash or garbage dumps will not be reviewed. A key component in many nonobliterative manipulations of natural marsh or impaired marsh systems is water management, which can range from the mere recognition of low and high (Chapman, 1974) or submerged and emergent (Ranwell, 1972) marshes to the sophisticated manipulation of water levels inside an impoundment over the course of a growing season. Drainage is water management used in land reclamation, insect control, and wildlife furtherance. Embankments are water-management structures that exclude water from reclaimed areas destined for agricultural exploitation, or that retain water for waterfowl encouragement. The hydraulics of the ebb and flow of the tide are an important consideration in the transport and retention of nutrients when the marsh is contemplated as a sewage treatment plant.

Chapter 2

Vegetation Management: Grazing, Fire, Weed Control, and Remote Sensing

GRAZING

Marsh Usage

Undoubtedly the first use of the tidal marsh was to provide food for human consumption. This is suggested by the identification and preparational procedures for various marsh plants described by Gibbons (1962) and MacLeod and MacDonald (1976). We know that man also sought animal food from the marsh in the form of fish, shellfish, and waterfowl.

The second use to which man put the tidal marsh was as a grazing site for domestic animals, primarily sheep and cattle. At first the marshes were used only in summer and the farmers and fishermen retired to higher ground in the winter. Later they constructed settlement mounds large enough for a family dwelling, a refuge for livestock during times of flood, or to protect a freshwater source from seawater pollution (Beeftink, 1975). Marshes were widely used for pasturage for many centuries throughout Western Europe (Gray, 1972; Larsson, 1976), but this use has decreased since World War II (Dalby, 1970; Møller, 1975; Larsson, 1976). When the Acadians first settled Nova Scotia, they used the salt marshes to provide pasture and hay for their livestock just as they had done in their homeland in northwestern France (Reed and Moisan, 1971; Harvey, 1973). The same use existed farther south along the Atlantic and Gulf coasts of the United States (Williams, 1955; Chabreck, 1968).

Table 2-1. The nutritive value of grasses found on Fenning Island, Bridgewater Bay, England (collected in November 1971)

	Puccinellia	*Agrostis*	*Festuca*
Crude protein	17.6	15.5	11.8
Oil (petrol extract)	3.6	3.2	3.0
Fiber	16.2	16.7	21.0
Crude carbohydrate	53.0	56.6	55.8
Ash	9.6	8.0	8.4
Value index[a]	57.6	52.5	31.4

Source: From Owen, M., 1973*b*, The winter feeding ecology of wigeon at Bridgwater Bay, Somerset, *Ibis* 115(2), 227-243, by permission.

Note: All results are percentages of dry matter after drying at 105° C.

[a]Approximate index of the nutritional value calculated as (% protein × % carbohydrate)/% fiber.

Desirable Species

In Iceland, where fertile lands are at a premium, the tidal marsh, or *flaedimyri,* is particularly valuable, growing as a self-sown field. Its fertility apparently has been unaffected by centuries of harvesting and, as long as the flaedimyri is flooded periodically, it will produce hay when other sites fail. Steindorsson (1975, p. 131) identified the flaedimyri as being exclusively associated "in watery tracts, especially near estuaries where rivers flow into fiords and fill them up with deposits." It may, however, appear wherever the river current loses strength to such an extent that sand and clay are deposited. *Puccinellia maritima* and *P. phryganodes* are the common marsh grass species in the vegetated lower intertidal zone of these Icelandic marshes. At higher intertidal elevations, *Carex Lyngbyei* is dominant, with *Calamagrostis neglecta* as a common accompanying species (Steindorsson, 1975).

Puccinellia maritima is the preferred pasture plant in the lower intertidal zone of European salt marshes for both sheep and cattle as well as water fowl (Table 2-1) (Ranwell, 1961; Cadwalladr and Morley, 1973; Owen, 1973*b*; Gray and Scott, 1977). *Spartina anglica (Spartina townsendii [Sensu lato])* has invaded marshes bordering the North Sea in England, Denmark, and the Netherlands at the expense of the lower zones of the *P. maritima* marsh. This is especially true where accretion rates are high (Ranwell, 1961, 1967; Beeftink, 1977*a*, 1977*b*). Gray and Pearson (unpublished manuscript to appear in a Nature Conservancy publication, made available by A. J. Gray in 1983) describe the continuing decline of *S. anglica* in Poole Harbour, in Dorset in southern England. This decline followed the peak of expansion in the 1920s and has been at the rate of 2 hectares per year, declining slowly to 1.7 hectares per year during the last decade. Higher in the intertidal zone, *Puccinellia* or *Spartina* is replaced by salt-tolerant forms of *Festuca rubra* and *Agrostis stolonifera* in grazed marshes. *Puccinellia* is confined to the intertidal salt marshes and is a poor competitor when grown in nonsaline conditions. *Festuca* and *Agrostis* are widely distributed in nonsaline situations. The three grasses can coexist because of different responses to factors associated with salinity and waterlogging. On the high marsh *Puccinellia* does best in the hollows, *Festuca* on the humps, and *Agrostis* on the edges of the humps. There is a minor reversal of this zonation at the extreme upper limits of *Puccinellia* as residual salt concentrates in the drier tops of the hummocks (D. S. Ranwell, oral communic.). *Puccinellia* is more competitive under conditions of higher salinity and high-water-table conditions while *Agrostis* does better in a less saline situation. (Gray and Scott, 1977).

Dominance of these grasses is maintained by intensive sheep grazing. Typical dicotyledenous plants of the English salt marsh such as *Halimione portulacoides, Limonium vulgare, L. humile, Suaeda maritima, Aster tripolium, Atriplex hastata,* and *Cochlearia officinalis* become dominant in ungrazed marshes or inaccessible sites in grazed areas (Gray and Scott, 1977). Møller (1975) found the grasses *Holcus lanatus, Agrostis stolonifera,* and *Lolium perenne* dominating an intensively grazed Danish marsh. Ponds and creeks were overgrown with *Batrachium fluitans* and *Scirpus maritimus,* the latter being grazed down by the cattle. The infrequently flooded higher portions of salt marshes that had not been grazed for years were dominated by the grasses *Deschampsia caespitosa, Anthoxantum odoratum,* and *Holcus lanatus. Phragmites australis* had overgrown the creeks. A mixture of low shrub (*Salix repens* and *Vaccinium uliginosum*), *Nardus* heath, and *Carex nigra* depressions had developed as the next successional stage.

The most desirable pasture vegetation found in the salt marshes along the Atlantic and Gulf coasts of North America include *Spartina patens, S. cynosuroides, S. alterniflora, Sporobolus virginicus,* and *Distichlis spicata. Paspalum vaginatum* and *P. lividum* are grazed, but their presence is usually the first evidence of overgrazing (Williams, 1955). *Scirpus olneyi, S. robustus,* and *S. americanus* are grazed by cattle to some extent, but their greatest value is for muskrats (*Ondatra zibethica*) and geese (Stearns, MacCreary and Daigh, 1940; Stearns and Goodwin, 1941; Lynch, O'Neil, and Lay, 1947). Snow geese (*Chen caerulescens*) consume large quantities of *Spartina alterniflora* (Ferrigno, 1958, 1976).

Growth Form

Beeftink (1977*b*) has compiled a list of grazing pressures from the literature (Table 2-2). The intensity of the grazing pressure by domesticated or wild mammals and waterfowl can have a variety of impacts on the marsh vegetation and various animal species. For example, intensive

Table 2-2. Recommended grazing pressures (animals per hectare) in salt marshes

References	Domestic Animals	Salt Marsh	Brackish Marsh	Beach Plains
Williams (1955) (Eastern America)	Cattle	0.62-1.25		
Gray (1972) (Morecombe Bay)	Sheep	Ave. 4.5, max. 6.5		
Ranwell (1972) (European saltings)	Sheep	5.0-7.5		
Beeftink and Duane (S.W. Netherlands)	Sheep	2	3	0.5-1.0
	Cattle	0.33	0.5	0.25

Source: From Beeftink, W. C., 1977b, Salt-marshes, in *The Coastline*, R. S. K. Barnes, ed., John Wiley & Sons, New York, pp. 93-121, by permission.

grazing can alter growth form and seed production. In the Dovey, England, salt marshes where horses and sheep were pastured, Yapp (1923) speculated that clipping the flower heads by grazing would enhance the rapid spread of *Spartina anglica* by rhizomes. Ranwell (1961) also noted that grazing favored tillering of *Spartina,* which in turn impeded the establishment of the annual *Atriplex hastata* on the strandline. The spread of *Spartina* temporarily reduced the number of bare spots in which *Atriplex* seedlings could become established. However, subsequent beach wrack formed by *Spartina* debris at the strandline would, in turn, smother out established *Spartina* plants producing bare spots, which *Atriplex* and other species could colonize. Ranwell attributed the year-to-year variability in the amount of *Spartina* and *Atriplex* to the extent of this smothering effect (Table 2-3).

Some inferences can be drawn from Table 2-3, which shows Ranwell's comparisons between grazed plots and ungrazed plots using point quadrant sampling. There was a greater range (0-228) but a lower average number (83.4) of hits/plot/year on mature *Spartina* plants in ungrazed plots than in the grazed plots ($\bar{x}$ = 158.4; range, 64-267). This would suggest that there were taller plants with more stem and leaf material in ungrazed plots at the end of the growing season to form more beach wrack, which in turn would be responsible for the lack of mature plants during some years. At the same time there were more *Atriplex* plants (80.1 hits/plot/year) and a greater range (3-276) in ungrazed plots than in the grazed plots ($\bar{x}$ = 23.2; range, 0-70). Thus grazing would stimulate tillering (shoot growth from base of stem), which would provide less material for beach wrack and create few bare spots for annual seedlings to become established.

Spartina anglica does well in the muddy situations of rapid accretion. Where grazing occurs near the landward limit of *Spartina,* it gives way to *Puccinellia maritima. Puccinellia* is spread by grazing sheep, which tread

(*Text continues on page 22.*)

Table 2-3. Presence data for four sheep-grazed *Spartina* plots contrasted with four ungrazed controls, 300 points per plot per annum, June 1955–1959 in an English marsh

| | Ungrazed Plots | | | | | | | | | |
| | *1* | | | | | *4* | | | | |
Species	*1955*	*1956*	*1957*	*1958*	*1959*	*1955*	*1956*	*1957*	*1958*	*1959*
Spartina (mature plants)	95	129	128	105	178	77	49		1	137
Spartina (seedlings)	54	26	4	120	57	66	9		71	49
Atriplex hastata	13	183	62	119	22	32	276	86	62	30
Puccinellia maritima			1	3	11	2			11	19
Phragmites australis					5			6	63	
Scirpus maritimus										3
Aster tripolium								1	4	2
Glaux maritima								8	5	3
Salicornia stricta			2	19				1		
Spergularia marginata								2		
Suaeda maritima				7			1		6	4
Bare ground or drift	160	60	129	77	86	149	21	207	160	71

18

Grazed Plots

	2					3				
	1955	1956	1957	1958	1959	1955	1956	1957	1958	1959
Spartina (mature plants)	73	131	258	130	255	64	85	226	81	267
Spartina (seedlings)	63	9	4	74	38	67	9	4	66	67
Atriplex hastata	10	70	29	50	7	8	63	36	26	2
Puccinellia maritima		1	1	1	18		9		1	45
Phragmites australis										
Scirpus maritimus										
Aster tripolium								8		
Glaux maritima										
Salicornia stricta			1	5					2	
Spergularia marginata										
Suaeda maritima				6	1				3	
Bare ground or drift	184	124	39	112	26	187	170	64	153	20

Source: From Ranwell, D. S., 1961, Spartina salt marshes in southern England. I. The effects of sheep grazing at the upper limits of Spartina marsh in Bridgwater Bay, J. Ecol. 49(2):325-340, by permission.

Table 2-3. Continued

Species	Ungrazed Plots 5 1955	5 1956	5 1957	5 1958	5 1959	8 1955	8 1956	8 1957	8 1958	8 1959	Hits/Plot/Yr.
Spartina (mature plants)	109	101			14	71	91	228	51	104	83.4 0–228
Spartina (seedlings)	32	12		44	34	63	30	1	38		35.5 0–120
Atriplex hastata	9	199	82	101	66	3	141	58	53	5	80.1 3–276
Puccinellia maritima	7				22	13	12				5.0 0–19
Phragmites australis		10	68	54	186						
Scirpus maritimus	8	12	75	91	83		17	47	1	28	
Aster tripolium	5				4		4				
Glaux maritima		7	8	2	1		13	12	4		
Salicornia stricta			3	2				2	2		
Spergularia marginata			1	1							
Suaeda maritima			1	11	4			3			
Bare ground or drift	162	52	107	97	24	166	88	34	193	168	

Grazed Plots

Species	6					7						
	1955	1956	1957	1958	1959	1955	1956	1957	1958	1959		
Spartina (mature plants)	93	108	250	129	252	68	113	241	152	192	158.4	64–267
Spartina (seedlings)	44	8	3	12	2	58	7	2	36	4	28.8	2–74
Atriplex hastata		31	43	6	1		19	49	13	2	23.2	0–70
Puccinellia maritima	5	36	35	21	78	13	35	46	6	50	20.0	0–78
Phragmites australis					6							
Scirpus maritimus										3		
Aster tripolium												
Glaux maritima								1				
Salicornia stricta				2			4	2				
Spergularia marginata								2				
Suaeda maritima				1		1		2				
Bare ground or drift	174	139	33	146	28	173	138	33	122	93		

Source: From Ranwell, D. S., 1961, Spartina salt marshes in southern England. I. The effects of sheep grazing at the upper limits of Spartina marsh in Bridgwater Bay, J. Ecol. 49(2):325–340, by permission.

in bitten-off fragments. Ranwell (1961) estimated that the transition from *Spartina* to *Puccinellia* marsh would take about 10 years to complete at the upper limits of a *Spartina* marsh in the Bristol Channel area. In ungrazed areas, *Phragmites australis* and *Scirpus maritimus* are favored; Ranwell estimated that the transition from *Spartina* to these tall marsh species would take about 8 years at the upper limits of this relatively low-salinity *Spartina* marsh.

Mowing has broadly similar effects as grazing. The rank growth associated with ungrazed areas is eliminated; flowering and seed production is greatly reduced while vegetative reproduction by tillering is enhanced (Cadwalladr et al., 1972; Cadwalladr and Morley, 1973, 1974). In the absence of intensive grazing or close mowing, *Festuca rubra* will take on a rank tussocky form, which grazing sheep avoid. This in turn enables *Festuca* to replace *Puccinellia maritima* and *Agrostis stolonifera*, both of which are preferred by sheep; Eurasian wigeon, *Anas penelope;* and white-fronted geese, *Anser albifrons* (Cadwalladr and Morley, 1973; Owen, 1975). Close mowing of the tussocky *Festuca* increases its palatability to a degree comparable with turf made up of *Puccinellia* and *Agrostis*.

Just as grazing enhances vegetative reproduction of some species by tillering, so the nibbling of the normal terminal inflorescence of other species stimulates the production of several lateral, short flowering stalks. Gillham (1955) demonstrated this effect by depicting comparative illustrations of specimens of grazed and ungrazed *Plantago maritima* and *F. rubra*. The typical growth form on intensively grazed sites was a dwarf prostrate rosette with more numerous inflorescences borne on very short peduncles. Gillham considered the prostrate form to have a selective advantage: it increases the rate of seed production and is more difficult to graze.

Gray, Parsell, and Scott (1979) have provided us with an interesting sequel on the effects of grazing on the growth form of salt marsh vegetation. In keeping with earlier work (Gray and Scott, 1975), they found significant differences between *Puccinellia maritima* plants taken from grazed and ungrazed marshes. The pioneer populations of both marshes contained a range of vegetation biotypes. The mature stage within the grazed marsh contained mainly small, prostrate, short-leaved plants with short flowering tillers and lower above-ground dry weights. The mature stage of the ungrazed marsh mainly comprised large, erect, long-leaved plants with long flowering tillers and substantial dry weights. These data supported the hypothesis that, as the marsh develops, grazing favors the selection of small, prostrate, short-leaved plants that divert a lesser amount of their resources to flowering, whereas in the absence of grazing, selection is for tall, erect, long-leaved plants with a larger proportion of flowering tillers.

Gray, Parsell, and Scott (1979) went further. Having obtained 400 tillers from grids set up in pioneer and mature sites of grazed and ungrazed *Puccinellia* marshes, grown them in culture solution, and examined extracts from the root tips using electrophoretic techniques, they tentatively identified various allelic patterns. The result was the establishment of differing clone structures on the two marshes. While the grids on both marshes contained three or four large clones of comparable size, in the grazed grids the spaces between the large clones were occupied by a small number of medium-sized clones. In the grids from the ungrazed marsh, the spaces between the large clones were occupied by many small clones. It was suggested such a contrast in clone structure could be explained if the space between colonists on grazed marshes is filled by the vegetative spread of the colonists while in an ungrazed marsh the spaces are filled more often by seedlings. As the marsh develops, grazing would be expected to reduce the number of seeds produced since the flower heads are nipped off, resulting in the differential survival of genotypes that direct resources to vegetative reproduction. Such rapid tillering would further reduce the space available for seedling attachment. In contrast, more spaces may appear in an ungrazed marsh, where taller plants will topple over after death. Seed production may be favored in such situations. In this way, Gray, Parsell, and Scott accounted for the differences observed between grazed and ungrazed *Puccinellia maritima* marshes brought on by differences in reproductive strategy. Such differences are induced by contrasts in selection that, because they determine the degree of genetic recombination, are self-reinforcing.

Number of Plant Species

Grazing helps determine which species are present in a marsh, for grazing animals are selective in what they eat. (Gillham, 1955; Ranwell and Downing, 1959; Ranwell, 1961; Gray, 1972; Cadwalladr and Morley, 1973; Owen, 1973a). Gillham (1955) described the selective effect of grazing on the plant species growing on the Pembrokeshire Islands off the southwest coast of Wales. While rabbits had the greatest impact, other animals did not necessarily avoid a plant avoided by rabbits. Plants were placed in three groups according to their ability to withstand heavy rabbit grazing: "rabbit-avoided" species, which are seldom eaten and which grow as well in grazed as in ungrazed areas; "rabbit-resistant" species, which are favored as food but whose survival is ensured by the resistant growth habit; and palatable species, which are favored as food and which do not undergo morphological adaptation to withstand grazing. Rabbits avoid plants such as *Arctium minus, Rubus ulmifolius, Holcus lanatus, Arum maculatum,* and *Senecio jacobaea* because of their woody tissue, spines and capacity to sting, dense felt of hairs, acrid sap, or toxicity. The majority of "rabbit-resistant" species are hemicryptophytes, which are perpetuated by the production of new shoots at or below ground level, where they are free from attack. The group includes both herbs and grasses; the growth of the latter is also facilitated by the basal position of the leaf meristem. In fact, grazing the leaf apices stimulates growth rather than curtails it. *Agrostis stolonifera* and *Festuca rubra* are widespread resistant grasses, while *Ranunculus repens* and *Trifolium repens* are examples of resistant herbaceous plants. Tallness, delicacy of texture, and a high moisture content characterize the nonresistant palatable species. Such succulent species include *Plantago maritima, Halimione portulacoides,* and the nonmarsh plant *Beta vulgaris maritima.* Such plants can survive as an important element in a marsh community only when grazing, particularly by rabbits, is slight or absent (Gillham, 1955).

Ranwell (1961) recorded 13 plant species in an ungrazed *Spartina* marsh plot on the Somerset coast; 2 of those (*Carex otrubae* and *Triglochin maritima*) were found only in such ungrazed plots. Of 12 species identified for the grazed plots, *Hordeum secalinum* was the only one found exclusively in the grazed plots. The restriction of *Limonium vulgare, L. humile, Halimione portulacoides, Suaeda maritima,* and, to some extent, *Aster tripolium* to ungrazed areas suggested to Gray (1972) that grazing eliminates these dicotylendonous species. These same species were observed by the author in the Norfolk marshes at Stiffkey and Wells-by-the-Sea in 1976 and 1980, respectively. Livestock had not been turned out on these marshes since World War II.

The removal of the *Spartina alterniflora* cover by clipping (simulated grazing) caused a significant decrease in both species diversity and the numbers of benthic diatoms in Canary Creek Marsh, Delaware (Sullivan, 1976). Shanholtzer (1974) and Reimold, Linthurst, and Wolf (1975), while working in Georgia marshes, noted *Distichlis spicata* on a grazed marsh and a formerly grazed site but none on an ungrazed area. Yet *D. spicata* is common in Delaware marshes that have not been grazed for at least 30 years. In another situation in Georgia, Reimold, Hardisky, and Adams (1978a) suggested that *D. spicata* did poorly where taller growing plants became established, presumably due to the shading effect. Chapman (1937) noted that mown tracts of *Spartina patens* in the Fundy marshes near Wolfville, Nova Scotia, were repopulated by a secondary association dominated by *Puccinellia maritima. S. patens* survived only in wetter areas where mowing could not take place. Since these marshes are no longer mown, *S. patens* has recovered its dominance.

Gillham (1955) noted an interesting relationship between grazing and wind exposure and the numbers of species and relative abundance of grasses on the Pembrokeshire Islands. Skokholm is heavily grazed and Grassholm Island is not grazed at all. Nearby Middleholm is grazed, but by a smaller population of rabbits and sheep. The number of species in the *Festuca rubra* community on these three islands portray the impact of grazing. The number ranged from 46 on Skokholm through 33 on Middleholm to 8 on Grassholm. The percentage of the ground covered by the dominant *Festuca* varied from 30 to 45% on Skokholm to 65 to 80% on Middleholm, to 80 to 90% on Grassholm. The average height of *Festuca* ranged from 1 to 3 cm on Skokholm to 3 to 8 cm on Middleholm, to 20 to 40 cm on Grassholm. The same pattern was recorded for the more sheltered *Agrostis* turf. (See also Table 2-4.)

Gillham (1955) observed that wind has much the same effect as rabbit grazing. The number of species tend to increase in the wind-exposed areas of Skokholm Island. The heavy grazing of the rabbits induces the prostrate growth form and also, because of accompanying trampling, increases the amount of bare soil. This allows colonization by easily established ephemerals, whose seeds are blown in from adjoining headlands and cliffs where the plants often thrive on soil swept bare by winter gales. Gillham concluded that in wind-swept habitats, low-growing dicotyledonous plants are more resistant to grazing than are the native grasses, which are thereby suppressed. In sheltered areas, the elimination of grazing leads to replacement of the grasses by dicotyledonous dominants; in exposed areas the elimination of grazing leads to a change from dicotyledon to grass dominance.

Grazing Selectivity

Owen (1971) and Cadwalladr and Morley (1973) commented on the high level of grazing selectivity exercised by both sheep and waterfowl (when feeding on the same site) in southwestern England. By analyzing two criteria, timing of usage and the relative quantity of food per unit area remaining after usage, Owen found the white-fronted geese to be highly selective in the choice of vegetation zone in the Slimbridge area of western England. On the basis of both criteria, the *Agrostis* zone was preferred to all others. *Lolium, Festuca, Hordeum,* and *Juncus,* in that order, were grazed later in the season. *Agrostis stolonifera* dominated the lowest grassy areas, while *Festuca rubra* was prevalent on well-drained sites next to the river. *Hordeum secalinum* occurred in the inland high regions and *Lolium perenne* was found slightly lower than the *Hordeum* zone. *Juncus gerardi* was situated in circular patches on the edges of the *Agrostis* and *Lolium* zones. Owen observed that selection by zone was not absolute; when large numbers of geese were present, all zones were occupied.

Sheep and wigeon displayed a preference for *Puccinellia maritima* and *A. stolonifera* over *F. rubra* (Cadwalladr and Morley, 1973). Early in the winter, wigeon select *P. maritima* over *A. stolonifera* and *F. rubra* (Owen, 1973a). The initial choice was made by selecting the broad zone in which

Table 2-4. Composition of *Agrostidetum tenius* in relation to grazing intensity in a Welsh marsh

Grazing Intensity (estimated by Ave. No. of Rabbit Pellets/½ m²)	No. of Species in Representative Area	% of Ground Covered by Grasses	% of Ground Covered by 2 Palatable Grasses, Agrostis and Festuca
None	2	100	100
	3	100	96
Very slight (0-10 pellets)	4	100	95
	4	100	75
Medium (5-100 pellets)	21	91	62
	16	75	68
Heavy (300-500 pellets)	23	54	50
	24	56	48

Source: From Gillham, M. F., 1955, Ecology of the Pembrokeshire Islands. III. The effect of grazing on the vegetation, *J. Ecol.* **43**(1):172-206, by permission.
Note: Most of the difference between the two final columns is accounted for by *Holcus lanatus*, and the rest by *Poa annua*.

to feed and then selecting feeding sites within zones and particular plant species from the mixed turf. The birds were more selective when feeding in less preferred zones. Late in the season, when the wigeon were in the *Festuca* zone, their feces contained a high proportion of *Puccinellia* fragments. Cadwalladr and Morley noted much the same kind of selection when they observed a considerable decrease throughout the grazing season in the height of *A. stolonifera* in an unmown *Festuca* plot. Comparable grazing of *F. rubra* occurred only after the sheep were given no choice and the size of the flock had increased. When the rank growing *Festuca* was closely mowed, its palatability was increased, making it comparable to that of *Puccinellia* and *Agrostis*. Thus height plays a role in selectivity. Owen (1972*a*, 1973*a*) noted that white-fronted geese (*Anser albifrons*) always kept the preferred *Agrostis* closely cropped throughout the winter, while taller *Hordeum secalinum* was cropped shorter late in the season. Wigeon, with their short legs, had difficulty moving through taller grass and had trouble manipulating the longer leaves.

Jerling and Andersson (1982) described the effects of selective grazing by cattle on the reproduction of *Plantago maritima* in Swedish salt meadows bordering the Baltic. *P. maritima, Triglochin maritima,* and *Phragmites australis* were grazed more heavily than the values of their percentage of cover indicated (Table 2-5). Like Cadwalladr and Morley (1973), Jerling and Andersson noted that the difference between species was small since the possibility to be selective decreased as grazing intensity increased. The study area comprised three vegetative zones. Jerling and Andersson observed that cattle visited the mid-zone, which was the area of peak abundance of *P. maritima,* less frequently. Flower spikes in this middle zone had a better chance to produce seeds. Conversely, the higher mortality of spikes in the inner and outer zones decreased the number of seeds available for dispersal. Therefore, the authors reasoned that the population of *P. maritima* could not increase under these conditions. In addition, they thought that, although heavy grazing restricted seed dispersal, grazing also kept the vegetation low, allowing light to reach the seedlings and thus enhance their survival. The prevention of grazing apparently would not foster population spread due to increased seedling mortality resulting from reduced light. In this particular example, the plant population would be maintained in a steady state through selective grazing.

Digestibility and physical characteristics may be important. The structure of the plants may affect digestibility, for waterfowl seem to rely more on mechanical rather than chemical methods of breaking up ingested material (Owen, 1973*b*). The physical character of these various grasses (*Puccinellia, Agrostis, Festuca*) and other vegetation differs in color, breadth of leaves, texture, and taste: grazers use sight, taste, or touch to

Table 2-5.   Percentage cover of five common species on a Baltic seashore meadow compared to the percentage of each species that had been grazed.

Species	% Cover ± S.E.	% Grazed ± S.E.	No. of Quadrants
Plantago maritima	20.9 ± 2.2	61.7 ± 2.9	80
Juncus gerardi	38.1 ± 3.1	33.4 ± 3.2	80
Triglochin maritima[2]	11.7 ± 1.3	71.9 ± 9.5	18
Scirpus maritimus	14.7 ± 3.6	10.8 ± 5.0	19
Phragmites australis	11.1 ± 1.4	40.9 ± 7.6	27

Source: From Jerling, L., and M. Andersson, 1982, Effects of selective grazing by cattle on the reproduction of *Plantago maritima, Holarctic Ecol.* 5:405-411, by permission.

recognize their preferred food plants. Gillham (1955) mentioned the dense felt of hairs on the leaves of *Holcus lanatus* and its acrid sap as repellants to rabbits. Owen (1972a, 1973b) noted the power of the broad bills of the white-fronted goose and the wigeon to grasp and cut several grass blades and the use of the tongue to move the grass backward to the esophagus. Such actions enable touch and taste to augment sight.

Owen (1973a, 1973b) stated that a number of animals select their food on the basis of nutritive value; earlier (Owen, 1971) he purported that geese select pasture on the basis of nitrogen and fiber content. Ydenberg and Prins (1981) found the protein content of food plants, primarily *Festuca rubra,* on grazed sites in Denmark to be significantly higher than elsewhere as a direct result of grazing by barnacle geese, *Branta leucopsis,* which sustained the regeneration of young, protein-rich plant tissues. The intensity of grazing maintained the standing crop at a constant level, and most grazing was concentrated where the plants grew most rapidly. Whether or not animals such as sheep, white-fronted geese, barnacle geese, or wigeon select on the basis of nutrition, the references cited here do clearly indicate a preference for foods that have a higher nutritive value (see also Table 2-1).

There seem to be some seasonal preferences in food consumption. Ranwell and Downing (1959) found the brent goose (*Branta bernicla*) ingesting greater quantities of *Zostera marina* in the fall and early winter and *Enteromorpha* and other green algae throughout the winter, but the higher salt marsh plants such as *Puccinellia maritima* and *Aster tripolium* in late winter and early spring. *Zostera* had the highest nutritive value, *Enteromorpha* the lowest, and *Puccinellia* and *Aster* were intermediate. Ranwell and Downing concluded that each type of food was favored in the diet during the season when it was in its most active growth phase: autumn, winter, and early spring, respectively.

The importance of the role of selectivity appears to be limited by an adequate source of desirable food items. Ranwell and Downing (1959), Cadwalladr and Morley (1973), and Owen (1972*a*, 1973*b*) have called attention to the decline in selectivity with a shift to less desirable foods as the preferred items become exhausted. Owen (1972*a*) found clear indications that maintaining a high rate of food intake was more important to the white-fronted goose, which digests its food inefficiently, than selecting the most nutritious diet possible. Owen found that juveniles ate more rapidly, were less selective, walked more quickly while grazing, and were less wary than the adults. Much of the daylight hours were taken up by feeding to maintain body condition. Geese ate between 650 and 800 grams of fresh food/day, which is more than 25% of their body weight. The feeding rate was rapid and increased with time of day to a maximum of 130 pecks/minute. In addition, the feeding rate increased to compensate for a decrease in the food supply toward the end of the winter.

Disturbance is another factor that can impinge on selectivity. Ranwell and Downing (1959) (brent goose), Cadwalladr et al. (1972) and Owen (1973*b*) (wigeon), and Owen 1972*b* (white-fronted goose) called attention to this factor. Owen (1972*b*) stated that up to one-half of the potential grazing area can be rendered unusable for the white-fronted goose because of disturbance. He went on to say that a review of the literature would lead one to believe that these geese prefer marsh vegetation. He suggested that this apparent preference may be due to the low disturbance values on such areas and the proximity to safe roosts. If undisturbed, however, the geese appear to prefer heavily grazed pasture where the grass is in a younger and more nutritious stage, and they may prefer the better-quality agricultural mixtures to the usually more fibrous wild grasses.

Production

To summarize, grazing influences not only growth form, species composition, and numbers of species but also the physical size and the amount of production. In a study of above-ground productivity of Baltic seashore meadows, Wallentinus (1973) and Jerling (1983) noted that the reed *Phragmites australis* was dense and tall in ungrazed areas but scarcely evident on a grazed site. When grazing ceased, the shoots grew to normal size and produced seed panicles. The immediate effect of grazing was the stimulation of growth characterized by the shoots remaining green for a longer time in the fall. In addition, both Wallentinus (1973) and Haslam (1972) observed that growth was stronger in the grazed areas after grazing ceased. Wallentinus also noted that *Agrostis stolonifera* had its greatest above-ground biomass on grazed areas at the time of the November sampling.

Table 2-6. Comparison of living and dead, wet and dry weights, for *Distichlis spicata, Salicornia virginica,* and *Spartina alterniflora* in a Georgia marsh

	Mean Wet Weight (g/m^2)	Mean Dry Weight (g/m^2)	% Dry Weight	Regression Equation $(Y = a + bX)$
Ungrazed				
S. alterniflora (live)	474.4	168.1	35.4	$Y = 2.05 + 0.35X$
S. alterniflora (dead)	326.2	129.5	39.7	$Y = 8.80 + 0.37X$
S. virginica	1,080.5	272.8	25.2	$Y = 13.47 + 0.24X$
Grazed				
S. alterniflora (live)	269.7	95.1	35.3	$Y = -4.69 + 0.37X$
S. alterniflora (dead)	147.1	53.0	36.0	$Y = -10.27 + 0.43X$
S. virginica	116.4	29.5	25.3	$Y = 1.57 + 0.24X$
D. spicata (live)	55.3	24.8	44.8	$Y = 1.56 + 0.42X$
D. spicata (dead)	35.3	14.8	41.9	$Y = 2.10 + 0.36X$
Formerly grazed				
S. alterniflora (live)	314.5	95.0	30.2	$Y = 3.79 + 0.29X$
S. alterniflora (dead)	353.0	89.6	25.4	$Y = 15.46 + 0.21X$
S. virginica	249.2	62.3	25.0	$Y = 17.45 + 0.18X$
D. spicata (live)	79.8	39.2	49.1	$Y = -3.87 + 0.54X$
D. spicata (dead)	72.4	30.9	42.7	$Y = 4.12 + 0.37X$

Source: From Reimold, R. J., R. A. Linthurst, and P. L. Wolf, 1975, Effects of grazing on a salt marsh, *Biol. Conserv.* 8:105-125, by permission.

Note: For the regression equation, $Y =$ dry weight, $X =$ wet weight. All regression equations have a correlation coefficient significant at the 99.9% confidence interval.

Reimold, Linthurst, and Wolf (1975) recorded a 70% reduction in primary production in a grazed *Spartina alterniflora-Distichlis spicata* marsh in Georgia as compared to an ungrazed site. Where grazing was prohibited for one year, production doubled (Table 2-6). When comparing living and dead as well as wet and dry weights of *S. alterniflora* and *Salicornia virginica,* the plants in an ungrazed system had a higher percentage dry weight biomass than those in a formerly grazed or a grazed system (Table 2-7). In addition, *D. spicata,* which was not present in ungrazed areas, had a greater percentage dry weight in the formerly grazed system than the grazed location. Examination of Tables 2-6 and 2-7 shows the greatest accumulation of dead material in an ungrazed marsh and the least in a grazed wetland. All this suggested to Reimold,

Table 2-7. Average yearly production of plant material per square meter in the three Georgia salt marsh areas considered

	$g/m^2/yr$	Total	N
Ungrazed			
S. alterniflora (live)	179.2		14
S. alterniflora (dead)	131.4		14
S. virginica	272.8		14
		583.4	
Grazed			
S. alterniflora (live)	92.5		16
S. alterniflora (dead)	53.0		16
S. virginica	36.8		16
D. spicata (live)	24.8		16
D. spicata (dead)	14.8		16
		221.9	
Formerly grazed			
S. alterniflora (live)	99.6		9
S. alterniflora (dead)	85.5		9
S. virginica	67.1		9
D. spicata (live)	39.2		9
D. spicata (dead)	30.9		9
		322.3	

Source: From Reimold, R. J., R. A. Linthurst, and P. L. Wolf, 1975, Effects of grazing on a salt marsh, *Biol. Conserv.* 8:105-125, by permission.
Note: N = number of observations.

Linthurst, and Wolf (1975) that the plants in a grazed (or mown) system are maintained in a younger stage of development due to harvesting by ungulates or waterfowl and are therefore more succulent than in an ungrazed marsh; this is supported by Wallentinus (1973), Owen (1972b, 1975), and Cadwalladr and Morley (1974).

As we have seen, intensive grazing in a local area for a short period can depress production. If this happens and the grazers turn to other vegetation, however, production can be reestablished (Ranwell and Downing, 1959; Reimold, Linthurst, and Wolf, 1975). When grazing is intensive and prolonged, it will have a destructive impact on the vegetation. Both Oliver (1913) and Rowan (1913) portrayed the very destructive habits of rabbits living on Blakeney Point, Norfolk, England, while Gillham (1955) did the same for the Pembrokeshire Islands off the Welsh coast. The depredation by these animals was emphasized in the comparison of grazed vegetation with those plots protected by fencing. Subsequent observations supported the view that cessation of grazing by rabbits results in a marked increase in the growth and flowering of grasses and sedges and a decline in the low-growing dicotyledons (Ranwell, 1960; White, 1961).

Other animals, by way of their feeding habits or numbers, can have a much greater, more lasting, or far-reaching impact. The snow goose, *Chen caerulescens,* as well as the Canada goose, *Branta canadensis,* feed on the rhizomes of *Spartina alterniflora, S. cynosuroides, Scirpus olneyi, S. robustus, S. americanus, S. californicus,* and *Distichlis spicata.* These rhizomes are "puddled out" by the geese, which use their feet when the marsh surface is just covered with water to excavate these underground plant parts. These geese also use their heavy, strong bills to pull up the rhizomes and to cut them into pieces before swallowing (Griffith, 1940; Lynch, O'Neil, and Lay, 1947). Since water levels determine where these

Figure 2-1. Effect of snow goose grazing in a *Spartina alterniflora* marsh in the Bombay Hook National Wildlife Refuge, Delaware. The previous year's stands of cordgrass are interspersed by denuded areas that had been grazed during the winter of 1983–1984. The denuded areas contained a few live sprigs of cordgrass in June 1984 and were covered with a mat of algae. The uprooted cordgrass, resulting from the grazing, formed extensive mats of wrack, which were deposited at the level of high tide, smothering existing vegetation. (Photo by F. C. Daiber)

geese feed and because they have enormous appetites, a large flock can denude a marsh in a short time (Lynch, O'Neil, and Lay, 1947). A flock of 5,000 greater snow geese, feeding extensively on *S. alterniflora,* can strip 300 acres of marsh in 6 weeks (Griffith, 1940). Smith and Odum (1981) reported that snow geese significantly reduced the below-ground biomass of *S. alterniflora, S. patens, D. spicata,* and *S. robustus* in North Carolina salt marshes. Grazing intensity, expressed as percent biomass removed, was 58%. The percentage plant cover and the type and amount of detritus were also significantly reduced. A follow-up report (Smith, 1983) stated that *S. alterniflora* production was reduced by two-thirds in grazed versus ungrazed areas but recovered when grazing ceased. *Scirpus robustus* increased under grazing pressure while goose activity did not affect *S. americanus.* Species of *Eleocharis* were found only in grazed areas. Total plant production was reduced by 16% where grazing occurred.

Such goose "eat-outs" have interesting side effects. The puddling activity of the geese make *Scirpus* seeds more readily available to feeding ducks. The marsh surface can be lowered by 1 or 2 inches (Griffith, 1940), or the soil may be broken to a depth of 5 to 8 inches (Lynch, O'Neil, and Lay, 1947). Water accumulates in such sites and can inhibit plant regeneration. Severe grazing can create ponds that other waterfowl use. Such expansive eat-outs can adversely affect nesting sites and food supplies, reducing the carrying capacity of the marsh for black ducks and other wildlife (Ferrigno, 1976). Small eat-outs produce shallow breeding depressions for large numbers of *Aedes* mosquitoes, while large depressions tend to form permanent ponds that discourage mosquito breeding. These large pools support populations of *Cyprinodon variegatus,* the sheepshead minnow, and *Fundulus heteroclitus,* the mummichog, giving these fishes access to any mosquito larvae that might still be produced. The recognition of this phenomenon has led to the establishment and maintenance of permanent shallow pools in the heavy mosquito-breeding areas of salt marshes as a means of mosquito control and waterfowl refuge (Ferrigno, 1958).

While goose eat-outs can have a severe effect on a marsh, an overpopulation of muskrats (*Ondatra zibethica*) can create an even greater impact. Goose damage may also generate a muskrat eat-out (Lynch, O'Neil, and Lay, 1947). Both geese and muskrats are attracted to the same food plants. Damage is inevitable when a muskrat population builds up, temporarily exceeding the carrying capacity of the marsh, or when wintering flocks of geese use the same marsh, or both.

Lynch, O'Neil, and Lay (1947) described in considerable detail the ecological consequences to a tidal marsh of goose or muskrat eat-outs. The magnitude of eat-outs was influenced by the extent of the dominant species. Pure stands of *Scirpus* or *Typha* were more subjected to a complete eat-out that were mixed stands of vegetation. Rate of recovery was determined by factors such as the amount of open water, the depth of soil damage, and the amounts of seeds and propagative pieces of vegetation that still remained. The "crevey," or dead marsh, may be attractive to some waterfowl, but geese and muskrats avoid it until recovery takes place (Lynch, O'Neil, and Lay, 1947). Not only is the marsh vegetation severely impacted by overexploitation by the muskrat, but the animals themselves are affected. Many will be driven from the marsh only to perish elsewhere (Errington, 1963). Those that remain suffer both a decline in numbers and a decrease in individual weights (Table 2-8). Harvesting is considered the only effective way to control muskrat overpopulation (Lynch, O'Neil, and Lay, 1947; Dozier, 1953). Dozier recommended that trapping begin when the density reaches one house per acre; a density of 2.5 dwellings per acre needs immediate attention to prevent an eat-out. He estimated that 2.5 animals per house would sustain an adequate breeding population.

Interspecific Impacts

Grazing by livestock, muskrats, waterfowl, or other primary consumers not only affects the vegetation of a tidal marsh but also spurs interaction among animal species occupying the area. Grazing or mowing tends to produce a more uniform environment (Larsson, 1969; Cadwalladr and Morley, 1973; Møller, 1975; Gray and Scott, 1977), and the bird fauna is inclined to be more limited (Larsson, 1969, 1976; Møller, 1975). Larsson (1969), working in the coastal marshes of southern Sweden, found a total of 23 bird species in areas influenced by grazing, whereas ungrazed sites supported 38. In areas of grazed pastures where the substrate was a quagmire, thus prohibiting grazing, the number of species was the same as in ungrazed locations. Larsson also noted qualitative differences: most species recorded in grazed areas were not found in ungrazed locations. The dunlin, *Calidris alpina*, was found only where intensive grazing took place. The black-tailed godwit, *Limosa limosa*, was recorded only where moderate to intensive grazing occurred, while the chaffinch, *Fringilla coelebs*, and four warblers were observed only at ungrazed sites. The common snipe (*Gallinago gallinago*) displayed the widest habitat amplitude, while the yellow wagtail (*Motacilla flava*) and the redshank (*Tringa totanus*) accepted varying grazing intensity.

In a subsequent study, Larsson (1976) noted that the yellow wagtail and the redshank and the broadest distribution of nest sites. The yellow wagtail displayed the highest incidence of nests in habitats with the highest incidence of tussocks. Most nests of the dunlin and the ruff, *Philomachus pugnax*, were found in patches with low tussocks.

Table 2-8. Progressive decrease in muskrat density, yield, and average weights, as affected by overpopulation, Blackwater National Wildlife Refuge, Maryland

Unit	Marsh	Trapping Season	Houses per Acre	Yield per House	Aver. Wt. (LBS)
17	Wolf Pit	1941	3.9	1.0	2.13
		1942	1.1	1.8	1.93
		1943	0.7	2.1	1.90
18	Rhode Island	1941	1.8	0.7	2.01
		1942	0.03	3.2	1.97
		1943	0.1	0.7	1.80
19	McGraws Island	1941	0.5	4.3	2.13
		1942	0.2	2.1	1.95
		1943	0.4	0.3	1.83
23	Sunken Island	1941	3.0	0.5	2.36
		1942	0.6	1.4	2.27
		1943	0.6	0.2	2.00

Source: From Dozier, H. L., M. H. Markey, and L. M. Llewellyn, 1948, Muskrat investigations on the Blackwater National Wildlife Refuge, Maryland, 1941-1945, *J. Wildl. Manage.* **12**(2):177-190, by permission.

Larsson (1969, 1976) noted that grazing tends to do two things: it keeps the tall herbaceous vegetation down, favoring a grass-dominated community; and the trampling by cattle greatly enhances the irregular, rough surface. Both factors favor the wading bird, which use such habitats for both feeding and nesting. The waders as well as the gulls and terns leave such habitats as the vegetation becomes taller and denser (Larsson, 1969, 1976; Greenhalgh, 1971; Møller, 1975). Møller (1975) has also noted that species dominance is lowest while the evenness index and species diversity are highest in plots that display the greatest habitat heterogeneity. As grazing ceases and the herbaceous and woody vegetation begins to replace the grass-dominated grazed areas, the social gulls and terns are the first to leave, followed by the less social waders. Only the snipe and the territorial passerine species increase in numbers (Møller, 1975).

In short, to maintain a high species diversity on salt marsh meadows, Møller (1975) recommended seed harvesting or hay production and cattle grazing, or both. Larsson (1976) suggested that the trampling and the selectivity exercised by the cattle speak in favor of grazing as a management tool. He believed that regular mowing means the reduction of some tussock-forming plant species, valuable to certain bird species but detrimental to others. As we have seen earlier (Cadwalladr and Morley 1973; Owen 1972*b*, 1975), the marsh manager must employ intensive sheep grazing or mowing, or both, to maintain a uniform grass-dominated turf in a young succulent stage to be attractive to wintering waterfowl. Such a procedure would not be conducive to maintaining a high diversity of nesting birds. If the management plan calls for enhanced diversity of nesting species, however, the creation of a habitat mosaic is suggested where the transition zones between different areas in regard to plant communities, water content, and the extent of land use should be extended as much as possible. Such habitat heterogeneity can be created by combinations of varying intensity and frequency of grazing (trampling) and mowing, and by leaving particular areas untouched. Controlled burning could also be useful in such situations. When stationary bird species are present, these management activities should not be carried out during the nesting season. By such marsh manipulation, a variety of nesting, feeding, and hiding sites can be provided in close proximity (Larsson, 1969).

Detritus Generation

Reimold, Linthurst, and Wolf (1975) found the lowest levels of detritus in grazed marshes, the highest in ungrazed sites, and intermediate levels in formerly grazed locations. They also found nitrogen levels to be highest in ungrazed areas and attributed this to detritus accumulation. Some species, such as the wading birds, may be attracted to grazed areas because the accumulation of litter in ungrazed locations may impede movements of their young (Larsson, 1976).

PRESCRIBED BURNING

Kozlowski and Ahlgren (1974) and Wright and Bailey (1982), among others, have identified fire as an important component in many ecosystems of the world. The role of fire in the tidal marsh ecosystem was little known before the 1940s (Garren, 1943), although Viosca (1928) and Penfound and Hathaway (1938) described the hazard that resulted when marsh soil dried out: subsequent fires consumed the peat down to the mineral soil. Such action removed a great deal of organic matter, thus impeding the increase in the elevation of the marsh and causing a reversion to an earlier hydric stage in the sere.

Much information comes from studies carried out along the Gulf Coast. Hoffpauer (1968) observed that marsh burning began after 1910 in Louisiana and Texas to facilitate hunting for alligators. A side effect was the enhancement of muskrat populations. Burning has a number of functions: it accelerates food production; it makes food available by removing the dense cover; it provides fire protection by removing rank growth; it enhances trapping operations; and under some circumstances the return from the mature stage to the hydrosere will create new habitat attractive to waterfowl (Lynch, 1941; Hoffpauer, 1968; Perkins, 1968).

There are three types of burns (Lynch, 1941; Hoffpauer, 1968): cover, or wet, burns, root burns, and deep peat burns. Cover, or wet, burns are used when the water level is at or above the root horizon. A clean cover burn is done over a wide area with a steady wind. Such a procedure is essential for goose management, which promotes extensive vistas for the geese to feed. A spotty cover burn is done on a diminishing wind or in damp weather and creates open areas in an otherwise uniform and dense vegetational cover. Marsh ducks and shore birds feed in such open spots, while the adjoining unburned portion of the marsh provides cover for ducks and fur bearers such as raccoons, mink, otters, and muskrats. The marsh structure is not changed; the dominant aerial vegetation is burned off but returns because the root system is not disturbed.

Root burns are carried out during dry periods so that the dominant or original vegetation is destroyed and can be replaced by an earlier seral stage. As an example, where *Spartina patens* high marsh is dominant and *Scirpus* is at a lower density, a root burn destroys the *S. patens* roots, which are closer to the surface. This allows the *Scirpus* to become dominant. Since *S. patens* has a much greater density potential, such root burns must be carried out to maintain *Scirpus olneyi* or *S. robustus* as dominant vegetation. Root burns must not be done when the marsh is too dry, or the *Scirpus* roots and other deep rooted species also will be destroyed.

A deep peat burn is usually confined to freshwater marshes during drought conditions. The overlying peat is burned down to the mineral soil or subsurface water level, where the fire is extinguished. An open pond devoid of vegetation will form; thus the climax marsh stage has reverted to the beginning hydrosere (Lynch, 1941; Hoffpauer, 1968).

Effects of Burning

Haslam (1968), in discussing the control of *Phragmites australis* in England, identified the effects of burning at different seasons of the year. A fire in winter produces a very rapid early emergence of buds in the spring, which gives the reed a competitive advantage. A spring fire yields a replacement crop, perhaps denser than the original because of the stimulating effect on the dormant axillary buds on the rhizomes. A spring fire, however, may result in late emergence because of the delay after the fire. A summer fire is considered less harmful than summer cutting since, while both remove existing shoots, only the fire produces a replacement crop. At any time the fire is severe enough to scorch the surface soil deeply, there will be up to a two-month delay in the next spring's emergence. The seeds will not complete their growth before the autumn frosts, so the crop is reduced the same way as crops coming up after a severe late frost or after a cutting in May or June.

A clean cover burn will remove the matted dead vegetation from a high marsh, and where *Scirpus* is prevalent, the presence of the exposed rhizomes will attract snow geese. Such activity, if concentrated in a particular area, will initiate an eat-out (Hoffpauer, 1968, as described by Lynch, O'Neil, and Lay 1947), which in turn will lead to a reversion to a more pioneer vegetational stage. This goose activity proves to be attractive to ducks, especially the pintail. There is an apparent symbiotic relation between ducks and geese, in that the ducks often feed on material left by the geese (Hoffpauer, 1968).

The borders of ponds created by deep peat burns can become vegetated by wild millet (*Echinochloa* sp.), spike rush (*Eleocharis* sp.). and cattail (*Typha*). Such vegetation will spread most rapidly under steady-state conditions (no flooding or drought) and becomes attractive to various duck species (Lynch, 1941; Hoffpauer, 1968).

Very few systematic studies have been done on the effects of fire on tidal marsh vegetation. On the Gulf Coast, de la Cruz and Hackney (1980) have examined the species composition, phenology, and primary production in a *Juncus roemerianus* and *Spartina cynosuroides* marsh to determine the frequency with which a winter cover burn or cutting could be used as a management device. They concluded that the *Spartina* marsh can be burned easily and uniformly every year since the plants leave enough litter to spread the fire effectively. The *Juncus* marsh does not burn well because the plants leave little dead material from one year to the next and much of the standing stems remain green. Experience suggested that such marshes can be effectively burned only every three to four years unless they are especially dry.

Winter burning or cutting of *Juncus* in this study enhanced primary production for only one year following the burn. Subsequently, production in the experimental plots was similar to that in the control plots. An analysis of the monthly standing dry biomass values of both the burn and harvest plots showed that they fell below the mean for the control values (Figure 2-2). The one exception was burn plot 1 of 1979. Winter fire and cutting had a negative effect on the height and weight of the *Juncus* plants, although the vigor of the plants seemed to return to that of the controls within three years of the original treatment. The fire did not affect plant density. Maximum flowering occurred one year after both fire and harvest treatment.

Primary production in both burn and cut *Spartina* plots exceeded production in the control. The plot that received two annual winter burns had 16 and 27 percent more biomass production than the controls, while the plot with one winter burn displayed 19 percent greater production than the control. The harvest plots showed some increase (15 to 17%) over the controls. In general, the monthly standing dry biomass values of both the burn and harvest values exceeded the mean for the *Spartina* control plots over the three-year study period (Figure 2-3). Usually more flower heads appeared directly after the burn than were present in the control plot.

Minor species biomass associated with the *Juncus* community did not change after one burn. There was an increase in minor species in the burn and harvest plots of *Spartina*. Both marshes showed higher below-ground standing crop at a depth of 0 to 10 cm in both the burn and harvest plots during the peak of the growing season than in the control plots.

De la Cruz and Hackney (1980) suggested that the initial increase in production of *Juncus roemerianus* following a fire could not be sustained because the plants had drawn on the reserved energy stored in the

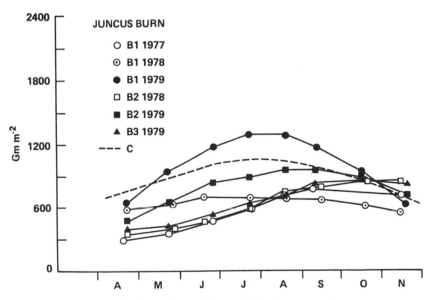

Figure 2-2.   Predicted values of monthly total live biomass of *J. roemerianus* in a Mississippi marsh, showing burn plots compared to the annual average of control plots (C). B_1 was burned in the winters of 1977, 1978, and 1979; B_2 in the winters of 1978 and 1979; and B_3 in the winter of 1979. *Source: After De la Cruz, A. A., and C. T. Hackney, 1980, The Effects of Winter Fire and Harvest on the Vegetational Structure and Primary Productivity of Two Tidal Marsh Communities in Mississippi, Miss.-Ala. Sea Grant Cons. MASGP-80-013, p. 24.*

rhizomes from earlier production. This could account for the three-year lapse for the plants in the experimental plots to return to the status of the plants in the control plots. While the density of *Spartina cynosuroides* plants did not increase following a burn, the treated plots produced heavier individual stems. They concluded that annual burning or harvesting of *S. cynosuroides* would not harm that plant community, but that the *J. roemerianus* community should not be so treated more frequently than every three or four years.

Vogl (1973) found that new growth of maidencane grass, *Panicum hemitomum,* in a Florida marsh appeared much earlier at the burned site. In addition, growth was more rapid and production was greater. The average yield showed a 50% increase in the burned area at the water's edge and a 2,739% increase at the landward edge of the burn site over that of the control plot. The previous year's growth appeared to suppress new growth at the unburned site.

De la Cruz and Hackney (1980) presumed that ashes were responsible

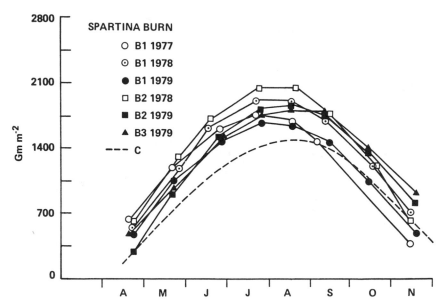

Figure 2-3.   Predicted values of total monthly live biomass of *S. cynosuroides* in a Mississippi marsh, showing burn plots compared to annual average of control plots (C). B_1 was burned in the winters of 1977, 1978, and 1979; B_2 in the winters of 1978 and 1979; and B_3 in the winter of 1979. *Source: After De la Cruz, A. A., and C. T. Hackney, 1980, The Effects of Winter Fire and Harvest on the Vegetational Structure and Primary Productivity of Two Tidal Marsh Communities in Mississippi, Miss.-Ala. Sea Grant Cons. MASGP-80-013, p. 26.*

for the increased production they had observed at their *Spartina* marsh site. Hoffpauer (1968) recorded an enhancement of soil nutrients following ash deposition, in the form of 82% and 30.5% increases in phosphorous and calcium, respectively. Total water alkalinity and pH increased by 560% and 10.8%, respectively. Such stimulated production is marked in light of earlier reports (Viosca, 1928; Penfound and Hathaway, 1938; Garren, 1943) that revegetation and production would be retarded because of the excessive leaching of the ashes.

Burns enrich the production of vegetation that serves as an attractive food source for wintering geese and muskrats (Penfound and Hathaway, 1938; Lynch, 1941; O'Neil, 1949; Perkins, 1968; Hoffpauer, 1968). Except for Vogl (1973), no one appears to have made a systematic attempt to assess animal usage of a burned-over marsh. Vogl observed no fire-induced mortality among birds or mammals in an experimental burn in a Florida marsh, although some frogs and snakes perished. He recorded a total of 754 birds during four months in the burned area, and 236 birds at the unburned site. Each sighting averaged 3.7 birds in the control area and 11.8 birds in the experimental plot. There were 290 "resident" birds in the burn site and 102 in the control area. "Transient" birds numbered 440 in the burn and 127 in the control tract. Only 5 of the total 35 species were found more frequently in the burned region. "Occasional" bird species (fewer than 5 sightings) numbered 24 in the burned plot and 7 at the control site. Vogl recorded 1 alligator in the control and 20 in the burned area. Based on limited sampling, mammal populations appeared to be similar in both tracts.

The timing of the burn is dictated by the intent. A spring cover burn will provide succulent vegetation for the muskrat. However, a summer or early fall burn will drive the muskrat out by destroying house-building material. In addition, such a late burn will attract cattle, which will destroy the muskrat houses. If the intent of the burns is to attract and hold flocks of wintering geese, it would be better to have periodic late summer and early fall burns, commencing two to three weeks before the anticipated first arrivals. Burning the marsh will attract snow geese, whereas burning the adjoining upland areas will be more attractive to Canada geese. Burning these adjoining upland sites will also tend to keep the cattle out of the marshlands (Lay and O'Neil, 1942; Lynch, O'Neil, and Lay, 1947; Neely, 1962; Hoffpauer, 1968).

WEED CONTROL

In the view of many wildlife refuge managers, weed species in the tidal marsh are those that do not attract and support substantial populations of waterfowl or marsh furbearers. Given the objectives of waterfowl or furbearer enhancement, management practices are designed to limit the growth of such "weed" species. This limitation of weed species is intended either to create desirable areas of open, non-plant-clogged water or to promote the growth and vigor of desirable food species. Steenis et al. (1954) described the successful use of flooding for weed control. Flooding the marsh through one or two growing seasons, with 18 inches or more of fresh water, killed species such as *Spartina* spp., *Distichlis spicata*, *Peltandra virginica*, *Hibiscus moscheutos*, and *Rumex verticillatus*. Flooding with as little as 6 inches of water in one growing season eliminated *Pluchea purpurascens*, *Panicum virgatum*, *Iva frutescens*, and *Baccharis halimifolia*, but *Nuphar advena*, *Nelumbo pentapetala* (Lutea), and water-tolerant species such as *Salix nigra*, *Alnus serrulata*, and *Cephalanthus occidentalis* were not affected. The latter woody species were killed when cut down and the stumps kept submerged for one growing season. A sudden rise of 30 or more inches of water for 2 weeks during the flowering and early fruiting period killed *Nelumbo*. Rises of several feet retarded the growth of *Nuphar;* however, Steenis et al. acknowledged that in most tidal marshes there is little opportunity for water-level changes of such magnitude.

Steenis et al. (1954) also reported that flooding with salt water could be used advantageously where freshwater weeds were abundant. Since this procedure might also kill desirable wildlife plants it must be carefully controlled and generally used only every several years. In the Steenis study, increases in salt up to 7‰ killed many submerged plants but did not destroy prime duck foods such as *Ruppia maritima*, *Potamogeton pectinatus*, and *P. bupleuroides*. Pad-leaf plants such as *Nuphar advena*, *Nelumbo pentapetala*, and *Nymphaea* spp. were controlled by salinities greater than 2‰, while *Hibiscus moscheutos*, *Peltandra virginica*, and *Pontederia cordata* could not withstand salinities greater than 4‰.

One of the most obvious and ubiquitous of weeds is *Phragmites australis*, commonly known as reed grass, common reed, or rosean cane. It is found throughout the world in both tidal and nontidal freshwater marshes and can withstand moderate to high salinities. A very aggressive plant, it can quickly invade a spoil site or any area where vegetation has been disrupted by mechanical means or by tidal restriction. It forms monospecific stands and spreads primarily by means of rhizomes, which often run on the surface of the ground for considerable distances. Most of the work pertaining to the biology and ecological requirements of this species has been carried out by European workers (for sources, see Haslam, 1972; Kvet, 1973; Mason and Bryant, 1975; Tyrawski, 1977).

In the past, *Phragmites* was used extensively as roofing thatch, particularly in England, where it is still harvested and used for this purpose in a limited way (Haslam, 1969; personal observation). It is used in Eastern Europe to produce paper of rather inferior quality (Silberhorn,

1976). Howard, Rhodes, and Simmers (1978) have briefly reviewed its limited value to wildlife species as a source of food, shelter, and nesting sites. In general, however, its ability to flourish and drive out all other vegetation has made it universally unpopular.

Steenis et al. (1954) suggested that *Phragmites* could be controlled by flooding with 10 to 12 inches of water, usually in early June after the young plants had become established. They warned that flooding later in the season after the plants were well established is not an effective control, although flooding with several feet of water might retard growth. Haslam (1968) reported that while *Phragmites* can tolerate chlorinity up to 1.2%, sudden increases are toxic. Flooding with sea water can cause severe damage by producing short, weak, sparse canes for several years. Haslam also observed that drainage can reduce plant vigor and enhances competition from other plants. Roman (1978), searching for the best way to rehabilitate Connecticut marshes that had been degraded by restricted tidal flushing, reported that reestablishing tidal flow reduced the height of *Phragmites* and allowed typical salt marsh vegetation to propagate.

Husak (1973) described the effects of cutting *Phragmites* as a means of control in a freshwater fish pond in Czechoslovakia. When the canes were cut at 180 cm above the water level, only a few leaves were produced at the end of the growing season. Secondary branching and an increase in stem density resulted after reeds were cut at only 120 cm above the water level. The next year's shoot biomass was very low for reeds cut at 120 cm. The highest stem biomass occurred among the 180-cm-high plants at the end of the second growing season. During the third season after cutting, the 120-cm-high plants produced short shoots in a very dense canopy, while the 180-cm-cut plants were the same as the controls. Husak suggested that for the greatest reaction, treatment take place when the shoots are drawing on rhizome reserves, that is, before mid-June or, at the latest, before flower head emergence.

Haslam (1972)—who was concerned not with the eradication of *Phragmites* but with its management as a source of thatch in England— found that cutting in July reduced the crop for the next year by 40%. Cutting in September was less damaging and, while the plants would be exposed to frost killing, cutting in the winter had no effect on the size of the next year's crop. Jerling (1983) noted that grazing (equivalent to mowing) in the *Phragmites* zone easily damaged the vegetation, and that bare ground could result. Haslam (1968, 1972), while quoting others, noted that grazing is effective if animals are available and the ground is not too soft. Grazing also deflected succession, and growth of *Phragmites* was accelerated after grazing ceased.

Van Der Toorn and Mook (1982) and Mook and Van Der Toorn (1982), working in the Netherlands, noted that there was little damage to *Phragmites* in wet-burned and wet-mown study plots if the procedure occurred before the new shoots emerged. Plants reacted to such preemergent fire (or early frost) damage by forming one or more thinner replacement shoots for each shoot in which the meristem was killed. While an increase in biomass was retarded by early frost and early burning, there was no significant reduction in later maximal biomass. This coincides with Haslam's (1968) observation that a winter burn produces a very early emergence of buds: the fire breaks the internal dormancy, allowing all preformed and about-to-be-formed buds to emerge about a month after the fire. Later burning during the period of emergence in both the wet and dry study plots led to the death of the majority of the shoots (Van Der Toorn and Mook, 1982). When a late ground frost occurred, there was a 25 to 30% reduction in the maximal shoot biomass. The authors also noted that frost damage was most severe in plots that received the dry-burned and dry-mown treatments. This supplements the observations of Haslam (1972), who noted extensive damage when a heavy spring frost was followed by a dry summer.

Howard, Rhodes, and Simmers (1978) provided an extensive review of the various methods used to control this weed. These include biological control by grazing; mechanical control by fire, cutting, dredging, plowing, draining, and altering salinity; and chemical control by means of a variety of herbicides. They concluded that the most effective control methods are cutting, draining, saltwater flushing, use of herbicides, and various combinations of these methods. Personal observations of cuttings along roadsides would suggest that repeated cuttings can be a way of controlling the reed by reducing its vigor. Cutting is expensive, however and will work only where specialized mowing equipment can get into the marsh. Based on work done to date (excluding herbicides), it appears that the most effective way to control *Phragmites* is to burn the canes in the winter just before the expected coldest time of the year or to burn in the spring after the shoots emerge.

Use of Herbicides

Herbicides have been given little attention in tidal marsh management. The vigor of the hybrid *Spartina anglica*, however, has prompted some concern by Ranwell and Downing (1960) in England and by Bascand (1968) in New Zealand. They reported that rapid and aggressive growth habits can enable *S. anglica* to replace most of the great variety of plant species usually found in the salt marsh, thus limiting the feeding grounds of various herbivorous waterfowl. Although its growth character can serve as a prime aid in stabilizing coastal mud flats, this same growth pattern has blocked small navigational channels and drainage outlets, resulting in flooding and water-logged soil. For these various reasons,

Ranwell and Downing explored the use of herbicides to control the spread of *S. anglica.*

Ranwell and Downing (1960) tested several herbicides, including Dalapon (sodium salt formulation of 2, 2-dichloropropionic acid [2, 2-DPA]), and substituted urea compounds such as Diuron and Fenuron on a *Spartina* marsh bordering the Severn estuary. They applied the herbicides 35 yards seaward of the high-water spring-tide level.

The spring application of Diuron was more effective than the summer application. Dalapon applied as 50 pounds/acre gave an 80% kill of the main growth one year after spraying. However, there was considerable regeneration by seedlings settling on the bare ground. Seedlings also reestablished in large numbers on plots treated with substituted urea compounds, with the exception of those treated with Fenuron. Applications of Fenuron at 40 and 60 pounds/acre gave a 95% kill 2 months after spraying, and seedling regeneration was inhibited in the year following application. The best results were obtained when the treated vegetation had the greatest exposure between spring tides. There was no significant difference between plots near the upper limits of *Spartina* marsh that had received a single application of Dalapon at 50 pounds/acre and those that had received a split treatment.

When pelleted applications of Fenuron were attempted, the seaward plots at a lower tidal elevation were more affected than the landward plots. The wetness seemed to aid the action of the herbicide in spite of increased tidal action. The sprayed plots had just the reverse result; the tidal action probably reduced the effects of the sprays in the seaward plots (Ranwell and Downing, 1960).

Bascand (1968) presented results indicating that various herbicides can temporarily control *S. anglica* growth in New Zealand. Paraquat was immediately the most potent, while Diuron the least effective. After 5 months, the potency of the Paraquat had been substantially reduced while the other substances enhanced their effects, with 2, 2-DPA being the most effective, followed by Bromacil. Bascand concluded that 2, 2-DPA was the most effective *Spartina* control regardless of substrate or whether applications were single or split. Administration rates varied with height of growth. Bascand as well as Ranwell and Downing concluded that repeated spraying may be necessary to control vigorous growth. He implied that livestock grazing can be an effective control where possible. Chemical control could then be restricted to areas below high-water neap tides and along shallow, navigable channels that are inaccessible to livestock. However, the tides would disseminate herbicides over a wide area with possible adverse effects.

Colonial shore birds and wading birds have turned to islands created from dredge material for nesting sites after nesting behavior has been disrupted on their normal beach habitat. Vegetation can become so densely established on such islands that available nesting space can be reduced. Worsham, Soots, and Parnell (1974) applied a variety of substituted urea-containing herbicides in early July on a 6-year-old dredge material island in North Carolina to recreate bare and sparsely vegetated nesting habitat. The 4% Bromacil-6% Diuron mixture, Tebuthiuro, and Karbutilate gave 98 to 100% control over *Spartina patens* and other vegetation. Promitons gave only 85% control, while Dichlolenil gave poor control over all plant species. On this basis, such herbicides show promise in altering plant succession on dredge islands to favor the nesting requirements of various shore birds.

Haslam (1968) deplored the use of chemicals to control *Phragmites* because the herbicides are not specific. Haslam did suggest that, because salt in high concentrations is toxic, it may serve as a good chemical control. Because of the quantity needed, it probably would be effective only in restricted areas. More recently, the Delaware Division of Fish and Wildlife has been evaluating the use of glyphosate (N-[phosponomethyl] glycine, the active ingredient in Roundup and Rodeo, Monsanto chemical Corporation products) as a chemical control for *Phragmites* in aquatic situations. Glyphosate is a phloem-mobile, broad-spectrum herbicide that translocates throughout the plant and into the root system. The ultimate purpose of the Delaware evaluation has been to determine an effective herbicide control of *Phragmites* on wet sites for enhancing the state's wetlands, in order to make them more attractive to game, nongame, and furbearing species.

Three 10-acre plots of *Phragmites* were sprayed by helicopter once in September 1981 with glyphosate. Vegetation on the plots other than *Phragmites* (90% surface cover) included *Polygonum* (5%) primarily *P. pennsylvanicum* and *P. hydropiperoides* (5%); *Amaranthus canabinus* (3%); and *Peltandra virginica* (2%). The application rate for all plots was 2 quarts of chemical in 5 gallons of water per acre. One plot was sprayed with Roundup (glyphosate plus a wetting agent), one plot was sprayed with Rodeo (glyphosate without a wetting agent), and one plot was sprayed using glyphosate plus X77 (another wetting agent). The manufacturer recommends that the herbicide be applied at low tide and that it not be applied if rain is imminent, since water from tide or rain washes the glyphosate off the vegetation, thus reducing its effectiveness. It is not effective on submerged vegetation. Examination of three plots in May 1982 showed better than 95% control in all three plots. In June the control was 95% for glyphosate alone (Rodeo), 98% for Roundup, and 85% for glyphosate plus X77. The last plot had been inadvertently burned during the winter, which may have affected the results. Regrowth of vegetation among the standing dead canes was primarily stunted *Phragmites* (less than 5% surface cover) with a small amount of *Impatiens capensis* on one plot. Fiddler crabs were abundant in all three plots.

All three applications provided good control. In no case, however, was control complete. In two or three years *Phragmites* displayed a substantial recovery. If cost is not a problem, a 2-year spray program would appear to provide complete control. If cost is a factor, at approximately $65/acre (in 1983 dollars), a single application will provide very good temporary control.

The herbicide must be applied after the *Phragmites* has tasseled. Earlier treatment will cause a whiskbroom-shaped stress-form of the plant, which will survive and grow back normally next year. The canopy will be much more open after the canes are killed, allowing greater light penetration. If the dead canes are burned or otherwise removed, new growth of more desirable species will be greatly enhanced. (The information dealing with this herbicide was made available from unpublished data through the courtesy of Anthony Florio and Thomas Whittendale of the Division of Fish and Wildlife, Delaware Department of Natural Resources and Environmental Control.)

The Monsanto Chemical Corporation claims that the active portion of Roundup (or Rodeo) has a negligible volatility; thus the transfer to nontarget sites or organisms is minimized. It is reported to be strongly adsorbed by soil colloids, bottom silt, and suspended soil particles in the water and is therefore not easily leached from the soil or moved laterally to nontarget sites. It is claimed to be biodegradable, that is, broken down aerobically and anaerobically by microorganisms into carbon dioxide, water, nitrogen, and phosphate. The microorganisms are reportedly unharmed in the process. The average half-life of the glyphosate is reputed to be 60 days, with 90% degradation in less than 6 months. Monsanto claims that it is practically nontoxic to the various terrestial and aquatic organisms tested. It was reported to be slightly toxic to oysters for a 96-hour TL 50 at > 10 mg/liter, and to trout for a 96-hour LC 50 at 86 mg/liter. Reportedly, it does not bioaccumulate in the food chain (derived from technical information provided by Monsanto Chemical Corporation).

In summary, because of the lack of specificity (Haslam, 1968), herbicides should be used on a tidal marsh only as a last resort (Beeftink, 1977*b*).

REMOTE SENSING*

Management of a resource requires a knowledge of the location, extent, and type of the resource. For wetlands, it is important to map and inventory the wetlands prior to developing management schemes. The

*Prepared by Dr. Michael A. Hardisky, University of Scranton. Much of what is presented here was also presented at the INTECOL International Wetlands Conference held at Trebon, Czechoslovakia, in June 1984.

vast majority of wetlands mapping has been accomplished with the aid of aerial photography. Although aerial photography remains the primary data source in many wetlands mapping and inventory programs, new remote sensors are likely to contribute to this effort in the future. This discussion of remote sensing in wetlands management will first provide some background concerning the development of remote sensing for evaluating natural systems and will include the use of particular remote-sensing media in wetlands systems.

Remote Sensing in Ecology

Remote sensing is the acquisition of information about an object without physical contact. Remote sensing as a tool for evaluating vegetative communities began with the camera. Soon after infrared film became available at retail outlets, ecologists began using it as an aid in vegetation surveys (Ives, 1939). By the 1940s aerial panchromatic films were being used extensively in forestry for timber stand identification and aerial quantification (Spurr and Brown, 1946). Although panchromatic films remained the best data medium in some areas (Jensen and Colwell, 1949), infrared films provided new and useful information in many forestry applications (Spurr, 1949). Infrared photography was used to detect diseased vegetation before the diseased tissue could be identified on panchromatic photography and was found to penetrate haze better than panchromatic films (Colwell, 1961). The unique spectral characteristics of infrared photography found increasingly numerous applications in forestry (Schulte, 1951), agriculture (Shay, 1967), and ecological studies (Colwell, 1967). Panchromatic black-and-white and color films were also being used for surveys of seaweed distribution in Nova Scotia (Cameron, 1950). The different tones found on photographs sparked interest in the reflectance pattern of various plant species. Spectrophotometric analyses of leaf reflectance were undertaken in an effort to increase our understanding of photographic tonal variations among plant species (Hindley and Smith, 1957; Olson and Good, 1962). With advances in the knowledge of the physics of remote reconnaissance (Colwell, 1963), and with advances in sensor technology, remote-sensing instrumentation was developed to probe areas of the electromagnetic spectrum invisible to panchromatic and infrared films (Colwell, 1968).

Remote Sensing and Wetlands

An awareness that wetlands might have value in their natural unaltered state began in the 1930s but did not surface as a national policy until the late 1960s. The first major manifestation of national concern for natural systems was the passage of the National Environmental Policy Act of 1969 (Darnell, 1978*a*). This action was reinforced in 1972 with the passage of the Coastal Zone Management Act, which focused directly on the coast and its wetlands. Coastal states, in some cases, had already enacted legislation or followed the federal lead and enacted legislation protecting and/or regulating activities within wetlands (Haueisen, 1974). Legislative mandates to protect wetlands generated a need and the financial support necessary to begin inventories of the wetland resource.

The result of these events has been close scrutiny of changes in wetlands acreage over time. The most cost-effective means of monitoring changes in areal extent of marshes has been through aerial photographic surveys and, recently, more advanced remote-sensing techniques (Carter, 1978, 1982). The low cost per acre and speedy analysis offered by remote-sensing techniques has recommended their use to monitor the effects of human activities on marshes. The major focus of remote-sensing activities has been the delineation and computation of marsh acreage.

Aerial Photography

Inventories of wetlands using primarily color infrared aerial photography began in the late 1960s as legislation protecting coastal wetlands was being formulated. Stroud and Cooper (1968) used color infrared photography and appropriate ground calibration to estimate the net primary productivity in North Carolina salt marshes. A similar study by Reimold, Gallagher, and Thompson (1973) in Georgia marshes reaffirmed the association between color tones on color infrared photography and different quantities of *Spartina alterniflora* net primary productivity. In both studies, ground harvesting of biomass in selected plant communities was used to estimate net primary productivity. Color tones on the aerial photography were used to differentiate a few community types (different species and/or different biomass quantities for a single species), and the productivity determined by harvesting was applied to the appropriate plant community. The aerial photography served primarily as a means of delineating plant communities and as a template from which the aerial extent of each community could be determined.

Efforts to extract more quantitative data from aerial photographs were also under way. Multispectral photographs and some microdensitometry were used to delineate wetland vegetation types in California (Pestrong, 1969), South Carolina (Guss, 1972), New Jersey (Russell and Wobber, 1972; Wobber and Anderson, 1972), Delaware (Klemas et al., 1974), Wisconsin (Scarpace et al., 1975), and Vermont (Howland, 1980). Different combinations of multiband photography were found useful for discrimination of plant associations in particular coastal and inland wetlands.

Overall, the combination of red and near-infrared spectral regions was found to be the best for species discrimination. Despite the efforts to dissect the spectral signature, color infrared photography was usually considered superior to multiband photos for species discrimination.

A series of investigations conducted on the Georgia coast identified color infrared photography at scales ranging from 1:2,500 to 1:40,000 as the best photographic product for discrimination of salt marsh plant communities (Gallagher et al., 1972a, 1972b; Reimold, Gallagher, and Thompson, 1972). Brackish tidal marshes required larger-scale photography (1:5,000) taken two to three times during the year to provide data necessary for plant association discrimination (Gallagher and Reimold, 1973).

Larger-scale photography in brackish or salt marshes provided more vegetation detail, yielding better discrimination. However, the cost of the photography rises with increases in scale. Aerial photographic missions for wetland mapping were designed to provide adequate resolution for species discrimination at a minimum cost. Small-scale (1:12,000 to 1:24,000) color infrared photography usually acquired in tandem with natural color photography became the standard for state wetland inventories. Reports describing the operational aspects of state wetland inventories are numerous. A few examples include Egan and Hair (1971) for Maryland wetlands, Anderson and Wobber (1973) for New Jersey wetlands, Klemas et al. (1974) for Delaware wetlands, Brown (1978) for New York and New Jersey wetlands, and Benton et al. (1977) for coastal Texas marshes.

Aerial photography was also useful for delineation and discrimination of plant associations in freshwater marshes. The diversity and complexity of freshwater marsh communities are much greater than those of salt marsh communities. More precise seasonal timing of photo acquisition and larger-scale photos are often necessary to differentiate the plant communities of interest. Inventories using aerial photography (usually color infrared) in freshwater marshes include studies of the Florida Everglades (Schneider, 1966, 1968), Nevada marshlands (Seher and Tueller, 1973), Lake Erie fringe marshes (Enslin and Sullivan, 1974), wetlands in glaciated regions of Minnesota (Cowardin and Myers, 1974), freshwater tidal wetlands of Maryland (Shima, Anderson, and Carter, 1976), forested and nonforested wetlands of Tennessee (Carter, Malone, and Burbank, 1979), riverine wetlands of Vermont (MacConnell and Niedzwiedz, 1979), and nontidal inland wetlands in Florida (Stewart, Carter, and Brooks, 1980). Seasonal aerial photographs contained the necessary information for determination of evergreen/deciduous boundaries and separation of deciduous canopy classes in the Great Dismal Swamp (Gammon and Carter, 1979). Color infrared aerial photography has also been used successfully for muskrat population inventories (Doiron and Wilson, 1974).

The documentation of areal change in wetland areas over time has been important data for wetland managers. Essentially all studies dealing with the determination of areal change employ some type of remote-sensing data. The usual procedure is to compare aerial photography from different years and to construct maps that reflect the changes that have occurred (Eyre, 1971; Wicker and Meyer-Arendt, 1982; Hardisky and Klemas, 1983). Many investigations of this sort have been undertaken and are summarized by Tiner (1984). To date, most studies use aerial photography as the data source since the coarse resolution of available satellite data (multispectral scanner) is inadequate to detect changes.

Photo Acquisition

Aerial photography for coastal wetland inventories presents some unique considerations for the mapping team. Sun angle, water turbidity, tidal stage, and seasonal weather conditions are all important factors. Thompson et al. (1973) provided an account of their experiences in conducting air surveys in Georgia marshes from the photogrammetrist's point of view, presenting a pragmatic account of the many unexpected difficulties that can hamper a photographic survey. Additional mapping considerations dealing with geodetic and tidal datums, contour mapping, and water refractions unique to coastal mapping have been presented by McEwen, Kosco, and Carter (1976) and by Masry and MacRitchie (1980). The massive effort to inventory and classify wetlands in a format useful to wetlands management personnel was not without problems. Penny and Gordon (1975) provided (from the manager's point of view) an interesting discussion of the problems in establishing boundaries between wetlands and uplands and the problems of wetland use regulation with large-scale map products. The manager often needs very detailed maps for specific site evaluations, yet the cost of such maps is prohibitive.

Satellite Remote Sensing

With the launching of the Landsat series of satellites in the early 1970s, multispectral scanner (MSS) data became available for wetlands surveys. MSS bands 4 (green region), 5 (red region), and 7 (near-infrared region) can be combined to yield an image that simulates color infrared photography. Although inexpensive per unit of ground area surveyed in comparison to aerial photography, the coarse resolution of the data (57 m × 79 m pixels) limited surveys using MSS data to relatively large tracts of coastal wetlands. As a result of the coarse resolution, MSS data were usually supplemented with high-resolution aerial photography. Usually the aerial photography provided a familiar data source for plant community identification, and the MSS data served as a template for extrapolation to large areas. Mapping and classification of marshlands using MSS data were accomplished in coastal South Carolina and Georgia marshes (Anderson, Carter, and McGinness, 1973); in Virginia coastal marshes (Carter and Schubert, 1974); in Delaware coastal marshes (Klemas et al., 1975); in Louisiana marshes (Butera, 1978, 1983); in lacustrine, palustrine, and riverine wetlands of Michigan (Lyon, 1979*a*); in the Columbia River wetlands of Oregon (Lyon, 1979*b*); and in prairie wetlands of North Dakota (Work and Gilmer, 1976; Gilmer et al., 1980). The combination of MSS data and aerial photography has also been used to develop vegetation maps of forested wetlands, such as the Great Dismal Swamp (Garrett and Carter, 1977; Carter et al., 1977). Zetka (1982) discussed some of the potential applications and types of information that Landsat can provide.

Radiometry

The advent of digital spectral data in specific spectral wavebands from the Landsat multispectral scanner sparked a new era in remote sensing. Data no longer had to be extracted from photographs. Instead, data were already in digital form, allowing direct quantitative treatment of the radiance data. Ground-gathered spectral reflectance data already collected for many agricultural crops (Thomas, Wiegand, and Meyers, 1967; Gausman, Allen, and Cardenas, 1969; Sinclair, Hoffer, and Schreiber, 1971; Gausman, 1974) were used to help interpret spectral signatures found on satellite images. Similar data were also being collected for wetland plants. Carter and Anderson (1972) and Pfeiffer, Linthurst, and Gallagher (1973) provided in situ spectral reflectance data for a number of wetland plant species. This spectroradiometric data constituted a basis for interpreting spectral signatures found on satellite imagery and also represented useful data for evaluating vegetative canopies from the ground.

Ground-based research not directly related to satellite imagery designed to equate fixed-band spectral data with vegetation canopy characteristics was also under way. Changes in the spectral quality of sunlight passing through a tropical forest canopy were found to be highly correlated with the leaf-area index of the canopy (Jordan, 1969). Similarly, Marshall (1970) used optical density measurements in *S. alterniflora* salt marshes as a rapid means of biomass comparison. By the early 1970s, ground-gathered spectral radiance data in the red region and in the near-infrared region were being successfully related to above-ground biomass of a variety of vegetation types. The first to report success in relating spectral data to gramineous biomass were Tucker, Miller, and Pearson (1973) and Pearson, Miller, and Tucker (1976*a*). They presented data indicating a very strong relationship between the biomass of blue grama grass (*Bouteloua gracilis*) and ratio of red to near-infrared radiance.

Similar research showed much the same results for gramineous wetlands species (Bartlett, 1976), but some difficulty was encountered in work with the broadleaf shrub *Iva frutescens* (Drake, 1976). Subsequent work with the hand-held radiometers in Delaware wetlands (Bartlett, 1979; Bartlett and Klemas, 1979, 1980, 1981) in marshes typical of the Danish Wadden-Sea area in Denmark (Jensen, 1980) and using optical density measurements from multiband photos in English bogs and marshes (Curran 1980, 1982, 1983) confirmed the correlation of spectral radiance data with selected canopy characteristics of wetland plant communities. One of the most important canopy parameters consistently related to spectral data was biomass. Other studies concerned primarily with species discrimination using hand-held radiometers included Best, Wehde, and Linder (1981) for hydrophytes occupying the glaciated wetlands of the Prairie Pothole region of South Dakota, Ernst-Dottavio, Hoffer, and Mroczynski (1981) for freshwater wetlands in northeastern Indiana, and Budd and Milton (1982) for a variety of salt marsh plants common to southern England marshes.

NASA has developed an upgraded multispectral scanner, the Thematic Mapper (TM). This instrument is spectrally, spatially, and radiometrically superior to the Landsat MSS for vegetative targets (Tucker, 1978). The TM has a nominal ground resolution of 30 m and has three more spectral bands than the original MSS. The spectral bands are narrower than the MSS bands and the addition of TM band 5 in the middle infrared (1.55-1.75 μ) will likely improve species-discrimination capabilities in wetland systems. Dottavio and Dottavio (1984), using simulated Thematic Mapper data, have suggested that the TM will have comparable classification accuracy to MSS for wetlands and that the addition of the middle infrared band greatly improved the separation between brackish low-marsh and brackish high-marsh communities. Butera, Browder, and Frick (1984), also using TM simulator data, have found that the spectral and spatial improvements of the TM are likely to enhance our ability to discriminate species as well as to estimate percentage cover in wetland systems.

Remote Sensing of Biomass

As indicated earlier, Pearson and coworkers (Pearson, Miller, and Tucker, 1976; Pearson, Tucker, and Miller, 1976) described a strong relationship between canopy biomass and a ratio of red to near-infrared radiance for prairie grass. In most cases the combination of red and near-infrared radiance provided the best correlation with canopy biomass. Apparently the combination of spectrally estimated chlorophyll density and biomass was a good indicator of the quality of the vegetation. Tucker

(1979) has provided an excellent summary of the relationships between vegetation canopy parameters and spectral data from the red and near-infrared regions.

Most literature pertaining to the estimation of vegetation biomass has been simply a correlation between spectral radiance (expressed as a ratio or various other transformations) and canopy biomass (Tucker, Elgin, and McMurtrey, 1979, 1980; Tucker et al., 1979, 1980, 1981; Hardisky, Smart, and Klemas, 1983). It was clear that the relationship between spectral radiance and biomass held for many different plant canopies.

Biomass classification was also being attempted with satellite imagery. Rouse et al. (1973) and Maxwell (1976) found significant correlations between ratios of MSS bands 5 and 7 and biomass classes for rangeland. Bartlett and Klemas (1980) also found good correlation between satellite-gathered spectral data and wetland biomass. Extensive testing of the technique had not been done, nor was an independent assessment of model performance presented. It was encouraging, however, that good correlations were also possible from orbital platforms.

The ground-based efforts to estimate wetlands biomass nondestructively were generally successful. Jensen (1980) was able to predict the amount of standing crop photosynthetic tissue in a *Halimione portulacoides* community to within 10% of harvest estimates using canopy radiance measurements in the near-infrared region. Jensen was the first investigator to describe the relationship between spectral reflectance and biomass, and then use the model to predict biomass in a different area and at a different time. Work in Delaware tidal marshes has been successful in predicting *S. alterniflora* biomass to within 10% of comparable harvest estimates (Hardisky, Klemas, and Daiber, 1983; Hardisky, Klemas, and Smart, 1983; Hardisky et al., 1984). A combination of red (TM band 3) and near-infrared (TM band 4) spectral data has been shown to be most effective for biomass predictions. Instantaneous measurements of aboveground biomass were combined over a growing season to yield a nondestructive estimate of annual net aerial primary productivity (NAPP). The accuracy of the NAPP estimate is a direct function of the accuracy of individual biomass estimates. The NAPP estimates were usually within 10% of comparable harvest NAPP estimates (Hardisky et al., 1984). This study was the first demonstration that canopy radiance measurements could be used in an operational framework to estimate marsh biomass and NAPP nondestructively. Subsequent research in this area has expanded the ground-based technique to brackish marsh canopies. Preliminary results and the complexities of working with a variety of canopy forms are discussed by Hardisky (1983). Investigations are presently under way to extend these ground-based remote sensing techniques to data gathered from orbital platforms. Although many problems remain, it appears that soon we may have the capability for quantitative biomass (or carbon or energy) assessments for large marsh areas via automated computer techniques.

Remote Sensing — The Future

Remote-sensing contributions to wetland management have essentially been in the areas of mapping and vegetative classification. The relative low cost and flexible format of aerial photography account for its wide use in the past and present for wetland management. As remote-sensing technology advances, more quantitative measurements will be available. Botkin et al. (1984) discussed the contributions satellite remote sensing has made to large-area surveys of biomass (or carbon) and suggested that remote sensing will contribute significantly to future global vegetation assessment.

New data sources of particular interest for wetland applications are the large-format camera (using 23×46-cm film) scheduled as payload on the U.S. space shuttle (Doyle, 1978) and the imaging spectrometer now under development and scheduled for future shuttle missions. The large-format camera will provide photography of specific areas of the globe at a 1:1,000,000 scale with a 15 m nominal ground resolution. The imaging spectrometer employs linear array technology, eliminating the need for moving parts, and will provide a continuous reflectance spectrum for each ground pixel. These advances in instrumentation and concomitant advances in computer analysis techniques will greatly enhance the types of data available for use by wetland managers.

Even with advances in remote-sensing technology, aerial photography alone or in combination with satellite multispectral images is likely to remain the primary data source for the wetland manager. Remote-sensing capabilities have crossed the threshold of simple areal inventories. Our management effectiveness in the future will be directly related to our ability to collect and analyze data on a regional, ecosystem, and, eventually, global scale.

Chapter 3

Water Management: Dikes, Impoundments, Ponds, and Ditches

RECLAIMED LAND AND IMPOUNDMENTS

Definition and Special Features

Reclamation involves the loss of paramaritime and intertidal habitat and sometimes the gain of terrestrial or brackish-water habitat (Gray, 1979). Reclaimed land signifies human activity; the habitats that are created are thus in some way "derived" or artificial. They may range from high-level salt marshes displaying relatively little human involvement to tracts of land that have been intensively cultivated for agriculture. Gray (1977) and Buchner (1979) characterized reclaimed land as resulting from the erection of a distinct dike or embankment and containing the land behind the dike as well as the subhabitats created by drainage ditches, small bodies of water, and the enclosing embankment itself. Gray excluded areas seaward of the dike that might comprise land-improvement activities such as ditching, brushwood groins and *Spartina* plantings to encourage accelerated accretion, and eventual grazing.

Reclaimed land may be created either directly for agriculture or industry, or indirectly through the construction of dikes for other purposes. The direct method is to enclose an area, pump it dry, or fill it in with

Note: For a more extensive coverage of land reclamation from the sea, see Knights and Phillips (1979).

dredge spoil, industrial waste, or domestic sewage. Such areas suffer varying degrees of impact. The ultimate degradation of marshland by fill for the purpose of erecting buildings defies restoration and is not germane to this discussion. Land is indirectly reclaimed when it is blocked off by dikes constructed for highways, railroads, and other uses. This land usually represents a vegetated intertidal area, but it may occasionally be a bare mud flat. One such example is the embankment, created in 1857, to carry the railroad across the northern portion of Morecambe Bay, England, which enclosed about 450 hectares of intertidal flats (Gray and Adam, 1974).

Reclaimed lands have certain special features. One is a temporal change in vegetation and animals from the condition at the time of embankment. There is also a spatial distinction between the marine and the terrestrial or freshwater habitats. In addition to these features, Gray (1977) characterized reclaimed lands as either temporary or permanent. The former is associated with those transitory marsh stages between the time of embankment and the final agricultural or industrial use. The latter is associated with reclaimed lands that have, or were designed to retain, a high level of wildlife interest as more or less permanent wetlands. Because of different ecological interests, these two types of reclaimed land should be managed differently.

Diked Lands for Agriculture and Animal Husbandry

Dikes and Aboiteaux.   In the early part of this century, Warren (1911) identified seven points of concern when considering any marsh reclamation: the nature of the soil and the level of its fertility; the elevation of the land surface relative to low tide and tidal range; the area and slope of the land; protection from storms; receding or advancing shoreline; the nature of upland drainage; and the market for the products of the land. These considerations are still valid today.

To reclaim a marsh three things are necessary: to shut out the sea, to wash out the salt, and to provide for removal of the water. Water to be removed includes fresh water falling as rain or draining from the upland and sea water intruding through a leaking sluice gate or topping the dike during storm tides (Ganong, 1903; Wright, 1907; Warren, 1911).

The sea can be excluded by the construction of a dike, which would be triangular in cross-section and usually built of marsh mud derived from a borrow pit paralleling the dike (Ganong, 1903; Warren, 1911; Dalby, 1957). There would often be a core of stakes and brush. Warren (1911) described a cross-sectional view of dikes in the Canadian Maritimes constructed with alternate layers of mud and trees. No tree trunk extended the full width of the dike since that would enhance the possibility of leakage. The seaward slope of the dike should be quite flat. When the dike was made of clay, the slope should be about 3 to 1, but with more sand the slope should be at least 4 to 1 and as much as 10 to 1. The seaward slope was often protected by stone riprap or a method of protection called picket and heading brush, where rows of horizontally placed logs on the face of the dike were kept in place by vertical timbers driven into the embankment. Away from the main tidal streams, the so-called running dike was often faced with vertical timber planking (Warren, 1911).

Ganong (1903) also provided us with a description of the process of dike construction in Acadia (the portion of New Brunswick and Nova Scotia occupied originally by the French). When a tidal stream was diked, five or six rows of large logs were driven into the ground and other logs were laid between each row. In the center an aboiteau (wooden clapper valve or sluice gate) was installed on horizontal hinges so that the fresh water from the streams and drains behind the dikes could flow seaward. The incoming tide forcibly closed the valve so the sea water could not enter. The original meaning of *aboiteau* (or *aboideau*) referred to the water-control structure (Ganong, 1903), but more recently it has come to refer to the dike as well. The term *aboiteau* was derived from the Saintonge region of France, where the term *aboteau* has been used. The aboiteau functions better when it is placed low in the intertidal range and when the tidal range is large to allow for a long period of drainage. For these reasons, reclamation of marshes has been more successful in the Bay of Fundy of Canada than in the United States (Warren, 1911). Warren stressed the importance of having a properly functioning sluice gate. He noted that at a number of marsh reclamation sites much of the water draining from the marsh actually resulted from seawater leakage at the sluice gate. This leakage could actually work to an advantage in such areas as the Bay of Fundy with its very heavy silt load. Due to continual drainage, the marsh surface tends to subside; infiltering would help restore the marsh elevation as well as add nutrients to the soil by way of sediments carried in the leakage (Ganong, 1903; Wright, 1907; Warren, 1911).

Before the reclaimed marshland can be used effectively, three to four years must elapse while the sea salts are leached from the marsh muds by rainwater or snow. To facilitate the leaching of these salts as well as enhance the production of the more desirable grasses and prevent bogs from forming behind the dikes, the accumulated water must be drained from the land. Once the dike is installed and the tide gate made operational, the natural drainage becomes intermittent. Therefore, the storage capacity must be large, and the ditches must be wider than would otherwise be necessary. The greater part of the storage area should be nearest the outlet so that the water can be discharged quickly. In this way water from remote lateral ditches can drain into the storage area (Wright, 1907).

Leaching by rain and snow is the only general—albeit slow—way to leach salt out of the soil. Frequent mowing will help remove the salt. Close pasturing by sheep and cattle help compact the soil and get rid of coarse grasses and weeds, but the animals tend to fill the ditches, which then must be cleaned to maintain drainage. As both Wright (1907) and Warren (1911) pointed out, well-functioning ditches, by being large enough and kept free of vegetation, are the key to good drainage. In the Low Countries and England, this drainage water was pumped out with the aid of windmills; the practice continues with modern electric pumps. In areas of the United States where the tidal range was small or where the marsh surface had subsided, pumping was also done. Otherwise the sluice gate was used, as it was in the Maritimes of Canada.

Some believe that the conversion of wetlands to farm land destroys the wetland character of the land and puts a stress on the remaining wetlands and estuaries that border the new farm land. Following such a conversion in North Carolina, there were reported changes in the nutrient loading and salinity pattern of an estuary. Further, the magnitude of such a change can be reduced if the runoff percolates through an intact marsh border before entering the estuary (Barber, Kirby-Smith, and Parsley, 1979).

History of Diking and Its Consequences.   In Western Europe, low sea walls were being thrown up by the seventh century; the practice was well established by the eleventh and twelfth centuries (Beeftink, 1975; Jéquel and Rouve, 1983). Kestner (1972), in describing the old coastline of the Wash on the east coast of England, stated that the "Roman Bank" was constructed around the Wash probably in the eighth century. These first walls were for protection against the sea, not to reclaim land. Such embankments did protect large areas from flooding and siltation, however. This, along with the advance and retreat of the sea, promoted accretion and maturation in the remaining salt marshes. Such actions stimulated the development of more progressive means of embankment, which, along with demographic factors, enhanced the shift from using salt marshes for livestock grazing to creating polders for tillage. Subsequently, during the Middle Ages, land subsidence, a rise in both the sea level and the water table, political and religious unrest, as well as military action wrought great changes in the landscape of the Low Countries and parts of England. In this way humans created their own environment and also changed the environment for plants and animals (Beeftink, 1975).

On the basis of his study of cores and trenching, Kestner (1962) found that an equilibrium had become established between accretion and erosion of the salt marshes forming outside the Roman Bank. This appears to have lasted for several centuries until hydraulic conditions changed suddenly. This change is represented by an accumulation of very fine sediments superimposed on the old marshes and a great extension of the salt marsh area. Kestner speculated that the sudden transformation might have been caused by the diversion of the river, the Great Ouse, at the beginning of the thirteenth century. These new marshes were enclosed by the mid-seventeenth century, and sediments began to accumulate on the seaward side of the embankments. The initially high accretion rates of these sediments were followed by a period of equilibrium between accretion and erosion; at such times, a new embankment would be thrown up to restimulate rapid accretion. In this way the salt marsh has advanced seaward through a whole series of dikes. In recent times accretion rates as high as 31 mm/year have been recorded from the lower salt marsh zones of the Wash; rates of 20 mm/year were average for the less-well-vegetated pioneer marsh zone (Corlett and Gray, 1976).

Kestner (1962, 1975), in discussing a loose boundary regime in the Wash, has proffered an explanation for this sediment-deposition pattern. Accretion is the result of continual circulation of large amounts of sediments by the tides. On the foreshore, or intertidal area, this sediment circulation occurs mainly in the creeks. During flood tides, the silt-laden water spills over creek banks and spreads onto the foreshore, where precipitation occurs as the velocity slows. The normal ebb flow, which is of longer duration and slower velocity, fails to remove all this accreted material, particularly in the upper, landward reaches. The erosion and accretion patterns, however, achieve equilibrium over an annual basis, for the spring floods move the sediments seaward again.

The creation of an embankment impedes the tidal flow, which reduces the velocity of the flooding tides and enhances the accretion rate. Since accretion rates are greatest along the sides of the sediment-laden creeks and channels and taper off across the face of the embankment, a band of sediment is laid down in a cusp pattern: the broad base rests against the embankment and triangular extensions project seaward along each creek. The area between the cusps is molded by the scouring action of the ebb tide. The accreted zone is stabilized by diatoms and other benthic algae (Coles, 1979). Eventually higher plants invade the area and trap more silt until the land rises above the normal high-tide level. At this stage the sediment deposits are contained in the creek bottoms, where they are carried back to sea by the ebb tide and the system enters a dynamic balance. The marsh front will then remain stationary until another embankment is built (or a natural catastrophe occurs).

The process of accretion can be hastened by the creation of sedimentation fields to trap silts and clays through a system of squares made of brushwood and earthen groins intersected by ditches. This process can be further reinforced by planting *Spartina townsendii (S. anglica)* and other species (Beeftink, 1977*b*). The marsh soils that are laid down display a successional change from immature, relatively organic, nutrient-poor soils of the seaward pioneer zone to more mature soils with higher organic and nutrient content at the landward edge (Gray and Bunce, 1972; Corlett and Gray, 1976).

Dalby (1957) suggested that there is an ideal height for reclaiming marshland that has accreted in front of a dike. Insofar as the Wash is concerned, with its spring tides of 22 ft this optimum elevation is 11 to 11.5 ft above ordnance datum (OD). Dalby found that the soil becomes very heavy at any higher elevations, mainly due to clay. *Spartina anglica* and *Salicornia stricta* become established at about 8 ft (OD) at the point where deposits change from fine sand to light clay. At 10 ft OD, *Spartina* gives way to the fescues. According to Dalby, when that stage is reached the marsh is "ripe" and ready to be banked. He cautioned that the dike should be high enough to take care of storm surges and should be made of clay to reduce erosion. He also advocated a soak-dike or ditch on the landward side of the levee for use in the final drainage of the land. Warren (1911) did not advocate such a drainage ditch, as he believed it weakened the foundation for the embankment.

Gray (1972) and Gray and Adam (1974) have provided an example of English salt marsh reclamation, in the Morecambe Bay area on the west coast of England. The recent history of the bay is one of progressive silting and salt marsh formation. Approximately 400 ha of salt marsh were added between 1845 and 1967. We can infer that much of this addition resulted from the periodic accretion process stemming from the reclamation activity described by Kestner (1972, 1975). The earliest seabanks were built in the area during the thirteenth century, and since then about 1,300 ha (3,300 acres) have been embanked, of which some 400 ha (1,300 acres) have been reclaimed directly for agriculture (Gray, 1972). The first major reclamation work took place in the late eighteenth century. Prior to that only small bits and pieces of embankment were erected. Following the turn of the nineteenth century, a variety of schemes, large and small, were developed to reclaim portions of Morecambe Bay. In addition, a grandiose plan to enclose some 46,000 acres during the 1840s did not materialize when the route for the London-Glasgow railroad line was changed. However, the completion in 1857 of the railroad from Ulverston to Lancaster allowed the incidental enclosing of about 1,000 acres, the single largest act of diking.

Soon after their arrival in North America, French Acadians began to dike the *Spartina* marshes in the Bay of Fundy region and the St. Lawrence estuary of Canada. They installed drainage ditches in the higher marshes and simple dikes along the seaward edge of the shoreline marshes (Reed and Moisan, 1971; Harvey, 1973). As the salt was washed out and the water table lowered by drainage ditches, the better grasses and clovers replaced the wild marsh vegetation behind the dikes (Clark,

1968). According to Harvey, the opinion that prevailed from the early seventeenth century to the early 1960s was that "the only good marsh was a diked marsh."

More than three centuries of agricultural history are associated with the tidal marshes of the Maritimes. The French first began to use them in the Annapolis Basin (Clark, 1968), and by 1672 they were reclaiming marshlands in the Tintamarre (Tantramar) district at the head of Chignecto Bay in southeastern New Brunswick. There are numerous sites of tidal marshes along the St. Lawrence estuary, Annapolis Basin, Musquash, St. John, St. Martins, and elsewhere, but the areas where the Bay of Fundy marshes are best developed are in the two heads of the bay: the Minas Basin and the Chignecto Bay. The largest block of tidal marshes are the combined Tintamarre-Aulac-Missequash marshes located along the New Brunswick-Nova Scotia border (Ganong, 1903; Jackson and Maxwell, 1971).

There were an estimated 34,300 acres of diked and undiked marshes in New Brunswick in 1895. In 1883 an estimated 12,600 acres were on the Nova Scotia side of the boundary, while New Brunswick had 19,400 acres in the Tintamarre, Aulac, and Missequash areas. In the Cumberland Basin portion of the Chignecto Bay, Ganong (1903) estimated approximately 40,700 acres of diked and wild marshland. Including the Minas Basin, he estimated a total of about 70,000 acres of wild and reclaimed marshland. More recently, Allan D. Smith of the Canadian Wildlife Service, Sackville, New Brunswick, provided an estimate of the salt marsh acreage in the Maritimes (Table 3-1) that is subject to change following a more critical examination of aerial photography (A. D. Smith, written communic., 1980). There appears to be some diversity of views regarding the fertility and quality of reclaimed marshes: earlier reporters extolled their virtues and more recent observers have questioned their value relative to the cost of establishment and maintenance. Nesbit (1885) and Means (1903) described reclaimed lands as being very fertile. Ganong (1903) portrayed them as being "wonderfully fertile, and in this respect they are unsurpassed, if they are equaled, by any land in eastern Canada." He and Warren (1911) acknowledged that they were not equally good for all crops. Grasses and grains did best. Although root crops can be grown in these heavy, compact soils, they do not do well. Hay production and pasturage are the almost exclusive current use (Retson, 1966; Jackson and Maxwell, 1971). In the South Atlantic states, rice was grown on great plantations of reclaimed marshland until the Civil War ended the slave labor that had made it so profitable (Bonsteel, 1909; McKenzie et al., 1980). Truck garden crops such as celery and corn, as well as cranberries, were important in the reclaimed marshes of the Middle Atlantic and New England states (Warren 1911). The upland grasses that grew on the best reclaimed lands in England yielded up to 3 tons per

Table 3-1. Approximate area of salt marshes in the Maritime Provinces (in hectares)

	Area of Remaining Salt Marsh	Area of Diked Former Salt Marsh	Total
Nova Scotia	12,370[a]	17,806	30,176
New Brunswick	6,070[b]	14,974	21,044
Prince Edward Island	4,879[a]	111	4,990
Totals	23,319	32,891	56,210
	(41.5%)	(58.5%)	(100%)

[a]Data extracted from the Nova Scotia and Prince Edward Island wetlands inventory, Canadian Wildlife Service, Sackville, New Brunswick, 1983 (calculated from 1974-1976 color air photos).

[b]Compiled by Canadian Wildlife Service, Sackville, New Brunswick (1980) from soil survey maps and topographic mapsheets. The figure is approximate and is probably on the low side.

acre with no fertilizers and with only an infrequent plowing (Ganong, 1903). Ganong attributed this production to three features: the appropriate nutrients and soil conditions were present; the fertility was very long-lasting; and the water conditions of the soil were such that the vegetation was less affected by dry seasons than that of the uplands.

There continues to be a positive relationship between agricultural efforts and marsh reclamation in parts of England. The influence of agriculture in western Norfolk extends to the sea margins of the Wash. A total of 48,500 ha (about 120,000 acres) has been reclaimed since Saxon times, for the most part in bits and pieces: some 250 ha were reclaimed in 1974 (Gray, 1976). The formation of new salt marsh keeps pace with continuing reclamation efforts, as already described.

On the other hand, some reports clearly indicate that reclamation of marsh land is not as attractive as it once was, particularly on the west coast of England. Gray and Adam (1974) quoted an early source, which stated that "the straw of the oat and other grain crops sometimes attained a height of six feet or more, the quality of the grain being far superior to any that ever appeared on the market." No such lush growth exists today, and the decline in fertility has been reflected in the reduction of the yearly rent. The present uses include intensive grass harvesting, rough grazing, a golf course, ornamental gardens, dock and harbor facilities, and industrial spoil heaps. While many acres of salt marsh continue to form, many of the formerly reclaimed agricultural acres have regressed to freshwater marsh or have been lost, reverting to intertidal salt marsh following the penetration of the dikes by the sea (Gray, 1972; Gray and Adam, 1974).

Although of primary importance to the Acadians, the diked lands have been of minor interest and importance to the people in the Annapolis Valley of Nova Scotia for the past two centuries. Although the diked lands covered only about 6% of the Annapolis Valley, the Acadians did little to use the non-marshlands because of the difficulty of clearing them, the acidity of the soils, and the early exhaustion of natural fertility. They were frequently criticized for their seeming laziness in not clearing the uplands for agriculture. The fertility of the diked lands, however, had given the Acadian upland soils a reputation they did not deserve (Clark, 1968), as the next wave of settlers soon discovered. Marsh reclamation was continued by New Englanders and British immigrants (Planters) after the Acadians were expelled. Ironically, the new settlers had to invite some Acadians back to teach them how to repair and maintain the dikes. (Even so, the Acadians were not allowed to return to their former farms [Clark, 1968].)

The new immigrants, however, were never fully successful in this unfamiliar farm land and began to cultivate the uplands as they had done in their former homeland. To enhance and restore the fertility of these lands, they used marsh mud as a fertilizer. They gathered it from the creek banks and bottoms in the fall and winter and spread it on the upland fields. This material added nutrients and body to the lighter upland soils, making them more moisture-retentive. In addition, the mollusk shells collected along with the mud helped reduce the soil acidity. Such mud was slower-acting but longer-lasting than commercial fertilizers (Warren, 1911; Eaton, 1972; Hocking, 1978).

The fact that many reclaimed acres of Canadian marshland lie idle, have become freshwater bogs, or have reverted to tidal marsh with the rupture of the dikes would suggest that these reclaimed lands no longer have much agricultural value (Reed and Moisan, 1971; Reed and Smith, 1972; Gray and Adam, 1974). Initially the marshes were reclaimed through the pooled efforts of the farmers in the community. In subsequent years the unwillingness of the poorer farmers to cooperate in the continual maintenance of the dikes caused many of the more proficient farmers to withdraw their own efforts (Ganong, 1903). In the early 1900s, unreclaimed marshland had values of $1 to $20 per acre in the United States and $1 per acre in Canada: reclaimed marshland usually averaged $50 to $60 and up to $200 per acre in Canada (Warren, 1911). Today the additional enclosure of marshland by diking would yield very expensive agricultural land (Harvey, 1973), and apparently the returns would not justify the financial outlays. While specifically discussing the diked lands along the St. Lawrence River estuary, Reed and Smith (1972) said that "under intensive management and care the capabilities of (the reclaimed) soil may approach those of the adjacent lowland plain." They observed that the low yields from diked lands provided insufficient incentives to maintain the dikes and water-control structures.

An examination of farming in the Tintamarre area of Sackville, New Brunswick, can serve as a portrayal of the agricultural use of reclaimed marshlands in the Maritimes of Canada. The status of agriculture in the area of Sackville is in sharp contrast to that of earlier times, when it was one of the most prosperous farming districts in the Maritimes (Retson, 1966; Jackson and Maxwell, 1971). These diked lands were ideally suited for forage production and the cash sale of hay, which was the basis for the prosperity of the area. Hay was needed to feed the many horses used in the forestry operations, which were prospering due to the shipbuilding industry. The demand for hay fell with the decline of shipbuilding and suffered still more with the advent of the automobile.

Between the world wars, agriculture declined in the Maritimes and little was done to maintain the dikes. Even though an increased market demand developed during World War II, a reduced source of labor made it difficult to keep up the dikes. Demands were initiated for restoration of reclaimed marshland. A major reclamation program was carried out by joint efforts of federal and provincial governments under the Maritime Marsh Rehabilitation Act (MMRA) of 1948. By the end of 1968-1969, a total of 232 miles of dikes, 408 aboiteaux, 5 major tidal dams, and 20 miles of river bank control installations had been constructed. Such work was done only because the provincial governments were willing to provide lands necessary for the works and to undertake reconditioning, construction, and maintenance of all protective works. Federal expenditures for construction and maintenance were nearly $19 million, while another $9 million went for design, supervision, and administration. When responsibility for all these dikes was turned over to the provinces in 1970, there were about 82,000 acres of protected marshland in the three provinces. Twenty-two thousand of these acres (27%) were located in the Tintamarre area of New Brunswick, and accounted for about $1.9 million (10%) of the total federal MMRA funds (Retson, 1966; Jackson and Maxwell, 1971). As a part of the MMRA, each farmer had the right to a certain number of hours of work provided by subsidized heavy equipment. Reed and Smith (1972) believed that the use of such equipment to dike off tidal land appeared to be more a question of "using up" the allotted subsidies rather than a sincere attempt to enhance land-surface production. They were equally pessimistic when they concluded that the time-consuming maintenance operations required to assure proper functioning of the water-control structures and dike maintenance appeared to be inconsistent with the local farmers' interests and abilities, further jeopardizing the success of such activities.

While the MMRA reclaimed marshland and restored dikes and water-control structures, it could not protect the farmers from the technological advances developing in North American agriculture. The Maritimes, because of their many small-scale enterprises, had great difficulty adjusting to these changes. The result was a decline in agricultural productivity and, correspondingly, farm income.

During the 40-year period 1921-1961, the total population in the Tintamarre district remained essentially the same: 4,500 to 4,600. However, the farm population declined from 3,131 to 1,251, the number of farms declined from 861 to 265, and the total farm acreage decreased from 92,740 acres to 45,909 acres. In the same 40-year period, the total pasture land declined gradually from 8,551 acres to 7,734 acres (1941) to 2,389 acres (1951), rebounding to 8,158 acres in 1956 and reaching a peak of 8,710 acres in 1961. This drop in 1951 and the increase from 1956 to 1961 reflected flooding by the sea and subsequent reclamation. Hay acreage had also shown corresponding declines over the years from 15,294 acres (1921) to 10,267 acres (1961). There were corresponding declines in grain and other cropland acreage as well as declines in the numbers of livestock (Retson, 1966).

The typical farm was located on an upland ridge with adjoining marshland. Frequently, individual lots of reclaimed marshland were located away from the farmstead—up to 3 to 4 miles away. This factor also worked against the enhancement of profitability. Intensively used reclaimed lands are no longer randomly distributed. They occur in well-defined concentrations related to drainage conditions, quality of access roads, distance from the farmstead, field size, and scale of farm operation. Into the early 1970s, hay and pasturage was the major crop and accounted for 92% of the improved acreage on each farm. Yields of hay (1.27 tons per acre) on marshland soils were lower than on upland soils (1.61 tons per acre). On the basis of species grown and dates of cutting, the quality of marshland hay was lower than that grown on the uplands. The yields of hay were directly related to applications of lime and fertilizer and to time spent on marshland improvements, mainly drainage (Retson, 1966; Jackson and Maxwell, 1971). Jackson and Maxwell believed that commercial agriculture should develop, or be encouraged, only where it makes good economic and social sense to do so; this is reflected in the shift from marshland agriculture toward upland farming.

There are a number of reasons why marsh reclamation has had limited success in North America, and particularly in the United States. Warren (1911) thought that people did not fully realize the true value of such improvements. A more cogent reason may have been the lack of sufficient capital. Means (1903, after Shaler, 1886) stated that the cost of reclaiming and reducing tidal lands to cultivation should not exceed one-fifth of the value per acre. The price per mile of dike in New Jersey ranged between

$3,700 to $14,300 (presumably 1911 dollars), while the construction of the aboiteau in the Aulac River in New Brunswick cost $27,500 in 1863. Another very practical reason for lack of success stemmed from a need for united and harmonious action on the part of all the landowners. A great deal of prolonged disharmony and lack of cooperation among the towns-people was evident in Warren's description of the reclamation in Marshfield, Massachusetts. A lack of cooperation among the landowners was also evident in Jackson and Maxwell's (1971) description of the changes that have occurred in the reclaimed lands of the Tintamarre district of New Brunswick. Additionally, there was either a lack of understanding or a disregard for the fact that marsh surfaces settled and periodically needed replenishment by an influx of sediments (Warren, 1911; Penfound and Schneidau, 1945). Early Canadian farmers, however, must have recognized this, as Ganong (1903) described the filing of bogs and lakes by letting silt-laden sea water flow through canals constructed for that very purpose. This technique, known as "warpin," was once widespread in Europe on large estuaries such as the Rhine, the Humber, and the Ems (A. J. Gray, written communic.). Buchner (1979) noted that an area can become "overwarped" by the addition of too much alluvial clay. The high clay content and probable lack of adequate drainage can make the soil unworkable during winter months. In Canada, the scarcity of skilled persons to design, construct, and maintain the dikes and aboiteaux properly became a serious problem. Dikes often were not high enough to keep storm tides from flooding over the top and washing out the levee. Sluice gates were poorly designed, badly constructed, and often too small. Ditches could not carry out their drainage function as they became silted up and choked with vegetation (Warren, 1911; Jackson and Maxwell, 1971).

There is substantial evidence of diking around and near Tinicum Island, located on the southern edge of Philadelphia. It is uncertain whether the Swedes engaged in diking during their 12-year sojourn there (1643-1655), but it seems reasonable that the Dutch who replaced them did. The earliest known reference to dikes is a historical statement that the banks were breached by British troops in 1777. The diked land apparently was used for pasturage and crops, and the owners of these dikes were expected to keep them in repair, clean, and mowed. Subsequently, during the nineteenth and twentieth centuries, these dikes fell into disrepair and the area was crossed and recrossed by isolated embankments to carry railroad lines and highways (McCormick, 1970).

Farther south in Cumberland County, New Jersey, along the Maurice River, extensive acreage of marshland had been diked and reclaimed early in the nineteenth century but allowed to regress. In the early years of the twentieth century (1903-1906), these dikes were restored and additional marshland tracts were embanked. At that time Smith (1907) advocated complete water removal from a diked marsh to enhance its value. Crops of timothy hay, wheat, corn, potatoes, and strawberries were harvested (Warren, 1911). Many of these marshland tracts bordering Delaware Bay still produce a crop of the salt marsh hay *Spartina patens*. Instead of forage for domestic animals, it is now used largely as garden mulch. Some of this hay has also been used as insulation and packing material for glass and other breakables as well as stuffing for pads lining coffins.

In addition to reclaiming land for crops, salt hay, and pasture, tidal restrictions have been created to enhance mosquito control and to provide flood control. Some workers (Ferrigno, 1959; Slavin, Shisler, and Ferrigno, 1978) have had grave reservations about diking because of possible conflicts between salt hay production and mosquito control and wildlife interests. Many workers have pointed out the relationship between vegetation and mosquito breeding (Smith, 1902; Connell, 1940; Darsie and Springer, 1957). These insects tend to be much more prevalent in the higher intertidal zone where *S. patens* dominates (Table 3-2.) Ferrigno

Figure 3-1. The edge of a salt hay *(Spartina patens)* meadow in early June, situated between Dividing Creek and Port Norris, New Jersey. (Photo by F. C. Daiber)

Table 3-2. Average number of *Aedes* larvae and pupae per dip in salt marsh vegetation in New Jersey

	Mosquito Species		
	A. cantator	A. sollicitans	Total
S. patens	0.31	6.95	7.26
S. alterniflora	0.01	0.37	0.38
Mixture	0.29	2.42	2.71

Source: From Ferrigno, F., 1958, A two-year study of mosquito breeding in the natural and untouched salt marshes of Egg Island, *New Jersey Mosq. Exterm. Assoc. Proc.* **45:**132-139.

Table 3-3. Abundance of mosquito larvae and pupae within the two work units on the Cadwalader Public Hunting and Fishing Grounds in New Jersey

Work Unit	Acreage	Average No. of Larvae per Dip per Genus			Seasonal Totals	
		Aedes	Anopheles	Culex	No. of Dips	No. of Larvae and Pupae
I	795	2.79	0.01	0.14	6,360	18,803
II	1,245	0.56	0.01	0.32	9,680	8,644
Total	2,040	3.35	0.02	0.46	16,040	27,447

Source: From Ferrigno, F., 1959, Further study on mosquito production on the newly acquired Cadwalader tract, *New Jersey Mosq. Exterm. Assoc. Proc.* **46:**95-102.

(1959) recorded the numbers of mosquitoes in two portions of tidal marshland that the state of New Jersey had recently acquired (Table 3-3). Eighty percent of Work Unit I was bounded by dikes to reclaim the land for salt hay production, whereas only 7% of Work Unit II was diked. Ferrigno found that 99.9% of mosquito production in Work Unit II came from the small diked area or the area adjacent to the uplands. (Table 3-4 provides an insight into the interrelationship of mosquito production, vegetation, and diking.) It is apparent that mosquitoes were more prevalent in the diked areas and among the vegetation of the higher intertidal zone. In addition, Ferrigno found an inverse relationship between mosquito production and the presence of avian fauna (Table 3-5). Populations of certain bird species such as the clapper rail (*Rallus longirostris*) and the black duck (*Anas rubripes*) are severely reduced by reduction of their food supplies in diked marshes (Ferrigno, 1959, 1961; Ferrigno and Jobbins, 1966; Roman, 1978).

Greenhalgh (1971) noted that, when salt marshes are embanked, the halophyte vegetation is replaced by farmland plants, and Glue (1971) observed that the floral state is determined by the age of the dike. The natural avian community of the salt marsh disappears, and passerine

Table 3-4. Summary of the dipping record for the different vegetational types in a New Jersey marsh

Vegetation Type	Larvae-Pupae per Dip		No. of Dips	No. of Larvae-Pupae
	C. salinarius	A. sollicitans		
Undiked				
S. alterniflora	0	0.0001	8,280	1
S. patens	0.11	2.74	1,080	3,293
P. virgatum	0.003	0	600	2
Woodland swamp	0.02	0.01	840	620
Diked				
S. alterniflora	0.26	4.22	360	1,701
S. patens	0.72	3.54	2,760	13,376
S. cynosuroides	2.94	4.66	240	1,988
P. virgatum	0.21	0.75	1,320	2,219
D. spicata	0	3.52	600	2,761
J. gerardi	0	2.86	240	780
Typha spp.	2.01	0.21	120	707

Source: After Ferrigno, F., 1959, Further study on mosquito production on the newly acquired Cadwalader tract, *New Jersey Mosq. Exterm. Assoc. Proc.* **46**:95-102.

birds become more abundant on these wet pastures. If poorly drained, fens and ponds will support more bird species; pools behind the dike and a high water table will allow a rich bird community to develop. When the land is drained and plowed, all species leave except for a poor farm-land bird community (Greenhalgh, 1971). Glue (1971) noted that each habitat is dominated by a different bird species: the salt marsh and brackish pools by the meadow pipit, the soft mud pans by the reed bunting, the hard mud pans by the yellow wagtail, and the grasslands by the skylark. In addition, Glue observed that enclosed salt marsh and adjoining grass-land stages hold the greatest variety and density of breeding birds: 15 species, 107 pairs/km^2 and 16 species, 157 pairs/km^2, respectively. As pointed out by Møller (1975), such numbers could reflect the size and heterogeneity of these particular habitats. Glue (1971) also noted an association between the loss of tidal mud flats and salt marsh, along with an increase in suitable roosting areas and a peripheral ditch system, and the changes in the incidence and absolute numbers of certain waders. Four species decreased, nine increased, and four showed no change.

Roman (1978) and Roman, Niering, and Warren (1984) observed a substantial reduction in soil water salinity on many Connecticut marshes. Tidal restrictions in the form of bridges, culverts, causeways, and dikes have directly reduced tidal flow to more than 90% of these wetlands with some restrictions dating back to the latter part of the seventeenth century. In marshes exposed to normal tidal flow, Roman noted that soil

Table 3-5. Comparison of waterfowl utilization, clapper rail usage and mosquito breeding within the main vegetational zone of a New Jersey marsh

	No. of Birds Flushed during 10 Censuses of 100-Acre Sample in Each Zone		Annual Total of Mosquito Larvae and Pupae per Dip
Vegetational Zone	Waterfowl	Clapper Rail	
S. alterniflora (tall)	1,742	29	0
S. alterniflora (short)	1,239	33	0.0001
S. patens	285	3	3.05
Diked hay meadow	111	1	4.13

Source: From Ferrigno, F., 1959, Further study on mosquito production on the newly acquired Cadwalader tract, *New Jersey Mosq. Exterm. Assoc. Proc.* **46**:95-102.

water salinity levels displayed average values of 25 to 30‰ among various marsh systems. On the restricted marsh sites in these same systems, the average salinity was 5 to 9‰, with one system fluctuating from zero to 20‰. He also observed a lowering of the water table, which was usually 2.6 to 13 cm below the surface on the normal, unrestricted marsh sites. For the restricted marsh sites, water levels averaged between 28 and 38 cm below the surface, with one reading at 19 cm and a maximum at 57 cm. There was a 30 to 50% decrease in tidal volume over these marsh surfaces, with the result that they averaged 35 cm below the surface of natural marshes.

These factors favored the establishment and spread of *Phragmites australis*, *Iva frutescens*, and other species. Cores demonstrated that *Spartina alterniflora* and *S. patens* beds lie under the *Phragmites* marsh. Generally the longer the period of restrictions, the more extensive the spread of *Phragmites*. This reed grass moves in at the same time or after the establishment of the seaside goldenrod (*Solidago sempervirens*) and the fireweed (*Erechtites hieracifolia*), which have a more open growth form than *S. patens*, thus encouraging the invasion of *Phragmites*.

Roman (1978) considered these *Phragmites* dominated marshes to be less productive than the *Spartina* marshes. The organic matter accumulated on the surface had a siltlike form rather than the matted stems and leaves found on the natural marsh. This was attributed to enhanced bacterial action of the drier (less waterlogged) surface on the restricted marshes. Because of reduced tidal flushing, however, this material could not be transported out of the restricted marsh sites into the adjoining estuarine systems. The increase of *Phragmites* was accompanied by a marked increase in the number of uncontrollable fires, resulting in personnel injury, property damage, and increased insurance rates.

The reintroduction of tidal flushing to a restricted marsh is probably the most positive way to rehabilitate such marshes. Controlled burning of *Phragmites* to open up sites and subsequent marsh plantings would hasten the process.

In the southeastern United States, reclamation was generally considered to be a failure (Penfound and Schneidau, 1945), with the exception of the very extensive diked rice fields of South Carolina and Georgia. Prior to the Civil War, these rice lands yielded greater and surer returns on the capital invested than any other agricultural venture in the country (Nesbit, 1885; Lawson, 1975; McKenzie et al., 1980).

Rice culture was introduced into the Charleston area during the last quarter of the seventeenth century (McKenzie et al., 1980) and was well established by 1691 (Salley, 1967). At first it was grown as an upland crop without irrigation. Irrigation is said to have begun about 1724 in the freshwater swamps. The shift to the tidewater region came during the late eighteenth and early nineteenth centuries. Due to ineffective methods of water control, upland rice culture never developed as it did in the tidewater areas. Silting and flooding—too little or too much water—were also problems. In 1758 a system was perfected that relied on tidal action to flood and drain the fields, providing greater control over the use of water and thus ensuring that rice culture would dominate the agriculture of the low country of South Carolina and Georgia, with the greatest development taking place in Georgetown County, South Carolina (Lawson, 1975; McKenzie et al., 1980). The ingenious adaptation to nature of this agricultural specialty was without parallel elsewhere on the continent. It depended on two conditions: sufficient tidal range (3 to 7 ft) to flood the fields, and a strong layering of fresh water to prevent the saline water from entering the rice fields (Hilliard, 1975).

There was a tremendous expenditure of labor to clear the cypress swamps and to create the dikes, ditches, and impoundments. Considering the technology that was then at hand, the extent of accomplishments with hand labor was prodigious; in fact, it is truly mind-boggling. It took years to transform a segment of tidal marsh into a productive rice field. Embankments were created and sluices or "trunks" were installed with floodgates at the ends of the sluices. These gates could be locked in position or act as one-way valves; during a flooding tide the outer gate was locked open and the inner one swung open, allowing the flooding tide to fill the field inside the dike. On the ebb tide, the inner gate was closed by the water pressure and the water was retained in the rice field.

McKenzie et al. (1980, after Hilliard, 1975) pointed out the factors that contributed to the success of the tidewater rice culture: the preciseness of the activity required very careful site selection; favorable conditions existed in the narrow coastal zone and nowhere else; massive time and labor commitments precluded the small farm operator; heavy and continual maintenance was required due to storm tides and floods; and a great deal of technical expertise was needed to convert a marsh into a productive rice field, more than any other form of agriculture of the time.

Ninety percent of the rice was produced in Georgia and South Carolina. During the 1850-1860 period, 39 plantations along the Santee River had 16,600 acres of tidal marsh under cultivation, with an average annual yield of 30 bu/acre. The rice plantation as a commercial venture lasted for 200 years. After 1860 production declined and never recovered. The loss of slave labor and capital started the decline. The ensuing deterioration in maintenance, coupled with hurricane damage, brought about the gradual demise of the dikes and sluice gates. Hand-grown rice could not compete with machine-cultivated and -harvested rice from Louisiana, Mississippi, Arkansas, and Missouri. The rice plantation at its peak (1840s-1850s) represented the most significant use of the tidewater marshes for crop agriculture ever attained in the United States (Lawson, 1975; McKenzie et al., 1980). While the evidence suggests that excellent crops of hay could have been produced if these lands had been drained, they never were (Nesbit, 1885).

The remnant fields and impoundments of the rice culture have had a tremendous impact on waterfowl management in the southeast United States. During the 200-year heyday of the rice plantations, waterfowl were attracted by the enhanced food supply. With the decline of rice production, many of the abandoned fields were taken over by desirable freshwater marsh plants such as wild rice, *Zizania aquatica*; duck potato, *Sagittaria*; squarestem spikerush, *Eleocharis quadrangulata*; Olney's three-square bulrush, *Scirpus olneyi*; wild millet, *Echinochloa*; softstem bulrush, *Scirpus validus*; and water hemp, *Amaranthus canabinus* (= *Acnida cannabina*). A perfect balance between food and cover for waterfowl was established. Some of the plantations were bought after the Civil War by wealthy northern industrialists, who restored dikes and water-control structures. Rice was planted and natural food plants were encouraged to attract waterfowl for hunting enjoyment (Lawson, 1975). In one study (McKenzie et al., 1980, after Morgan, 1974) of the South Edisto, Ashepoo, and Combahee rivers, it was shown that 54,087 acres of tidal lands had never been diked, and 21,828 acres were abandoned diked lands, of which 21,400 were former rice fields. There were 213 waterfowl impoundments comprising 22,536 acres, of which 69% or 15,670 acres were rediked former rice fields. Including abandoned rice fields, a minimum of 37,070 acres in Morgan's study area had once grown rice commercially and are now maintained as waterfowl habitat under private control. Comparable and larger acreage under state and federal jurisdiction are also subject to waterfowl management.

In their examination of projects in southeastern Louisiana, Penfound and Schneidau (1945) found that reclamation work had started in 1893 and, up to the time of their report, 284,217 acres had been reclaimed through publicly organized activities on 67 projects. In addition, 3 private projects had been initiated. Of the total 70 projects, only 7 were in actual operation in 1940; 34 existed only as legal entities. Most had been failures due to the high initial costs of dike construction, canalization, clearing and soil preparation, high maintenance costs, and soil subsidence after drainage. Penfound and Schneidau estimated that one project would have produced $2 million over the 20-year period (at $5/acre) if it had been left alone. As it was, less than 10% of the reclaimed area was under cultivation at the time of their report. At another site, what had been a productive muskrat marsh was drained so that long-staple cotton and truck garden crops could be produced. Over a nine-year period, however, less than 5% of the reclaimed land had been cultivated. A break in the levee later flooded the whole area, turning what had been an excellent brackish marsh into a 12-square-mile lake. From an agricultural point of view, it was a total loss—although the lake became a fishermen's paradise as well as a mecca for waterfowl hunters. A third project was reclaimed from a cypress-gum swamp and was a successful sugar cane producer from 1908 until 1919, when it was abandoned. Subsequently it became a prime wildlife and fishing area.

Penfound and Schneidau (1945) noted that a few reclaimed lands that had been reflooded not only became excellent wildlife areas but produced a wider variety and greater quantity of wildlife than the original marsh or swamp. They did not, however, recommend that marshes be reclaimed for wildlife purposes. In general, the long-term effects of reclamation (draining) and subsequent abandonment (reflooding) usually result in catastrophic destruction of the flora and fauna. Wildlife areas were destroyed by the invasion of such plants as the giant reed (*Phragmites australis*), the goldenrod, *Solidago mexicana*, and groundsel bush (*Baccharis halimifolia*), which have little wildlife value.

Tidal marshes are much less extensive and more dispersed on the west coast of the United States. The San Francisco Bay estuary has the greatest concentration of marshes, and these areas have been subjected to the greatest manipulative change. About 95% of the approximately 2,200 square kilometers of marshes in the bay region have been diked or filled. By 1900 about half of the freshwater marshes around the Delta and Suisun Bay had been diked for agriculture. In the more saline San Francisco Bay area, about one-fifth had been diked. Later in the twentieth century, most of the marshes were converted to salt-evaporation ponds, to sites for residential or industrial structures, or to transportation facilities, or were lost to garbage dumps. The erection of these dikes has added about 75 km^2 of new marshland (see the discussion of the loose boundary regime [Kestner 1972, 1975] in the section on the history of diked lands). New marshes have also been formed on dredge spoil in the San Francisco Bay area (Atwater et al., 1979).

Many acres of formerly reclaimed marshlands have reverted back to the wild condition, as noted in the rice fields of the South. The John Lusby National Wildlife Area outside Amherst, Nova Scotia (Van Zoost, 1969), is another example of a diked marsh that was used intensively for agriculture (until 1947). Since then the dikes and aboiteaux have been destroyed by storms or allowed to deteriorate. The area has reverted to wild salt marsh colonized by *Spartina alterniflora*, *S. patens*, and *Puccinellia maritima*; in the process, sediment accretion has raised the surface of the marsh by 2.5 feet. Van Zoost noted that the area has become a feeding and resting area for waterfowl. *P. maritima* is the main source of food for the Canada geese. For the ducks, the seeds of *S. alterniflora* and *Atriplex* sp. are the most available food in the spring. These two plants and *Ruppia maritima* make up the major food for ducks such as the American black duck and blue-winged teal. Van Zoost noted that the geese sometimes move to the adjoining upland farmland, where they pull up clover by the roots from frost-loosened soil. He considered the destruction to be minimal and saw no evident damage to the marsh vegetation caused by the feeding birds.

However, much of the once-improved and reclaimed lands that were used for agriculture are now extensive acres of idle or intermittently used land. This is especially true in the Canadian Maritime Provinces. Many of these acres have considerable potential for waterfowl habitat. In fact, Shaw and Crissey (1955) believed that the best waterfowl areas also have the best agricultural capability. Ever since marsh reclamation began, human activities have greatly reduced wildlife habitat. Diking and ditching have forced present-day waterfowl populations into increasingly limited areas. In places like the Tintamarre area of the New Brunswick-Nova Scotia border, agriculture and waterfowl have been in competition until recently. Agricultural needs can now be satisfied in those more productive upland areas that have been clearly defined (Jackson and Maxwell, 1971). Very substantial accomplishments have been made by the Canadian Wildlife Service, the provincial governments of the Maritime Provinces, and Ducks Unlimited to restore the original meaning to the word "Tantramar." This name is derived from the French *tintamarre*, which means racket or hubbub and referred to the noise created by the huge flocks of waterfowl that used the marsh during migration. Public awareness of the need to preserve and enhance wildlife resources places a high priority on waterfowl enhancement in tracts of marshlands outside prime agricultural areas (Jackson and Maxwell, 1971).

There is no question that Ferrigno (1959) and others (Ferrigno, Jobbins, and Shinkle, 1967; Ferrigno, MacNamara, and Jobbins, 1969; Slavin,

Shisler, and Ferrigno, 1978; Shisler, 1978*b*) had reservations regarding the tradeoffs and value of marsh reclamation for salt hay production, especially in the Middle Atlantic area. While the hazards of mosquito breeding might be mitigated by seasonal manipulation of proper water levels, hay production would suffer under such a procedure. Their preference was to open the dikes permanently to permit free access to the tides, which would terminate hay farming but provide restorative benefits. This procedure would not only reduce mosquito breeding but restore original marsh vegetation, enhance the tidal food web, and reinstate such delicacies as the fiddler crabs to attract waterfowl and clapper rails. When salt hay farming is a viable interest, however, Ferrigno (1959) reluctantly suggested application of chemicals for mosquito control. Wherever the tripartite interests of the hay farmer, mosquito control, and wildlife enhancement are in conflict, management recommendation for dike removal would have to be considered very carefully.

Impoundments for Wildlife Habitat and Mosquito Control

Water can be retained in various ways. High-level impoundments are designed so that water, other than rain, normally does not enter and the water level is maintained at or near high-tide level (MacNamara, 1949; Catts et al., 1963; Provost, 1968; Whitman, 1974). Plugs placed in ditches or natural channels stabilize water levels, reduce salinity and turbidity, and restrict tidal flow behind the plugs. If the plugs accomplish their task, desirable vegetation is enhanced and waterfowl are attracted. Low-level impoundments, or weirs, are designed to retain water behind a sluice gate as the tide recedes. These weirs stabilize water levels by allowing water to recede to a fixed level, prohibiting excessive drainage during low tides (Chabreck, 1968b; McKenzie et al., 1980). Permanent, shallow pools are often created on the marsh surface by blocking drainage from a low area or by blasting (Provost, 1948). Clarke (1938) likened the action of mosquito predators (larvivorous fishes) at the surface of these basins to champagne bubbles; thus they are often called "champagne" pools. They can be difficult to manage since water levels are hard to control and the development of the natural vegetation may reduce the time they are useful to waterfowl (Chabreck 1968b; McKenzie et al., 1980). Ditches often radiate outward from these pools across the marsh surface, forming an interconnecting network that permits fish access and movement for mosquito control. These pools can be associated with low-level impoundments (Smith, 1968), thus overcoming the problem of controlling water level. Marshes with potholes and ponds are much more attractive to waterfowl than marshes with a solid stand of vegetation (Chabreck, 1968b).

The concepts for integrated mosquito control and wildlife management in marshes had their inception in three papers presented in 1938 at a wildlife management conference. Clarke (1938) characterized three categories of freshwater marshes: permanent—holding water at all times; intermittent—periodically wet and dry; and temporary—holding water for only a few days. Clarke advocated that permanent and intermittent marshes need not be drained, since mosquitoes can be controlled best by encouraging their aquatic predators in permanent pools on these marshes. A wildlife oasis can be provided by creating a relatively deep central water hole with channels connecting shallow pools throughout the marsh. Protection and a resting site would be provided to wildlife by the central pool, while mosquito-eating fish, living in this permanent pool, could radiate outward through the channels as the water level rose.

At the same time, Price (1938) advocated a new approach to water management without draining the marshland. The procedure was to dig a series of shallow, blind ditches about 12 in below the mean high-tide mark; these ditches would not be connected to tidal streams, or guts. Each high tide would flush the marsh potholes, bringing in a new supply of fish that would move out over the marsh and, on the ebb, collect in the ponds, potholes, and ditches. The water-table level would be raised throughout the marsh, keeping water in potholes and ponds that otherwise would dry up. Such depressions would be freed of mosquitoes and would maintain a good stand of *Ruppia maritima* (wigeon grass), a prime habitat for ducks. It should be pointed out that such a scheme would be effective in the low marsh and less effective in the high marsh zone.

In wildlife habitats where permanent ponds are involved, Cottam (1938) believed that mosquito control should be attempted by biological methods that would be less destructive to the marsh than mechanical drainage. Cottam also advocated the establishment of permanent pools

Figure 3-2. Great egrets at a high-level impoundment in the Little Creek Wildlife Area, Delaware. (Photo by F. C. Daiber)

to serve as reservoirs for mosquito-eating fish with channels radiating outward to permit these fish to get out over the marsh surface. Diking and water impoundment were advocated, with the use of weir boards and sluice gates that would not restrict tidal flow yet would maintain a proper head of water in the marsh area. Christopher and Bowden (1957) and Provost (1968, 1977) considered water management, properly employed, as the single most potent means of mosquito control. Mosquito breeding can be prevented by filling with spoils or draining the breeding depressions on the high marsh surface, eliminating egg deposition or larval development sites; channelizing the marsh surface with shallow ditches to permit access for larvivorous fishes; and keeping the marsh continuously flooded via impounding to prevent oviposition by many species of the genus *Aedes*. The last technique is the most expensive and involves loss of marsh to permanent open water; the first two are not as expensive but also have a potential for marsh destruction if care is not taken. Whether ditching or impounding is employed depends on the cost, which in turn is determined by soil character, availability of water for flooding, and location of the mean high-water level (Provost, 1968). Provost noted that, since the high marsh in Florida is above the mean high-water level and streams are few, it is necessary to pump in brackish water to maintain impoundments. Where extensive pumping is required to maintain appropriate water levels, electricity costs will add very substantially to maintenance costs. Streams are more adequate in the Middle Atlantic region and impoundments can be more easily shifted to a freshwater situation. Provost believed that an impounded marsh should be flooded initially during the breeding season and, once mosquito production has been stopped, supplemented by other water-management regimes.

Provost (1968) also noted that Florida has been the only state to seriously consider impounding for just mosquito control. Christopher and Bowden (1957) proposed that, for proper management, the purpose of the impoundment must be decided; this in turn would dictate the necessary form of management, which would determine the resultant changes in that part of the marsh ecosystem. As Provost (1968) queried, how does the practice of impounding affect the natural resources of the marsh as well as the adjoining estuary, and what are the possibilities of modifying the practice to render the effects less damaging or possibly to produce positive benefits?

Effects of Impoundments.   The presentations by Clarke (1938), Price (1938), and Cottam (1938) have stimulated numerous studies to evaluate the effects on mosquitoes and wildlife of water management through impounding and permanent pothole development (MacNamara, 1949, 1953; Chapman and Ferrigno, 1956; Catts, 1957; Catts et al., 1963; Darsie and Springer, 1957; Florschutz 1959a, 1959b; Lesser, 1965). Tracts of marsh-

Table 3-6. Maximum and minimum average nitrate concentration in the Delaware Murderkill River marshes, July 1966–December 1967 (in microgram-atoms per liter)

	Maximum Concentration			Minimum Concentration		
	Month	*h.s.w.*	*l.s.w.*	*Month*	*h.s.w.*	*l.s.w.*
Murderkill River	Feb.	84.3		June	1.2	
	Nov.		97.2	Sept.		6.1
Natural Marsh	Nov.	100.4		Aug.	4.2	
	Mar.		26.7	Oct.		5.0
High-level impoundment	Oct.	46.7		Sept.	3.5	
	Oct.		42.3	Aug.		4.8
Low-level impoundment	Jan.	69.1		Sept.	4.1	
	Jan.		67.4	May		5.6
Champagne pool	Mar.	36.4		June	2.9	
	Feb.		32.7	Nov.		3.5

Source: After Aurand, D., 1968, *The Seasonal and Spatial Distribution of Nitrate and Nitrite in the Surface Waters of Two Delaware Marshes,* Master's thesis, University of Delaware, pp. 61, 62.

Note: h.s.w. = high slack water; l.s.w. = low slack water.

land formerly diked and reclaimed for agriculture have been recommended for wildlife use (Penfound and Schneidau, 1945; Van Zoost, 1969; Jackson and Maxwell, 1971) and are being converted to waterfowl habitat (Smith, 1967; Landers et al., 1976; McKenzie et al., 1980).

Retaining water behind a dike will markedly change the marsh vegetation along with the associated fauna, nutrient flows probably will be reduced (Hawkes, 1966), and the nutrient chemistry will be modified.

As part of a study to examine the impact of water manipulation in a Delaware tidal marsh, Aurand (1968) and Aurand and Daiber (1973) demonstrated a marked seasonal pattern in nitrate levels in the Murderkill River marshes with maximal mean levels during the cold half of the year and minimal mean levels during the warm months (Table 3-6). The low and high slack water values for the Murderkill River proper and the manipulated marshes generally tracked each other (Figure 3-3). In contrast, there was a marked difference in concentration between high and low slack water maximum nitrate values for samples taken from the surface of the natural, uncontrolled marsh (Table 3-6). The high- and low-level impoundments and the champagne pool in the marsh displayed the typical winter nitrate highs and summer lows. However, the difference between the maximum and minimum values tended to be less than for the river or the natural marsh (Table 3-6 and Figure 3-3). What is more significant is that there was much less difference between high and low slack water, especially for the high-level impoundment and champagne

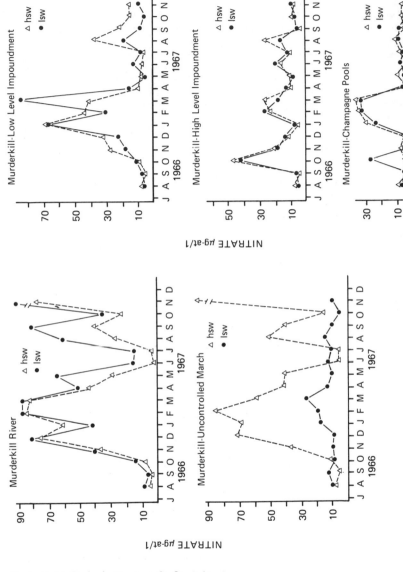

Figure 3-3. Monthly average nitrate concentration at high and low slack water for each of the areas of Delaware marshland sampled. Values are in microgram-atoms of nitrate per liter. *Source: After Aurand, D., and F. C. Daiber, 1973, Nitrate and nitrite in the surface waters of two Delaware salt marshes, Chesapeake Sci. **14**(2): 105–111, by permission.*

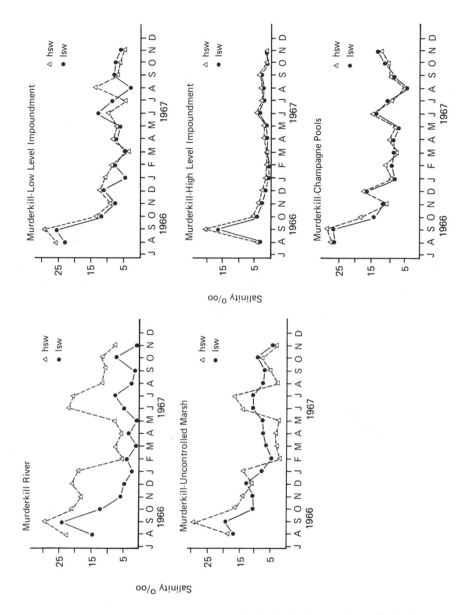

Figure 3-4. Monthly average salinity at high and low slack water for each of the areas of Delaware marshland sampled. Values are in parts per thousand. *Source: After Aurand, D., and F. C. Daiber, 1973, Nitrate and nitrite in the surface waters of two Delaware salt marshes, Chesapeake Sci.* **14**(2):105–111, *by permission.*

pool. Some difference was observed in the low-level impoundment. The greatest difference between slack waters was evident on the natural marsh surface; somewhat less of a difference for the river. The magnitude of difference in nitrate concentrations between the slack water values paralleled the salinity values recorded (Figure 3-4). Slack water salinity variations were the greatest for the Murderkill River and the natural marsh, reflecting the greatest exchange of water. The least exchange of water was evident in the champagne pool and the high-level impoundment, where there was the least variation in salinity. The isolation of the high-level impoundment from tidal exchange was also made evident by the almost freshwater conditions inside the dike.

A similar pattern of lowered impoundment concentration maximums was demonstrated for the various forms of phosphorus in this same Murderkill River marsh (Reimold, 1968). The levels of phosphorus in the river and natural marsh were significantly higher than levels found in the impoundments and champagne pools. Seasonal patterns of phosphorus concentration were evident, but opposite to those observed for nitrate: highest in the summer and lowest during the cold months (Reimold, 1968).

In a two-year-old impoundment along the Northumberland Strait, Nova Scotia, Hatcher (1977) noted that monthly concentrations of all nutrients were generally higher within the impoundment than in the natural creek. She observed a pulse of NH_4-N in July while NO_3-N displayed a peak in October. Due to a leakage, nutrient levels below the impoundment spillway were higher than in the creek of the natural marsh. Hatcher recorded a decline in nitrogen fixation (acetylene reduction) on the soil surface from 5.15 ± 2.93 mg fixed $N/m^2/hr$ in the natural marsh to 0.05 ± 0.04 mg N fixed/m^2/hr within the impoundment. There was a reduction in the export of carbon and other nutrients, which she attributed to impounding. Higher nutrient levels within the impoundment were attributed to agricultural runoff and decomposition of organic matter. Along with this there was a high fish mortality in the impoundment, apparently caused by high water temperatures and low oxygen levels. Hatcher expected the nutrient levels to decline, presumably because they would be bound up in plant tissue and, with the agricultural runoff, she anticipated eutrophication. If so, the best management procedure would be to flush the impoundment periodically with tidal water.

In a study on the John Lusby National Wildlife area on the border of Chignecto Bay, Nova Scotia, Morantz (1976) noted that 71% of the August standing crop was removed during the winter by ice scour. He estimated that, from an area of 18,460 m^2, some 83.8 and 49.4 metric tons would be removed from the marsh in the winter and spring, respectively, and transported into the bay waters. Morantz estimated the natural marsh was supplying about 5 metric tons per hectare (4,450 lbs/acre) of dry organic material (= 2.25 metric tons of carbon/hectare, or 2,000 lbs/acre) annually to the Cumberland Basin. Impoundments prevented the transport of this material to the Bay of Fundy through ice scour and winter storms.

It is evident from the foregoing that impounding the marsh surface inhibits the free tidal exchange of nutrients in the various forms of carbon, nitrogen, and phosphorus. This inhibition was recognized by farmers who periodically allowed tidal waters to flood their fields behind the dikes to restore fertility (Ganong, 1903; Warren, 1911). The elevation of the impoundment may be important. Even in a natural marsh, it is unclear what role the high marsh plays in providing nutrients to the estuary (Provost, 1968). Impoundment of the high marsh would presumably further reduce any nutrient exchange. Ruber and Murray (1978) speculated on the effect of biannual drawdowns to remove accumulated organics. The construction of these impoundments could also provide for the periodic flushing by spring tides. By such means there could be an increased export from the high marsh areas during spring and storm tide periods. In the same vein, Ruber and Murray wondered whether the installation of sills in ditches (stop ditching) would not enhance the accumulation of organic material while maintaining the water level in the marshes. Presumably stop ditching might enhance organic accumulation in compared to ditched marshes with standard ditch depths but not in comparison to unditched natural marshes. Spring and storm tides would likewise flush these sediments to the estuary. Provost (1974) demonstrated that seasonal flooding of Florida impoundments could control mosquito populations as well as permit nutrient exchange with the estuary. Shisler (1978a) has suggested that the permanent ponds associated with the high marsh may serve as mini-farms, where biomass in the form of fishes, invertebrates, and plant material would increase until storm tides flood the marsh and "harvest" such ponds through pulse outflows to the open estuary.

The objectives of impoundment for wildlife enhancement are to provide an interspersion of open water and vegetative cover and to produce a maximum quantity and quality of food supply, all of which are to benefit selected species. Food is the most important requirement on the wintering grounds of waterfowl; thus, effort is directed toward the control or elimination of undesirable plants and the corresponding encouragement of desirable waterfowl food plants (Provost, 1968; McKenzie et al., 1980).

The retention of water by impounding in Delaware produces vegetation changes from *Spartina alterniflora-S. patens* to the pondweeds *Potamogeton berchtoldi* and *P. pectinatus*, wigeon grass (*Ruppia maritima*), and algal mats (principally *Rhizoclonium* during low water). Around the edges a variety of emergent species will appear: three-square, *Scirpus americanus*; rose mallow, *Hibiscus moscheutos*; cattail, *Typha*; reed, *Phragmites australis*; and switch grass, *Panicum virgatum* (Springer and Darsie, 1956). Prior to impoundment of marshland in 1973 on the border of Northumberland Strait, Nova Scotia, Hatcher (1977) recorded 13,050 ± 5,850 (S.D.) m^2 of *S. alterniflora*. Following impoundment, *Spartina* declined to 10,512 ± 2,880 (S.D.) m^2 with a corresponding decline in production from 90.9 gm carbon/m^2/yr to 37 gm carbon/m^2/yr. Production of *S. patens* and *Zostera marina* plummeted to zero. The area weighted mean macrophyte production declined in 1973 from 161.9 gm carbon/m^2/yr to 37 gm carbon/m^2/yr in two years of impoundment. After two years of flooding, macrophyte production was replaced by filamentous algae.

This same pattern of both species shifts and lost productivity was noted by Florschutz (1959a, 1959b) and Tindall (1961) in the Assawoman and Little Creek wildlife areas in Delaware, respectively, and by LaSalle and Knight (1974) for Pamlico and Carteret counties, North Carolina. All reported that salt marsh vegetation (*Spartina, Distichlis, Scirpus, Hibiscus, Cladium, Juncus, Baccharis, Iva*) was reduced and replaced by open-water and emergent types: *Potamogeton* and *Ruppia* beds, *Typha, Echinochloa, Cyperus,* and *Chara*. Florschutz noted that *Typha* tended to expand in some places and decrease elsewhere. *Spartina patens* was greatly reduced on the inner portions of the marsh but flourished along the edge of the impoundment. LaSalle and Knight noted that very little *Ruppia* appeared in the Carteret County impoundment and that isolated patches of *Typha* appeared instead.

Farther north, in the Shepody and Tintamarre districts of New Brunswick, Malone (1976) reported a rather complex change in vegetational resources following impoundment. The preimpoundment vegetation in 1970 at Shepody was dominated by *Carex paleacea* and *Spartina pectinata*. The vegetation at Tintamarre prior to impoundment in 1968 reflected the changes in surface topography. The higher elevation was a hay meadow with moderately drained soil supporting *Calamagrostis canadensis, Phleum pratense, Agropyron repens,* and *S. pectinata*. The meadow fen was dominated by *Carex lasiocarpa*. The lowest elevation was a mesotrophic marsh with floating peat, the cinquefoil (*Potentilla palustris*), cattail (*Typha glauca*), and the water smartweed (*Polygonum natans*).

Following impoundment at Shepody, wild rice, *Zizania aquatica*, was planted in 1975. By 1976 the rice was dominant, although some *C. paleacea* and *S. pectinata* were still present. The submergent bladderwort *Utricularia vulgaris* became abundant, while some duckweed *Lemna minor,* common bed straw (*Galium palustre*), arrowhead or duck potato (*Sagittaria latifolia*), and pondweed (*Potamogeton pusillus*) became evident. Moss (*Fontinalis* sp.) became common, and dense stands of *Phragmites australis* developed. In the former tidal creek channels, pondweed (*Potamogeton epihydrus*) and giant bur-reeds (*Sparganium eurycarpum*) flourished while meadow-sweet (*Spiraea latifolia*) and blue-joint grass (*Calamagrostis canadensis*) appeared along the former creek banks (Malone, 1976).

Floating mats of peat became common in the Tintamarre impoundment. Species associated with disturbance—such as bur-marigold (*Bidens frondosa*), tearthumb (*Polygonum sagittatum*), *S. eurycarpum, G. palustre, S. latifolia,* and water plantain (*Alisma triviale*)—were common in the former hay meadow. The abundance of *Carex lasiocarpa* was unchanged in portions of the meadow fen that had not been plowed. In the plowed portions the cattail *Typha* became abundant, *S. eurycarpum* and *C. lasiocarpa* were common, and scattered plants of *S. latifolia, Juncus effusus, Agrostis scabra, Lemna minor,* and dock (*Rumex orbiculatus*) were observed (Malone, 1976).

Mangold (1962), Shoemaker (1964), Smith (1968), and Harrison (1970) noted the replacement of *S. patens* by *S. alterniflora* during the flooding of low-level impoundments and a champagne pool system in marshes of the Middle Atlantic area. This was particularly true in the beginning. *Distichlis* associated with *S. patens* survived and flourished (Shoemaker) but, when associated with *J. gerardi,* survived with difficulty (Mangold). Flooding caused the disappearance of *Baccharis* and *Iva* while the submergent horned pondweed, *Zannichellia palustris,* increased and flourished. In contrast, Shisler and Lesser (1979) reported no significant changes in vegetational zonation (*S. alterniflora, S. patens, D. spicata*) because of increased water levels during the first two years of impoundment. The short form of *S. alterniflora,* which dominated the marsh surface, showed the most dramatic effect by reaching heights over 6 ft throughout the impoundment. This seems strange, as it would be expected that the impounding would decrease soil aeration and thus stunt *S. alterniflora* growth. Shisler and Lesser attributed the increased height and biomass to increased water levels and associated nutrients. *Baccharis, Iva,* and other ecotonal species were unaffected.

In impoundments in formerly diked agricultural tracts in the Cape Jourimain, New Brunswick, marsh complex, *Spartina patens* and *Festuca rubra* dominated in those portions not always covered by water. *Ruppia maritima* as usual was the dominant vegetation in the permanently flooded areas (Cairns, 1974; Shisler and Lesser, 1979). Smith (1968) noted the increase of *Baccharis,* common reed (*Phragmites australis*), poke-weed (*Phytolacca americana*), and the foxtail grasses *Setaria faberii* and *S. magna* on the higher ground created by the embankments and spoil piles. The pokeweed and foxtail grasses provided excellent food and shelter for terrestrial wildlife. He also noted a decline of wigeon grass in the older impoundments, although it had flourished in younger pools. In summary, just as J. B. Smith had noted in 1907, impounding a tidal marsh will change the salt marsh vegetation to that of a freshwater marsh or that of drier ground along the embankments.

Water-level manipulation is an effective management technique for acquiring and maintaining the less aggressive but desirable vegetation attractive to waterfowl. Any practice that reduces the coarse vegetation or causes a reversion to an earlier stage is beneficial to waterfowl. Baldwin (1968) was of the opinion that the most waterfowl food with the least amount of management can be provided by a good wigeon grass *R. maritima* impoundment in the lower intertidal zone of a *S. alterniflora* marsh. Steenis et al. (1954) noted that small bodies of water with constant water levels to encourage the growth of submerged aquatics could be achieved by constructing small ponds, blind ditches, or blasted potholes or by plugging small ditches or natural guts in the marsh. The maintenance of a stable water depth of 18 to 24 in and a salinity of one-third sea water will encourage submergent waterfowl foods such as sago pondweed, wigeon grass, and other pond vegetation (*Potamogeton, Najas, Zannichellia*). Reducing the water level or decreasing salinity will encourage the growth of emergents such as cattails, which can benefit muskrats but not waterfowl. Fluctuating salinities will enhance desirable species production such as that of *Scirpus robustus*. The shallow-water borders of impoundments can be maintained in desirable species such as bulrushes (*Scirpus*), spikerushes (*Eleocharis*), and annual grasses by periodic drawdowns and disking to discourage the cattail *Typha* (Baldwin, 1968; Landers et al., 1976; McKenzie et al., 1980).

Freshwater and brackish-water impoundments require different kinds of manipulation to enhance waterfowl food production. In the freshwater marshes, desirable foods such as the annuals *Echinochloa crusgalli, E. walteri*, and annual *Polygonum* spp. cannot maintain themselves on a permanently flooded site. Since they require a moist but not flooded area, the water level must be drawn down to the ground surface by midsummer, which encourages these rapidly growing annuals to flourish and produce abundant seed. Reflooding in the fall makes this seed crop available to waterfowl. There is a late winter drawdown to dry out the soil for subsequent burning or mechanical cultivation and this is done before the seeds germinate in the spring. The water level is then raised to the surface without any accumulation of standing water. The soil must be kept moist throughout the growing season. If allowed to dry, undesirable plants like beggar-tick (*Bidens*), plume grass (*Erianthus*), and foxtail grass (*Setaria*) will become established. Flooding will induce the establishment of undesirable species like the cattail, giant cutgrass (*Zizaniopsis miliacea*), pickerel weed (Pontederia), and others (MacNamara, 1949; Steenis et al. 1954; McKenzie et al., 1980). Steenis et al. considered a marsh area with 80% open water to be ideal for ducks and geese.

The usual way to manage mid- and south Atlantic brackish-water impoundments to encourage waterfowl is to dewater in late winter or early spring. This is done to encourage the salt marsh bulrush (*Scirpus robustus*) and the dwarf spikerush (*Eleocharis palustris*), which begin to grow at this time. During the spring the impoundment is reflooded to a depth of 6 in. Water is added in 6-inch increments at monthly intervals, to a depth of 2 ft. Wigeon grass becomes established in open areas and the bulrush and spikerush continue to grow. Once a 2-foot depth is achieved, it has been recommended that a flow of water be kept up to maintain the salinity level and to forestall the buildup of algal blooms. By fall wild millet (*Echinochloa*), sprangle top (*Leptochloa fascicularis*), and fall panic grass (*Panicum dichotomiflorum*) are among the desirable species dominating the shallow edges of the impoundments. Valuable muskrat plants such as *Typha* and *Scirpus validus* are adversely affected by salinities above 7‰. Among duck food plants, *Polygonum* spp. and *Leersia oryzoides* are inhibited by salinities greater than 2‰, and *Zizania aquatica* and *Echinochloa crusgalli* by salinities greater than 4‰. Marsh plants such as *Scirpus olneyi, S. robustus, Amaranthus canabinus, Spartina* spp., and *Phragmites* can stand salinities greater than 18‰ (Steenis et al., 1954). Letting a brackish-water impoundment dry out will encourage *S. alterniflora* to become established, while permanent flooding will allow *Typha* to become established if the salinity remains low. Algal mats, primarily of *Cladophora*, will cover the open water areas if a flow of water is not maintained (McKenzie et al., 1980).

Steenis et al. (1954) have recommended that a drawdown in the spring is best for muskrat management and should be done no later than May. This will expose the mud flats for the germination of seeds of perennial plants such as *Typha* spp., *Scirpus olneyi, S. robustus*, and *S. validus*. They caution that care should be taken that the marsh bottom does not dry out, since seedlings require moist beds for successful growth. Because the muskrats should have access to open water for parasite control and for escape from predators, these authors considered a marsh with 20% open water to be ideal.

An early spring drawdown, however, will encourage growth of such plants as *Distichlis spicata, Spartina* spp., *Hibiscus moscheutos*, and *Phragmites australis*. This can be controlled by reflooding in June to a depth of 10 to 12 inches. Established, desirable species such as *E. crusgalli, E. walteri, Polygonum* spp., *Typha* spp., *L. oryzoides*, and *A. canabinus* tolerate the flooding and continue to grow. The maintenance of the water level throughout the summer prevents *Phragmites* runners

Table 3-7. Mosquito immatures dipped (collected) from April to October, 1959 and 1960, Little Creek Wildlife Area, Little Creek, Delaware

| | *Inside Impoundment* | | | | *Outside Impoundment* | | | |
| | *1959* | | *1960* | | *1959* | | *1960* | |
	No.	*%*	*No.*	*%*	*No.*	*%*	*No.*	*%*
A. sollicitans	56,137	96.1	76	0.4	1,502	96.5	7,203	99.9
Aedes sp.	62	0.1	10	—	1	—	—	—
Total	56,199	92.6	86	0.4	1,503	96.5	7,203	99.9
A. bradleyi	19	—	677	3.5	1	—	1	—
Anopheles sp.	—	—	161	0.8	—	—	—	—
Total	19	—	838	4.3	1	—	1	—
C. salinarius	2,143	3.7	17,163	88.7	25	1.6	—	—
Culex sp.	69	0.1	743	3.8	27	1.7	—	—
Total	2,212	3.8	17,906	92.5	52	3.3	—	—
Uranotaenia sapphirina	—	—	512	2.7	—	—	—	—

Source: From Tindall, E. E., 1961, A two year study of mosquito breeding and wildlife usage in Little Creek impounded salt marsh, Little Creek Wildlife area, Delaware, 1959-1960, *New Jersey Mosq. Exterm. Assoc. Proc.* 48:100-105.

Note: 1959 was the first year of impoundment.

from becoming established. Steenis et al. (1954) noted that additional benefits include the elimination of the temporary pools, which are prime mosquito-breeding sites, and the access of fish to mosquitoes breeding in permanent pools. In the fall, the additional rise in the water level further enhances the muskrat food supply and affords trappers more easy access to the marsh.

Impounding sharply alters the numbers and species composition of biting fly populations as compared to that of a natural tidal marsh (Chapman et al., 1954, 1955; Chapman and Ferrigno, 1956; Catts et al., 1963; Shoemaker, 1964; LaSalle and Knight, 1974). *Aedes sollicitans* is the most abundant mosquito in natural marsh conditions along the Atlantic and Gulf coasts, making up as much as 96% by number of immatures collected (Table 3-7) (Darsie and Springer, 1957; Tindall, 1961). Chapman et al. (1954) identified *A. sollicitans* and *A. cantator* along with *Anopheles bradleyi* and *Culex salinarius*, the salt marsh group of mosquitoes, as being typical of a natural salt marsh. *Aedes* spp. can be essentially eliminated from impoundments; *Culex* and *Anopheles*, *Uranotaenia sapphirina*, and *Coquillettidia (= Mansonia) perturbans* will increase after impoundment but are considered a lesser nuisance (Chapman et al., 1954; Chapman and Ferrigno, 1956; Tindall, 1961; Franz, 1963).

Healthy fish populations (e.g., *Fundulus heteroclitus, F. diaphanus, Gambusia affinis*) within the impoundments can substantially curtail mosquito production. *Coquillettidia* deposits its eggs in sedge tussocks and beneath mats of cattail debris under flooded freshwater conditions (Hagmann, 1953). Since *Coquillettidia* larvae and pupae develop within muddy pond bottoms, attached to subsurface plant roots and stems, they are not as susceptible to control by chemicals or fish predation as are other species. Temporary impoundments can control tabanid flies (*Chrysops fuliginosus*) since flooding at the time of larval-pupal and pupal-imaginal molts will devastate the populations (Olkowski, 1966; Anderson and Kneen, 1969). Rogers (1962) reported that sand fly breeding was controlled in 94% of the larval habitat by flooding. The sand flies (primarily *Culicoides furens*) were reduced from 619 larvae per sample in an intermittently flooded site to 0.1 larvae per sample from two flooded plots.

Manipulation of water levels within impoundments also seems to control species composition and the magnitude of breeding (Hagmann, 1953; Chapman and Ferrigno, 1956). Springer and Darsie (1956) reported the elimination of *Anopheles* along with the two *Aedes* species. Darsie and Springer (1957) and LaSalle and Knight (1974) noted that many of the permanent water mosquitoes are unimportant because of short flight patterns, biting habits, and other behavior. MacNamara (1952) reported that constant water levels produced mosquitoes while drawdown decreased breeding. Chapman and Ferrigno (1956) noted heaviest breeding at water depths 5 to 10 in below salt hay meadow surface level for *Aedes*, slightly below meadow surface level for *Culex*, and slightly above meadow surface level for *Anopheles*. LaSalle and Knight (1974) found that water depths greater than 1 foot tended to submerge or disperse vegetation and reduce *Anopheles* and *Culex* populations. Chapman and Ferrigno (1956) reported that summer drawdown controls *C. perturbans*, but along with Darsie and Springer (1957), they reported greatly increased *Aedes* broods following rains or reflooding. Catts et al. (1963) recommended moderate water levels of 9 to 12 inches as compatible with reduced mosquito production and enhanced waterfowl usage. Tindall (1961) suggested that the higher water levels would reduce vegetation and expose the mosquito larvae to wave action and predators.

As might be expected, impounding a portion of a tidal marsh will also have an impact on the other invertebrate fauna. Cairns (1974) recorded larger numbers of taxa/sampling site/day from an undiked salt marsh (7.5 taxa) in the Cape Jourimain, New Brunswick, salt marsh complex than from impounded sites (4.2 taxa). The mud flats in the natural marshes yielded the highest numbers of organisms. In addition, more individuals were found associated with the natural marsh sites than impoundment sites, and this difference was more pronounced late in the summer. Impounded sites with a higher salinity tended to be more productive in terms of numbers of invertebrates than the sites in the fresher portions of the diked brackish systems. MacInnis (1979) found numbers of invertebrates to be lower in the impoundment than on the tidal marsh. He reported that invertebrate diversity and abundance were similar in both habitats during the waterfowl brood season for these same Cape Jourimain marshes. Across the peninsula in the Chignecto Bay area, Van Zoost (1969) found the number of faunal species on the natural marsh surface to be low; the most common were *Hydrobia minuta, Gammarus* sp., *Chaoborus* sp., and *Culex* sp. *Microtus pennsylvanicus* was the most abundant mammal.

Whitman (1974) found the age of the impoundment to be a major factor affecting the production of macroinvertebrates, which are an important food source for waterfowl. He examined seven different age impoundments and a natural marsh in the Missaquash marsh and Tintamarre National Wildlife area of the New Brunswick-Nova Scotia border. He found that cattails, sedges, and other rooted aquatics dominated the impoundments after seven years. During this aging process, water quality (total alkalinity, specific conductance, dissolved chlorides, and magnesium) declined. Whitman recorded 115 genera, representing 60 families and 18 orders of invertebrates. More than 90% of the numbers were in 20 taxa. About 90% of all the taxa appeared during the first growing season after the impoundments were flooded. Zones of emergent vegetation had the highest numbers of invertebrates. High numbers were associated with *Spartina pectinata, Spiraea latifolia, Carex lasiocarpa,* and *Calamagrostis canadensis.* Whitman also noted peaks of invertebrate abundance during the first half of May, in June, and in August, with July being relatively low. It was observed that the high levels of abundance in May and June coincided with high protein requirements of breeding pairs of waterfowl and the broods, respectively. Invertebrates most commonly eaten by ducks were most abundant in the new impoundments. Species diversity among the invertebrates reached its highest level and stable position in four years or less, and diversity declined after that. By age seven a dense emergent vegetation producing little vegetable food for waterfowl became established. Invertebrate populations were composed of less abundant species and were not as available to the waterfowl as food. Waterfowl production reached a plateau or declined as the impoundments reached seven to eight years of age. On the basis of these observations, Whitman (1974) concluded that impoundments younger than four years of age are the most desirable for waterfowl production. He recommended that water-level drawdown be done for impoundments five to seven years of age. Such drawdown was to be done in conjunction with other habitat manipulation such as plowing, burning, and fertilizer application.

As noted earlier, one basic premise of water management and mosquito control on marshes has been to provide a suitable habitat for mosquito-eating fish and the means for these fish to get to the mosquitoes. *Fundulus* spp. can survive in impoundments and will provide an effective control over mosquito larvae if water levels are high enough to permit the fish to forage among the vegetation (Alls, 1969). Darsie and Springer (1957) noted that the numbers of fish species increased following impoundment and tended to shift toward freshwater forms, including the bullhead (*Ictalurus nebulosus*), the pickerel (*Esox americanus*), and the sunfish (*Lepomis gibbosus*). The bullfrog (*Rana catesbiana*) and the snapping turtle (*Chelydra serpentina*) also appeared. Mangold (1962) and Shoemaker (1964) believed that the attraction of birds like herons, bitterns, and terns to such impoundments was due to the increase in fish. Following the examination of a number of sites in New Jersey employing different management procedures, Able, Shisler, and Talbot (1979) and Talbot et al. (1980) categorized the fish fauna into freshwater and estuarine groups. The freshwater species consisted of *Fundulus diaphanus, Gambusia affinis, Lepomis gibbosus,* and *Notemigonus chrysoleucas.* The estuarine species comprised *Fundulus heteroclitus, F. luciae, Cyprinodon variegatus, Lucania parva,* and *Menidia beryllina.* A salinity of 10‰ tended to separate the two groups (which accounted for 97% of the total fish population). Low-level impoundments and stop ditches with average low salinities were occupied by the freshwater species, while estuarine species were prevalent in higher-salinity waters. Lesser and Saveikis (1979) also found a similar dichotomy for open, tidal ponds and ditches (estuarine fish species) versus closed, nontidal ponds and ditches (freshwater species) in open marsh water management systems on Maryland's eastern shore. Seasonal salinity and temperature variations noted in New Jersey also caused changes in species composition and accounted for observed high winter mortalities. These factors appear to create an unstable habitat, which in turn can create a less than optimal habitat for the maintenance of fish populations for mosquito control. Harrington and Harrington (1982) have reported a study on the effects of impounding a Florida salt marsh. Eleven of 16 fish species present in the natural marsh were absent from the impoundment. The populations of three more were reduced, and stomach contents indicated an increase in plant tissue in the diet of all five remaining species, presumably due to the impoverishment of the invertebrate fauna. No new species were reported.

Impounding studies carried out in southern coastal marshes, particularly in Louisiana, have provided evidence that impoundments (weirs) will reduce the numbers of fish species that spawn away from the marsh, decrease the number of herbivorous species, and increase the number of zooplankton- and diverse-feeding fishes (Provost, 1968). Circumstantial evidence suggests that these weirs present physical and ethological barriers to fish migrations. A number of forage and predatory species congregate in the immediate vicinity of the weirs. Some species, like the spot, *Leisostomus xanthurus*, may not pass over the weir even when physically possible. *Brevoortia* were unaffected and *Anchoa* found the habitat satisfactory above the weir. *Mugil cephalus* apparently did not go over the weir, as their greatest numbers were found just below the sluice gate. Estuarine forms such as *Lucania parva* and freshwater species were enhanced by the establishment of weirs (Herke, 1968, 1979).

Impoundments have been established and developed mainly for the enhancement of wildlife, particularly waterfowl and shore birds. Bradbury (1938) reported on such a restoration for the Duxbury, Massachusetts, marshes. Other investigators have reported the increased use of impoundments by birds (Catts, 1957; Darsie and Springer, 1957; Florschutz, 1959a, 1959b; Tindall, 1961; Mangold, 1962; Chabreck, 1963; Shoemaker, 1964; Lesser, 1965; Smith, 1968; Provost, 1968, 1969). Darsie and Springer (1957) identified 86 bird species in an impounded area, versus 55 in the same area prior to impoundment. Tindall (1961) reported a threefold increase. Smith (1968) cited 62 species on the impoundments and 39 on the natural marsh areas. Several of these workers reported increased numbers of broods of young after impoundment, particularly among the black ducks. These impoundments offered emergent and submergent vegetation as food for ducks, scattered emergent vegetation as important cover for new broods, fish and invertebrates as food for wading birds, and open water for resting areas (Catts et al., 1963).

The significance of freshwater impoundments in waterfowl management is evidenced by the work of MacNamara (1949) and Landers et al (1976). The impoundments on the Tuckahoe, New Jersey, marshes were capable of producing large quantities of desirable waterfowl food by a complete drawdown. MacNamara reported a kill of 1.9 ducks/hunter/day for the 1948 season following impoundment, compared to 0.8 in 1947. After restoration, several uncommon ducks, including the redhead, ring-necked duck, surfscoter, and the shoveler, were observed.

Landers et al. (1976) studied impoundments derived from former abandoned rice fields in South Carolina; they recorded that 43% of the total area was covered by duck food plants, which made up 85.7% of the total food volume ingested by 15 different waterfowl species. These plants were found only occasionally in undiked marshlands. Six of the plant species predisposed to impoundment contributed 66% of the food volume ingested. Fifty-five percent of the impounded area was freshwater marsh, and 62% of the ducks were associated with these freshwater impoundments. Except for the American wigeon (*Anas americana*), gadwalls (*Anas strepera*), and scaups (*Aythya*), the ducks derived about 87% of their food from such impoundments rather than from the brackish or saline habitats. The seeds of the dotted smartweed (*Polygonum punctatum*), fall panic grass (*Panicum dichotomiflorum*), and the rhizomes and seeds of redroot (*Lachnanthes caroliniana*) were the main food items from freshwater impoundments drained in the summer, variously treated, and flooded in the fall. In the brackish ponds, the seeds and vegetative parts of wigeon grass (*Ruppia maritima*) were the main food in the deeply flooded sites, areas particularly attractive to wigeon, gadwalls, and scaups. The seeds of the salt marsh bulrush *Scirpus robustus* were the dominant food item from the shallower ponds with fluctuating water levels. Coarse perennials dominated undiked, poorly managed areas.

While impoundments play a key role in providing food, they also serve as an assembly and resting area when waterfowl feed elsewhere. MacInnis (1979) noted that the American black duck (*Anas rubripes*), green-winged teal (*A. crecca carolinensis*), and blue-winged teal (*A. discors*) were the most common species on an impounded brackish and adjacent tidal salt marsh at Cape Jourimain, New Brunswick, during spring-fall 1972 and 1973. He noted very distinct patterns of activity. During most of the daylight periods, densities of teal and black ducks were greater on the impoundments, where they rested in large flocks, than on the tidal marsh. In the evening the waterfowl flew to the tidal marsh to feed, returning to the impoundments in the morning. While most of the feeding took place on the marsh surface at night, the ducks did do some feeding during the day, mostly on the impoundments. MacInnis attributed such behavior patterns to fear of the northern harrier (*Circus cyaneus*) and the availability of invertebrate prey. He found that teal and black ducks fed mainly on animal foods that were more abundant in locations free of emergent vegetation for both impoundments and the marsh surface. In the fall, blue-winged teal fed primarily on gastropods, whereas black ducks ingested *R. maritima* and *Potamogeton pectinatus*.

In addition to distinctive feeding behavior pattern differences, MacInnis (1979) found that the numbers of waterfowl broods were five times greater on the impoundments than on the marsh. Pintails (*Anas acuta*) and black ducks were the only species to raise broods on the natural marsh. The high concentrations of dissolved salts and fluctuating water levels in the salt marsh were proffered as an explanation for lower brood densities.

Some bird species have declined in number with the advent of impoundments. The frequent disappearance of the clapper rail *Rallus longirostris* has been associated with the absence of such food as fiddler crabs *Uca* (Darsie and Springer, 1957; Mangold, 1962; Shoemaker, 1964). Long-term inundation would also reduce the nesting areas for this rail. Mangold (1962), Shoemaker (1964), and Provost (1969) also noted declines in the small birds: song sparrow (*Melospiza melodia*), seaside sparrow (*Ammospiza maritima*), sharp-tailed sparrow (*Ammospiza caudacuta*), and yellow-throated warbler, (*Dendroica dominica*), primarily through loss of nesting sites and food. Smith (1968) reported marsh wrens (*Telematodytes palustris*) and seaside sparrows to be relatively abundant, especially where the tide bush grew along ditch or pool margins; however, no comparative quantitative data were given. Provost (1969) indicated the decline in the dusky seaside sparrow following impoundment on Merritt Island, Florida, where it preferred the *Distichlis* habitat. Fish-eating birds also declined on Merritt Island, especially the merganser. Provost could give no reason for such declines and went on to say that, while six species of birds were reduced, there was no apparent effect on seven species and an increase in number was noted for 22 species.

Evidence of mammalian activity has increased with the creation of impoundments (MacNamara, 1952; Catts, 1957; Darsie and Springer, 1957; Tindall, 1961; Mangold, 1962; Shoemaker, 1964; Smith, 1968). Darsie and Springer noted that continued maintenance of high water levels within an impoundment tended to restrict use by muskrats, but the recession of water from the vegetated margin during the summer enhanced plants attractive to muskrats and waterfowl. MacNamara (1949) observed that 8 in was the optimum water level for growth of muskrat food. MacNamara (1952) and Tindall (1961) reported increased numbers of muskrat houses, while Mangold (1962) found muskrats to prefer the fresher-water impoundments. Smith (1968) noted no direct increase in mice populations, but increased evidence of their predators about the impoundments suggested that the small mammal populations had indeed expanded. Increased mammal activity was attributed to greater variety of habitat and an increase in prey concentrations due to the edge effect associated with embankments (Florschutz, 1959*b*).

Springer (1964) has provided a good summary for this section. Many marshes do not realize their full potential as wildlife habitats because they do not have enough open water. This can be remedied by diking to impound and by deepening existing areas. Permanent pools can control mosquitoes and provide clear water, enabling submergent plants, which are important waterfowl food, to become established. Pool-breeding mosquitoes can be controlled by raising the water level to reduce interspersed vegetation, increase wave action, and enhance fish production. Too much deepening, however, will reduce the emergent vegetation and make the area less attractive to waterfowl. Temporary impounding can be used where it is not possible to maintain permanent pools or where the water is too dark to permit plant growth.

Water management for wildlife enhancement depends on keeping the area partially or completely dewatered during the growing season to encourage germination and growth of moist-soil plants used by muskrats and waterfowl. Some cultivated plants can be used to augment the native species. Dewatering during the summer also inhibits the development of larvae. At times it may be necessary to flood earlier than usual because of migrating waterfowl. Then it is advisable to delay as long as possible and restrict the duration of flooding to reduce mosquito egg deposition. Through such restricted flooding, the waterfowl are given a place to rest and provided with food to encourage them to disregard the yet-to-be harvested upland crops.

DITCHING AND PONDING FOR MOSQUITO CONTROL

As we have seen from the discussion of diked lands, ditching to drain water from the marsh surface was once an important aspect of marshland reclamation. Some ditching was done at various points along the east coast of the United States to facilitate the harvesting of salt hay (*Spartina patens*).

In the early 1900s people became aware of the mosquito's role in disease transmission and recognized that control of the mosquito would check diseases such as malaria. Means (1903) and Wright (1907) noted that east coast tidal marshes breed mosquitoes in sufficient numbers to detract from the comfort and well-being of residents and their livestock, thus hindering the development of such localities.

Smith (1902), in describing the life cycle of *Culex (= Aedes) sollicitans,* advocated filling depressions where the mosquito breeds in the high marsh zone adjoining the uplands. Smith (1902, 1907) was also an early advocate of selective ditching as a means to control mosquitoes in portions of the marsh that had high levels of breeding. Over the years a general pattern of ditching became established. Ditches were run in a grid system, about 100 to 150 ft apart, across the surface of the marsh. This activity was carried out whether or not various marsh sites were heavy mosquito-breeding areas. Drainage by ditching for the rapid removal of water from the marsh surface became the primary means of mosquito control. With the passage of the years, many thousands of tidal marshland acres were ditched; progress was evaluated in miles of ditches dug each year. Such ditching probably reached its peak during the depression years of the 1930s, when federal and state agencies with large appropriations for the relief of unemployment became involved in such activities (Stearns, MacCreary, and Daigh, 1940). Stearns, MacCreary, and Daigh pointed out that the ecological side effects may be greater than the original objective. They noted that the water table was lowered by ditching; this finding was supported by Singh and Nathan (1965), who added that the rate of lowering was determined by ditch spacing and soil type. As described earlier, drainage and lowering the water table by ditching have been key components in marsh reclamation (Ganong, 1903; Warren, 1911; Dalby, 1957; Gray, 1977).

Effects of Parallel-Grid Ditching

Up to this point, ditching was concerned only with the elimination of mosquito breeding. Little or no consideration had been given to other consequences. While relief workers were measuring progress by the numbers of miles of ditches dug, people with wildlife interests began to express concern for other organisms, both plant and animal, associated with these tidal marshes. Urner (1935) pointed out that ditching adversely affected game birds, waterfowl, and other bird species. Bradbury (1938) described the adverse effects of such mosquito-control measures on waterfowl and shore bird populations in the Duxbury, Massachusetts, marshes. Stearns, MacCreary, and Daigh (1939, 1940), Cottam et al. (1938), and Bourn and Cottam (1950) portrayed a degrading effect on vegetation; plants useful as food and shelter for various wildlife species were replaced by a colorful but "useless" expanse of greenery. They found a decline in the muskrat population corresponding to the reduction in food plants. Waterfowl were affected not only by reduction in food but through the drainage of marsh pools that had served as feeding and resting areas. Cottam (1938) likened ditching as relief work to scalping someone to cure dandruff or burning a granary to get rid of rats. However, mosquito-control advocates were not easily swayed. Cochran (1935), for instance, believed that ditching was not detrimental to muskrat populations and that the water level could be maintained at a couple of inches below the marsh surface by the use of flood gates. Later he stated that ditching improved muskrat trapping (Cochran, 1938). Both Headlee (1939) and Travis, Bradley, and McDuffie (1954) asserted that ditching had no adverse affect on vegetation and did not lower the water table. Provost (1974) found no evidence of a lowered water table in Florida marshes due to the construction of ditches or canals. He did note, however, that the interior ditches of a project designed to facilitate water movement for mosquito control needed to be as wide as the perimeter canal but not as deep in order to encourage proper water movement and aeration.

Ditches that are dug deep and that drain into the natural channels are generally considered to have a marked impression on tidal marsh vegetation: they lower the water table and replace species of the lower intertidal zone such as *Spartina alterniflora* with less desirable species from the higher intertidal zone, such as salt marsh fleabane (*Pluchea purpurascens*) and salt marsh aster (*Aster subulatus*), followed by *Iva frutescens* and *Baccharis halimifolia* (Cottam et al., 1938). Prior to ditching, the mallows *Hibiscus moschuetos* and *Kosteletzkya virginica*, the seaside goldenrod (*Solidago sempervirens*), *Aster novi-belgii*, *Bidens trichosperma*, *P. purpurascens*, and the swamp milkweed (*Asclepsias incarnata*) were scattered throughout most of the *Scirpus* marsh area adjoining Delaware City, Delaware, but they never became dominant. Within three years (1936-1938) after ditching, however, they dominated the marsh, replacing *Scirpus olneyi* (Stearns, MacCreary, and Daigh, 1940). The lowering of the water table and subsequent intrusion of salt water had a greater effect on *S. olneyi* than on *Spartina alterniflora* or *S. patens* (Cory and Crosthwait, 1939). A pure stand of *S. alterniflora* covering 90% of the Mispillion River marshes was replaced to a large degree by *Baccharis* (Bourn and Cottam, 1950). Ditching drained the permanent pools, destroying the resident wigeon grass (*Ruppia maritima*), and dried out the marsh surface, leaving it more vulnerable to destructive fires (Cottam et. al., 1938). On the other hand, Cory and Crosthwait (1939) advocated ditching as a means for maintaining water levels in pools containing wigeon grass by permitting intrusion of water on the flooding tide. They stressed, however, that the ditches had to be shallow so that the pools would not be drained. In a more recent study of irregularly flooded North Carolina salt marshes dominated by needlerush (*Juncus roemerianus*), Kuenzler and Marshall (1973) found that ditching had increased the area of aquatic habitat by almost 500%. These ditches were inhabited by many juvenile fish, crabs, and shrimp, thus serving as a nursery area. Because they were dealing with a high marsh, Kuenzler and Marshall found no appreciable change in the density and growth of *Juncus*. Brushy vegetation, particularly *Baccharis* and *Iva*, had invaded the spoil piles. They noted that many of the spoil piles had not become covered with vegetation and that erosion was occurring. In addition, they expressed concern about the retention of water behind the levees along the ditches.

Marsh surfaces uncut by ditching are relatively level. After a New Jersey marsh was ditched, Rockel (1969) observed an almost 1 ft depression of the banks bordering the ditches and extending approximately 7 m. back from the ditch. The effect of such a depression would be to increase the amount of marsh surface at the lower intertidal level. Rockel estimated that, for a marsh having ditches at 100-ft intervals, at least 42% of the marsh surface would have been lowered in elevation. Such an increased submergence would enhance the greater production of the taller forms of *S. alterniflora* on the gently sloping banks (Stewart, 1951; Ferrigno, 1961; Rockel and Hansens, 1970) and total production in general (Shisler, 1979). This enhancement of production was also demonstrated by Shisler and Jobbins (1975), who found a significantly higher mean vegetational biomass (1,461 gms/m^2 dry wt.) in a ditched New Jersey marsh than in a natural marsh (850 gms/m^2 dry wt.). The ditched marsh produced 1,562 gms/m^2 in 1974, a significant increase over the

1,360 gms/m^2 produced in 1973. There was no significant difference in productivity of the natural marsh during that time. The increased production in the ditched marsh was attributed to enhanced water circulation. Shisler and Jobbins suggested that the marsh was reverting to a more productive low marsh community, as evidenced by the greater number of fiddler crabs and isopods, fewer *Melampus*, and increased individual *S. alterniflora* stem biomass. It is possible that populations of *Fundulus heteroclitus* may be enhanced as the marsh surface becomes more accessible for feeding and spawning (See Taylor et al., 1979; Weisberg and Lotrich, 1982). These various results would presumably best take place where the ditch banks had been slumping and the level of the water table had not receded.

As stated earlier, Smith (1902, 1907) advocated selective ditching as a means to control mosquitoes in those portions of the marsh identified as prime breeding areas. During an experimental ditching study of the Appoquinimink marshes of Delaware, Stearns, MacCreary, and Daigh (1940) proclaimed that breeding was completely eliminated, as no mosquito larvae or pupae (*Aedes cantator, A. sollicitans, Culex salinarius*) were observed. However, another study in Delaware (Connell, 1940) demonstrated that ditching the lower intertidal marsh dominated by *S. alterniflora* did not reduce the mosquito population. Several years later, eight species of mosquitoes were collected from a ditched marsh in the Assawoman wildlife area of southern Delaware, where *Aedes* spp. constituted 92% of the collections (Catts, 1957). Population size varied with local tidal and rainfall fluctuations, and little breeding progressed beyond the first instar larval stage. Such results were attributed to the effectiveness of the drainage system as a means of controlling mosquito production. A continuation of this work by Florschutz (1959a) reiterated the effectiveness of ditching as a means of mosquito control. Florschutz recorded an increase in the numbers of *C. salinarius* during a rainy season in contrast to low numbers during a dry year. He attributed this increase to the greater permanence of puddles on the marsh surface in the wet year.

MacCreary (1940) was of the opinion that ditching for mosquito control may have helped control biting flies. Other authors, however, have reported that ditching increased available breeding areas for the biting fly family Tabanidae (Bailey 1948; Hansens, 1949). Wall and Doane (1960) found the greatest numbers of punkies (Ceratopogonidae) along the edges of the bays and drainage ditches where tall *S. alterniflora* was the dominant cover or from the moist mud where other vegetation dominated. MacCreary (1940) found ditching to be effective to control tabanids only when the ditches were free of overhanging vegetation. Rockel (1969) observed increasing cordgrass density but decreasing plant height with an increase in elevation. Both greenhead flies (*Tabanus nigrovittatus*) and deer flies (*Chrysops* spp.) displayed population peaks in marsh areas that were 0.2 ft below mean high water (Rockel, 1969) and where the cordgrass *S. alterniflora* was 2 feet tall (Rockel and Hansens, 1970). Rockel (1969) emphasized that 42% of the marsh surface could be lowered by ditching. It is somewhat ironic that in an attempt to reduce mosquito populations the numbers of greenheads and deer flies could be increased through an increase in low marsh area resulting from ditch bank slumping.

In addition to alterations in the populations of mosquitoes and other biting flies, ditching has been deemed responsible for the marked declines in the invertebrate fauna of tidal marshes. Balling and Resh (1982) found that diversity of arthropods (primarily insects such as midges, brineflies, and leafhoppers, plus spiders) in a San Francisco Bay *Salicornia* marsh was high near mosquito ditches during the dry season, but during the wet season was lower near new mosquito ditches in comparison to nonaltered marsh areas. They observed no difference, however, in arthropod biomass between areas adjacent to ditches and undisturbed marsh. In a nearby, more floristically diverse salt marsh they found no difference in arthropod diversity between ditched and natural areas. Balling and Resh suggested an eventual convergence of arthropod community structure between disturbed areas adjacent to mosquito ditches and undisturbed areas adjacent to natural channels. During their examination of the effects of ditching the Mispillion River marshes of Delaware, Bourn and Cottam (1950) recorded a reduction in the number of all invertebrates in the *S. alterniflora* zone ranging between 39.3% and 82.2% depending on the season. Reductions in successive plant zones relative to marsh elevation ranged as follows: *Distichlis spicata* zone, 63.7 to 87.9%; *Spartina patens* zone, 41.2 to 97.3% and *Scirpus robustus* zone, 49.6 to 97%. Bourn and Cottam considered the reduction in mollusks and crustacean populations to be most significant because of their food value for waterfowl and other wildlife: in the *S. alterniflora* association, the reduction ranged from 31.6 to 95.2% depending on the season; in the *D. spicata* association, from 82.4 to 94.3%; in the *S. patens* association, from 54.6 to 99.9%; and in the *S. robustus* association, from 57.6 to 98%. They stressed the seriousness of this situation by pointing out that in 1938 some 90%, or 562,000 acres, of the total original tidal marshland acreage along the Atlantic coast from Maine to Virginia had been ditched. However, Lesser (1975), Lesser, Murphy, and Lake (1976), and Provost (1977) have challenged the idea that ditching produced the changes in vegetation and invertebrates observed by Bourn and Cottam. They suggested that dredging the Mispillion River by the Corps of Engineers was responsible for the changes. Daiber (1982) suggested that the decline in invertebrates with the change in marsh vegetation was induced by the concomitant downward trend in sea level while the more recent restoration of *S. alterniflora* was brought about by the reestablishment of the general rise in sea level.

Ditching with an associated decline in the water table (Provost, 1977) has a direct effect on marsh animals through desiccation, by reducing their ability to move onto the marsh, by leaching, and by oxidation of the soil. More acidic conditions are produced (Neely, 1962) with an adverse impact on the mollusks and crustacea, which depend on alkaline conditions for shell building. Under anaerobic conditions, sulfates in the sea water are reduced to sulfides in the presence of organic matter. These sulfides combine with iron in the clay to form polysulfides. No further changes will occur if the soils remain wet. If they dry out, the sulfides oxidize to form sulfuric acid, which can reduce the pH to 2.5 or less (Neely, 1962).

Most shore birds and waterfowl are directly affected by the reduction in the invertebrate populations used as a food resource (Bourn and Cottam, 1950; Ferrigno, 1959; Shisler, 1973). Another effect is the reduction of marsh pools that are used as a food source as well as a nesting or resting area (Reinert, Golet, and DeRagon 1981). Birds that need a fairly constant water supply, like the American bittern (*Botaurus lentiginosus*), pied-billed grebe (*Podilymbus podiceps*), and American coot (*Fulica americana*) will be seriously affected by such drainage. American black ducks (*Anas rubripes*), willets (*Catoptrophorus semipalmatus*), Virginia rails (*Rallus limicola*), and some herons can be adversely affected (Urner, 1935). Herring gulls (*Larus argentatus*) nesting in the tidal marsh can be adversely affected by ditches open to tidal flow. Burger and Shisler (1978*b*) reported that an increased growth of *Baccharis* and *Iva* bushes caused the gulls to seek less brushy areas. Post (1974) found fewer seaside sparrows (*Ammospiza maritima*) (mean of 0.9 pair/hectare) in a ditched marsh than in an unditched one (mean of 24.8 pairs/hectare).

On the other hand, Florschutz (1959*a*, 1959*b*) observed little difference between a natural marsh and a ditched marsh for some species. Birds that use a low *S. alterniflora* marsh, such as the clapper rail (*Rallus longirostris*), will not be affected as long as the salinity and water level are not changed. As pointed out earlier (Stewart, 1951; Rockel, 1969), ditching can enhance *S. alterniflora* production, which in turn can encourage the clapper rail to nest in the taller grass (Oney, 1954; Stewart, 1951). The willet, which normally nests on higher ground along the landward edge of the marsh, has taken to nesting on the old spoil piles bordering ditches (Burger and Shisler, 1978*a*).

Balling, Stoehr, and Resh (1980) found twice the number of fish species in a ditched San Francisco Bay salt marsh compared to an adjacent unditched marsh surface three times greater than on the ditched marsh. Lorio, Capeyya, and Dakin (1979) reported that Mississippi salt marsh mosquito ditches do not serve as significant nursery areas for important marine sport or commercial fishes, although several brackish-water centrarchids spawn in the ditches.

According to Cochran (1938), ditching would not have an adverse impact on muskrat populations. Stearns, MacCreary, and Daigh (1939, 1940), however, strongly refuted this contention. Their work demonstrated that the vegetation needed for food and house building was much reduced in quantity, causing muskrats to leave.

The consequences of ditching are not simple, straightforward interactions. In general, the water table is lowered and the resulting vegetation shifts toward that of the high *S. patens* marsh. This is usually less desirable for waterfowl due to a reduction in invertebrate populations as a food source. Therefore indiscriminate ditching of a whole marsh is no longer recommended. Flooding mosquito-breeding areas by means of properly designed ditches can remove mosquitoes and, at the same time, enhance the habitat for other species. Such selective ditching has the potential for extending the natural tidal channels, thus increasing the flow of nutrients and organic materials as well as enabling fish to move onto the marsh surface (Springer, 1964; Provost, 1969, 1974). Any management practices will induce some changes in the habitat, which will cause changes in species composition, density, and distribution of the marsh flora and fauna.

Open Marsh Water Management: Selective Ditching and Ponding

History of the Concept.   During the late 1960s, a different form of water management for mosquito control began to be espoused (Ferrigno, Jobbins, and Shinkle, 1967; Ferrigno, MacNamara, and Jobbins, 1969; Ferrigno and Jobbins, 1968). This concept of water management, which advocated the use of biological control rather than mechanical drainage, evolved from the recommendations of Clarke (1938), Cottam (1938), and Price (1938), discussed in the section on impoundments. This concept, which became known as quality ditching, was fostered to replace the grid ditching that had been practiced for some 30 years. Quality ditching has since become transformed into what is known as open marsh water management (OMWM) and is based on the following assumptions: that not all parts of a tidal marsh breed mosquitoes; that mosquitoes are greatly reduced or absent from portions of the marsh where tidal action circulates water over the surface and removes excess water; that biological control in the form of predation by marsh fishes will reduce mosquito populations; and that permanent pools of water on the marsh surface serve as reservoirs for mosquito-eating fish, which can forage among the grass stems at high tide.

The objectives of OMWM are to control mosquito populations by inhibiting the larvae through permanent suppression or habitat manipulation; to eliminate insecticides and other temporary procedures; and to enhance tidal food webs by encouraging nutrient exchanges between the marsh and the adjoining estuarine habitat or embayment. It has been proposed that these objectives can be accomplished without manipulating or disturbing nonbreeding areas. In marshes where breeding occurs, most existing ditches are cleared of choking vegetation and deep ditches are dug to the breeding areas, not for drainage but to enhance water circulation. It is possible, however, that these deep, circulation-enhancing ditches also cause water-table drainage and depression, especially in high marshes, where ditch channels are usually dry for the major portion of a tide cycle. Stop, or blind, ditches have plugs and have no dredged connection to a creek channel, so they can alleviate this problem. These stop ditches are used to keep the water table at or near the soil surface, thus reducing breeding but without excluding storm tides from the area (Shisler, 1978a). Permanent pools are dug on the marsh to provide a reservoir for fish. Pools dug to a depth of 6 to 12 inches encourage waterfowl use, and deeper holes (depths of 18 to 30 inches) provide refuge for the fish during dry periods. Ditches radiate outward onto the marsh surface, permitting the fish to penetrate the surface of the marsh to graze on immature stages of mosquitoes.

Smith (1902, 1904, 1907) proposed the basic concept of OMWM early in this century when he observed that all areas of a salt marsh do not breed mosquitoes. He stated the concept clearly in his 1904 paper:

> Safe areas are wherever fiddler crabs run; wherever high tides cover frequently; wherever fish are carried in with the tide, and solid flat areas where water draws off completely within two or three days. Dangerous marsh is that which is broken up by little holes and pools—rotten marsh, so to speak—or which contains shallow, depressed areas surrounded by grasses so dense that, while the water may work its way in, the fish cannot. Old ditches, grass-grown at the mouth or choked so as to prevent free circulation of water and the entrance of fish, are prolific breeding places. . . . The larger, more permanent salt ponds are always stocked with fish, and are safe; it is the smaller, grassy pond, which is often dry, that is dangerous.
>
> The problem is, in brief, to drain or fill such parts of the salt marsh as are dangerous. . . . Simply, that means be provided for the surface water to make its way out, within three or four days, after the marsh becomes covered by rain or tide. To do this effectively requires ditches two feet deep and not more than six inches wide. . . . Sometimes it may happen that there is a bad, depressed area some distance from a possible outlet for ditches; in such cases the centre should be deepened to make a permanent pool, and that should be stocked with some of the "killies" that swarm in every ditch.

These little fish are great wiggler hunters, and will get at them in the shallowest water if not too densely grass-grown. But they must have a retreat that will not dry up between showers. Very frequently it is only necessary to open up a way for them through dense growth to enable them to work into a dangerous area. . . .

Oil is useful as a temporary expedient only; it is effective enough but must be used everytime a brood develops, and one is no better off at the end than at the beginning of the year. Permanent improvement should be the objective.

Smith (1902, 1904, 1907) found high marsh sites that are infrequently flooded by high or storm tides and dominated by *Spartina patens*, short-form *S. alterniflora, Distichlis spicata*, and *Juncus gerardi* to be prime mosquito-breeding areas. Ferrigno, Slavin, and Jobbins (1975), Shisler (1978a), and others have reaffirmed this observation. Connell (1940) and Fultz (1978), among others, substantiated Smith's observation that mosquitoes are absent from portions of the marsh that are frequently flushed by the tides. Such circulation can be enhanced by ditches leading to breeding sites (Fultz, 1978). Ferrigno and Jobbins (1968) have concurred with Smith's advocacy of deeply cut, straight ditches rather than wide, shallow ditches for enhanced tidal circulation, wildlife usage, and long life. Smith's recognition of biological control through fish predation has been borne out by subsequent observations (Seal, 1910; Headlee, 1915; Chidester, 1916; Harrington and Harrington, 1961) wherein the mummichog (*Fundulus heteroclitus*) is the dominant predator, along with other cyprinodontiform fishes.

Method of Construction.   The creation of such ditches, ponds, and pond radials—as well as the filling of low spots—can be most effectively handled by a rotary ditcher. Only one piece of equipment is needed, and the cost of moving a cubic foot of material is about half that required for a drag line. Greater operator skill is needed, but more precise alterations to the breeding depressions and pond and ditch construction are possible and can be accomplished in less time with a rotary ditcher (Shisler et al., 1978). Hansen et al. (1976) considered OMWM to be the most economical method for mosquito control in New Jersey marshes; 1974 costs varied between $5.05 and $63.45/acre, and the estimated life span of the ditching is 20 years. Over the same 20-year period, larvicide applications (which are considered temporary) were estimated to cost $285/acre in 1974 dollars. In Florida, Provost (1977) also propounded the economic advantage that OMWM has over the use of insecticides. Shisler and Lesser (1979) produced similar kinds of cost estimates for a low-level impoundment in New Jersey. Prorated over a 20-year period, the permanent control established by the impoundment was estimated to be $26.15/acre/year, whereas larviciding was estimated to cost $34.80/acre/year. Shisler and Lesser estimated that the cost of constructing the impoundment would be recovered in approximately 15 years. They also pointed out that nondollar costs had to be considered in the use of larvicides: for example, in the effect on other organisms, timing of application to be effective, and the accuracy of the application. Shisler (1979) indicated that some water-management projects have not required any chemical treatment in 20 years. Boyes and Capotosto (1978) described the positive results of their efforts to use OMWM in Rhode Island. The ditches, pond radials, and other excavations had been done by hand—clearly an immense effort. Apparently the results were worth the exertion.

One of the problems with the older methods of ditch construction was the creation of spoil piles paralleling the ditches. Such spoil piles permit the invasion of ecotonal species, such as *Iva*, onto the marsh surface and foster growth of *S. patens* on the spoil. These piles also impede the flushing of the marsh surface by both normal and storm tides, trapping water and creating wetter conditions that favor the short form of *S. alterniflora* (Ferrigno and Jobbins, 1968; Ferrigno, Slavin, and Jobbins, 1975; Shisler, 1978a; Niering and Warren, 1980). The spoil from the rotary ditcher is broadcast as a mulch or crude slurry over the adjoining marsh surface so that the marsh surface is not substantially elevated (Ferrigno and Jobbins, 1968; Shisler, 1978a; Shisler et al., 1978; Bruder, 1980). The mulch appears to have a stimulatory effect, at least temporarily, since the vegetation takes on a deeper green color than the adjoining grasses not covered by the mulch (Burger, Shisler, and Lesser 1978; personal observation).

Bruder (1980) has established a set of OMWM standards for the state of New Jersey based on the discussion of objectives given earlier. While Boyes and Capotosto (1978) reported positive results for OMWM in the Barrington, Rhode Island, marshes, Lesser, Altman, and George (1978) have questioned whether the techniques that have been so well worked out in New Jersey marshes can be transposed totally and effectively to other marsh systems. These workers observed different tidal regimes, marsh soils, salinity patterns, and species assemblages in Maryland marshes on the Chesapeake Bay side of the Delmarva peninsula, where marshes are encroaching on former woodlands. Drowned stumps and roots, along with the clay layer beneath the shallow peat zone, create problems in excavating functional ditches, radials, and ponds. Lesser and Saveikis (1979) reported good mosquito control in all three of their experimental treatment types within two high marsh areas (treatments were tidal, or open; semitidal, or sill; and nontidal, or closed). The nontidal, or closed, systems produced the least change in plant community structure as a result of ditching when compared to tidal and semitidal systems, presumably because water tables were least affected in the nontidal plots. In some of the tidal and semitidal systems, a substantial incursion of *Iva frutescens* occurred within one year following excavations (with a maximum change noted in percentage of *Iva* cover, from less than 1% to 43% of surface area). The observed *Iva* incursions were correlated to measured water-table depressions caused by open or semiopen ditching, and/or surface elevation increases due to excessively deep or clumped spoils. Lesser and Saveikis found subtle differences in fish use among treatment types, no substantial changes in water quality parameters with the exception of lowered salinities in nontidal systems, and surface-dwelling invertebrates. Subsequent to the Lesser and Saveikis study, nontidal OMWM systems were installed on Maryland's eastern shore in several irregularly flooded marsh areas that are low-elevation basins behind bayside levees. In these types of marshes, nontidal OMWM systems did not provide satisfactory mosquito control, so open systems were belatedly installed and control achieved (C. Lesser, oral communic.). Whigham, O'Neill, and McWethy (1980) studied OMWM's impacts on marshes adjacent to several of the Lesser and Saveikis sites. They observed similar incursions of *Iva*, but they also noted fluctuations in the dominance of *Distichlis spicata* versus *Spartina patens*, depending on the type of OMWM treatment. They found no major differences among sites in water-quality parameters between treatment types and no indication that OMWM resulted in any deterioration of water quality in adjacent estuarine streams. Whigham (in Howe, 1981) stated that undesired changes in vegetation caused by OMWM could be avoided or corrected by controlling the water-table levels. In his opinion, the OMWM technique has not led to any problems with either the vegetation or water quality in the adjacent estuary. While the basic OMWM concept remains sound, it appears that modifications to accommodate local situations are in order.

The Delaware Department of Natural Resources and Environmental Control, through its Mosquito Control Section, is presently evaluating the effects of the various facets of OMWM on surface elevation, water-table height, nutrient supply, emergent vegetation, zooplankton and fish populations, mosquito production, and bird and mammal use (W. H. Meredith, oral communic.). Control areas have been set up adjacent to the experimental plots. Personnel are examining the environmental effects of several types of OMWM alterations: shallow surface pools with deeper reservoirs for fish; pool radial ditches; open, tidally connected ditches; blind ditches; and ditches with sill outlets.

The Delaware group's preliminary observations suggest that, wherever OMWM has been practiced and the water table has dropped 5 in or fluctuated widely as in open-ditched high-marsh areas, *Baccharis, Iva,* and other drier-soil plants such as *Pluchea purpurascens* will invade the ditched area. This observation is consistent with that of Stearns, Mac-Creary, and Daigh (1940), who recorded a similar plant invasion and subsequent departure of muskrats from a ditched marsh when the water table dropped 5 in.

Part of the Delaware plan has been to dig a ditch up to 30 inches deep in the interior marsh and then, as a creek edge is approached, to raise the cutting head of the rotary ditcher to create a shallow sill outlet (Figure 3-10). It was proposed initially that the sill outlet bottom be about 5 in below local marsh surface and about 4 in below the normal water-table

Figure 3-5. A pothole or depression in a *Spartina* marsh, which depicts a typical breeding site for *Aedes sollicitans;* Bombay Hook National Wildlife Refuge, Delaware. (Photo by F. C. Daiber)

Figure 3-6. An overgrown grid ditch in Canary Creek Marsh, Lewes, Delaware, with typical slumping banks. The positions of such drainage channels can be detected by the presence of the tall form of *Spartina alterniflora* that flourishes in these ditches. The *Baccharis* bush in the middle of the picture denotes an old spoil pile. (Photo by F. C. Daiber)

Figure 3-7. A stop, or blind, ditch at Delaware's experimental OMWM site in the Bombay National Wildlife Refuge. Such a ditch has no connection with adjoining tidal creeks; therefore, the water table in the marsh is not lowered. It serves as a refuge for the mummichog, a mosquito-eating fish, during low tide. (Photo by F. C. Daiber)

Figure 3-8. A sill ditch at Delaware's experimental OMWM site in the Bombay Hook National Wildlife Refuge. Such a shallow ditch allows the surface water to drain off the marsh into a tidal creek, but is designed to prevent lowering the water table in the marsh. (Photo by F. C. Daiber)

level, but subject to later possible modification dependent on results. The approximate 100-foot length of the sill would start behind any creek-bank levee, and usually would be excavated in the areas of relatively hard soils and salt hay cover on the backside of the creek-side berm. An extra-deep ditch (36 inches) would be cut from the end of the shallow sill outlet through the creekside levee (with its associated vegetation of *Phragmites, Spartina cynosuroides, Iva,* and *Baccharis*) to connect with an open tidal creek; sometimes this levee cut would be made extra wide (up to 5 ft). This wide, deep cut of relatively short length (about 30 ft) would serve as a catch basin for sediment that would accumulate more rapidly along the creek edge than in the marsh interior. Thus, the longevity of the recessed sill outlet (behind the deep cut) would be promoted, since sediments would be deposited at the creek edge, in the excavated catch basin. The long length of the sill proper, and its construction in relatively hard substrate, should reduce the chances of erosion through normal ebb and flood of tide and also limit the effects of any muskrat burrowing.

It was anticipated that the use of such a sill outlet would allow

Figure 3-9. A shallow surface pool with a deep reservoir for fish at Delaware's experimental OMWM site in the Bombay Hook National Wildlife Refuge. The fish move out across the surface of the marsh at high tide to graze on mosquito larvae and pupae, returning to the pool as the tide ebbs. The reservoir serves as a refuge if the shallow portion of the pool dries out. The island was created as a potential nesting site for waterfowl such as black ducks. (Photo by F. C. Daiber)

enhanced tidal circulation in the pools and ditches, a critical component of open marsh water management, and yet maintain the water table at near its normal level so that the marsh surface and pools would not dry out and no undesirable vegetation changes occur. There appears to be a high potential for success, but the final decision must await completion of the experiment. (W. H. Meredith, oral communic.).

Productivity and Effect on Species.   One of the purposes of OMWM is to enhance the estuarine food web by tidal action. Nutrient exchange is part and parcel of such a food web. While information is very sparse, one paper (Shisler and Jobbins, 1977*b*) has demonstrated that ditched (OMWM) marshes release significantly lower levels of total organic carbon (TOC) and particulate organic carbon (POC) than natural marshes. Reimold (1968) obtained similar results when he reported significantly lower levels of phosphorus coming from a grid ditched marsh than from natural marsh systems during a three-year study in Delaware.

While there is some uncertainty about nutrient exchanges, there is considerable evidence of a progression in several localities in New Jersey to a low-marsh habitat. Ferrigno (1970) found some reduction in the quantity of the short form of *Spartina alterniflora* as well as *Salicornia*. He found no change in the amount of *S. patens* or in *Distichlis spicata* and an increase in *Ruppia maritima* and *Limonium* (sea lavender). Later, Shisler and Jobbins (1977*a*) found stem densities of *S. alterniflora* to be significantly lower (397 shoots/m^2), on a ditched (OMWM) marsh in contrast to the natural marsh (2,647 shoots/m^2). They discovered that the individual plants were much more robust in the ditched marsh; they

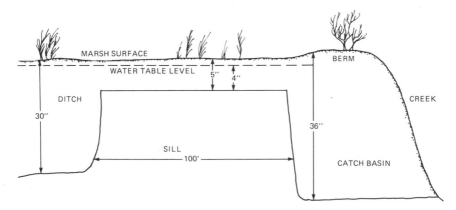

Figure 3-10.   Schematic profile of OMWM ditching developed by the Mosquito Control Section of the Delaware Department of Natural Resources and Environmental Control. Not drawn to scale.

calculated the average individual stem biomass to be 1.8 and 0.2 gms/shoot for the ditched marsh and control area, respectively. In addition, the vegetational biomass was significantly higher (1,462 gms dry wt/m^2) in the experimental site than in the control area (852 grams). Ferrigno (1970) reported mosquito production to be greatly reduced from more than 10,000 larvae/ft^2 in the pretreatment stage to 948 in the first post-treatment sampling and to zero in subsequent sampling. Both Ferrigno (1970) and Shisler and Jobbins (1977*a*) recorded a reduction in the salt-marsh snail (*Melampus bidentatus*) at the ditched site in contrast to the natural marsh. Ferrigno noted a decrease from 529/m^2 to 403/m^2 while Shisler and Jobbins noted a 10-fold decline, from 850/m^2 to 85/m^2. In contrast, both the fiddler crabs and the isopods showed an increase after ditching. Ferrigno noted a change from 3.7 to 13.1 crabs/m^2 in the control and ditch sites, respectively. Shisler and Jobbins (1977*a*) reported a greater change (from 2.5 to 80 crabs/m^2), while the isopods increased approximately 80 times (from 27.5 to 215/m^2) from the natural to the ditched habitat, respectively. Ferrigno reported an increase of the ribbed mussel (*Geukensia demissa*) in the ditched site but noted that snow geese displayed a marked preference for the natural marsh (605 birds from three counts) in contrast to the treated area (8 birds). Ferrigno (1970) concluded that the OMWM method decreased mosquitoes, encouraged the shift in vegetation toward that of a low marsh, increased marsh species, and, with the exception of the snow geese, had no effect on waterfowl. Shisler and Jobbins (1977*a*) attributed the progression toward the low-marsh habitat to the OMWM procedures, which induced greater tidal circulation and nitrogen availability. In other localities (e.g., Maryland's eastern shore), however, the installation of OMWM open ditches may cause a progression toward high-marsh habitat because of excessive surface and subsurface drainage.

Among others, Ferrigno and Jobbins (1968) and Fultz (1978) found that tidal circulation, enhanced by ditches, replenished the mosquito-eating fish in the high-marsh ponds. In California, Balling, Stoehr and Resh (1980) found 10 fish species occupying ditched areas, versus five in unditched sites. Fish density was three times greater in ditched areas (11.0 fish/m^2) than in unditched areas (3.7 fish/m^2). The size and age structure of the dominant species, *Gambusia affinis*, indicated that the population at the ditched site had a greater proportion of immatures than was found in the unditched marsh. These investigators, working in a San Francisco Bay salt marsh, believed that ditching increased diversity and density through enhanced tidal circulation, improved habitat accessibility for fish from other areas, and allowed water retention at low tide, providing refuge for the fish and their food.

In another New Jersey study (Able, Shisler, and Talbot, 1979), the species composition varied significantly between the various types of water management. These differences appear to be due primarily to salinity differences. In OMWM sites with higher average salinities, *Cyprinodon variegatus* and *Fundulus heteroclitus* were dominant, with *F. luciae* and *Lucania parva* being common. Similar results were observed in an unaltered natural marsh. In low-level impoundments and stop ditches with low salinities, freshwater species such as *Notemigonus chrysoleucas, Lepomis gibbosus, Fundulus diaphanus*, and *Gambusia affinis* were prevalent. The estuarine species dominated in the higher salinities of low-level impoundments.

As stated earlier, it has been recognized for some time that the cyprinodontiform fishes play an important role in the biological control of mosquitoes. Only recently has the significance of the marsh surface in the lives of these fishes, particularly *F. heteroclitus*, been appreciated. Prinslow, Valiela, and Teal (1974) and Katz (1975) demonstrated that the mummichog is unable to grow or even survive on diets of aged plant detritus. Kneib and Stiven (1978) reported that a major portion of the caloric requirements of this fish is met by the intake of animal matter, particularly marsh invertebrates. Weisberg (1981) and Weisberg and Lotrich (1982) have shown that *F. heteroclitus* has a higher-than-average assimilation efficiency (87%); no organic nitrogen wastes were excreted and the total nitrogen excretion was higher than that recorded for other fish. They also found a high fraction of ingested nitrogen that is later excreted. Metabolic costs were high, with an average of 69% of ingested energy; correspondingly, gross growth efficiency was lower than average ($\approx 12\%$). All this would point to the fact that *F. heteroclitus* has a high nitrogen demand in the form of animal tissue and at the same time releases a great deal of inorganic nitrogen into the water column.

The work of Weisberg, Whalen, and Lotrich (1981) has shown the mummichog to feed primarily on the high tide during the daylight hours, supporting Clymer's (1978) contention that *F. heteroclitus* is a visual feeder. Weisberg, Whalen, and Lotrich found some feeding activity at nonpeak hours, which might be important for an individual fish — but, for the population as a whole, they considered such activity to be inconsequential. During nonpeak tidal periods, the mummichog usually fed on subtidal invertebrates, insects, and fish. Food items prevalent in the guts during high-tide periods (e.g., detritus, marsh animals) were virtually absent in the guts of nonpeak feeders. The authors suggested that the observed feeding pattern is not necessarily stimulated by food availability. A conditioned response to increased water volume or associated chemical changes at high tide may initiate feeding behavior.

A feeding exclusion experiment (Weisberg and Lotrich, 1982) has demonstrated that growth rates of *F. heteroclitus* were significantly higher for fish allowed access to the marsh surface. Food availability per fish, rather than behavioral responses due to fish crowding, was deemed responsible for the increased growth. While food was available in the subtidal areas, it was insufficient for fish at normal densities to grow at a normal rate. Weisberg and Lotrich concluded that the mummichog must use the marsh surface during flooding tide conditions for at least a portion of its energy intake.

The marsh surface also affects the life cycle of *F. heteroclitus* through the spawning cycle. Taylor et al. (1979) found a semilunar periodicity in the spawning cycle. They reported that the gonadosomatic indices (GSIs) for both sexes were significantly higher during the spring tide periods. Spawning readiness (percent ripe fish) was nearly 100% in both sexes at gonadal peaks and less than 50% between peaks. Peaks of spawning readiness and GSIs for both sexes were evident on the night high tides for over 80% of both sexes for those days defining the spring tide peak. Ovaries examined on night tides were filled with many mature eggs, of which 100 or more were regularly found in the posterior portion of the ovary; during the day, however, the eggs were uniformly dispersed throughout the ovary.

Mummichog eggs have been found in the empty shells of ribbed mussels, *Geukensia demissa* (Able and Castagna, 1975; Kneib and Stiven, 1978), and on the inner surface of the older, dying primary leaves of *S. alterniflora* (Taylor, DiMichele, and Leach, 1977). Taylor, DiMichele, and Leach found eggs situated 5 to 10 cm above the marsh surface. None were found on the surface or among the plant roots. They were distributed in a narrow zone high on the banks of ditches and creeks at a level exposed at low tide but covered by the night high tides.

The timing of the peaks of spawning readiness, the placement of the eggs above the marsh surface, the kinds of food items in the gut, and the accelerated growth rate clearly demonstrate that the mummichog depends on the marsh surface, and that it can do so only during flood tide (primarily spring tide) periods. The OMWM design, by enhancing ingress to the mosquito-breeding sites on the marsh surface, ensures that *F. heteroclitus* is an effective biological control agent.

The former practice of grid ditching, with its concomitant spoil piles or levees, created a varied habitat, which OMWM does not normally do. These old spoil piles in some instances enhanced bird usage. Burger and Shisler (1978a) found that the willet *Catoptrophorus semipalmatus* showed a strong preference for nesting on spoil piles with few birds nesting in areas devoid of ditches. These spoil piles, as the highest areas around, are drier and provide more visibility for courtship and territorial displays. They also provide nesting material, opportunity for concealment and the nests would be better protected from washout. Presumably the use of OMWM, which avoids the creation of spoil piles, would keep the nesting willet from penetrating the marsh surface.

Burger and Shisler (1978b) found herring gulls (*Larus argentatus*) also using spoil piles to advantage. When OMWM was practiced in a well-established herring gull breeding area just before the gulls returned in the spring, Burger, Shisler, and Lesser (1978) found that fewer breeding birds were using the site. Apparently the birds found that the bare, exposed site had been altered enough to be less attractive. One might presume that clapper rail (*Rallus longirostris*) populations could be enhanced by OMWM since this practice appears to develop a progression in some localities toward the low-marsh habitat (Ferrigno, 1970; Shisler and Jobbins, 1977a), and since Stewart (1951) and Oney (1954) found many more nests in the edge between the tall and medium-height cord grass *S. alterniflora*. Interestingly enough, Shisler and Shulze (1976) and Shisler (1979) found that clapper rails were using spoil piles not covered by bushy vegetation for nesting sites. The birds were attracted to the ditches because of increased numbers of fiddler crabs. Where there has been a decrease in cord grass and an increase in bushy vegetation, clapper rail populations have declined. As Burger, Shisler, and Lesser (1978) noted, the effect of ditches on clapper rails depends on the particular marsh and the management technique used.

In summary, tidal marsh management must satisfy the environmental needs of wildlife and provide some control over biting flies. The enhancement practices used to encourage wildlife must not foster mosquito breeding. The control methods to eradicate biting flies must not destroy the wildlife habitat. Management procedures will vary depending on the object of the exercise and on the type of marsh vegetation, tidal range, frequency of flooding, presence of natural pools, and drainage patterns. A mix of physical and biological control methods are considered most effective. The combination of properly designed ditches to facilitate water movement without lowering the water table and the creation of pools to provide reservoirs for mosquito-eating fishes will also furnish feeding and resting sites for waterfowl and shore birds.

Effective management procedures are based on a knowledge of the species concerned and the ecological requirements necessary to increase or decrease their populations. Chemical control has the disadvantage of possible toxicity to beneficial animals and the development of resistant strains in the pest species. When chemical control must be used, it must be safe and should be coordinated with physical and biological control methods (see Chapter 6 for further discussion).

CANAL CONSTRUCTION

As a footnote to this chapter, it is interesting to note a comparatively recent and totally different impact on salt marshes due to the construction of canals by gas and oil companies. These canals, dug through the marshlands for transport of equipment, have been identified as one of the prime causes for the loss of wetlands in Louisiana (Sperling, 1982). There is considerable debate about the role the canals play in the loss of these wetlands. Some claim that they may account for as much as 90% of the loss, whereas others say it is well under 50%. According to Sperling, the mechanism for such losses is unclear. One explanation states that the canals enable salt water to penetrate into freshwater marshes, thus killing the vegetation. Once the vegetation is destroyed it is not replaced. The underlying peat then decomposes, creating large open-water areas. Tidal action is amplified, which aggravates the situation. Another view attributes the losses to a lack of sediments rather than the decomposition of vegetation. In addition, the levees created during canal construction may impound water with a resultant waterlogging of the soil (Sperling, 1982).

Stone, Bahr, and Day (1978) determined, through direct observation and the use of models, that these canals in Louisiana can change the hydraulic regime. The magnitude of change can range from 1 to 35% of normal flow depending on canal alignment and local elevations. This change in turn accelerates wave action, which increases land loss. Stone, Bahr, and Day also reported that these canals, especially the straight ones, create a condition whereby runoff water from agricultural and urban areas is shunted through the marsh directly into the open-water areas. Eutrophication is thereby enhanced with negative impacts on most species in the local fishery. When such runoff is directed through the marsh, the area is purged of the nutrients that would normally be incorporated into primary production. Consequently, the food web no longer receives the heavy load of detritus necessary to support the marsh community.

Chapter 4

Sewage Disposal and Waste Treatment

Wetlands have always served as natural filters and water-conservation devices, using the sun as a source of power. They serve already as interfaces, both consciously and in an inattentive way, between human wastes and aquatic habitats (Odum, 1978). There are several properties more or less common to wetlands that give tidal marshes an affinity for such contaminants (Valiela, Vince, and Teal, 1976). Anoxic organic sediments probably contribute to the retention of various chemical species. Through the accretion process, and because the majority of contaminants adsorb on particulate material, many contaminants are buried in the sediments, thus preventing the dispersal of pollutants. Soluble substances are converted into less mobile forms through incorporation into plant tissues. Furthermore, the plants that dominate wetlands tolerate a wide variety of stresses and have a wide variety of opportunistic characteristics.

A host of studies have evaluated the effects of nutrient enrichment on the wetland ecosystem. Valiela, Vince, and Teal (1976) reviewed much of the literature of nutrient enrichment and sewage applications as they apply primarily to tidal wetlands, while Kadlec and Kadlec (1978) reviewed work with emphasis on freshwater wetlands. Odum (1978, p. 9) asked, "Can scattered wetlands interspersed among urban, industrial, and agricultural activities of humans provide the human-dominated landscape low cost water quantity management, water quality, and other high values?" He suggested that perhaps wetlands can be used to exploit solar energy for water management. This notion is derived from the idea that most sewage treatment is based on a trickling filter system derived from the natural gravel bed of lakes and streams. Since such a system does work, why not use the marsh ecosystem with its comparable filtering and water-quality capabilities? Odum suggested that this would be a way to protect our wetlands by coupling them to the economic system.

EFFECTS ON VEGETATION

Additions of nutrients in the form of commercial fertilizer or dried sewage tend to encourage the growth of vegetation. Tyler (1967) found an approximate 30% increase in dry weight when ammonium chloride and sodium orthophosphate were added to *Juncus gerardi* in a Swedish tidal marsh. Sullivan and Daiber (1974) recorded a threefold increase in fresh weight of the dwarf form of *Spartina alterniflora* in a Delaware marsh with the addition of ammonium nitrate at the rate of 20 gm/m^2/month for a year. They perceived no appreciable response, however, when calcium superphosphate was applied at the rate of 3 gm/m^2/month. Valiela and Teal (1974) obtained similar results in Massachusetts. The standing crops of *S. alterniflora, S. patens* and *Distichlis spicata* increased when urea nitrogen was administered, but there was no increase in production in response to the phosphate ion (Fig. 4-1). The addition of ammonium nitrate produced a significant increase in the above-ground biomass along with a sharp reduction in the carbon-to-nitrogen ratio in the dwarf *S. alterniflora* of Georgia (Gallagher, 1975). One year later, biomass differences between the treated and control plots were even greater, but the C/N ratios had risen to that of the controls. During a study of the effects of ammonium chloride enrichment on a diatom community in Mississippi, Sullivan (1979) noted that the *D. spicata* yield following nitrogen enrichment was increased by 62% in the natural area and 128% in the regrowth of shoots in areas where the grass had been clipped.

Similar above-ground biomass increases can be obtained by the addition of sewage effluents. A North Carolina marsh (Calico) receiving effluent produced significantly greater weights of *Spartina* per square meter than at comparable sites in a control (Dill) marsh (Marshall, 1970). Not only did the waste-receiving marsh in Calico Creek produce a greater plant biomass, but it reached its peak biomass sooner (Fig. 4-2). There was a consistently greater accumulation of dead grass in the control marsh. It was suggested that, without a steady supply of nitrogen, decomposition would take place more slowly. Valiela, Teal, and Persson (1976) found substantial increases in above-ground production with both high (25.2 g/m^2/wk) and low (8.4) levels of dried sewage as well as urea when compared to the control plots (Table 4-1).

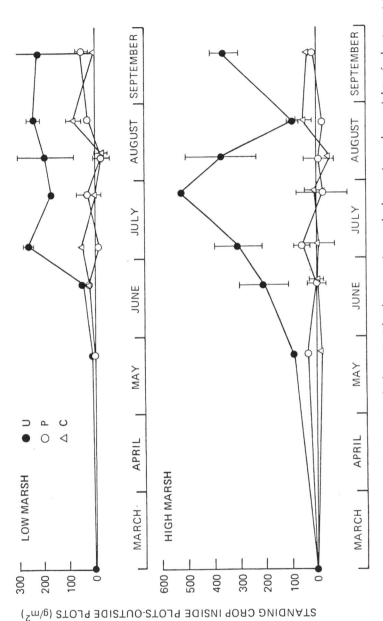

Figure 4-1. Dry weight (mean ± standard error) of plants inside the experimental plots minus dry weight of plants outside the experimental plots for 1972, Sippewissett marsh, Massachusetts. (U = urea, P = phosphate, C = control.) *Source: After Valiela, I., and J. M. Teal, 1974, Nutrient limitation in salt marsh vegetation, in Ecology of Halophytes, R. J. Reimold and W. H. Queen, eds., Academic Press, New York, pp. 547–563, by permission.*

119

Using an overland flow method for disposing of menhaden fishery waste in a Louisiana marsh, Turner et al. (1976) found that the mean *Phragmites* biomass was 1,128 g/m² in the treated plot as compared to 726 g/m² at the control site (Table 4-2). The 55% increase was not significantly different, however, due to the variability of plant density and distribution over the study site. Following the direct application of waste material onto study plots, the live standing crop was significantly higher in the experimental plot. The total biomass was increased and the mean live-dead standing crop was greatly enhanced in the experimental plots for *Scirpus validus* and *Spartina patens*, and approached a significant level for *Sagittaria falcata*. The annual net primary production was 32.5% greater in the experimental plots for all three species (Table 4-3).

It is apparent that marsh vegetation responds to nitrogen additions by enhanced production, but there is little evidence of increased biomass

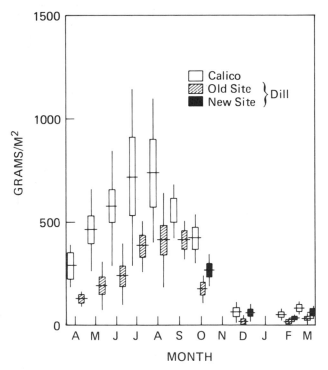

Figure 4-2.   Live *Spartina* weights from a North Carolina marsh receiving sewage effluent (Calico) and from a control site (Dill). *Source: After Marshall, D. E., 1970, Characteristics of* Spartina *marsh which is receiving treated municipal sewage wastes, in Studies of Marine Estuarine Ecosystems Developing with Treated Sewage Wastes, H. T. Odum and A. F. Chestnut, eds., University of North Carolina Institute of Marine Science Annual Report 1969–1970, pp. 317–359.*

Table 4-1.   Estimates of annual production (g/m²) by the various components of salt marsh grasses under the various treatments in Sippewissett marsh, Massachusetts. The values for HF, LU, and C are means for three years; the urea plots are means for two years

	HF	*LU*	*C*	*U*
Low Marsh				
Above-ground	1,320.9	956.4	423.7	834.3
Rhizomes	2,943.0	5,490.0	3,291.0	4,014.0
Roots	372.0	147.0	207.0	414.0
Total	4,635.9	6,593.4	3,921.7	5,262.3
High Marsh				
Above-ground	1,255.6	1,379.5	631.8	1,193.5
Rhizomes	3,384.0	3,402.0	1,614.0	4,505.0
Roots	156.0	210.0	906.0	474.0
Total	4,795.6	4,991.5	3,211.8	6,172.5

Source: From Valiela, I., J. M. Teal, and N. Y. Persson, 1976, Production and dynamics of experimentally enriched salt marsh vegetation: below ground biomass, *Limnol. Oceanogr.* 21(2):245-252, by permission.

Note: HF = high sewage level; LU = low sewage level; C = control; U = urea addition.

resulting from phosphorus additions. The work by Dolan et al. (1981) is an exception. Secondarily treated effluent was added to a Florida freshwater marsh dominated by *Sagittaria lancifolia, Pontederia cordata, Panicum* spp., and *Hibiscus* sp. The marsh removed phosphorus from the effluent during the first year as evidenced by an increased net production of plant shoots, increased litter production, increased root and rhizome production, and higher concentrations of phosphorus in living and dead plant tissue compared to that of the control plot. Bender and Correll (1974) found that a low marsh site in Maryland did take up large amounts of phosphorus, retained it for variable lengths of time, and then released it into the marsh channels. Such a process occurred because the phosphorus was removed from the sediments by plants that later died and redeposited the phosphorus into the detritus zone. Tyler (1967) found both phosphorus and nitrogen to be limiting factors in a Baltic marsh. Work carried out by Woodhouse, Seneca, and Broome (1974) on a natural marsh at Ocracoke, North Carolina, indicated that additions of nitrogen alone could increase yields significantly, but phosphorus availability quickly became the limiting factor when nitrogen rates were increased (Fig. 4-3).

While macrophytic production is definitely stimulated by nitrogen enrichment and in a few instances by phosphorus additions, the edaphic algal standing crop is limited by the availability of inorganic nitrogen or phosphorus, or both, throughout a yearly cycle (Sullivan and Daiber, 1975). Gross algal production is lowest during the fall and midwinter due

Table 4-2. Tissue nutrients and live biomass of *Phragmites australis* in the overland flow area in a treated Louisiana marsh

	Experimental						Control	
	Distance down slope (m)							
	7.5		*15.0*		*22.5*		*Control*	
	% N	*% P*	*% N*	*% P*	*% N*	*% P*	*% N*	*% P*
Tissue nutrient concentration (dry wt basis)								
June	2.30	0.2	1.80	0.15	1.60	0.14	1.30	0.15
July	2.03	0.22	1.62	0.19	1.78	0.16	1.40	0.19
August	1.95	0.19	1.68	0.17	1.83	0.15	1.04	0.13
Live standing crop								
No. of stems/m^2	25		21		26		17	
kg/m^2	1.17		1.03		1.10		0.73	
g/stem	46.5		50.7		44.0		43.0	

Source: From Turner, R. E., J. W. Day, Jr., M. Meo, P. M. Payonk, J. H. Stone, T. B. Ford, and W. G. Smith, 1976, Aspects of land-treated waste applications in Louisiana wetlands, in *National Symposium on Freshwater Wetlands and Sewage Effluent Disposal Proceedings*, D. L. Tilton, R. H. Kadlec, and C. J. Richardson, eds., Ann Arbor, Mich., pp. 147-167.

to decreased light intensity and temperature. Phosphorus availability, not nitrogen, limits the quantity of soil algae during the fall months. During the spring both phosphorus and nitrogen limit algal growth and, because light intensity is greatest during the spring, phosphorus levels are more limiting than in the fall. Gross algal productivity is highest in the spring. During the summer, nitrogen severely limits both algal and cordgrass production. Gross algal production falls during the summer probably because the greater grass canopy allows less light to penetrate to the marsh surface. With the addition of nitrogen to the marsh surface, the grass canopy is greatly increased, which in turn decreases algal productivity (Sullivan and Daiber, 1975).

The evidence suggests that low and high marsh sites respond to nutrient enrichment in different ways. Marshall (1970) observed that maximum live weight was attained in July in a low marsh, and in August for the mid- and high marsh sites. Flowering occurred in early August in the same low marsh but later in the month at higher elevations. Gallagher (1975) noted that availability of nitrogen appears to limit *S. alterniflora* in the middle portions of the marsh but not in the tall *S. alterniflora* occupying the low marsh zone. The differences in growth forms of *S.*

alterniflora can be attributed to the availability of nitrogen (Table 4-4). Valiela, Teal, and Sass (1975) ascribed this to decreased flushing and lower levels of denitrification on the high marsh. For this same reason, low levels of sewage sludge applied to the high marsh produced as much yield as high dosage levels (Table 4-4). The short form of *S. alterniflora* on the high marsh took on the deeper green color, stem density, and height of the tall form following fertilizer application (Sullivan and Daiber, 1974; Valiela, Teal, and Sass, 1975). The same was observed for *Distichlis spicata* (Sullivan, 1979).

Some reports suggested that there is no increase in below-ground biomass with fertilizer additions (Valiela and Teal, 1974; Turner et al., 1976). Dolan et al. (1981), however, did observe an enhancement of below-ground production in a freshwater marsh. Valiela, Teal, and Persson (1976) noted no change in the standing crop of rhizomes for either *S. alterniflora* or *S. patens*, although fertilization did affect root production (Table 4-1). There was a marked reduction in root biomass following the spring peak, particularly where fertilization was the highest. Roots

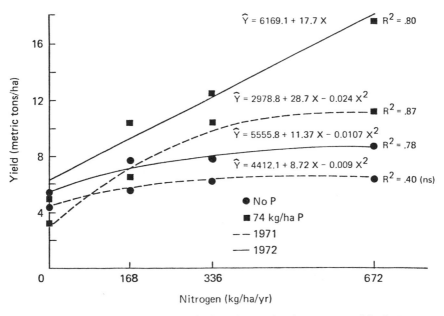

Figure 4-3. Effect of nitrogen and phosphorus fertilizers on yields during two successive growing seasons in a planted North Carolina marsh. *Source: After Woodhouse, W. W., Jr., E. D. Seneca, and S. W. Broome, 1974, Propagation of Spartina alterniflora for Substrate Stabilization and Salt Marsh Development, Technical Memo 46, U.S. Army Corps of Engineers Coastal Engineering Research Center, Ft. Belvoir, Va., 155 pp.*

Table 4-3. Above-ground biomass, adjusted mean live, dead, live-dead, and total tissue standing crops sampled in a treated Louisiana marsh, March–November Units are g/dry wt/m^2. Also given is the annual net production determined using Smalley's method

Species	Live		Dead		Live-Dead		Total		Annual Net Production	
	Control	Exp.	Control	Exp.	Control	Exp.	Control	Exp.	Control	Exp.
S. falcata	247	308*	192	146*	—	—	439	455	608	918
S. validus	501	603**	417	441*	279	301	1,243	1,369*	1,313	1,738
S. patens	760	1,031*	415	285*	293	426	1,569	1,742 (p+.06)	2,128	2,939
All species	503	547**	357	304*	336	363	1,083	1,188*	—	—

Source: From Turner, R. E., J. W. Day, Jr., M. Meo, P. M. Payonk, J. H. Stone, T. B. Ford, and W. G. Smith, 1976, Aspects of land-treated waste applications in Louisiana wetlands, in *National Symposium on Freshwater Wetlands and Sewage Effluent Disposal Proceedings*, D. L. Tilton, R. H. Kadlec, and C. J. Richardson, eds., Ann Arbor, Mich., pp. 147-167.

*p < .05.
**p < .01.

Table 4-4.   The effect of sludge fertilizer on the net annual production and peak above-ground biomass on low-marsh and high-marsh vegetation in Sippewissett marsh, Massachusetts (in kg/m^2)

	Low Marsh		High Marsh	
Treatment	Net production	Peak biomass	Net production	Peak biomass
High dosage	1.32 ± 0.12	1.18 ± 0.20	1.26 ± 0.11	1.00 ± 0.18
Low dosage	0.86 ± 0.04	0.74 ± 0.66	1.38 ± 0.23	0.97 ± 0.04
Control	0.51 ± 0.11	0.32 ± 0.05	0.63 ± 0.05	0.44 ± 0.05

Source: After Valiela, I., J. M. Teal, and W. J. Sass, 1975, Production and dynamics of salt marsh vegetation and effect of sewage contamination. I. Biomass, production and species composition, *J. Appl. Ecol.* **12**:973-982 by permission.

Note: Mean values are based on three years of observations.

disappeared during the autumn, leaving the rhizomes as the only part of the plant to winter over. Woodhouse, Seneca, and Broome (1974) observed a significant increase in the root and rhizome biomass of *S. alterniflora* following nitrogen fertilizer additions to a natural marsh in Ocracoke, North Carolina (Table 4-5). There was no further response to nitrogen additives above 168 kilograms per hectare, indicating that such a quantity was sufficient for maximum below-ground production. When Woodhouse, Seneca, and Broome broke root and rhizome biomass down from 0-10 and 10-30 cm depths, they noted a variable response. In the 0-10 cm layer there was a significant response to nitrogen stimulation and no response to phosphorus enrichment. In contrast, the 10-30 cm layer showed a significant response to phosphorus additives but not to nitrogen. The authors speculated that, because there is a higher proportion of rhizomes in the 10-30 cm zone, it was possible that the response to phosphorus in this layer was due to rhizome growth: that there was a greater response to phosphorus by the rhizomes than by the roots. Coincidentally, the increased dry weight in the 0-10 cm layer might have been the result of nitrogen stimulation of root growth.

Along with general increases in biomass following additions, there is evidence of increases in the concentration of both nitrogen and phosphorus in the above-ground tissues (Tyler, 1967; Valiela and Teal, 1974; Turner et al., 1976; Dolan et al., 1981). Turner et al., while investigating an overland flow method of disposing of fishery wastes, noted three patterns in seasonal concentrations of nutrients: (1) experimental and control concentrations were the same (molybdenum and barium in *Scirpus validus*; calcium in *Spartina patens*); (2) seasonal trends in the experimental sites tracked the controls but at a higher level (iron, potassium, and zinc in *S. patens*); (3) concentrations of nutrients in the experimental

Table 4-5. Effect of nitrogen and phosphorus on below-ground standing crop in a planted North Carolina marsh, 1972

Below-Ground Dry Weight (kg/ha)

P Rate (kg/ha)

N Rate (kg/ha)	0-10-cm Depth			10-30-cm Depth			0-30-cm Depth		
	0	74	$\overline{X}^*$	0	74	$\overline{X}^*$	0	74	$\overline{X}^*$
0	13,714.0	11,900.0	12,807.0	4,170.0	5,525.0	4,847.0	17,884.0	17,425.0	17,654.0
168	17,308.0	16,333.0	16,820.0	4,276.0	6,136.0	5,206.0	21,584.0	22,469.0	22,026.0
336	16,162.0	16,300.0	16,231.0	5,267.0	4,972.0	5,119.0	21,429.0	21,272.0	21,350.0
672	15,702.0	16,864.0	16,283.0	4,537.0	6,613.0	5,575.0	20,239.0	23,477.0	21,858.0
$\overline{X}^*$	15,721.0	15,349.0	—	4,563.0	5,812.0	—	20,284.0	21,161.0	—
LSD 0.05:									
N		2,295.0			n.s.			2,763.0	
P		n.s.			695.0			n.s.	
N × P		n.s.			n.s.			n.s.	
CV (%)		28.8%			37.0%			26.0%	

Source: From Woodhouse, W. W., Jr., E. D. Seneca, and S. W. Broome, 1974, *Propagation of Spartina alterniflora for Substrate Stabilization and Salt Marsh Development,* Technical Memo 46, U.S. Army Corps of Engineers Coastal Engineering Research Center, Ft. Belvoir, Va., 155pp.

Note: $\overline{X}$ = main effects; LSD = least significant difference; n.s. = not significant; CV = coefficient of variation.

Table 4-6. Five-month average nutrient concentrations in the overland flow during operations (mg/l) in a Louisiana marsh

		Distance down slope (m)				Marsh edge	% Reduction
	Source	7.5	14.0	24.2	36.4		
Organic Carbon							
Dissolved	480	360	380	288	272	120	44
Particulate	206	196	137	167	64	15	69
Total	800	559	518	456	337	136	58
Nitrogen							
NH_4-N	547	484	419	359	227	37	59
Organic	95	62	55	48	49	23	49
Total	642	546	476	408	312	58	51
Phosphorus (PO_4-P)							
Available	28	15	14	15	15	7	47
Organic	22	11	9	8	7	5	68
Total	51	26	23	24	24	13	53

Source: From Turner, R. E., J. W. Day, Jr., M. Meo, P. M. Payonk, J. H. Stone, T. B. Ford, and W. G. Smith, 1976, Aspects of land-treated waste applications in Louisiana wetlands, in *National Symposium on Freshwater Wetlands and Sewage Effluent Disposal Proceedings*, D. L. Tilton, R. H. Kadlec, and C. J. Richardson, eds., Ann Arbor, Mich., pp. 147-167.

sites tended toward higher levels later in the year (calcium, potassium, and barium in *Sagittaria falcata*; potassium, magnesium, molybdenum, and strontium in *S. patens*). They also observed a significant increase in nitrogen (47%) and phosphorus (13%) in *Phragmites* leaves and stems from the top to the bottom of the slope. Correspondingly, they recorded a decrease in carbon (58%), nitrogen (51%), and phosphorus (53%) from the waste water as it moved down the slope (Table 4-6). In spite of these appreciable declines in the nutrient load of the waste water, Turner et al. (1976) determined that the amount of nitrogen and phosphorus absorbed by the plants was less than 5% of the total added.

In contrast, Woodhouse, Seneca, and Broome (1974) found the nitrogen content of the plant tissues to be closely related to the rate of nitrogen applied as a fertilizer (Fig. 4-4) on a natural marsh at Ocracoke, North Carolina. Also, there was a surprisingly high recovery of nitrogen in relation to the amount applied (Table 4-7).

While the vast majority of references have recorded an increase in biomass with fertilizer additions, and an associated increase in tissue uptake, a few have not. The artificial enrichment of saw grass (*Cladium jamaicense*) in a Florida freshwater marsh did not increase biomass even though nutrients were assimilated (Steward and Ornes, 1975). This species has low nutrient requirements and thus could not be used efficiently

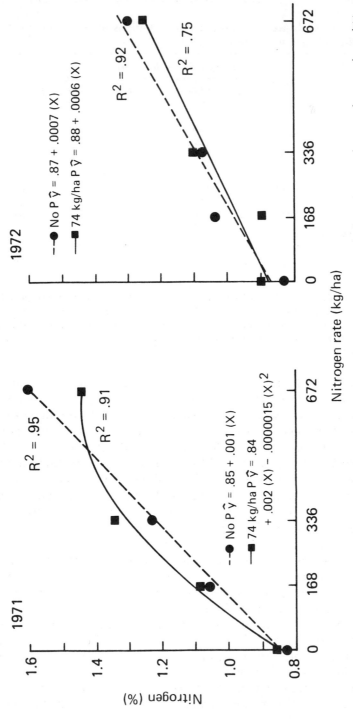

Figure 4-4. Relationship between nitrogen fertilizer applied and nitrogen content of plant tissue at harvest from a planted North Carolina marsh. *Source: After Woodhouse, W. W., Jr., E. D. Seneca, and S. W. Broome, 1974, Propagation of Spartina alterniflora for Substrate Stabilization and Salt Marsh Development, Technical Memo 46, U.S. Army Corps of Engineers Coastal Engineering Research Center, Ft. Belvoir, Va., 155 pp.*

Table 4-7. Apparent recovery of fertilizer nitrogen in the shoots at harvest in a planted North Carolina marsh site

			Apparent Recovery (% of Total N Applied)				
	1971		*1972*				
	0^a	74	0^a			74	
N Rate				*Roots and*			*Roots and*
kg/ha	*Shoots*		*Shoots*	*Rhizomes*	*Total*	*Shoots*	*Rhizomes*	*Total*
0	—	—	—	—	—	—	—	—
168	15.2	24.3	20.2	33.3	53.5	30.3	31.5	61.8
336	12.2	33.0	11.9	22.9	34.8	28.0	16.7	44.7
672	9.6	19.9	9.7	14.7	24.4	26.3	16.7	43.0

Source: From Woodhouse, W. W., Jr., E. D. Seneca, and S. W. Broome, 1974, *Propagation of* Spartina alterniflora *for Substrate Stabilization and Salt Marsh Development*, Technical Memo 46, U.S. Army Corps of Engineers Coastal Engineering Research Center, Ft. Belvoir, Va., 155pp.
[a]Rate of P (kg/ha).

to renovate waste water with high nutrient concentrations. This suggests that the physiological requirements and nutrient requisites of the various (or at least the dominant) plant species need to be known for the individual marsh sites being proposed for waste-water rehabilitation.

PORE WATER CONTENT

Valiela and Teal (1974) observed increases in sediment pore water nutrient levels associated with increased biomass and tissue nutrient content following fertilization (Figure 4-5). Turner et al. (1976) noted increased groundwater nutrient levels at the bottom of the slope receiving fish wastes. Dolan et al. (1981), however, did not observe any increase in phosphorus concentration in the ground water.

HEAVY METALS

The marshes appear to retain a considerable portion of the nutrients that have been added (Valiela, Teal, and Sass, 1973; Valiela, Vince, and Teal, 1976; Bender and Correll, 1974). This probably involves adsorption and absorption on organics and clay particles. Nutrients are incorporated into the plant tissues during the growing season and then dropped to the soil as the plants die. This is also true for heavy metals such as lead, cadmium, zinc, and mercury (Valiela, Banus, and Teal, 1974; Banus, Valiela, and Teal, 1975; Windom, 1975, 1976; Windom et al., 1976) (Table

4-8). Windom (1975, 1976) and Valiela, Banus, and Teal (1974) noted that *S. alterniflora* concentrates metals to a high degree. The plants are subsequently harvested by the tides, degenerating to form detritus. Much of this detritus is then exported from the marsh (Valiela and Teal, 1974; Valiela, Teal, and Sass, 1973; Valiela, Vince, and Teal, 1976; Roman, 1981), increasing the possibility that heavy metals will enter the estuarine food web. The flocculation of organic matter at the river-estuary boundary acts to scavenge metals from the water column with their accumulation in the sediments. The salt marsh serves as a sink for iron

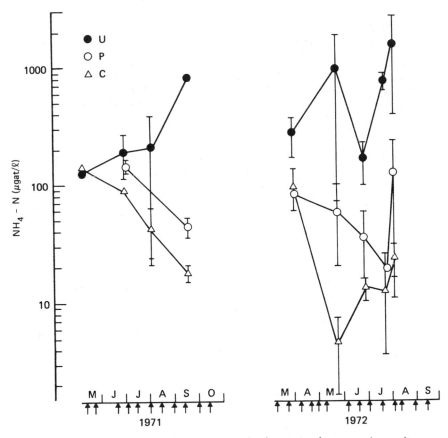

Figure 4-5. Concentration (mean ± standard error) of ammonium nitrogen (NH₄-N) in the sediment water in low marsh plots subjected to urea (U), phosphate (P), and control (C) treatments in Sippewissett marsh, Massachusetts. The arrows along the horizontal axis indicate the dates of fertilization. *Source: After Valiela, I., and J. M. Teal, 1974, Nutrient limitation in salt marsh vegetation, in Ecology of Halophytes, R. J. Reimold and W. H. Queen, eds., Academic Press, New York, pp. 547-563, by permission.*

Table 4-8. Concentration of lead, zinc, and cadmium (mean ± standard error) in the acid-soluble fraction of cores 0 to 2 cm deep from plots subjected to the fertilizer treatments in Sippewissett marsh, Massachusetts. Four replicate cores were used to obtain each mean. Vertical lines joining means indicate no significant differences among those means at the 0.05 level

	Concentration of acid-soluble fraction (in ppm)		
	Pb	Zn	Cd
High fertilizer dosage	117.0 ± 22.7	514.0 ± 43.5	11.8 ± 2.2
Low fertilizer dosage	113.0 ± 5.0	228.0 ± 18.6	13.4 ± 2.5
Control	62.3 ± 2.0	113.0 ± 11.6	1.7 ± 0.3

Source: From Valiela, I., M. D. Banus, and J. M. Teal, 1974, Response of salt marsh bivalves to enrichment with metal-containing sewage sludge and retention of lead, zinc and cadmium by marsh sediments, *Environ. Pollut.* 7: 149-157, by permission.

and manganese along with an accumulation of particulate cadmium and mercury. Mercury is lost from areas of local concentration so slowly that such concentrations will persist for some time (Windom, 1976). Windom et al. (1976) noted that the presence of higher concentrations of mercury in the surface layers of the sediments suggested recent inputs from particular industrial activities.

While Windom (1976) suggested that heavy metals may enter the estuarine food web, Banus, Valiela, and Teal (1975) noted that, although lead is largely retained by surface sediments, only 6 to 8% is taken up by marsh grasses. This incorporated lead is exported as detritus but accounts for only 3 to 4% of the entering lead. About 2% of the zinc added to this same marsh was exported in grass detritus, while 16% (from the low-level [15 mg/m^2/yr] addition) and 45% (from the high-level [43 mg/m^2/yr] addition) were lost by unknown means. About 80% of the low-level addition of cadmium was retained in the sediments but, at a higher dosage, 65% of the added cadmium left the study plot, probably in the dissolved form. Apparently very little of the metals was released into the water column; the metal levels in the ribbed mussel, hard clam, and oyster were very uniform and were not different from the controls, except for much higher cadmium levels in the high-fertilizer-dosage plots. Increases in zinc and particularly cadmium, but not lead, were detected in the creek-bottom detritus downstream from the plots (Valiela, Banus, and Teal, 1974). Fiddler crabs showed increased lead and cadmium in the high-dosage plots but no increase in zinc. On a dry-weight basis, however, the crabs did not accumulate as much as the detritus food sources. The amount of metals decreased up through the food chain according to Valiela, Vince, and Teal (1976). At the same time, Banus, Valiela, and Teal (1975) reasoned that since fiddler crabs feed from the marsh mud, they should be good biological indicators of metal contaminations of the surface layer.

Valiela, Vince, and Teal (1976) have pointed out that metals are present in considerable quantities in sewage sludge and, while much of such metals are trapped in the marsh sediments, they can be recirculated through the uptake process in plants. Through the export of detrital carbon (see Roman, 1981), these metals can be moved into the estuarine environment. This export can be enhanced by the concomitant nitrogen load in the sewage sludge. Since nitrogen increases the standing crop, it is likely that larger amounts of heavy metals will leave the marsh in the increased quantities of dead grass (Banus, Valiela, and Teal, 1975). Currently cadmium is the only metal to appear in appreciable amounts in the detrital food web of the marsh. However, full-scale sewage applications with accompanying heavy metal concentrations have not been studied for sufficient time to determine the long-term effects, if any, on the marsh biota and adjoining estuarine community.

ANIMAL POPULATIONS

The addition of fertilizers can alter animal populations. Marshall (1970) noted an increase in the number of *Littorina* snails in a North Carolina marsh associated with a sewage outflow. This was attributed to the steady supply of nitrogen, which was hastening the decomposition of plant material to detritus upon which the snails fed. McMahan, Knight, and Camp (1972) attributed increases in amphipod populations in the same marsh to increased detritus formation. Spider densities were also exaggerated in the sewage-treated marsh. The increased spider population was attributed to a probable increase in herbivores resulting from intensified grass growth. The lack of significant difference between herbivore populations of the two marshes studied was ascribed to increased spider predation. The growth of the hard clam *Mercenaria mercenaria* and oyster *Crassostrea virginica* was not affected by metal-containing sewage sludge and urea fertilizers added to New England salt marsh plots. Growth of *Geukensia demissa* was enhanced, however, (Valiela, Banus, and Teal, 1974). In this same marsh Meany, Valiela, and Teal (1976) observed that larval tabanid populations (*Tabanus nigrovittatus* and *Chrysops fuliginosus*) were greatly reduced in plots treated with sewage sludge but unaffected in plots treated with phosphate and urea fertilizer.

COMMUNITY ORGANIZATION

Valiela, Vince, and Teal (1976) noted that nutrient additions could change not only the biomass but also plant densities; species composition remained the same. Grant and Patrick (1970) were of the opinion that a healthy marsh can have a normal population balance and maintain a reasonable species diversity, and that the marsh can serve as a reservoir from which a polluted stream can be repopulated should a catastrophic event befall the creek. If the marsh is heavily polluted, however, it will lose its ability to repopulate such an inflowing stream. McMahan, Knight, and Camp (1972) observed species diversities to be higher in a polluted North Carolina marsh than was typical, but they attributed some of this increase to reduced tidal action. Clipping or shading or phosphorus enrichment of a pure stand of dwarf *S. alterniflora* caused significant decreases in both species diversity and the number of diatom species in a Delaware marsh; nitrogen enrichment decreased only the latter (Sullivan, 1976). In a subsequent study in Mississippi, Sullivan (1979) reported that clipping had a greater effect on species diversity and the number of diatom taxa than did nitrogen enrichment. He did say, however, that two diatom species, *Nitzschi perversa* Grun. and *Nitz. gandersheimiensis* Krasski, may represent bioindicator organisms for detecting nitrogen enrichment in Gulf Coast salt marshes.

LIMITATIONS OF WASTE-TREATMENT APPLICATION

In 1973, Valiela, Teal, and Sass stated that salt marsh systems are flexible enough to use as much nitrogen as is available regardless of the mechanism of supply. Such marshes may act as effective removers of excess inorganic nitrogen and may be considered as potential tertiary treatment systems for sewage effluent. Grant and Patrick (1970) presented data indicating that the freshwater Tinicum marsh near Philadelphia was able to treat the polluted inflow from Darby Creek. They estimated that, with a marsh surface area of 512 acres, there would be a reduction of approximately 7.7 tons of biological oxygen demand (BOD)/day, 4.9 tons of PO_4-P/day, and 4.3 tons NH_3-N/day along with an increase of 138 pounds of NO_3-N/day and 20 tons of oxygen/day where waste treatment occurs. It was concluded that this marsh had a remarkable capacity to reduce the nutrient load and at the same time enhance the oxygen content. Marshall (1970) cautioned that the effects of such nutrient additions to the underwater communities had not been studied. At the same time he was of the opinion that the effects of sewage additions could be judged as beneficial. Whigham and Simpson (1976) predicted that the freshwater tidal marsh they were examining along the Delaware River would be able to handle effluent two and a half times the daily flow from a treatment plant into the creek. In 1978 they found, after a three-year study, that the biomass and standing crops of nitrogen and phosphorus did not differ between the experimental and control areas following spray application of chlorinated secondarily treated sewage effluent. The only consistent result was an increase in percent nitrogen and percent phosphorus concentrations in the treated marsh. Total nitrogen, percent nitrogen, total phosphorus, and percent phosphorus of the plant litter were significantly greater in the experimental areas. There were no significant substrate responses due to the spray irrigation. Their tidal flux studies showed that the irrigated wetland was a sink for nitrogen. The input of NH_3-N, NO_3-N, and total nitrogen was greater than the output. The evidence suggested that wetlands may assimilate up to 40% of the total nitrogen and well over half the NO_3-N received. All evidence indicated the marsh exported PO_4-P as well as total phosphorus. Because Whigham and Simpson found an accumulation of phosphorus and nitrogen in the litter but not in the vegetation or the sediments. They concluded that the high-marsh habitat of freshwater wetlands would not have the tremendous nutrient-removal characteristics of other wetlands. Where limited removal of nitrogen from sewage is a management goal, however, they concluded that such freshwater tidal wetlands can play an important role.

Valiela, Vince, and Teal (1976) thought that wetlands are better processors of wastes than open estuarine and coastal waters. They believed the properties of wetlands and the effects of nutrients, heavy metals, hydrocarbons, and pathogens to be features of wetlands as they function normally. These authors proposed that wetlands provide free waste treatment for contaminated waters and that wetland conservation be implemented to maintain such a subsidy. Kadlec (1978), working on freshwater wetlands, also recognized their potential as tertiary treatment plants. He did raise important questions dealing with how much waste water could be safely added, at what particular timing schedule, in what physical distribution manner, and at what cost to the community. Valiela, Teal, and Sass (1973) stressed that there are strong seasonal patterns for retention of any nutrients applied to the marsh surface. This retention was considered to be related to primary production; such patterns should be part of important management considerations. Ryther et al. (1978) have suggested that, at least for freshwater sites, not only can aquatic vegetation remove excess nutrients but the biomass produced may be converted to fuel by anaerobic digestion.

In contrast to this positive evidence, a precautionary note is found in a publication by Bender and Correll (1974), who reported that a Chesapeake Bay low marsh did take up large amounts of phosphorus, retained it for variable times, and then released it into the marsh channels. The phosphorus was taken up by plants from the sediments and the detritus, and when the plants died the phosphorus was redeposited in the detritus zone. When the high marsh was loaded at the rate of 430 mg $P/m^2/day$, (about the equivalent of 29,000 gallons of secondary sewage effluent per acre per day, or about 1.1 inches of effluent per day), the capacity of the marsh to bind up phosphorus was exhausted in 45 days. Such binding was restricted to the upper few inches of the sediment. Lighter rates of loading could proportionately extend the time frame of loading. Bender and Correll suggested that, once the marsh had been loaded to capacity with phosphorus, it could not be expected to have a significant phosphorus-binding capacity again for many years. They estimated that approximately 0.05 acres/person/year would be needed, assuming sewage generation at a rate of 150 gallons/day/capita. They concluded that the use of marshes of any type as nutrient-removal systems was questionable. Dolan et al. (1981) found that sewage additions to a Florida freshwater marsh enhanced production of plant shoots and root rhizomes, and increased litter production during the first year. While higher levels of phosphorus were found in living and dead plant tissues, concentrations did not increase in the groundwater. They concluded that the marsh successfully removed phosphorus from the effluent during the first year and suggested that the long-term result will be determined by the phosphorus-adsorption capacity of the soil and the rate of peat production. Steward and Ornes (1975) found that, because of the low nutrient requirements of the saw grass (*Cladium jamaicense*) in the Florida Everglades, there would have to be 5.7 times more saw grass area than was then available to recycle secondarily treated waste water successfully. Their experimental plots were overwhelmed in eight weeks at a continuous weekly application of 2.5 kg phosphorus/ha/week. In addition, dense algal blooms developed over the experimental plots, with the resultant loss of several components of the floral community.

The nature of the substrate may have an effect on the rate at which a tidal marsh is overwhelmed by such excessive nutrient loading. Woodhouse, Seneca, and Broome (1976) observed a continued increase in total growth and response during the fourth year of nitrogen and phosphorus additions to a young natural stand of *Spartina alterniflora* growing on a sandy substrate near Hatteras Inlet, North Carolina. In the absence of applied phosphorus, nitrogen had a slightly depressing effect. It is evident from Table 4-9 that both nitrogen and phosphorus were sharply limiting at this site. This fourth-year response also demonstrated the capacity of this vegetation to withstand and benefit from a rather high input of nutrients on a regular basis (Woodhouse, Seneca, and Broome, 1976). It should be pointed out that nutrient applications were applied in three stages (late April-early May; June; and late July-early August) rather than the daily flow basis that one would expect from applications of sewage effluent.

Table 4-9.   Effect of the fourth year of fertilizer[a] on growth of *Spartina alterniflora* at Ocracoke, North Carolina. Plots 4 by 25 feet, three replications; harvested 19 September 1974

N Rate (kg/ha)		*Aerial dry Weight (kg/ha)*		
		P rate (kg/ha)		
		0	*74*	*Average*
0		4,085	3,831	3,958
168		4,671	8,592	6,632
336		3,635	11,192	7,413
672		3,484	17,029	10,257
Average		3,969	10,161	
LSD				
Nitrogen	0.01	1,573		
	0.05	1,133		
Phosphorus	0.01	1,112		
	0.04	801		
Nitrogen	0.01	2,224		
plus				
Phosphorus	0.05	1,603		
CV	(%)	13.0		

Source: From Woodhouse, W. W., Jr., E. D. Seneca, and W. S. Broome, 1976, *Propagation and Use of* Spartina alterniflora *for Shoreline Erosion Abatement*, Technical Rept. 76-2, U. S. Army Corps of Engineers Coastal Engineering Research Center, Ft. Belvoir, Va., 72pp.

Note: LSD = least significant difference; CV = coefficient of variation.

[a]Nitrogen from ammonium sulfate and phosphorus from treble superphosphate applied in split applications in April, June, and August of each year.

The very nature of sewage effluent dictates concern about the release of pathogenic microorganisms in a marsh. Seidel (1971) demonstrated the removal of pathogenic bacteria from water during its passage through a stand of freshwater macrophytes. Valiela, Vince, and Teal (1976) noted that fecal and total coliform bacteria in the water were halved as water flowed over the marsh surface during tidal inundation (Table 4-10). In addition, they observed a decline in the numbers of coliform bacteria leaving a tidal creek from those in the Hackensack River (northern New Jersey) water entering the marsh. The total coliform count increased again in the ebbing tide. The authors attributed this increase to possible abundant bird populations in the marsh vegetation.

While Valiela, Vince, and Teal (1976) called attention to the reported bactericidal effect of sea water, Jensen and Tyrawski (1978) found total and fecal coliform concentrations to be extremely high in tidal creeks where high-tide salinities are typically 27 to 28‰ (Figure 4-6). They suggested that significant coliform export on a long-term basis is likely.

Table 4-10.   Mean ± standard error of bacterial counts (cells/100 ml) in flooding and ebbing tides in tidal creeks within Hackensack Meadows, New Jersey, 31 January 1975. Numbers in parentheses are the number of creeks involved in each mean

	Flooding Tide	*Ebbing Tide*	*Test*
Fecal coliforms	667 ± 303 (3)	329 ± 35 (8)	significant at 0.01 level
Total coliforms	1,820 ± 180 (4)	935 ± 132 (8)	significant at 0.01 level

Source: From Valiela, I., S. Vince, and J. M. Teal, 1976, Assimilation of sewage by wetlands, in *Estuarine Processes*, vol. 1, M. Wiley, ed., Academic Press, New York, pp. 234-253, by permission.

Flux results of a 24-hour study in Canary Creek, Delaware, were variable due to light levels and other factors. A model development of the adjacent Broadkill River revealed the average marsh total coliform export to be between 2×10^9 and 2×10^{10} colonies/ha/day, depending on tidal range and adjacent water coliform levels. Jensen and Tyrawski (1978) also proposed that tidal wetlands appear to have a strong effect on total and fecal coliform levels. Removal of point sources from the model substantially lowered the coliform level. When the point sources remained and the wetlands were removed, however, total coliform levels decreased significantly (Figure 4-7). Since these wetlands appear to be a "natural" source, the authors deemed it appropriate to question the validity of total coliform data for shellfish-harvesting regulations. It also appears appropriate to question the role wetlands appear to play in the removal of pathogenic microorganisms following any sewage effluent applications.

Perhaps the best summary for this section is derived from the paper by Kadlec and Kadlec (1978), which deals with two basic categories: interest in understanding the natural functions of a wetland ecosystem and human impact on the wetland. Some studies show marshes to be net exporters of nitrogen and phosphorus while other marshes retain larger portions of both when these elements are added to the system. The amount of nitrogen and phosphorus in plants and soils is a function of both concentration and quantity of material containing the concentration. The bulk of the nitrogen and phosphorus for plant growth apparently comes from and returns to the sediments with only an ephemeral existence dissolved in surface waters. Sediments appear to be the action zone for most uptake and storage. Uptake by vascular plants, and subsequent cycling, is an important route, which requires months to complete. For epiphytic plants, on the other hand, the time scale is measured in hours. One needs to know whether harvest is required in order to prolong the lifetime of a particular waste-treatment project.

The toxicity of heavy metals and the possible tendency of these materials to accumulate in the food chain are problems associated with human impact on the wetlands. Vascular plants may accumulate even low concentrations. Heavy metals are reduced in their passage through the wetlands ecosystem by being retained in the sediments or taken up by the plants, all of which may enter higher food chains. Suspended solids are important in the total ecosystem function, for they transport large quantities of nutrients, heavy metals, and other substances. These may be carried as part of the solid itself or as adsorbed material.

Much remains to be learned about the actual cycle and uptake processes under circumstances of altered water quality. A still larger gap concerns

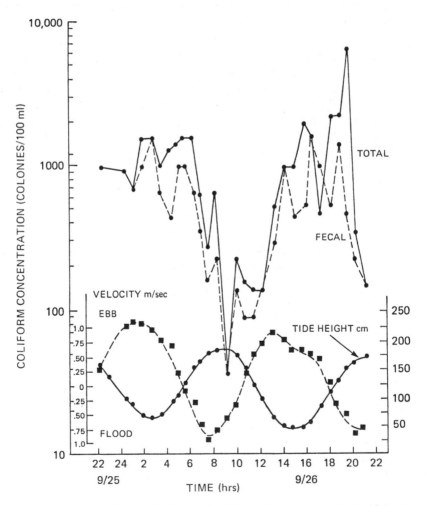

Figure 4-6.   Canary Creek, Delaware, coliform flux data on September 25-26, 1977. *Source: After Jensen, P. A., and J. M. Tyrawski, 1978, Wetlands and water quality, in Coastal Zone '78, vol. 2, Symposium on Technical, Environmental, Socioeconomic and Regulatory Aspects of Coastal Zone Management, American Society of Civil Engineers, New York, pp. 201-223, by permission.*

the various time effects that will be important. Sewage discharges may alter the amplitude of seasonal fluctuation and the mean of seasonal variables. While some wetlands appear to be successful in processing waste water, there is some question about the removal of certain constituents. There is evidence that some wetland systems have become saturated and have lost the ability to function as tertiary treatment plants. Hydrologic flow patterns in both space and time play an important role in the effectiveness of a particular wetland for renovating waste water. Channels through a wetland allow waste water to bypass the ecosystem and result in poorer renovations. Periodic tidal flushing appears to negate any possibility for permanent nutrient storage (Kadlec and Kadlec, 1978).

Lastly, data are needed to determine the limits of human disturbance that a particular wetland can withstand. Odum (1978) believed that natural wetlands can develop a modified association of organisms to process wastes of human developments, as long as the loads are not excessive and the contents are not too toxic. At the present time we do not know what those limits are. We need to act with dispatch but proceed with caution.

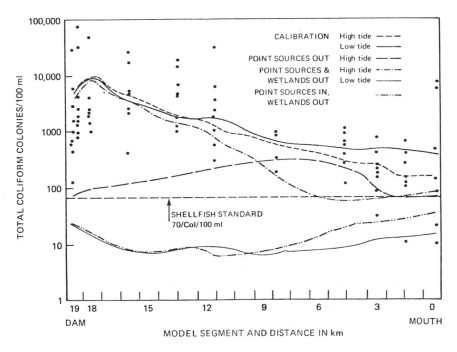

Figure 4-7. Model average flow total coliform simulations on Broadkill River, Delaware. *Source: After Jensen, P. A., and J. M. Tyrawski, 1978, Wetlands and water quality, in Coastal Zone '78, vol. 2, Symposium on Technical, Environmental, Socioeconomic and Regulatory Aspects of Coastal Zone Management, American Society of Civil Engineers, New York, pp. 201–223, by permission.*

Chapter 5

Dredge Material for Wetland Restoration

The growing concern over the years about the extensive losses of our tidal wetlands has generated an interest in finding ways to mitigate such losses.* At the same time there has been growing anxiety about the disposal of spoil resulting from navigational channel dredging. A conflict has arisen between those who object to dredge material being deposited in a wetland and the economic merit of maintaining navigable waterways for commerce and recreation (Reimold, 1978). Historically, site selection for spoil disposal was determined by the discharge capabilities of the dredging equipment. This is no longer an acceptable criterion in the face of a shortage of accessible lands in general and the emerging environmental awareness that has further reduced available lands. Thus new site-selection processes are emerging. It has been long recognized that dredge spoil is a resource (de Nekker and d'Angremond, 1976; Beeman and Benkendorf, 1978), but little recognition has been given to the need for the future use of recommended disposal sites. Continued estuarine modification from dredging has intensified the need for mitigation and positive approaches to the use of dredge spoil (Eleuterius and McClellan, 1976). This should be integrated with long-term land use planning and

---

*Zedler (1984) provides a guide for salt marsh restoration with particular reference to Southern California. It identifies the goals for restoring and enhancing coastal wetlands and discusses the techniques to accomplish those goals.

development. It is also evident that dredged material-disposal sites could be used more productively if the federal government were to take greater interest in (or responsibility for) the use of the sites and if local communities were to take greater interest in navigation and channel maintenance (Beeman and Benkendorf, 1978). The numerous reports of the Dredged Material Research Program of the U.S. Army Engineer Waterways Experiment Station dramatically demonstrate a satisfactory resolution to the concerns of tidal marsh losses and spoil disposal through the restoration or creation of new wetlands by using dredge spoil.

CRITERIA AND GUIDELINES

La Roe (1978) cited the Estuarine Resources Goal of the Oregon Land-use Program as setting the tone in regard to any relationship between wetlands and dredging. ". . . plans and activities in estuaries . . . 'shall protect the estuarine ecosystem, including its natural biological productivity, habitat diversity, unique features and water quality.'" It specifies that any degradation of these values would be permitted only if navigation or other water-dependent uses were to require an estuarine placement; if public need were manifested; if no upland alternatives were available; and if adverse effects were minimized as much as possible. La Roe went on to quote from the Estuarine Resources Goal: "When dredge or fill activities are permitted in intertidal or tidal marsh areas, their effects shall be mitigated by creation or restoration of another area of similar biological potential to ensure that the integrity of the estuarine ecosystem is maintained." "Similar biological potential" and "integrity of the estuarine ecosystem" are the key phrases. These were deliberate efforts to couple legal requirements to sound but involved biological principles. The intent should be to maintain the ecosystem as a complete and functionally unimpaired unit. Any created or restored area should produce similar flora and fauna both qualitatively and quantitatively. The emphasis should be on similar potential, not on substitute productivity (La Roe, 1978).

Lunz, Diaz, and Cole (1978) expressed concern about such substitute productivity, which they identified as habitat displacement. They questioned the resource value of the new habitat relative to that of the displaced habitat. According to Lunz, Diaz, and Cole, new habitats should not be developed at the expense of relatively more valuable existing habitats. That such evaluations are not easy to assess may be demonstrated by the controversy over the value of marshes to estuarine systems in regard to the contribution of detritus (see Odum and de la Cruz, 1967; Darnell, 1967; Reimold, Linthurst, and Wolf, 1975; Haines, 1979). Five points need to be considered in evaluating displaced habitats:

accommodation characteristics of the existing habitat; extent of existing habitat; lifespan of existing habitat; functional aspects of both existing and developed habitat; and external factors influencing target populations.

Habitat development using dredged material offers an alternative disposal method that is feasible from biological, engineering, and economic standpoints. Alternatives can best be determined through a combination of public opinion and local biological and engineering expertise. The selection of habitat development should be considered with other options if one or more of the following exist: opposition to other alternatives; recognition of habitat need; use of enhancement measures on existing disposal sites; demonstration of feasibility at the local level; need for stability of dredged material; and economic feasibility (Johnson and McGuinness, 1975; Smith 1978a, 1978b).

Marsh rehabilitation can serve as a means to mitigate impacts from concurrent or past disposal, a means to reclaim or develop an existing site to increase its value, and a means to restore a marsh that has been damaged or to protect a marsh that is eroding. The careful use of this alternative also could significantly increase the extent of wetland and wildlife resources in many parts of the country (Smith, 1978a, 1978b; Synthesis of Research Results, 1978). Procedural guidelines have been detailed by Smith (1978a); see Figure 5-1.

Kruczynski, Huffman, and Vincent (1978) cautioned that a study of flora in adjacent marshes should be conducted before any habitat development is initiated. Also, prior to any large-scale artificial propagation effort, a small-scale feasibility study should be performed. If these two preliminary steps are carried out, the opportunity to develop the desired wetland will be enhanced.

A number of constraints must be considered when dealing with the use of dredge material for habitat development. Site selection should be based on energy conditions, foundation character, salinity, tidal influence, and bottom topography. Operational constraints relate directly to the design, availability of equipment and its capabilities, scheduling, and spoil transport distance (and cost alternatives). Social factors focus on public concern of a project that may be near residential areas or may replace one resource for another, such as a marsh for a fishing site. Development of a current project may preclude a more desirable choice for the future. Although subject to all the usual government regulations, ownership of newly created sites in tidal or riparian areas has not been fully established, resulting in legal conflicts. Biological factors are probably the least restrictive and variable. Most important, the plant community must be able to compete successfully. The nature of the sediments and the uptake of various contaminants by the plants with their subsequent release into the environment must receive careful attention. Given

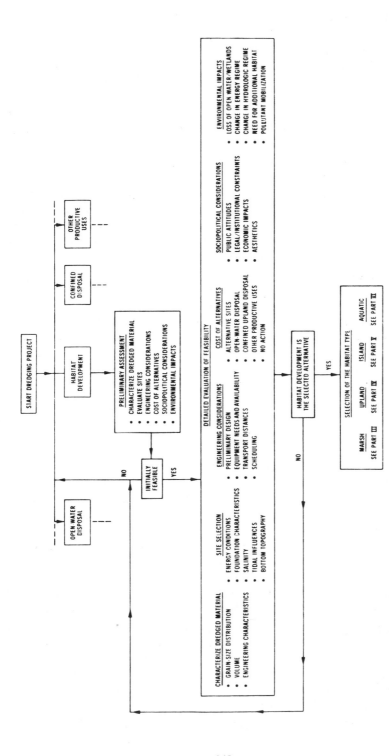

Figure 5-1. Procedural guidelines for selection of habitat development alternatives. *Source: After Smith, H. K., 1978, An Introduction to Habitat Development on Dredged Material, U.S. Army Corps of Engineers Dredged Material Res. Prog. Tech. Rept. DS-78-19, 37 p.*

the correct hydrological regime and timely completion of the disposal operation, biological requirements should not present major problems, if habitat selection is based on knowledge of the local environment and existing patterns of vegetation change. In short, planners should be aware of regulations, problems, and delays that could surface during the project, special interest groups, contaminant uptake, and local, state, and federal concerns; in addition, they should have a good comprehension of ecological principles (Smith 1976, 1978a; Synthesis of Research Results, 1978).

Despite the constraints, the selection of a marsh site for habitat development has certain advantages: public appeal; creation of desirable biological communities; release of contaminants; and loss of the site for subsequent disposal. Johnson and McGuinness (1975) recognized eight types of marshes, based on three interrelated factors created from dredged material: frequency of dredging (incremental or one-time); confinement requirements (confined or unconfined); and surcharging requirements (overfilling to increase settlement or not overfilling). The probability of occurrence of a marsh type was determined to be 36 and 54% for incremental unconfined and not surcharged, respectively, and 10% for all four types of marsh involving one-time frequency of dredging.

Once a marsh is the selected alternative, Smith (1978a, 1978b) advised choosing the appropriate wetland type on the basis of salinity and tidal range. His design for the marsh habitat would be influenced by location, elevation, orientation, and shape as well as size (Figure 5-2). Low-energy areas and sandy material are deemed best. Cost will become a factor, however, if the distance to a low-energy site is long. A reevaluation would then be required; if it is favorable, construction would be followed by propagation, natural invasion, or artificial means. Smith pointed out the necessity of evaluating the productivity of the various plant species to aid in the design of highly productive manmade marshes. It is also important to assess the response of plants to physical and physiological stress. In high-energy situations, perpetuation of the marsh may require planned periodic maintenance of protective structures.

Other papers dealing with this subject have identified the basic goals as those that will lead to or reduce the time required for the establishment of productive marsh communities, which would aid in substrate stabilization, water-quality improvement, biomass production and export, and use by wildlife (Woodhouse, Seneca, and Broome, 1974; Eleuterius and McClellan, 1976; Synthesis of Research Results, 1978). Habitat development is an extension and enhancement of physical and ecological principles: a habitat is important because of its vital function in a biological system. It is not an isolated entity; rather, it depends on the transfer of matter and energy for structural and functional integrity. The general ecological

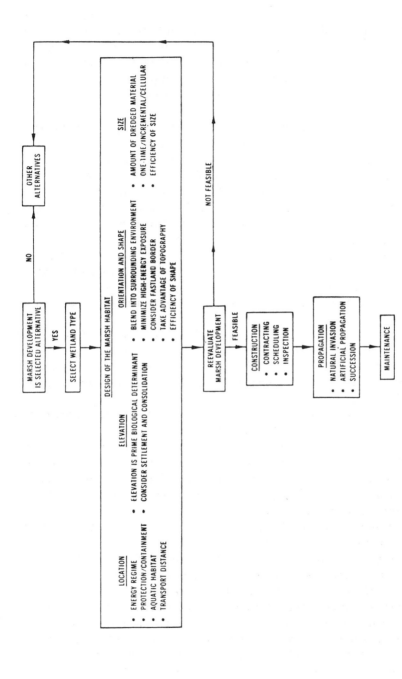

Figure 5-2. Procedural guidelines for selection of marsh habitat development. *Source: After Smith, H. K., 1978, An Introduction to Habitat Development on Dredged Material, U.S. Army Corps of Engineers Dredged Material Res. Prog. Tech. Rept. DS-78-19, 37 p.*

management objective of habitat development with dredged material would be to maintain or increase the distribution, abundance, and/or biomass of target animal populations and their support populations (plant or animal). Target animals are those of primary interest to the manager or conservationist while support populations provide cover, or food for the target species. The animal-habitat interaction is a common denominator that will determine the success of a developed habitat. Without a balance between the needs of target and support populations and the ability of a habitat to provide these needs, habitat development will not fulfill its function. Cover provided by the physical structural characteristics of marsh vegetation is perhaps as important to target populations as is trophic support. The diversity of habitats should be enhanced but such an enhancement should be developed through a progression of habitats rather than human creation of a variety of habitat types all at once (Lunz, Diaz, and Cole, 1978).

Summarizing work that has been largely supported by the Dredged Material Research Program of the U.S. Army Engineer Waterways Experiment Station, Hunt (1979) identified a set of principles, based on ecological concepts, that should enhance such marsh habitat establishment.

1. Elevation and inundation are the major determinants of vegetation success; magnitude, frequency, and duration of inundation are critical. Hunt concurs with Boyce (1976) that successful artificial propagation should mimic the strong plant zonation that is a reflection of inundation in natural marshes.
2. The number of invading species may be high, but usually only two to four will become established and dominant.
3. Protection is needed against excessive wave and wind energy, and grazing by herbivores. Dikes, fencing, and planting in low-energy sites provides protection for the planted or invading vegetation. Such protection enhances sedimentation and enables the site to resemble a natural marsh more quickly.
4. Sprigs and seeds may be used for establishing vegetation with the former generally more successful.
5. Fertilization has no long-term effects. Results, if any, will be seen the first year and will be overwhelmed by sedimentation.
6. Spacing the individual plants will be important.
7. Spring plantings display better shoot production, but there is little significance between the time of planting and overall survival.
8. There are differential rates of survival, growth, spread, and colonization among species and sites. The magnitude of invasion and extent of planting determines the adequacy of cover.

One needs a knowledge of soil-plant relationships in dredged material marshes and natural marshes in order to facilitate plant establishment on varying types of dredged material, understand the factors influencing water quality in estuaries, and evaluate the potential threat of substrate-derived heavy metals and other contaminants to the detrital food chain (Boyce, 1976).

METHODOLOGY

The two most important factors in site preparation are slope and surface elevation (Garbisch, 1977). Slopes should be as low as possible without impounding water and should not exceed inclines considered unstable under normal conditions in the absence of plant cover (Garbisch, 1977). Surface elevation must be tied in with the various zones of marsh types existing in the region, and the final elevation to be chosen for the design of the marsh will be strongly influenced by the type of vegetation that is to be grown (Johnson and McGuinness, 1975). Surface elevations are most critical in areas subject to tidal amplitudes of 2 ft or less (Garbisch, 1977).

Another important factor is the time required to complete site preparation, so that marsh establishment can proceed on schedule. This is especially necessary if vegetation is to be established by seeding and sprigging dormant or growing plants. There is no limitation to the use of uncontaminated sediments, and substrate characteristics do not appear to limit plant establishment. With or without fertilization, however, *Spartina alterniflora* production is poorest on substrate in gravel and well-sorted sand with high percolation and a low nutrient level, and highest in poorly sorted but permeable substrate. High compaction does not limit the establishment of *S. alterniflora* (Garbisch et al., 1975; Garbisch, 1977).

The selection of plant species for establishment in the various elevation zones at the site is governed by a number of factors: the objectives of the project; the plant species that are known to grow in the area; the relative growth rates and sediment-stabilizing capabilities of the various plant species; and the relative food value of the candidate species, which will be determined by available surface elevations, exposure of the site to physical stresses, and time of planting.

Various workers have used several forms of propagation, including seeds, rhizomes, cuttings, transplants, root stocks, and seedlings. They may take the form of bare-root stock from natural marsh sources or nursery stock, soil plugs from the same sources, robust rooted cuttings, and dwarf rooted cuttings. The most important factors to consider in planting design are salinity, tidal range, elevation, flood stages, soil texture, wave and wind action, contaminant tolerance, outside influences, cost, protection, plant spacing, species selection, and relationship to natural vegetation adjacent to the work site. The selection of species is determined by the project goal, location, climate and microclimate tolerance, soil characteristics, growth characteristics, availability of species, maintenance, and cost. The criteria for selection of propagule include cost and availability, collection and handling ease, storage ease, planting ease, disease, urgency for vegetative cover, site selection, and time of planting (Woodhouse, Seneca, and Broome, 1972; Garbisch et al., 1975; Dredge Disposal Study San Francisco Bay and Estuary, 1976, Appendix K; Reimold, Hardisky, and Adams 1978a; Synthesis of Research Results, 1978).

The use of peat-potted nursery stock is considered most suitable— although the most expensive—because these plants are less disturbed and there is greater flexibility in the planting schedule. It is also possible to fashion the age or development of the plant material to accommodate the various stresses prevailing at the site. Nursery stock is considered superior to all other types when subjected to wave and debris deposition stresses, and for summer, fall, or winter planting. Increased maturity of nursery transplant material will generally result in better survival as the lower intertidal elevations are planted (Garbisch et al., 1975; Garbisch, 1977). Such potted nursery material is particularly effective on small sites. Bare-root stock or plugs are especially useful for large tracts, where mechanical planters can be used effectively to reduce planting time and labor costs (Woodhouse, Seneca, and Broome, 1972, 1974; Garbisch et al., 1975).

Both seeds and transplant material should be obtained from local stands that are exposed to the same tidal regime as that of the proposed restoration site (Woodhouse, Seneca, and Broome, 1974; Seneca, Woodhouse, and Broome, 1975). Since *S. alterniflora* is one of the most widespread plants used for marsh restoration, most of the techniques that have been developed deal with this particular species. It is best to collect transplant material from young stands of smooth cordgrass, as the old stands have very dense root and rhizome mats, which make it difficult to obtain intact individual plants (Woodhouse, Seneca, and Broome, 1972, 1974; Dredge Disposal Study San Francisco Bay, 1976, Appendix K). If the sprigs or plugs are not to be immediately planted, they can be heeled in until planting time. When they are set out by hand or by machine, the individual plants should have the soil firmly packed around the roots and stem to keep the plant from floating out on the flooding tide. Spacing at 0.9 to 1 meter has been found to be a good compromise between cost and substrate stabilization. In North Carolina, Woodhouse, Seneca, and

Broome (1974) found that it takes only 111 *S. alterniflora* plants per 1,000 square feet at a spacing of 0.9 m but 1,000 plants in the same space at a planting interval of 0.3 m. While vegetative cover was developed much more quickly, labor costs were markedly higher at the closer spacing interval. In Florida, Kruczynski, Huffman, and Vincent (1978) found that *S. alterniflora* did well at spacings of 0.3 to 0.9 m but poorly at the greater spacings of 1.8 and 2.7 m. In contrast, they found that *S. patens* grew best at the spacing intervals of 1.8 and 2.7 m.

Transplants can be made at any time from December through July, but the appropriate time is a compromise. The greatest biomass and vegetative cover can be achieved during a growing season if the plants are set during the late fall through late winter. The chances for losses due to storm damage will be high, however. Therefore, planting is best done from late March into early May, when a long growing season is still possible. Summer is not a good time (Woodhouse, Seneca, and Broome, 1972, 1974; Garbisch, 1977). Georgia marsh sites that are inundated for longer than 14 hours can be planted with smooth cordgrass with moderate success at any time of the year. Although Reimold, Hardisky, and Adams (1978a) found winter and early spring to be the best for optimal growth, Woodhouse, Seneca, and Broome (1972, 1974) pointed out that the planting operation can be more efficiently carried out during milder weather.

S. alterniflora will usually grow in any area, roughly between mean high water (MHW) and mean low water (MLW) for sites with a reduced tidal range and from neap high water (NHW) to mean spring low tide (MSL) for the greater tidal ranges. There is a lower limit of survival in the intertidal zone; the best growth is just above this level. In the San Francisco Bay area, the mean tide level appeared to be the lower elevational extreme suitable for the marsh flora, specifically *Spartina foliosa* (Dredge Disposal Study San Francisco Bay and Estuary, 1976, Appendix K). The upper limit of growth grades into the growth zone of other species. Such growth is determined by the time of exposure and inundation. Therefore the upper and lower limits of growth in natural stands should be checked before any transplants are made (Woodhouse, Seneca, and Broome, 1972, 1974).

All other species—such as *Spartina patens, Distichlis spicata,* and *Salicornia*—grow better at higher elevations. Reimold, Hardisky, and Adams (1978a) found that water hemp (*Amaranthus canabinus* [= *Acnida cannabina*]), marsh fleabane (*Pluchea purpurascens*), and panic grass (*Panicum* sp.) can grow at an intermediate elevation in Georgia. While many plants grow at higher elevations, they found *S. patens* and *D. spicata* to be best for substrate stabilization. Woodhouse, Seneca, and Broome (1972, 1974) found some overlap in survival at the end of the first growing season between *S. patens* and *S. alterniflora*, but there was a fairly sharp cutoff at the lower end, near the upper zone of best growth for *S. alterniflora*. Thus, they expected the two species to be limited to their respective elevations.

The use of seeds for propagating *S. alterniflora* has limited success. The seeds can be scattered by hand or by mechanical means (a seed drill) at about 100 seeds/m^2 but care must be taken to cover the seeds by incorporating them into the substrate thorough raking or tilling. Such a procedure will result in complete coverage by the end of the first growing season. Seeding is considered feasible only in the spring and in sheltered areas protected from wave action. There is a much narrower zone of survival located at an elevation above mean tide level (upper 20% of the mean tide range). While seeding is more economical, transplants can be used in a greater variety of conditions and over a greater tidal range (Woodhouse, Seneca, and Broome, 1972, 1974; Seneca et al., 1976; Garbisch, 1977).

The best seed production is obtained from young stands of *S. alterniflora* and, as the site matures, production drops off markedly. Seed maturity is highly variable even in a single stand, so the seeds must be harvested shortly after maturity before their heads shatter. Floyd and Newcombe (1976) recorded a viability of less than 5% for *S. foliosa*; usually only the first seed on an inflorescence contained an embryo. Seeds must be stored in a cold, wet condition at a temperature of 2 to 4°C in sea water of 25‰. Webb et al. (1978) reported that the viability of *S. alterniflora* seeds in Texas was appreciably reduced after five months of cold, wet storage. Woodhouse, Seneca, and Broome (1972, 1974) and Seneca et al. (1976) noted that germination is greatly impaired if the seeds are allowed to freeze or dry.

After seeding or transplanting, a maintenance program should be established. A lack of maintenance may lead to an invasion of unwanted species; smothering of seedlings or transplants by litter; colonization or grazing by domestic animals or wildlife, which will exclude or destroy desirable species; and a change in topography such as a breached dike would produce. If there is high wave stress, the site may require annual maintenance fertilization (Garbisch, 1977; Synthesis of Research Results, 1978; Reimold, Hardisky, and Adams, 1978*a*).

The cost of marsh rehabilitation depends on the plant materials used, planting density, planting techniques, size of the project, use of fertilizer, maintenance of the project after planting, distance between the site and the contractor, and site accessibility (Garbisch, 1978). Seeding was the most economical method for propagating *S. foliosa* and *S. alterniflora*; $3,050 (1976 dollars) per ha in the San Francisco Bay area and $4,940 per ha ($2,000/acre) on the east coast. On the west coast the cost per ha for plugs of *S. foliosa* was $8,600; for seedlings, $11,600; and for rooted cuttings, $12,100. Rooted seedlings of *Salicornia* cost $11,300/ha, while rooted cuttings cost $11,700/ha. In 1975 dollars, the cost to construct

Table 5-1.   Comparison of starter types of cordgrass after one and two growing seasons

Starter Type	Plants/m^2 Season 1st	2nd	Coefficient of Variation Season 1st	2nd	Dry Weight (grams/plant) Season 1st	2nd	Coefficient of Variation Season 1st	2nd
Control	0.02	0.20	254	165	—	—	—	—
Seeding	1.29	4.28	90	53	0.72	9.43	60	32
Seedlings	0.52	5.60	32	61	—	13.87	—	57
Robust rooted cuttings	0.28	1.04	81	125	7.39	12.07	52	70
Dwarf rooted cuttings	0.68	7.80	23	48	3.23	10.54	67	62
Plugs	0.80	8.92	18	48	20.16	14.17	74	46

Source: From Dredge Disposal Study San Francisco Bay and Estuary, 1976, Appendix K. Marshland Development. U.S. Army Engr. Dist., San Francisco, Corps Engr., San Francisco, Calif., 61pp. (manuscript form).

and plant the Alameda Creek marsh using the seeding method was estimated to be $26,000/ha (Dredge Disposal Study San Francisco Bay and Estuary, 1976, Appendix K). Garbisch (1978) calculated the cost of planting a 1- to 5-acre tract with peat-potted stock on a 2-ft (0.6-m) grid to be $6,000/acre ($15,820/ha) for mechanical and $9,000/acre ($22,230/ha) for semimechanical planting and fertilization.

Newcombe and Pride (1975) found that planting *S. foliosa* seeds required abut 30 man-hours/1,000 m^2. The corresponding times for rooted cuttings, seedlings, and plugs were 121, 116, and 86 man-hours, respectively. Planting *Salicornia* required 117 man-hours for rooted cuttings and 113 man-hours for seedlings.

RESULTS

Method of Propagation

Five methods of propagating *S. foliosa* were used during marsh rehabilitation in the San Francisco Bay area (Dredge Disposal Study San Francisco Bay and Estuary, 1976). Three forms of transplants (seedlings, dwarf rooted cuttings, and plugs) survived above the 50% level (Newcombe and Pride, 1975), while robust rooted cuttings and seeds did not. At the end of the first growing season, the seeded plots had the largest number of plants. A plant was recorded as a new individual if its culms (stems) were more than 15 centimeters from its nearest neighbor. Due to their large size at the start, the plugs had the largest amount of plant material at the end of the first season (Table 5-1). During the second season, all plant propagules reproduced vegetatively. Plant densities increased from an average of 0.71 plants/m^2 in October 1974 to 5.53 plants/m^2 by October 1975. The number of seedlings, dwarf rooted cuttings, and plugs increased by a factor of approximately 10 during the second growing season. In contrast, vegetative reproduction in the seeded plots and the robust rooted cutting plots increased only by a factor of approximately three. The unplanted plots were virtually bare after the first growing season, with 0.02 plants/m^2; by the end of the second season, they averaged only 0.20 plants/m^2.

The number of culms increased rapidly during the second growing season (Table 5-2). Newcombe and Pride (1975) considered the number of stems to be a good index of growth. The original height of *Spartina* plants was not exceeded during the first season, but height and lateral spread increased rapidly during the second. The absolute growth from seeds averaged 17 cm during the first season while seedlings averaged 12 cm. The continuous growth of *S. foliosa* undoubtedly accelerated the repopulation of the experimental site. As soon as an inflorescence developed and matured, new shoots arose around the base of the plant and rhizomes elongated, sending out additional shoots (Floyd and Newcombe, 1976).

Based on the number of culms/m^2 produced during the second growing season, plant densities in the plug, dwarf rooted cuttings, seedlings, and seeded plots would be similar to that of a natural marsh midway through the third growing season. It was estimated that the control and robust rooted cuttings plots would take an additional three years to resemble a natural marsh (Dredge Disposal Study San Francisco Bay and Estuary, 1976; Floyd and Newcombe, 1976).

At least along the mid- and south Atlantic coasts, spacing *S. alterniflora* transplants abut 0.9 to 1.0 m apart will produce a complete cover in two years. A closer spacing will produce a greater above-ground cover but will take 2 years to develop a network of roots and rhizomes that will bind the substrate. Transplants put out in November to early March will have a higher production rate but a low survival rate, while those put out later in the spring will produce the opposite results. If immediate cover is not required, warm-weather planting can be more easily accomplished. Seeding early in the spring will produce a more dense stand by the end of the first growing season but, by the end of the second growing season, there should be no difference between April and June seeding. Second-year production for an April seeding will be similar to transplants done at the end of the first growing season (Seneca, 1974; Woodhouse, Seneca, and Broome, 1974; Seneca, Woodhouse, and Broome, 1975; Webb et al., 1978). Growth during the first season is primarily tiller production from the original plant (Reimold, Hardisky, and Adams, 1978a). Woodhouse, Seneca, and Broome (1976) observed that by the spring of the second growing season, new shoots of smooth cordgrass so populated the area

Table 5-2. Comparison of cordgrass culm abundance, October 1974 vs. 1975

Planting Method	Number of Culms/m^2		Factor of Increase
	1974	1975	
Control	0.07	2.52	36.0
Seeding	3.24	52.22	16.1
Seedlings	3.68	64.74	17.6
Robust rooted cuttings	0.99	6.55	6.6
Dwarf rooted cuttings	3.79	85.72	22.6
Plugs	5.26	88.13	16.8

Source: From Dredge Disposal Study San Francisco Bay and Estuary, 1976, Appendix K. Marshland Development. U. S. Army Engr. Dist., San Francisco, Corps Engr., San Francisco, Calif., 61pp. (Manuscript form).

that original hills and rows were no longer identifiable. Ristich, Frederick, and Buckley (1976) successfully transplanted cattail (*Typha angustifolia*) into a tidal marsh from April through June and found the clones to survive best in May and June. Vigorous growth culminated in fruiting in the third growing season.

Plant Zonation

Seneca (1974) reported that *S. alterniflora* seeds will germinate and young seedlings will grow over most of the intertidal zone, but survival is limited to the zone near mean high water (MHW). Woodhouse, Seneca, and Broome (1974) and Webb et al. (1978) observed that plants can be grown at any elevation. Webb et al. had the best survival, growth, and tiller production at approximately 0.5 to 1.0 ft below MHW. Survival was slightly limited and plant height and stem density somewhat reduced at a position slightly above MHW. In areas with a narrow tidal range, *S. alterniflora* does best between MHW and mean low water (MLW). With an expanded tidal range, plants grow best between MHW and mean spring low tide (MSL) (Woodhouse, Seneca, and Broome, 1974). Thus elevation becomes more critical in areas of low tidal amplitude. Woodhouse, Seneca, and Broome (1976) recommended that the upper and lower limits of growth of natural stands of *S. alterniflora* in the vicinity should be checked before any planting.

Woodhouse, Seneca, and Broome (1974) observed some overlap in survival between *S. alterniflora* and *S. patens* at the end of the first growing season in North Carolina. They expected to find a separation in zonation in subsequent years, as would be seen under natural conditions. They also noted that the lower limit of vigorous growth for *S. patens* was about 1.25 m above MLW. The upper limit was not sharply defined, but growth was poor in higher and drier elevations. Webb et al. (1978) reported that *S. patens* survived and grew successfully only at elevations above MHW, with the best growth at the highest elevation at their Texas dredge spoil site.

Seneca, Woodhouse, and Broome (1975) suggested that in areas of low salinity the lower half of the tidal range will provide the best habitat for smooth cord grass. Working in the low-salinity waters of Buttermilk Sound in Georgia, Reimold, Hardisky, and Adams (1978a) noted that the elevational range for each seeded species was narrower than for the transplants. By the third year after planting, all the planted species excelled within their particular elevational range. *S. alterniflora* dominated the middle and upper portions of the lower intertidal zone.

Reimold (1978) and Hardisky (1979) observed *S. alterniflora* in all portions of the intertidal zone, but the best growth occurred in the lower and middle segments with 6 to 18 hours of inundation. No plants survived with more than 18 hours of inundation. *Borrichia frutescens, Distichlis spicata, Iva frutescens, Juncus roemerianus, Spartina cynosuroides,* and *S. patens* were restricted to the upper third of the intertidal zone. *D. spicata, S. patens,* and *B. frutescens* were most important for substrate stabilization and the creation of new habitat, while the others materially enhanced diversity.

As the result of tidal inundation, Doumlele and Silberhorn (1978) found the vegetation segregated into four zones at an essentially freshwater study site on the James River (Virginia). Arrowhead (*Sagittaria falcata*) and pickerelweed (*Pontederia cordata*) dominated the lower zone; in the lowest portion they were codominant. Higher in the zone, beggarticks (*Bidens* sp.), barnyard grass (*Echinochloa crusgalli*), and rice cutgrass (*Leersia oryzoides*) became more common, blending into the next zone, which was dominated by *Bidens.* Along with the *Bidens* were barnyard grass, water smartweed (*Polygonum punctatum*), jewelweed (*Impatiens capensis*), cattail (*Typha*), and water hemp (*Amaranthus canabinus*). The upper zone, which was the only one artificially planted, was dominated by panic grass (*Panicum amarulum* and *P. virgatum*) along with jewelweed (*Impatiens*), beggar-ticks (*Bidens*), pigweed (*Amaranthus*), and cocklebur (*Xanthium*). Isolated patches of black willow (*Salix nigra*), cottonwood (*Populus deltoides*), and common alder (*Alnus serrulata*) constituted the fourth zone. The rest of the dredge site was a mixture of vegetation. It is apparent from the foregoing that plant zonation is a reflection of the frequency and duration of tidal inundation.

Role of Invasion

The role of invasion by plant species in the restoration of marshes on dredge spoil has some distinctive characteristics. Invasion appears

Table 5-3. Mean above-ground biomass for four tidal zones for *S. alterniflora* and invading plants over three years on dredge spoil at Snow's Cut, North Carolina. Salinity of the groundwater and estuarine water was 8 to 10‰

Period Inundated Daily (hr.)	Aerial biomass (g dry wt/m²)			
	1971[a]	1972[b]	1973	
	Spartina	Spartina	Spartina	Invaders
2.5	—[c]	1,180	408	282
5.5	—[c]	1,298	726	104
8.5	203[d]	989	988	76
11.5	—[a]	790	1,290	4

Source: From Seneca, E. D., W. W. Woodhouse, and S. W. Broome, 1975, Salt water marsh creation, in *Estuarine Research*, vol. 2, L. E. Cronin, ed., Academic Press, New York, pp. 427–438, by permission.

[a]No invaders.
[b]Too few invaders to sample.
[c]Not sampled.
[d]Most productive zone in 1971.

to be most significant at fresh and brackish-water sites (Reimold, Hardisky, and Adams, 1978a). Ristich, Frederick, and Buckley (1976) recorded 40 species of vascular plants and 63 genera of algae in a tidal marsh along the Hudson River during the first two years after transplantation of *Typha* onto the site. Doumlele and Silberhorn (1978) recorded 217 species (including six planted species) at a tidal freshwater site on the James River.

Seneca, Woodhouse, and Broome (1975) stated that both salinity and inundation must be maintained to sustain production of *S. alterniflora* (Table 5-3). By the third year of their study, invaders made up 41% of the production in the uppermost zone; as the inundation period increased, the numbers of invaders diminished. Reimold, Hardisky, and Adams (1978a) and Hardisky (1979) found only *S. alterniflora* and a few invaders in the lower and middle intertidal zones. Doumlele and Silberhorn (1978) also noted that the extent of tidal inundation determines plant distributions. They observed the greatest diversity on the dike and the original island, where the plants did not have to contend with frequent tidal inundation. Reimold, Hardisky, and Adams (1978a) observed that transplanting *D. spicata* and *S. patens* excluded many invading species. Hardisky (1979) reported that *D. spicata* is a good candidate for stabilization of a dredge material in an essentially freshwater tidal site in Georgia because of its rapid spreading ability and dense aerial and root biomass. It deteriorates as the marsh matures, however, because the influx of invaders provides an overstory, which shades the *Distichlis* from the sun.

Such invasions by both annuals and perennials occur by means of floating seeds and plant parts, or seeds buried in the spoil (Seneca,

Woodhouse, and Broome, 1975; Ristich, Frederick, and Buckley, 1976; Doumlele and Silberhorn, 1978). Natural colonization can be considered an alternative for marsh rehabilitation that will work well in sheltered areas not requiring rapid colonization. It can be a slow and haphazard process, however, (Eleuterius and McClellan, 1976; Kruczynski, Huffman, and Vincent, 1978; Synthesis of Research Results, 1978). Reimold, Hardisky, and Adams (1978*a*) and Hardisky (1979) observed that invading plant species were spreading over most of the Georgia site, with *Amaranthus canabinus* and *Panicum* sp. the principal invaders. The upper zone contained all the invading species and generally had the highest densities and biomasses. It was observed that these invaders maintained a lower aerial and below-ground biomass than was found in the planted areas. Therefore, Hardisky recommended that the spoil sites be colonized by transplanting rather than by natural revegetation.

We can infer from the above that the more saline habitats would be associated with slow invasion. In studies on the west coast, however, high-salinity plants such as *Salicornia pacifica* rapidly colonized a spoil site by seed, while *Spartina foliosa* was slow to invade (Newcombe and Pride, 1975; Floyd and Newcombe, 1976; Dredge Disposal Study San Fransico Bay and Estuary, 1976).

Density and Biomass

Newcombe and Pride (1975) noted a die-back in cuttings and plugs after planting in a San Francisco Bay site. Reimold, Hardisky, and Adams, (1978*a*) observed that during the first year in Georgia, whatever growth there was came from the original plants. Woodhouse, Seneca, and Broome (1974) recorded the typical die-back of the stems at the end of the first growing season in North Carolina, but below-ground production continued.

During the subsequent growing seasons there was an expanding production of new plant material, which resembled that of natural marshes. New shoots arose at the base of the plants after inflorescence in late fall (Woodhouse, Seneca, and Broome, 1974; Newcombe and Pride, 1975; Floyd and Newcombe, 1976; Seneca et al., 1976; Reimold, Hardisky, and Adams, 1978*a*). The continuous growth of *S. foliosa* accelerated seed production. Both Newcombe and Pride and Seneca et al. reported that plants spread rapidly during the second year. The former recorded an absolute growth of 17 cm from seeds and 12 cm from seedlings. The latter workers observed that, by the end of the second growing season, above-ground biomass derived from seeds approached that produced by transplants. However, Reimold, Hardisky, and Adams (1978*a*) and Hardisky (1979) reported that transplants produced a much greater biomass than seeds.

Table 5-4. Growth and Development of an *S. alterniflora* Planting at Snow's Cut, North Carolina over Three Growing Seasons (transplanted 8 April 1971)

Period Inundated (mean hr/day)	No. of Culms/m² Center	No. of Culms/m² Rhizome	Flowers/m²	Basal Area (cm²/m²)	Height (cm)	Below-ground Yield[a] (kg/ha)	Above-ground Yield (kg/ha) Spartina	Above-ground Yield (kg/ha) Invaders
14 September 1971								
[b]0.0–3.6	17	11	5	9.6	95	183	280	None
3.6–13.0	48	42	18	40.1	147	920	2,275	
13.0–16.6	10	5	1	4.5	97	106	240	
19 September 1972								
[b]0.0–3.6		179	80	58.0	101	4,348	3,260	[c]
3.6–8.9		237	82	86.0	148	7,176	7,850	
8.9–13.0		324	104	81.0	125	13,647	7,910	
13.0–16.6		232	71	49.0	138	3,837	5,740	
18 September 1973								
[b]0.0–3.6		273	7	173.0	131	32,949	9,296	442
3.6–8.9		419	84	110.0	136	20,918	10,760	[c]
8.9–13.0		448	79	95.0	142	21,673	10,856	[a]
13.0–16.6		361	45	75.0	132	7,406	5,460	[c]

Source: From Woodhouse, W. W., Jr., E. D. Seneca, and S. W. Broome, 1974, *Propagation of Spartina alterniflora for Substrate Stabilization and Salt Marsh Development,* Tech. Memo No. 46, U.S. Army Corps of Engineers Coastal Engineering Research Center, Ft. Belvoir, Va., 155pp.

Note: 1971 samples were three individual plants from three elevation zones. 1972 samples were four, 0.25 m² samples from each of four elevation zones. 1973 samples were three, 0.25 m² samples from each of four elevation zones.

[a]All species.
[b]Barely covered by spring tides.
[c]Too few invaders to sample.

Table 5-5. Distribution of below-ground growth by depths, Snow's Cut, North Carolina, 1972

Inundation Zones (hr/day)	Dry-Weight (kg/ha) Roots		Dry-Weight (kg/ha) Rhizomes	
	0–10 cm	*10–30 cm*	*0–10 cm*	*10–30 cm*
0.0–3.6	3,093.0	1,499.0	6,734.0	4,015.0
3.6–8.9	2,831.0	1,783.0	5,695.0	4,261.0
8.9–13.0	2,553.0	1,304.0	3,987.0	3,990.0
13.0–16.6	2,318.0	934.0	3,664.0	2,723.0
LSD 0.05	n.s.	n.s.	n.s.	n.s.
CV (%)	37.5	73.2	84.3	73.9

Source: From Woodhouse, W. W., Jr., E. D. Seneca, and S. W. Broome, 1974, *Propagation of* Spartina alterniflora *for Substrate Stabilization and Salt Marsh Development,* Tech. Memo No. 46, U.S. Army Corps of Engineers Coastal Engineering Research Center, Ft. Belvoir, Va., 155pp.

Note: Samples were four core samples (8.5 cm in diameter and 30 cm deep) from each elevation zone. One core was taken from each 0.25 m^2 sample area.

LSD = least significant difference; CV = coefficient of variation (%); n.s. = not significant.

Woodhouse, Seneca, and Broome (1974) observed a large increase in plant cover between the end of the first and the end of the second growing season. This growth was reflected in the number of culms and the aerial and below-ground production of dry matter, with increases ranging from three- to tenfold. By the end of the third growing season, the real change was in the below-ground production (Table 5-4). Woodhouse, Seneca, and Broome concluded from these three years of data that, from the standpoint of vegetative cover, substrate stabilization, and primary production, marsh development after transplanting can be very rapid. Production was estimated at 7,000 kg/ha the second year and reached 10,000 kg/ha in the third year. This compared to 5,100 and 16,000 kg/ha for short and tall *S. alterniflora* in long-established natural marshes. By the fourth year Woodhouse, Seneca, and Broome (1976) noted that production at Snow's Cut, North Carolina, had leveled off to about 12 metric tons/ha and was visually similar to an adjoining natural marsh. At another site (Drum Inlet), production was good as long as nutrients were added. At a seeded site in Beaufort, North Carolina, production was low ($\simeq$ 4 metric tons/ha) and was attributed to the source of seed. This finding implies that seeds and transplants should be acquired locally.

The evidence suggests that the rate of underground production declines during the third year. Cores taken during the second year (1972) showed two-thirds of the roots in the upper 10 cm while the rhizomes were more evenly distributed between the 0-10 and 10-30 cm zones. There was little penetration of either roots or rhizomes below 30 cm, and there was a distinct tendency toward less total below-ground production as the period of inundation increased (Table 5-5) (Woodhouse, Seneca, and Broome, 1974).

The continuous growth of *S. foliosa* undoubtedly accelerated the repopulation of an experimental site in California (Floyd and Newcombe, 1976). As soon as an inflorescence developed and matured, new shoots arose around the base of the plant and rhizomes elongated, sending out additional shoots. This latter growth took place in late fall and early winter. The following spring there was a sharp decline in root biomass concomitant with an increase in stem biomass (Figures 5-3 and 5-4).

Reimold, Hardisky, and Adams (1978a) observed the most dramatic change during the third growing season in Georgia. The various plant species excelled within their particular optimum elevational range. The integrated biomass of the various species demonstrated that *S. patens* had the best overall aerial production. *S. alterniflora* and *Borrichia frutescens* ranked second and third and reversed their position for below-ground production (Table 5-6). *S. patens* and *Juncus roemerianus* had

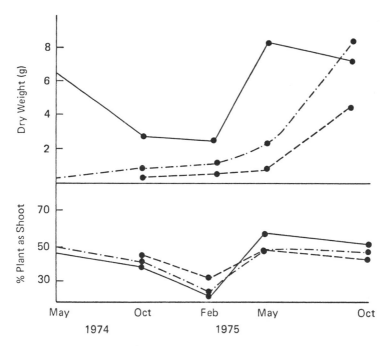

Figure 5-3. Dry-weight analysis of *S. Foliosa* shoot growth from a San Francisco Bay marsh.
Symbols: seeds (......), seedlings (_._.), plugs (___).
Source: After Floyd, K. W., and C. L. Newcombe, 1976, Growth of Intertidal Marsh Plants on Dredge Material Substrate, San Francisco Bay Marine Research Center, Richmond, Calif., 101p.

greater aerial biomass than any other species in the upper portion of the intertidal zone. Reimold, Hardisky, and Adams (1978a) and Hardisky (1979) noted no significant differences in the mean root biomass concentration among different plant species in this zone. *S. alterniflora* survived in all three elevations of the intertidal zone but, based on greater aerial biomass and culm densities, the optimum elevational range was in the middle and lower zones. In contrast, *S. patens* far exceeded the production of other species in the uppermost zone (Table 5-7). The production foremost transplanted species in the Buttermilk Sound study was somewhat lower in aerial and below-ground biomass than in mature Georgia marsh communities. *Iva frutescens* and *S. patens* were the only plants to equal or exceed the aerial biomass from such mature sites. *B. frutescens* and *S. patens* yielded below-ground biomass values similar to other Georgia marshes. The lag in biomass production for most species suggested

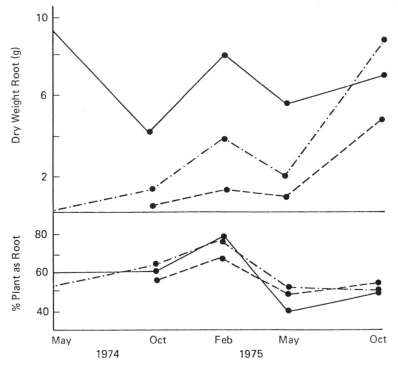

Figure 5-4.   Dry-weight analysis of *S. foliosa* root growth from a San Francisco Bay marsh. Symbols: seeds(......), seedlings (._._), plugs (___).
Source: After Floyd, K. W., and C. L. Newcombe, 1976, Growth of Intertidal Marsh Plants on Dredge Material Substrate, San Francisco Bay Marine Research Center, Richmond, Calif., 101p.

Table 5-6. Mean integrated biomass for Buttermilk Sound, Georgia, experimental species, November 1977

	Propagule	*Aerial Biomass (g/m²)*	*Root Biomass (g/m²)*
Borrichia frutescens	sprig	6.7 ± 1.4[a]	12.2 ± 5.0
	seed	0.8 ± 0.1	0.4 ± 0.2
Distichlis spicata	sprig	6.2 ± 2.4	15.6 ± 8.7
	seed	3.5 ± 1.1	2.9 ± 0.7
Spartina alterniflora	sprig	11.7 ± 3.2	6.4 ± 1.8
	seed	0.1 ± 0.1	0.4 ± 0.4
Spartina cynosuroides	sprig	1.3 ± 0.4	3.0 ± 1.4
	seed	1.6 ± 0	3.4 ± 0
Spartina patens	sprig	41.4 ± 11.7	66.2 ± 28.9
	seed	— —	— —

Source: From Reimold, R. J., M. A. Hardisky, and P. C. Adams, 1978[a], *Habitat Development Field Investigations, Buttermilk Sound Marsh Development Site, Atlantic Intracoastal Waterway, Georgia*; Appendix A: Propagation of Marsh Plants and Post Propagation Monitoring, U.S. Army Corps of Engineers Dredged Material Res. Prog. Tech. Rept. D-78-38, 223 p.
[a]mean ± standard deviation

that more than three years would be needed for the development of a mature marsh ecosystem at the Buttermilk Sound experimental site.

Effect of Fertilization

Woodhouse, Seneca, and Broome (1974) demonstrated that the application of nitrogen and phosphorus fertilizer to a natural stand of *S. alterniflora* increases aerial and below-ground biomass. While additions of nitrogen alone could significantly increase yields, it was also noted that the availability of phosphorus quickly becomes limiting when nitrogen rates are increased (Figure 4-3). The nitrogen content of the plant tissues was closely related to the rate at which nitrogen was applied (Figure 4-4), and the results clearly revealed a high rate of recovery by the various parts of the plants (Table 4-7).

When nitrogen was added to an experimental spoil site, the dry weight of *S. alterniflora* seedlings at the end of the first year increased from 3,470 kg/ha to 9,340 kg/ha. When both nitrogen and phosphorus were added, the aerial yield increased to 10,800 kg/ha (Table 5-8). When nitrogen alone was added up to a rate of 224 kg/ha all parameters increased. Yields declined at higher application rates, and additions of phosphorus enhanced production, but again the highest application rates of phosphorus generally produced declining yields. Below-ground yield at the highest applica-

Table 5-7.   Mean plant biomass and density, and crab burrow density by species and zone in Buttermilk Sound, Georgia, November 1977

	Zone[a]	Stems/m^2	Crab Burrows m^2	Biomass (g dry wt/m^2) Aerial	Root
Borrichia frutescens	1	0	0	0	0
	2	0	4	0	0
	3	105	23	244	297
Distichlis spicata	1	0	0	0	0
	2	0	3	3	1
	3	742	66	209	225
Iva frutescens	1	0	0	0	0
	2	0	4	2	0
	3	126	28	317	382
Juncus roemerianus	1	0	0	0	0
	2	0	3	11	0
	3	599	30	518	409
Spartina alterniflora	1	78	0	177	141
	2	181	9	288	146
	3	35	22	108	170
Spartina cynosuroides	1	0	0	0	0
	2	8	5	20	20
	3	79	18	241	300
Spartina patens	1	0	0	0	0
	2	0	1	0	0
	3	1,894	31	1,046	1,109
Control (no plant)	1	—	0	—	—
	2	—	7	—	—
	3	—	11	—	—
LSD 0.05		341	11.4	227	249
LSD 0.01		—	—	299	328

Source: From Reimold, R. J., M. A. Hardisky, and P. C. Adams, 1978[a], *Habitat Development Field Investigations, Buttermilk Sound Marsh Development Site, Atlantic Intracoastal Waterway, Georgia*, Appendix A: Propagation of Marsh Plants and Post Propagation Monitoring, U.S. Army Corps of Engineers Dredged Material Res. Prog. Tech. Rept. D-78-38, 223 p.

LSD = least significant difference.

[a]Zone 1 = lower intertidal zone; zone 2 = middle zone; zone 3 = upper zone.

tion rate was the exception (Table 5-9). As noted in the discussion of waste disposal, Turner et al. (1976) reported an increase in levels of nitrogen and phosphorus as well as in biomass when *Phragmites* was treated with fish wastes. Such increased responses to fertilization should

Table 5-8. Aerial dry weight (kg/ha) of the standing crop of seedlings at Beaufort, North Carolina, to which nitrogen and phosphorus fertilizers were applied

	Fertilizer Treatment[a]		
Replicate	*Check*	*N*	*NP*
1	4,450	11,100	14,180
2	2,860	9,430	10,200
3	3,100	7,480	8,010
$\overline{X}$	3,470	9,340	10,800

Source: From Woodhouse, W. W., Jr., E. D. Seneca, and S. W. Broome, 1974, *Propagation of* Spartina alterniflora *for Substrate Stabilization and Salt Marsh Development*, Tech. Memo No. 46, U.S. Army Corps of Engineers Coastal Engineering Research Center, Ft. Belvoir, Va., 155p.

Note: Plots were seeded 4 April 1972 and harvested 5 October 1972.

[a]N rate = 224 kg/ha N; P rate = 49 kg/ha P; half the fertilizer was applied on 26 June 1972 and half on 26 July 1972.

enhance the colonization—and thus the stabilization—of a spoil site. As Woodhouse, Seneca, and Broome (1976) noted at Drum Inlet, however, production of *S. alterniflora* was sustained only as long as nutrients were continually added.

Elsewhere results were less well defined. Newcombe and Pride (1975) noted that fertilizer applications in California produced an increase in the number of stems of *S. foliosa* but had no effect on the height of the plants or the overall dry weight of the shoots or roots. In contrast, they reported an overall positive effect of fertilizer on shoot weights of nursery-rooted *Salicornia pacifica* seedlings, with a ratio of 3:1 fertilized to unfertilized and absolute growth increments of 30 g and 11 g, respectively. In a subsequent study, Floyd and Newcombe (1976) observed no fertilizer or elevational effects on the growth of *S. foliosa* or *S. pacifica*. Fertilization did not result in significant differences in survival, tiller production, height, or seed production in planted *S. alterniflora* or *S. patens* at a Galveston Bay, Texas, spoil site (Webb et al., 1978) or in planted or invading species in Georgia (Reimold, Hardisky, and Adams, 1978a).

These divergent results may be explained by the nature of the substrate available at the spoil site. Where the substrate was sandy there was a significant response to both nitrogen and phosphorus (Woodhouse, Seneca, and Broome, 1974) and a response could be maintained only by repeated fertilizer applications (Woodhouse, Seneca, and Broome, 1976). Where the sediments were finer (Woodhouse, Seneca, and Broome, 1974) and where there was an appreciable accumulation of organic material as well as nutrient-laden water (Reimold, Hardisky, and Adams, 1978a), fertilizer additions produced little or no response. At the same time,

Table 5-9. Effect of nitrogen and phosphorus fertilizers on growth of seedlings on South Island near Drum Inlet, North Carolina. Seeded 18 April 1973; sampled 8 November 1973

N Rate (kg/ha)	*P Rate (kg/ha)*								
	0	49	$\overline{X}$	0	49	$\overline{X}$	0	49	$\overline{X}$
	No. Flowers/m^2			*No. Culms/m^2*			*Height (cm)*		
0	10.7	10.3	10.5	142.0	144.0	143.0	24.0	29.0	26.0
112	4.7	10.0	7.3	144.0	137.0	141.0	23.0	30.0	27.0
224	10.3	21.3	15.8	171.0	285.0	228.0	30.0	35.0	33.0
448	5.7	17.0	11.3	109.0	219.0	164.0	23.0	31.0	27.0
$\overline{X}$	7.8	14.8	—	141.0	196.0	—	25.0	31.0	—

LSD[a]									
N 0.01		n.s.			n.s.			n.s.	
0.05		n.s.			67.0			n.s.	
P 0.01		7.1			n.s.			n.s.	
0.05		5.1			47.0			5.0	
Coeff. of variation (%)		52.1			32.0			21.2	

	Basal Area (cm^2/m^2)			*Aerial Dry Wt. (kg/ha)*			*Below-Ground Dry Wt. (kg/ha)*		
0	8.6	9.1	8.8	66.0	86.0	76.0	529.0	1,615.0	1,072.0
112	8.6	12.2	10.4	70.0	132.0	101.0	705.0	1,586.0	1,145.0
224	18.8	23.9	21.3	129.0	247.0	188.0	1,469.0	2,056.0	1,762.0
448	6.0	20.5	13.2	53.0	170.0	111.0	1,204.0	2,937.0	2,071.0
$\overline{X}$	10.5	16.4	—	80.0	158.0	—	977.0	2,049.0	—

LSD[a]									
N 0.01		n.s.			n.s.			n.s.	
0.05		n.s.			69.0			790.0	
P 0.01		n.s.			68.0			757.0	
0.05		n.s.			49.0			559.0	

Source: From Woodhouse, W. W., Jr., E. D. Seneca, and S. W. Broome, 1974, *Propagation of* Spartina alterniflora *for Substrate Stabilization and Salt Marsh Development*, Tech. Memo No. 46, U.S. Army Corps of Engineers Coastal Engineering Research Center, Ft. Belvoir, Va., 155p.

[a]LSD = least significant difference. (There were no significant N × P interactions.) n.s. = not significant.

numerous examples (Woodhouse, Seneca, and Broome, 1974, and others) clearly establish that fertilization in natural marshes can produce significant positive results.

Sediment and Organic Accumulations

Gray and Bunce (1972) have demonstrated a relationship between physical structure and chemical characteristics and thus soil maturity on one hand and plant distributions on the other hand in a natural marsh. Wetzel and Powers (1978), in their study at Windmill Point marsh, Virginia, found an extreme spatial heterogeneity of soil characteristics. Doumlele and Silberhorn (1978) suggested that the plant zonation at this same site probably resulted from both elevation and soil characteristics. In nearly all cases, a significant and positive correlation was found between percent silt-clay, percent volatiles, and organic carbon. The soils at the reference site had higher values, including soil nitrogen, than those at the experimental spoil sites. Such differences may have accounted for the height variations observed for *Pontederia* from site to site. These various data suggested to Wetzel and Powers that the soil system at their experimental site had not yet reached maturity.

Reimold, Hardisky, and Adams (1978a) determined that the development of soil types was a function of elevation; the soils that did develop resembled the natural soils associated with each plant species. By the second year of their study, up to 8 cm of silt had accumulated in the lower and middle portions of the intertidal zone (where a silty anaerobic soil developed), while the upper zone remained sandy. There was a corresponding reduction in redox potential in these two zones. At the Galveston Bay site, Webb et al. (1978) noted that, at the end of two and a half years, the marsh had two distinct sediment zones separated by a zone of intermediate composition. Because the lower portion was inundated much of the time, there was a marked increase in clay content, organic content, total Kjeldahl nitrogen, and extractable phosphorus. These accumulations were associated with surface sedimentation and active algal growth. The sediment composition at the higher elevation remained essentially unchanged chemically and physically. The area between the two zones was intermediate in both chemical and physical parameters. It was evident to Webb et al. (1978) as well as to Cammen, Seneca, and Copeland (1974), Reimold, Hardisky, and Adams (1978a), and Wetzel and Powers (1978) that the changes in sediment properties were largely controlled by elevation, which in turn influenced the duration of inundation and the establishment of algae and *Spartina*. Whereas most investigators, including Gray and Bunce (1972) and Wetzel and Powers (1978), have found some relationship between sedimentation or chemical composition of the sediments and the presence of plants in the marsh, Webb et al. (1978) found no such association.

While the tidal accumulation of sediments can influence the plant species composition, the deposition of spoil on the marsh surface can have a profound influence on the well-being of the marsh vegetation. In one study reported from Georgia (Reimold, Hardisky, and Adams, 1978b), the short form of *S. alterniflora* was able to penetrate up to 23 cm of material consisting of coarse sand, sand or clay mix, or clay material. Biological growth and production nearly equaled those in an undisturbed marsh. The sandy dredge material allowed a larger number of culms to penetrate than did the pure clay spoil. There was a more luxuriant growth of *S. alterniflora* in the clay material, however, probably due to the nutrients incorporated with the clay. The amount of biomass was related to the depth of the spoil, type of spoil, and month of smothering. Smothering in July produced lower biomass levels than smothering in November or February. Reimold, Hardisky, and Adams (1978b) concluded that smothering a high marsh under dredge spoil was a feasible way to dispose of such material. However, they believed that this kind of disposal should be used only as a last resort. It would appear that the feasibility of such spoil disposal would be largely determined by the long-term viability of the marsh vegetation. This viability in turn would be markedly influenced by the elevation of the spoil surface relative to the frequency and duration of tidal inundation.

Toxic Materials

Not only may dredge spoil physically smother marsh biota if applied too deeply, but there may be accumulative effects from heavy metals and other toxic materials working their way through the marsh-estuarine food chains. (See earlier discussion of heavy metals in the section on waste treatment.) Many of these materials found in the marine and estuarine sediments result from human industrial activity. The production of toxaphene to use in pesticides is one example: Reimold and Durant (1972) and Reimold (1974) found significant levels in *S. alterniflora*. The greatest uptake was in the roots and rhizomes and the least in the leaves. Measurable quantities of toxaphene were found in the snail *Littorina*, suggesting that the snail was involved in the *Spartina* detritus food chain. At the same time the supposed detritivore *Uca* did not show any measurable levels of toxaphene. Measurable quantities were found in the white shrimp and such fin fish as killifish, mullet, menhaden, and anchovies, implicating them in the detritus food chain. Concentrations of toxaphene were highest in the surface sediment layer and decreased with depth. Analyses of water samples indicated that the toxaphene appeared to be confined to the suspended material in the water and was not dissolved in the water. This could account for the low levels of toxaphene found in the oyster (Durant and Reimold, 1971), its incorporation into fish and shrimp tissue, and concentrations of 33 ppm found in the dredging spoil. It does not explain how the toxaphene was changed into a soluble form taken up by *Spartina* on one hand from a form that became concentrated in the marsh sediments on the other. Following the reduction of toxaphene discharge into a tidal creek from 2,332 ppb to 6.4 ppb over a two-year period, there was a corresponding enhancement of species diversity from 0.70 to 2.26 ($\overline{H}$) (Reimold, 1974).

Fine-grained dredge spoil appears to have considerably higher levels of lead, zinc, and manganese than do natural marsh sediments. Drifmeyer and Odum (1975) reported large differences in concentration depending on sediment type. As dredge effluent flowed over the marsh, the concentration of metals (iron, manganese, cadmium, copper, nickel, and zinc) was reduced by as much as 15 to 32%. The most important mechanism of removal appeared to be due to inorganic chemical processes, which lead to accumulation of nutrients and metals on particles, which are then deposited in the sediments. Biological processes may be more important during periods of greater production. The removal process may be controlled to a high degree by the formation of hydrated iron and manganese oxides, which scavenge both nutrients and metals. Since these compounds form more readily at high pH and high oxygen concentrations, removal is more efficient during daylight hours. The efficiency of this removal also appears to be a function of concentration in the effluent (Windom, 1977).

Drifmeyer and Odum (1975) found lead in *Palaemonetes pugio, Fundulus heteroclitus, Phragmites australis, Spartina alterniflora,* and *S. patens* to be significantly higher from a dredge spoil site than in organisms taken from a natural marsh. Zinc was significantly higher ($p < .01$ level) in the three plant species at the dredge spoil site and manganese was significantly higher ($p < .05$ level) in the grass shrimp from the same site. Thus it is apparent that dredge spoil used in the creation of a new marsh may act as a source of heavy metals that are potentially toxic to biota. Estuarine food chains based on the ingestion of such sediments would be particularly prone to contamination with variable toxic effects at the higher trophic levels. Windom (1975) found decreasing concentrations of lead and manganese with increasing trophic level but no consistent pattern with zinc. De Nekker and d'Angremond (1976) cautioned that dredge spoil may have a high level of fertility for agricultural crops but also high concentrations of heavy metals.

Marsh Maturity

How long does it take a manmade marsh located on a dredge spoil site to achieve the same level of maturity as adjoining natural marshes? By measuring the rate of horizontal spread of *S. alterniflora*, Woodhouse, Seneca, and Broome (1974) were able to estimate the time required for stands established by seeds in the upper part of the tidal range to advance down slope to the lower limit of growth. At Snow's Cut, North Carolina, Woodhouse, Seneca, and Broome estimated it would take 30 years. For them such a rate justified the expense of using transplants rather than seeds, especially where early stabilization was needed. Based on sediment carbon content, Seneca et al. (1976) estimated that it would take 4 to 25 years for a planted marsh to resemble a natural marsh. Cammen, Seneca, and Copeland (1974) were more specific for the same sites. Also using organic carbon content as a criterion, they estimated that the area at Drum Inlet, North Carolina, would resemble a natural marsh in 3.7 to 4.5 years. At Snow's Cut it was calculated to take 22 to 26 years. In both places the major source of carbon was benthic algae, since the rate was the same in bare as in planted plots. Increasing species diversity was used to indicate a shift toward achieving maturity, but all the experimental spoil sites were still in various developmental stages (Floyd and Newcombe, 1976; Reimold, Hardisky, and Adams 1978a; Doumlele and Silberhorn, 1978; Webb et al., 1978). The criteria were focused on the plant species; only modest examination was made of the faunal component of the marsh habitat.

Microbial and Faunal Communities

Relatively little has been done to examine the development of the microbial community on dredge spoil destined for marsh rehabilitation. Silty organic material begins to accumulate in the lower and middle portions of the intertidal zone, and the rate appears to be related to the presence of vegetation (Cammen, 1976; Doumlele and Silberhorn, 1978; Wetzel and Powers, 1978; Reimold, Hardisky, and Adams, 1978a). In time, as the sediments become more anaerobic, a microbial community, similar to that found in the natural marsh, begins to develop. Associated with this microbial development are increases in the mineralization of the substrate and in nutrient levels. There is a general increase in microbial biomass and viable cell counts. Reimold, Hardisky, and Adams (1978a) calculated that this biomass accumulated at the rate of 13.3 g $C/m^2/yr$. (Figure 5-5). They also estimated that 22% of the biomass was bacterial and yeast in origin while the remaining 78% was derived from algae, diatoms, meiofauna, and macrofauna in the dredge material. It was presumed that most of this latter component was derived from the algae (primarily blue-greens) and diatoms.

An intensive examination of the macrofauna on dredge spoil was carried out in North Carolina by Cammen (1976) and Cammen, Seneca, and Copeland (1974). The sediments consisted of 98 and 96% sand, and salinities were 28 to 35‰ and 7 to 10‰ at Drum Inlet and Snow's Cut respectively. The level of organic carbon in the lower intertidal zone was high at both sites. A positive correlation was reported between the different elevations of the bare and planted spoil plots and the differences between their invertebrate macrofauna. At Drum Inlet, where elevational difference between plots was slight, the faunal communities were qualitatively and quantitatively similar. At Snow's Cut, where the difference in elevation was large, the faunal communities were dissimilar. Each transect could be expected to have a lower creek fauna and an upper intertidal zone or marsh fauna (Figure 5-6). The change in biomass corresponded in each area to the true boundary of the *Spartina* marsh (i.e., the lower limit of *Spartina* growth).

The dominant fauna (Table 5-10) of the creek natural assemblage were polychaetes, *Laeonereis culveri*, and the Capitellidae. At Drum Inlet they made up 80% of the biomass of the creek transects, about 60% in the natural marsh, and about 36% in the bare and planted spoil marsh. The

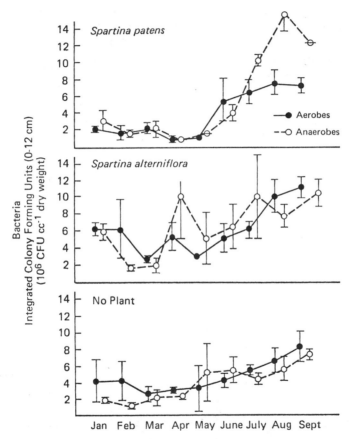

Figure 5-5. Integrated number of bacteria in the top 0 to 12 centimeters of dredged materials from *S. patens*, *S. alterniflora,* and no plant plots in middle third of the tidal zone of a Georgia site. Vertical bars represent standard error for three cores. *Source: After Reimold, R. J., M. A. Hardisky, and P. C. Adams, 1978a, Habitat Development Field Investigations, Buttermilk Sound Marsh Development Site, Atlantic Intracoastal Waterway, Georgia, Appendix A: Propagation of Marsh Plants and Post Propagation Monitoring, U.S. Army Corps of Engineers Dredged Material Res. Prog. Tech. Rept. D-78-38, 223p.*

bare and planted marsh fauna were predominantly insect larvae, which constituted 56 to 63% of the biomass in contrast to 7% in the natural marsh and less than 1% at the creek stations.

The high faunal affinity between the bare and planted plots at Drum Inlet indicated that the growth of *Spartina* did not have an appreciable effect on the macrofauna. The "marsh" species accounted for 14 of the 16 species found in the natural marsh. The natural marsh had 8 species in common with the planted spoil, and these made up 67% of the total natural marsh biomass and 94% of the planted spoil biomass. These species' relatively higher success at the spoil site was presumably the result of the lack of competition from the 8 other marsh species that had not colonized the spoil. The bare and planted spoil sites at Drum Inlet had similar faunal biomass, but there were differences between them in the average number of individuals per sample.

Biomass was greatest in May at both planted and bare spoil sites at Drum Inlet due to a spring peak of insect larval biomass. The natural

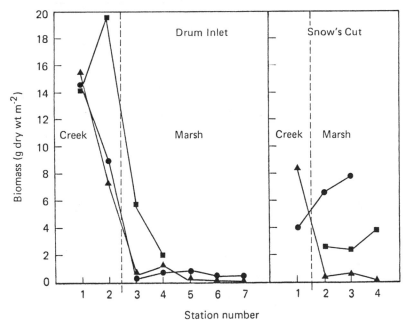

Figure 5-6.   Change in faunal biomass between creek and marsh stations of a North Carolina site. Values are the overall means for each station. ●—●, Bare, ▲—▲, Planted; ■—■, Natural. Vertical dashed lines separate the creek and marsh stations. *Source: After Cammen, L. M., 1976, Microinvertebrates. Colonization of* Spartina *marshes artificially established on dredge spoil, Estuarine Coast Mar. Sci.* **4:**357–372, by permission.

Table 5-10. The dominant taxa of the marsh stations for each transect in a North Carolina marsh

	Drum Inlet	Snow's Cut
Bare spoil	Capitellidae (36%) Ephydridae (36%) Dolichopodidae (10%)	*Laeonereis culveri* (88%)
Planted spoil	Ephydridae (44%) Capitellidae (32%) Dolichopodidae (12%)	*Lepidactylus dytiscus* (57%) Dolichopodidae (17%) *Gammarus palustris* (11%)
Natural marsh	Capitellidae (51%) *Melampus bidentatus* (12%)	*Cyathura polita* (31%) *Nereis succinea* (27%) *Geukensia (= Modiolus) demissa* (18%) *Laeonereis culveri* (18%)

Source: From Cammen, L. M., 1976, Microinvertebrates. Colonization of *Spartina* marshes artificially established on dredge spoil, *Estuarine Coast. Mar. Sci.* 4: 357-372, by permission.

Note: Only those taxa accounting for more than 10% of the total biomass have been included.

marsh had more individuals and a higher biomass than either spoil site at the end of June, but by October these differences had disappeared. The late June biomass of the natural marsh was about 9 times greater than the peak of the spoil areas in May, and about 50 times that of June. Cammen (1976) observed that, overall, the natural marsh at Drum Inlet had significantly more individuals and a higher biomass than the spoil plots.

The number of taxa per sample and the Shannon-Weaver diversity index were not significantly different between the bare and planted plots at Drum Inlet. Since this was the case, *Spartina* had no apparent effect on the plots' community structure or their biomass. Just as with numbers and biomass, the natural marsh had a much greater diversity and more taxa per sample than either spoil plot in late June, but this difference had disappeared by August. Overall the natural marsh differed significantly in diversity and numbers of taxa from the bare or planted spoil sites. Coincidentally, when there was a high biomass in late June in the natural marsh, there was also a high degree of diversity (Figure 5-7).

In contrast to Drum Inlet, the bare and planted sites at Snow's Cut differed significantly in numbers of individuals and total biomass. Most of the difference was due to the absence of the polychaete *Laeonereis culveri* from the planted site and its abundance in the bare spoil site. The differences were attributed to the role of *Spartina*. The natural marsh had significantly more individuals than either spoil site, but the biomass was greater than that for the planted plot and less than that for the bare plot.

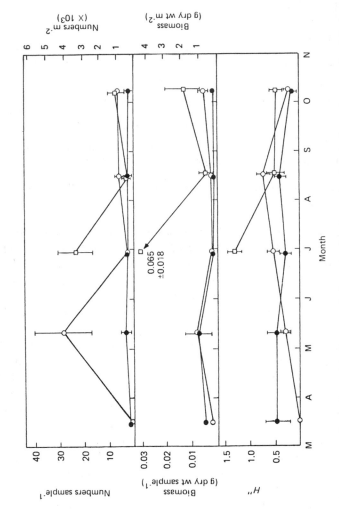

Figure 5-7. Seasonal variation of numbers, biomass, and diversity for the macrofauna from the marsh stations at Drum Inlet, North Carolina. Vertical lines represent ± 1 standard error. Number of taxa per sample has not been shown since it was significantly correlated with diversity ($r = .88$, $p < .001$). O——O, Bare; ●——●, Planted; □——□, Natural. Source: After Cammen, L. M., 1976, Microinvertebrates. Colonization of Spartina marshes artificially established on dredge spoil, Estuarine Coast Mar. Sci. **4**:357–372, by permission.

There were no significant differences among the natural marsh and the two spoil sites with regard to diversity and number of taxa per sample. The calculated values for overall faunal affinity showed that the bare and planted spoil plots differed greatly (Figure 5-8). The polychaete *L. culveri* was dominant in the bare plot while the amphipod *Lepidactylus dytiscus* was the major taxon in the planted spoil. The main species in the natural marsh were the polychaete *Nereis succinea* and the isopod *Cyathura polita*; both were insignificant at the spoil sites. In fact *Cyathura*, which comprised the greatest number of individuals in the natural marsh, was completely absent from the spoil sites. The lower creek elevations favored the polychaetes; their numbers dropped at the higher elevations of the marsh stations.

There was considerable difference in the development of the planted spoil of both sites when compared with the local natural marsh. At Drum Inlet the planted spoil had an overall faunal affinity of almost 40% during the second growing season. At Snow's Cut the faunal affinity between the planted site and the natural marsh was lower than 10% after three seasons. The main cause for these faunal differences may have been the rapid accretion at Snow's Cut, as *Spartina* trapped water-borne sediments, raising the elevation above the optimum for natural marsh species. The spoil fauna was considered to be responding more quickly to elevation than to vegetation change, with the result that what appeared to be a typical *Spartina* marsh did not have the typical marsh fauna. Cammen (1976) proposed that the length of time for the development of a natural fauna would depend on elevation, sediment particle size, rate of sedimentation, proximity to a natural marsh, and relative maturity of the natural community.

The faunal development of a marsh created from dredge spoil will be a reflection of faunal components in adjacent marsh sites. While Cammen (1976) identified the natural creek assemblage to be polychaetes, Diaz et al. (1978) found a James River, Virginia, site to be dominated by tubificid oligochaetes and chironomid larvae. These differences in part reflected the water salinity, which is essentially freshwater at the Virginia site but ranges from brackish to almost full salinity at the North Carolina sites.

The oligochaete *Limnodrilus* was dominant in numbers and biomass in most situations at the Virginia site, while the chironomids were secondarily dominant. The introduced bivalve *Corbicula manilensis* was dominant in some habitats. The total density and biomass of the macrobenthos were highest in the low and subtidal channels of the experimental site. Intermediate densities and biomass were found in the high marsh at the experimental sites as well as in the low marsh at the reference site. Lower values were found outside the marshes on the adjacent tidal flats and were attributed to the populations of oligochaetes. There were seasonal varia-

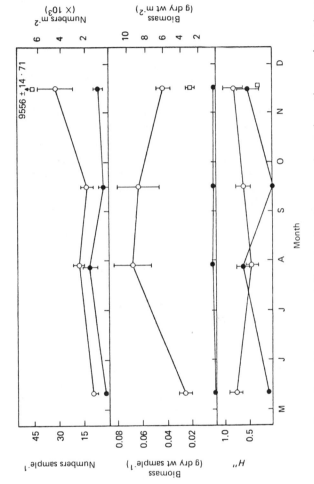

Figure 5-8. Seasonal variation of numbers, biomass, and diversity for the macrofauna from the marsh stations at Snow's Cut, North Carolina. Vertical lines represent ±1 standard error. Number of taxa per sample has not been shown since it was significantly correlated with diversity ($r = .74$, $p < 0.001$). O————O, Bare; ●————●, Planted; *Source: After Cammen, L. M., 1976, Microinvertebrates. Colonization of Spartina marshes artificially established on dredge spoil, Estuarine Coast Mar. Sci.* **4:**357–372, *by permission.*

tions in both density and biomass with the highest values in the summer and lowest in the winter. Life-cycle patterns, the presence of plant cover, and increased physical stress in the winter were presumed to be responsible.

Species diversity of the macrobenthos was higher in the natural marsh on the James River than at the experimental site. This was due to a greater richness of species and a greater evenness (less dominance by a few species) in the natural marsh. Species composition of the macrobenthos was different between the two sites. The natural marsh had more unique species, while widely distributed species were more evident at the dredge spoil site. This undoubtedly reflected the sandy nature of the spoil site and the higher incidence of silt and clay in the natural marsh sediments.

The meiofaunal populations also displayed the greatest estimated biomass in the natural marsh, due largely to the crustacea. Production estimates indicated that the meiofauna was almost as important as the macrofauna in the natural marsh while macrobenthos, largely owing to the oligochaetes, dominated at the experimental site. Densities of organisms, on the other hand, were much greater in the low marsh and subtidal portions of the spoil site (Diaz et al., 1978).

The benthic fauna at a site like the James River is highly opportunistic and can quickly exploit a dredge spoil site. The invasion and long-term fate of such benthos depend not on further biological accommodation but on changes in the physical environment. Elevation, tidal-level fluctuations, composition of the dredge material, sedimentary structure, subsidence, and erosion, as well as accretion of organic and mineral sediments, will have a pronounced effect on species composition and abundance (Seneca et al., 1976; Diaz et al., 1978; Webb et al., 1978).

Cole (1978) and Hardisky (1979) found that fiddler crab burrows tended to decrease at lower intertidal elevations but became more abundant as the vegetation density increased. Reimold, Hardisky, and Adams (1978a) reported that bird species associated with open, sandy spaces began to disappear as vegetation became established and were replaced by marsh species such as sparrows, egrets, and the marsh hawk (*Circus cyaneus*). The lack of a sedimentary structure and the absence of such species as the ribbed mussel (*Geukensia demissa*) led Reimold, Hardisky, and Adams (1978a) and Webb et al. (1978) to consider the fauna in their dredge spoil marshes to be in an early successional stage. As pointed out earlier, the rapid colonizing ability of some benthic forms does not signify maturity in a tidal marsh community.

The data presented indicate that none of the dredge spoil sites used to establish a tidal marsh has achieved a level of maturity similar to that of the adjoining natural marshes. Superficially the vegetation has begun to take on the character of a mature marsh. However, the soil structure does not display the same characteristics found in the natural situation. The opportunistic and rapid colonizing ability of the faunal and microbial populations with short life spans is a transitional stage. Species richness and evenness, as compared to local natural sites, will give an insight to the level of maturity of a developing manmade marsh.

SYNTHESIS

Reimold, Hardisky, and Adams (1978a), in addressing approaches to mitigation, have drawn several overall conclusions regarding the use of dredge spoil as a means to establish or restore tidal marsh land. Marsh habitat can be developed on dredge spoil. Transplanted *Spartina alterniflora* performs best in the lower to middle portion of the intertidal zone; *S. patens* and *Distichlis spicata* best stabilize the substrate in the upper third of the intertidal zone. Species such as *Borrichia frutescens, Iva frutescens, Juncus roemerianus,* and *Spartina cyanosuroides* are not as useful for rapid stabilization but provide diversity in the maturing marsh. The development of the soil is a function of elevation and stability: the soil tends to resemble the natural condition associated with each particular plant species. Vegetated soil enhances colonization by the marsh fauna. Faunal composition and rate of development, wildlife use, microbial development, invasion pressure, interstitial water nutrients, and plant mineral content directly depend on soil development and plant success at each elevational regime.

If these conclusions can be utilized in the mitigation of tidal wetlands, they should become part of the requirements of regulatory agencies to reduce environmental harm or restore unavoidable losses. Mitigation measures must be determined as part of any long-range estuary management plan. Hershman and Ruotsala (1978) have identified four requirements for workable mitigation: a definition of terms necessary for communication between environmental managers, developers, and the public; a wider range of financing strategies; a methodology to determine an equitable amount of mitigation; and established procedures for plans and management programs so that mitigation rules and costs are known in advance.

Interest in building new marshes to replace those that have been destroyed is both an acknowledgment of the environmental and social values of such wetlands, and an attempt to ensure the continuation of these marshland values in the face of development. Mitigation involves more than establishing vegetation in an intertidal area and calling the result a marsh. Race and Christie (1982) raise a very serious question about the purpose of marshland mitigation. There are value judgments about the relative importance of the various functions attributed to tidal wetlands, and such judgments directly or indirectly become a part of any coastal management program.

In areas where new marshes are needed most, there is the danger that marsh creation may be used as a bartering device to destroy natural marshes one at a time. Mitigation by marsh creation will be of little value if it maintains the quantity of marshes by substituting equal areas of inferior quality and uncertain duration. The critical determination must be whether marsh creation and restoration techniques are used to compensate for the unavoidable loss of wetlands and enhance estuarine systems or to justify the destruction of wetlands. Marsh creation as a mitigation technique should not serve as the basis for bartering away natural marshes (Race and Christie, 1982).

Chapter 6

Insecticides

Chemical control of aquatic insects that we consider pests has been available for many years. Before the advent of DDT, oil and oil with pyrethrum were the only materials used (Smith, 1902; National Academy of Science, 1976). The successful use of DDT to control insects during World War II resulted in a sharp increase in postwar use of this compound, followed by the proliferation and use of other synthetic organic pesticides. Soon there were more and more reports of fish and wildlife mortalities following such use. Since the coastal waters are the habitats of many fish and shellfish, concern began to develop about persistent chemical pesticides disseminating into, and accumulating in the estuaries. Butler (1966) pointed out that many of the crustaceans used as food are representatives of the same group of arthropods that these insecticides are designed to kill. Table 6-1 lists the insecticides that have been used on or near tidal marshes.

Since it is well established that chemical control has significantly enhanced human health and economic well-being, crops and domestic animals, it seems ironic to argue against the use of pesticides. Rudd

Note: There will be no attempt to provide an exhaustive review of the role of pesticides in the control of tidal marsh biting flies. A voluminous literature already exists on the use of insecticides and their environmental impacts. For selected reviews, see Johnson (1968) and National Academy of Science (1976).

Table 6-1. Insecticides that are used, or have been used, for the larviciding and/or adulticiding of biting dipterans (mosquitoes, tabanids, gnats) in or near tidal marshes

Surface films (sprayed on water surface)	kerosene, diesel oil, fuel oil No. 2, Flit MLO, monomolecular organic surface film of isosteryl alcohol.
Copper arsenite	Paris Green
Chlorinated hydrocarbons	DDT, dieldrin, chlordane, endrin, lindane (BHC), heptachlor, methoxychlor. All have been discontinued for control of biting marsh dipterans, with the exception of methoxychlor.
Organophosphates (cholinesterase inhibitors)	malathion, parathion, fenthion (Baytex), trichlorfon, fenitrothion, chlorpyrifos (Dursban), diazinon, naled (Dibrom), temephos (Abate).
Carbamates (cholinesterase inhibitors)	propoxur (Baygon), carbaryl (Sevin).
Botanicals	pyrethrum (insecticidal compound from the flowers of chrysanthemums); synthetic pyrethroids (resmethrin, permethrin). Pyrethrins are sometimes used with a synergist such as piperonyl butoxide.
Insect growth regulators (IGRs)	methoprene (Altosid), a juvenile hormone mimic; diflubenzuron (Dimilin), a chitin inhibitor.
Toxin-producing bacterial spores	*Bacillus thuringiensis* var. *israelensis* (Serotype H-14), commonly known as BTI (Bactimos, Teknar); *Baccilus spaericus.*

(1964), however, has provided a number of reasons to do so: (1) most pesticides are nonselective; (2) the manner of use has not been precise, being restricted neither to the pest species nor to the area of application; (3) insufficient attention has been given to alternate means of crop protection; (4) many of the earlier (as of the mid-1960s) insecticides were stable and persist in the environment; (5) insidious pathways of biological transfer of toxic chemicals have become identified; (6) as of the mid-1960s, use was entirely too single-minded in relation to the manifold effects produced; (7) the technically supported views of the conservationist, resource analyst, biologist, and sociologist were too frequently overlooked; and (8) equally lacking was the overt concern for the aesthetic and moral values that must be considered in any application of technology to the satisfaction of human needs and desires. Rudd specifically emphasized that continued heavy dependence on chemical-control systems must ultimately be self-defeating, that such controls have departed from fundamental biological principles, and that the limited goals of pest-control practices fail to serve either long-range productive values or the varied interests of the public. Such chemical controls have generally been initiated only when it appeared that habitat manipulation would fail. The reasons for this failure were, according to Rudd, often social or economic rather than biological. Chemical pest-control measures have often been an inconsistent mixture of actual need, superficial appraisal, unbalanced perspective, and expediency. Table 6-2 is a representative list of some of the adverse consequences resulting from specific insecticide use in or near tidal marshes.

A major problem with most insecticides has been the high level of toxicity to nontarget organisms. Aquatic invertebrates as well as fish have been found to be very sensitive to chemical insecticides, especially those that contact the gill surfaces. This is particularly true for the organochloride pesticides like DDT and the early forms of organophosphates such as Parathion and Malathion. For example, the suppression of shell growth in oysters has increased uniformly with each tenfold increase in DDT concentration in the range of 0.0001 to 0.1 ppm at a water temperature of 17°C. Growth was almost nil at the highest concentration, while at the lowest concentration it was 20% of the control. Fishes are also indirectly affected by the reduction of food organisms affected by pesticides (Rudd, 1964; Butler, 1966; O'Brien, 1967; National Academy of Science, 1976).

A great many chemical compounds have been screened in an attempt to find a specific, highly effective mosquito larvicide with short residual properties and the least harmful effect to wildlife. Wilkinson (1967) initiated a study to determine the effect of such larvicides on selected nontargeted tidal marsh organisms. The mummichog (*Fundulus heteroclitus*), the grass shrimp (*Palaemonetes pugio*), and the blue crab (*Callinectes sapidus*) were tested against the insecticides Abate, Malathion, Baytex, and SD7438. Abate was deemed the least toxic, with a 24-hour LC-50 value (concentration at which 50% of organisms are killed in a 24 hr period) for the mummichog in the acute test at 10.2 lbs/acre. The accumulative tests following three applications at 0.032 lbs/acre resulted in a 3% mortality for fish and no mortality for shrimp or crab. The other three insecticides were moderately to highly toxic to one or more of the test organisms. Toxicity increased for the fish as the salinity increased, resulting in higher mortalities. Abate and Baytex were found to be relatively nonpersistent and could not be detected by bioassay at 72 and 120 hours after application, respectively.

Later, Tripp (1974) reported that well-fed oysters (*Crassostrea virginica*) showed almost no detectable effect, including reproduction, after exposure to pesticides even when chemical concentrations greatly exceeded what might be expected under field conditions. Adult oysters were subjected to regular but intermittent exposure to the mosquito larvicide Abate and the adulticide Dibrom. Exposure to two concentrations (1 and 10 ppm) of either insecticide did not cause dramatic acute mortality. However, oysters chronically exposed to 10 ppm of Dibrom did display much higher mortalities than the controls. There was no evidence of tissue damage that could be attributed to either pesticide. Overall, gonad maturation and spawning were not dramatically inhibited. Abate-treated oysters, however, did not show the early spawning peak of the controls but did spawn normally in August. Dibrom-treated (10 ppm) oysters did not mature quite as rapidly and spawned less fully when compared to the controls.

Another major problem with pesticides is the development of resistance. Pesticides exert strong selective pressure on pest species, and resistant strains have quickly developed. There is also considerable evidence of preadaption either through biochemical or physical modifications or by behavioral changes which reduce exposure to lethal doses of the insecticide. In addition, some studies have produced evidence of multiple resistance to several pesticides as well as cross-resistance (Moore, 1967; National Academy of Science, 1976). Since 1946 mosquitoes have developed resistance to DDT and other organic insecticides. For the most part, this has been a matter of genetic selection for resistance. The use of larvicides will exert selection pressure against the entire mosquito population, while adulticiding will exert such a pressure only against that portion of the population that creates a nuisance in populated areas. By the mid-1950s mosquitoes had developed resistance to all the organochlorides; the degree of resistance has been greatest where the most larviciding has been done. Where the insecticides failed to control mosquitoes because of enhanced resistance, mosquito-control personnel have felt the wrath of the people being bitten (National Academy of Science, 1976).

In 1956 Hoskins and Gordon acknowledged that, while little was known about the genetic aspects of resistance to toxicants, the basic explanations must be sought in the physiological and biochemical reactions in which the pesticides take part. Later, Plapp (1976) suggested that the ultimate resistance mechanism would be a change in the target enzyme acted on by an insecticide. Plapp went on to say that such precision is possible only if we understand the biochemical target of the insecticide. This fits in with the view expressed by Hoskins and Gordon (1956) that insecticides kill by interfering with some "sensitive mechanism" essential to life. As an example, the rate of absorption of pesticides by insects is an important determinant of insecticide toxicity. A decrease in the absorption rate would allow more time for the detoxification of the insecticide (Plapp, 1976). Such resistance is enhanced by the creation of a protective mechanism that prevents the interaction with the sensitive

Table 6-2. Representative list of insecticides and any adverse consequences resulting from their use in tidal marshes or with selected animals characteristic of that habitat

Study	Location	Insecticide Used	Application Rate	Impacted Organism	Adverse Effect Observed
Rio (1970)	Laboratory, New Jersey	Abate	0.4 to 8 mg/l	Fiddler crab	No immediate effect for first 2 days. By day 4 increasing mortality with increasing concentration.
Campbell & Denno (1976)	Field, New Jersey	Abade, Dursban		Marsh community	Selective mosquito larvicide. No significant change in diversity, richness, or density of nontarget salt marsh insect community.
Ward and Busch (1976)	Laboratory, New Jersey	Abate	ppm	Fiddler crab	24-hour LC 50 at 9.12 ppm. at 4.13 ppm, crabs either killed or eliminated escape response in 50% of animals tested.
Fitzpatrick and Sutherland (1978)	Field, New Jersey	Abate, Dursban	Repeated applications	Coffee-bean snail	No significant change in snail densities when subjected to granular form. Temporary significant depression of snail densities when Abate used in an emulsion.
Butler et al. (1960)	Laboratory, Florida	Chlordane DDT Dieldrin Endrin Sevin Toxaphene	0.01 ppm 0.1 ppm 0.1 ppm 0.1 ppm 1.0 ppm 0.1 ppm	Oyster	Sublethal inhibition of shell growth after 24-hr exposure.
Croker and Wilson (1965)	Field, Florida	DDT	0.2 lb/acre	Fish and shrimp	Significant fish and *Palaemonetes* mortalities soon after application.

Reference	Location	Chemical	Concentration/Units	Species	Observation
Harrington & Bidlingmayer	Field, Florida	Dieldrin	1.0 lb/acre	Fish and invertebrates	Significant fish and invertebrate mortalities.
Christiansen et al. (1978)	Laboratory, North Carolina	Dimilin (insect growth regulator)	0.5, 1, 3, 5, 7, and 10 ppb	Larvae of mud crab Rhithropanopeus harrisii, and Sesarma riticulatum	Survival of larvae of both species decreased with increased concentration of Dimilin.
Hansen (1969)	Laboratory, Florida	Endrin	ppm	Sheepshead minnow	24-hour LC 50 at 0.003 ppm.
Katz (1961)	Laboratory, Oregon	Lindane	ppb	Stickleback	Estimated 96-hr TLm for 5‰ was 44 ppb
Hansen (1969)	Laboratory, Florida	Malathion	ppm	Sheepshead minnow	24-hr LC 50 at 0.3 ppm
Rio (1970)	Laboratory, New Jersey	Malathion	8 to 16 mg/l	Fiddler crab	No survival at day 1 in 16 mg/l, no survival at day 3 in 12 mg/l, only 20% survival by day 3 in 8 mg/l with increasing mortality to days 7 and 8 with 5% survival.
Butler (1963)	Laboratory, Florida	Sevin	ppm	Long nose killifish	24-hr LC 50 at 1.75 ppm
Stewart et al. (1967)	Laboratory, Oregon	Sevin	ppm	Stickleback	24-hr LC 50 at 6.7 ppm
Hansen (1969)	Laboratory, Florida	Sevin	ppm	Sheepshead minnow	24-hr LC 50 at 2.8 ppm
Katz (1961)	Laboratory, Oregon	Toxaphene	ppb	Stickleback	96-hr TLm at 5‰ was 8.6 ppb

Note: LC50 = Lethal concentration; 50% mortality
TLm = Median tolerance Limit

mechanism, or by changing or replacing the sensitive action by some insensitive mechanism not affected by the insecticide. Behavior changes, impermeability, detoxification devices, storage mechanisms, and highly sensitive ways for concentration all may serve as potential protective mechanisms against the action of insecticides (Hoskins and Gordon, 1956).

All known means of detoxification of organophosphates and carbamates are also mechanisms of resistance. The detoxification devices confer resistance by occurring at abnormally high levels in resistant strains. All are inherited as if controlled by simple semidominant genes, even when they appear to involve complex series of biochemical changes. Although it is not well understood, the development of resistance to chlorinated insecticides seems to be associated with their action on the nervous system (Plapp, 1976).

The persistence of many of the organochloride insecticides, as well as the propensity of shellfish and fish to concentrate and store these pesticides at levels many thousand times greater than are present in their environment, had become a major concern by the 1950s and 1960s. In some locations, it was found, the biological concentrations of DDT may have been more than 70,000 times the background levels, depending on water temperature, duration of exposure, and concentration in the surrounding water. DDT in the water column that may not be detectable by ordinary chemical methods could be concentrated in oysters and other organisms and thus incorporated into the food web within a relatively short time (Butler, 1966).

Another ecological impact of nonselective pesticides is the accumulated evidence that many pesticides greatly reduce the pests natural enemies. The conclusions of Ripper (1956), although derived from studies of crop pests, seem to indicate that the use of broad-spectrum insecticides on the tidal marsh could be the cause of the resurgence of certain tidal marsh pests. An ecosystem normally has a built-in defense against pests: a population of their natural enemies. This defense mechanism can cope only with moderate infestations, however. Applications of insecticides are most effective against the pest if they are selected so as to eliminate or reduce the offending pest population only, and thus supplement the means of natural defense, not destroy it. Resistant forms of prey that accumulate pesticides can be a great hazard to predators (Moore, 1967). Where natural enemies already exist, the use of nonselective insecticides must be considered a costly and potentially dangerous interim measure. In addition, the use of selective pesticides should help prevent the development of resistant strains in ecosystems where natural enemies are present (Ripper, 1956).

When Croft and Brown (1975) reviewed the responses of arthropod natural enemies to insecticides as used in pest management for crops, they arrived at two conclusions that are relevant to pest control in the tidal marsh: (1) the addition of a selection pressure from the natural enemies that are not harmed by the use of a selective pesticide would delay the development of resistance in the pest, and (2) the survival of sufficient prey or host species would allow the natural enemy to multiply and respond by becoming resistant to a wider spectrum of insecticides. It follows that enough prey and hosts must remain to serve as food for the resistant genotypes of natural enemies surviving the pesticide applications. The natural enemies of biting flies in the tidal marsh include such birds as sharp-tailed and seaside sparrows, marsh wrens, and tree and barn swallows. Damsel flies, dragonflies, and a host of spiders also serve as predators. Natural enemies that can find prey or hosts at low densities may develop resistance at the same time as their prey. It is important to make a periodic assessment of the insecticide-susceptibility levels of both prey (host) and predators. A greater understanding of selection in both groups could result in an optimization of spray practices, leading to a greater balance in the adaptation of both groups to insecticides and a greater balance in the ecosystem, thus avoiding the destruction of natural enemies as well as limiting resistance in the pest (Croft and Brown, 1975).

In his synopsis, Moore (1967) considered pesticides to be an ecological problem with a solution to be achieved through an interdisciplinary approach. Pesticide management in tidal marshes requires interaction among entomologists, wildlife managers, toxicologists, biochemists, soil and water chemists, hydrographers, ecologists, and pesticide manufacturers. Ruesink's (1976) suggestion of a need for a broad range of expertise for systems analysis of pest management for crop protection is also applicable to management of the tidal marsh. Evidence of this approach can be seen in the ongoing activities in open marsh water management (OMWM) described elsewhere.

Pesticides are an ecological problem because they always affect ecosystems even though they are applied to control only a single or very few species. Most pesticide problems arise because they are nonspecific. Because most pesticides are density-independent, they do not control a pest in the biological sense. Also, they may kill only a portion of the surplus that would be eliminated by such density-dependent means as predation. As pointed out earlier, however, insecticides have had a particularly harsh effect on predators. This has been particularly true of the organochlorides in pesticides because their persistence and fat solubility have caused them to be widely dispersed, to be concentrated in the food chains, and eventually to have an impact on the top predators (National Academy of Science, 1976).

Pesticides may kill, have sublethal effects, or have no effect at all. Some remain active for years, and others are broken down or deactivated almosτ as soon as they are applied. In general, biotic concentrations appear to be greater in the aquatic habitat than in terrestrial systems. This can be expected, as aquatic organisms must pass large volumes of water through their bodies for respiration, thus picking up pesticides directly from contaminated water as well as indirectly through the food chain. Fat-soluble pesticides can be eliminated temporarily from systemic circulation by being stored in the fat. Once the fat is remobilized, the insecticide is put back into circulation. Females of the species may eliminate such insecticide residues from their systems by transferring it to the yolk of the eggs, which are subsequently released through ovulation (Moore, 1967).

Pesticides affect diversity, usually reducing it, and thereby enhance the instability of the ecosystem. The decline in diversity is not random; some groups are affected more than others. The extent to which such a decrease in diversity persists will depend on the rate at which the treated area can be recolonized. This in turn will depend on the size of the treated area and what has happened in adjoining areas (Moore, 1967).

Norgaard (1976) believed that the components and dynamics of the socioeconomic system as it pertains to agricultural pest control are still little understood. Humans use their existing knowledge and materials according to market incentives, government regulations, social and political pressures, and a sense of responsibilities. Cost is often a prime factor in determining a course of action. Norgaard noted that solutions will come only by changing human behavior. He recommended the use of fewer and narrower-spectrum pesticides and the development of biological controls consistent to the ecosystem's dynamics. Accordingly, the most favorable results would come through a better comprehension of the ecosystem.

Control of tidal marsh pests seems to be moving in this direction. Many years ago, public criticism forced the termination of larvicide programs using organochloride compounds. By the early 1950s, the use of chlorinated hydrocarbons was eliminated in the southern and western United States. A series of court cases involving the use of DDT resulted in a ban throughout the country (National Academy of Science, 1976). Currently, OMWM practices are attempting to develop biological controls within the framework of tidal marsh dynamics.

Much remains to be done, however. Provost (in National Academy of Science, 1976) has provided an excellent description of the present status of the use of insecticides in biting-fly control in tidal marshes. Where there is no organized mosquito control, people protect themselves as best they can. Areawide control has become more and more dependent on complicated technology, and the quality of the control is determined by the fund of knowledge available. A sizable effort has been expended on an ad hoc basis. All too often, where demands for such control have developed, the personnel involved with such insecticide sprayings have known little (or nothing) about which mosquito species is involved, its behavior, or ecology. Provost believed that good mosquito control is available and should not be left in the hands of the uninformed.

Aedes sollicitans and *A. taeniorhynchus* are the two major species associated with the extensive salt marshes of the Atlantic and Gulf coasts. Accordingly, their biology and behavior should largely dictate control methods. The work of an organized mosquito-control program can be divided into the following components: education, preventive planning, surveillance, environmental manipulation, larviciding, and adult-iciding. Education is the most effective and least expensive way to eliminate mosquito breeding in urban areas. However, preventive planning, which eliminates some kinds of breeding sites, is not effective in areas where the major nuisance species originate on temporarily flooded sites such as tidal marshes. No amount of planning can prevent breeding if rain, thaw, or tide is the breeding determinant. Surveillance is an integral part of every control district's program: it involves locating mosquito sources, measuring and identifying the nuisance, and evaluating the control effort. Environmental manipulation can provide the most sure and permanent control by modifying the larval habitat to such an extent that breeding success is reduced. While the aquatic environment can be retained in an essentially natural condition, salt marsh mosquitoes can be controlled by proper drainage, flooding, or impounding of tidal lands. Such environmental manipulation is one of the most diligently applied mosquito-control methods. With the recent enactment of legislation in the coastal states, however, such control programs will be increasingly constrained by these laws, which are designed to protect the tidal areas from human modification.

Larviciding has been carried out in all the mosquito-control districts of the United States. Before the advent of DDT, oil and/or pyrethrum were used. Between 1946 and 1966, organic insecticides were used everywhere, although Paris Green (a copper-arsenite insecticide) was used in some southeastern marshes and small amounts of oil were still used in spot larviciding. Since 1966, largely as a reaction to the development of multiple resistance to organochloride insecticides, some mosquito-control districts have increasingly used oil/surfactant larvicides. Some districts have reverted to pyrethrum larvicides while others have turned to organo-phosphates, such as Abate and Dursban, which are presumably more environmentally acceptable. The use of larvicides is waning, however, because of the development of resistance, the lack of effective and economical substitutes for the available organic insecticides, and ecological concern over toxicants in the environment. In 1972, 21 to 23% of the district mosquito-control budgets was earmarked for larviciding. Adulticiding is not a general procedure. Most districts rely on spot control for reducing adult populations at specific sites. Malathion, an organophosphate, has been the most widely used adulticide, but Dibrom (another organophosphate) has become increasingly popular because it is not as toxic to fishes. While adulticides have not been extensively used in the northeast, about 10 to 20% of district mosquito-control budgets have been involved in the salt marsh areas of the southeast (National Academy of Science, 1976).

In summary, the strategy in mosquito control is to kill mosquitoes in such a way that produces the greatest relief at a minimum cost and with the least environmental disruption. The strategy is a reflection of the nature of the problem, whether it be man-induced or not. In states with extensive tidal marshes, the problem is not manmade. Controlling mosquitoes in such a situation is not easy because it is difficult to alter the terrain in a cost-effective fashion and to avoid ecological disruption. Before the advent of DDT, the basic strategy of mosquito control was the prevention of breeding (e.g., the alteration of suitable ovipositioning habitat) and secondly killing the larvae. DDT and related insecticides permitted a third form of response: adulticiding. Even though mosquitoes have developed resistance to many insecticides, and earlier insecticides were highly toxic to nontarget animals and persisted in the environment, Provost (in National Academy of Science, 1976) believed that organic insecticides will be useful everywhere and indispensable in some but not all areas. He stated that "wherever the major mosquito nuisance arises from terrain refractory to environmental manipulation for reasons physical, ecological, economic, or political, mosquitoes will be controlled with insecticides or they will not be controlled at all." If this be so, the future development of insecticides even more specific than Abate or the juvenile hormone mimic methoprene could herald another generation of even more environmentally acceptable insecticides. Better yet, the further development of open marsh water management, plus the development of pathogens specifically designed to infect mosquitoes and other forms of biological control, will further reduce and even eliminate the need for chemical control. One such pathogen might be a biological insecticide, the spores of a bacterium, *Bacillus thuringiensis* var. *israelensis* (BTI). A variant of the bacterium used regularly against gypsy moths, BTI is toxic only to mosquitoes, black flies, and a few closely related species. The sporulated cell of BTI contains an endotoxin that becomes lethal after ingestion and exposure to a larva's digestive tract.

Another group of biting flies that are even more voracious in the tidal marsh than the mosquitoes are the deer flies (family Tabanidae). Pechuman

(1972) has stated that little of a routine nature can be said about the control of horseflies and deer flies. Insecticides have been of little value in restricted areas, and applications over wide areas have been only moderately effective while increasing the danger to nontarget organisms. Insecticides have been more effective in controlling the larval stages than the adults, but damage to other organisms has been even greater (Jamnback and Wall, 1959).

The females deposit their eggs in clusters on vegetation close to moist or wet substrate (many over water). These sites may be leaves and stems of marsh grass and emergent vegetation (Axtell, 1976). In restricted areas, the removal of such vegetation could be useful in the control of deer flies. Such a procedure would not be practical, however, for the expansive areas of tidal marshes.

Most promising, at least in restricted areas, is a trapping device. Catts (1970) and Pechuman, Webb, and Teskey (1983) described traps that are very effective in capturing adult tabanids. Baited with dry ice, they consist of a pyramidal canopy of clear plastic with a lower apron of black polyethylene. Catts reported captures of 1,000 tabanids per hour during peak seasons, and the capture of large numbers of mosquitoes, punkies, snipe flies, black flies and stable flies. Subsequently, Catts and Hansens (1975) described an effective box trap. They recommended it over the canopy trap, as it is easier to build and maintain and does not require dry ice. Its shiny black sides contrast with its surroundings and absorb heat from the sun. This lures greenhead flies, which are attracted to glistening, warm targets.

Chapter 7

Oil Pollution

The increase in demand for petroleum products has been accompanied by an increase in oil spills resulting from ship groundings, spillages in transfer operations, and oil-contaminated refinery discharges. An enormous effort is under way to devise methods to prevent such spills, to handle them when they occur, and to assess the effects of oil contamination on the afflicted habitats and associated organisms. For a general coverage of the effects of oil spills in the marine environment, see the following published symposia: Cowell (1971); Beynon and Cowell (1974); Vernberg and Vernberg (1974); Baker (1976); Stevenson (1978); Neff and Anderson (1981); and the Ecological Study of the Amoco Cadiz Oil Spill (1982).

PETROLEUM HYDROCARBON INTERACTIONS

Vegetation

Effects of Single and Chronic Spills. A number of papers have described the effect of oil on marsh vegetation: the damage appears to depend on the species, kind of oil, season of year, and other variables. *Puccinellia maritima* took on a yellow cast, wilted in May, and subsequently died after heavy contamination from the Torrey Canyon spillage on the Cornwall (England) coast in March 1967. Sea pink (*Armeria maritima*), sea aster (*Aster tripolium*), sea plantain (*Plantago maritima*), annual sea-blite (*Suaeda maritima*), and glasswort (*Salicornia* spp.) were damaged to some degree in the same accident (Ranwell, 1968). Oil killed the upper parts of well-developed clumps of sea purslane (*Halimione portulacoides*), while sea rush (*Juncus maritimus*) appeared unaffected. The extent of damage was most evident in sites where the oil persisted into May (Cowell, 1969).

In the case of a spillage on the south coast of Wales at Martinshaven, Pembrokeshire, on January 12-13, 1967, the damage caused by a heavy layer of oil was intense and extensive (Cowell, 1969). Damage was less intense when spring tides carried the oil higher up the intertidal zone. *Puccinellia maritima* remained healthy up to the level of the January 14 tide. Most of the oil was deposited at that level and the species was totally killed. On two transects there were 37 and 14% mortalities of *Spartina anglica*. The presence of drainage channels on the marsh surface prevented higher mortality. At Bentlass, farther from the initial contact at Martinshaven, the vegetation was clearly damaged, mostly at levels below that of the January 14 high tide. In general, however, the effects of oil at all levels were less severe than at Martinshaven. *Puccinellia* was killed at the level of the high tide, while above and below that level, little harm was done. *S. anglica* was little affected, and there was some damage to *Festuca rubra. Spergularia media, Armeria maritima*, and *Halimione portulacoides* were slightly reduced in quantity, and the amount of *Aster tripolium* was substantially reduced. Annuals such as *Salicornia* spp. and *Suaeda maritima* were markedly diminished.

By June 1967, six months after the spillage of Kuwait crude oil on the Pembrokeshire coast, *S. maritima, Salicornia* spp., *H. portulacoides*, and filamentous green algae showed the greatest reduction in plant frequency, while *A. tripolium, Cochlearia* spp., *Triglochin maritima, Puccinellia maritima, J. gerardi, Limonium humile*, and *S. anglica* showed some reduction. The frequencies of *F. rubra, Plantago maritima, Armeria maritima, Artemisia maritima, Glaux maritima*, and *Spergularia* spp. were not significantly lower than the pre-spill levels. By June 1968 most species affected in 1967 showed some recovery, the exception being *T. maritima*, on which the ill effect had increased. The species with the greatest coverage—*F. rubra* in the upper marsh, *Puccinellia maritima* in the mid-marsh, and *S. anglica* in the lower marsh—had recovered more or less completely by June 1968 (Cowell and Baker, 1969). New, vigorous shoots appeared where oil had previously killed all above-ground parts (Dalby, 1969).

Salt marshes on the Brittany coast of France recovered from heavy oil coverage with only slight floral changes. Stands of *Agropyron pungens*,

J. maritimus, Scirpus maritimus, and *F. rubra* displayed vigorous growth, seemingly deriving nutrients from the oil. *J. gerardi, T. maritima, H. portulacoides,* and *Puccinellia maritima* were especially able to withstand the heaviest pollution. These observations by Stebbings (1970) are somewhat in variance with those of Ranwell 1968), Cowell (1969), and Cowell and Baker (1969). One possible explanation for the reported extent of floral damage may be the age of the oil and the time of year it comes in contact with the marsh vegetation (Cowell, 1969; Dalby, 1969; Stebbings, 1970).

Dalby (1969) and Baker (1971) have noted that perennials will generally survive better than annuals because new growth can form from large underground vegetative systems even after the leaves and shoots have been destroyed. Annuals can be expected to return, however, because they are opportunistic species adapted to shifting sites that are often of temporary duration. The low levels of two annuals, *Suaeda maritima* and *Salicornia* spp., noted by Cowell and Baker (1969) after the January 1967 spill, could not have been due to oil killing the seedlings because germination normally takes place in March. Instead, the oil appeared to inhibit germination, probably by preventing water and oxygen from entering the seeds. The sharp decline in filamentous algae was attributed to the large algal surface area and the absence of a cuticle. The observed rapid recovery was ascribed to a fast growth rate and asexual reproduction (Cowell and Baker, 1969).

Spartina alterniflora suffered heavy mortalities, persisting for over a year after the initial spill of Bunker C oil in February 1970 in Chedbucto Bay on the south coast of Nova Scotia. Recovery became evident two years later, and the flora had essentially returned to normal by 1975 (Thomas, 1978).

The damage to *S. alterniflora* caused by a spill of No. 6 fuel oil in the Hackensack Meadows of New Jersey in May 1976 resulted primarily from physical properties of the oil. The oil coating the plants prevented gaseous exchange, which caused the underground parts to suffocate. Mortality was highest when *S. alterniflora* plants were neither cut nor washed clean by the tides. Cutting soon after contamination was beneficial, reducing long-term physical damage despite the trampling that occurred (Dibner, 1978).

A similar pattern of cutting and removing the previous season's plant growth after a spill of No. 6 fuel oil in the lower Chesapeake Bay caused an immediate and substantial loss of primary production from the marsh. Such a loss was readily compensated by the significant increase in net productivity as expressed by the standing crop, increased stem density, and increased flowering success despite a decrease in mean plant height (Hershner and Moore, 1977). While cutting and burning had been recommended if vegetation was severely contaminated, Gundlach and IIayes (1978) suggested that such action be taken only as a last resort. They feared that heavy machinery and trampling by untrained personnel could exacerbate the damage and warned that burning would destroy the benthic community. They suggested that, where tidal action is strong or where there is normally extensive seasonal plant growth, physical marine processes will naturally clean the marsh.

A much different outcome followed a spill of the more refined No. 2 fuel oil adjacent to the Falmouth marshes in Massachusetts. The spill occurred on October 9, 1974. By October 23 the *Spartina, Salicornia,* and *Limonium* in Winsor Cove exhibited a brownish discoloration. Three years later *Spartina* was still completely absent from the lower marsh zone. Generally these lower marsh quadrats appeared to be subjected to a continual stress that retarded or restricted plant growth and regeneration. High concentrations of oil were found in the sediments wherever plant mortalities were high. The continual stress on the plants resulted from the slow chronic discharge from the sediments (Hampson and Moul, 1978).

Among experimental oilings carried out by various investigators, Slavin, Good, and Squiers (1975) found no significant difference in the dry weight of *S. alterniflora* between controls and test plots subjected to three different mosquito-larviciding oils. The evidence suggested that these oils may reduce production in *Spartina patens.* It was noted that there was more yellowing on the leaves of both species with oil applications. In contrast, when Lytle (1975) poured 15 gallons of Empire Mix crude oil into an intertidal pond in Mississippi with well-established growths of *S. alterniflora, Juncus roemerianus,* and *Distichlis spicata,* all the plants looked dead after ten days. Within three weeks new shoots were forming and recovery was good within two months. Some species that had not been present before the spill showed up in the oiled pond but not in the control pond.

Phytoplankton populations suffered reductions immediately following an oiling but displayed a subsequent resurgence (Lytle, 1975). Thirty days after the oiling there was a lower phytoplankton population and a higher zooplankton population in the oiled pond than in the control. As the oil dissipated, the zooplankton bloomed. During the following spring, both phytoplankton and zooplankton were more abundant in the oiled pond than in the control. By summer, phytoplankton in the oiled pond remained high while zooplankton became more abundant in the control pond.

When Bender et al. (1977) applied both fresh and artificially weathered South Louisiana crude oil to a mesohaline marsh off the York River, Virginia, phytoplankton rebounded to the level of the control within a week. The effects of initial reduction and stimulation were more acute for

Table 7-1. Standing crop of *Spartina alterniflora* from oiled and control plots in a York River, Virginia, marsh

	Sept. 1975		March 1976		June 1976		Sept. 1976	
	Live	*Dead*	*Live*	*Dead*	*Live*	*Dead*	*Live*	*Dead*
Control	426	189	37	416	424	452	657	441
Fresh oil	356	288	18*	522	154**	499	213**	244
Weathered oil	467	298	17**	634**	157**	561	267**	343

Source: From Bender, M. E., E. A. Shearls, R. P. Ayres, C. Hershner, and R. J. Huggett, 1977, *Ecological Effects of Experimental Oil Spills on Eastern Coastal Plain Estuarine Ecosystems*, 1977 Oil Spill Conference Proceedings, American Petroleum Institute Publ. 4284 Washington, D.C., pp. 505-509, by permission.
*Significant difference from control P < .05.
**Significant difference from control P < .01.

weathered crude than for fresh crude. There was no significant difference in the numbers of individuals and numbers of species of phytoplankton. Periphyton biomass was consistently higher in the marshes receiving oil than in the controls.

Oilings can very substantially depress production of *S. alterniflora*. Prior to the experimental application of oil, Lytle (1975) clipped a 1-square-meter plot in both the oiled and control ponds. Thirty days after the spill, the grass from both plots was cut. The weight of the 30-day growth was 173.2 g from the control and 96.9 g from the oiled pond. Bender et al. (1977) recorded *S. alterniflora* production in the oiled plots to be less than half the biomass of the control (Table 7-1).

De la Cruz, Hackney and Rajanna (1981) recorded a variable reduction in *Juncus roemerianus* biomass following single oilings applied in March. The monthly regrowth was completely suppressed following an application of 1,500 ml/m². Results of a 750 ml/m² application were also significantly different from the control, but not those of a dosage of 250 ml/m². Plants in the 1,500 ml oiled quadrat showed brownish color followed by early senescence and death. There was a definite and visible reduction in new growth, which was not evident in the 250- and 750- ml quadrats. The estimated relative production values/m² were as follows: control, 372 g; 250-ml oiled quadrat, 232 g; 750-ml oiled quadrat, 136 g; 1,500-ml oiled quadrat, 44 g (Figure 7-1).

However, not all research efforts recorded declines in marsh plant production. De Laune, Patrick, and Buresh (1979) added South Louisiana crude at the rate of 1, 2, 4, and 8 l/m² to enclosed 0.25-m² plots in a marsh of the Barataria Basin of Louisiana. The oil was added onto a 15-cm layer of water during May and the grass was harvested in September. The added oil did not significantly increase or decrease the above-ground biomas of *S. alterniflora*, nor was the second-year growth (as biomass measurement) significantly different. The numbers of new shoots and stem density were not affected (Table 7-2).

De Laune, Patrick, and Buresh (1979) observed no effect on biomass of *S. alterniflora* with oil applications of up to 32 liters/m^2 in a greenhouse study. They did record a depressed plant growth by a reduction in the number of new shoots developed after the first harvest at applications of 4 and 8 l/m^2. No new shoots formed at rates of 16 and 32 l/m^2. If a new shoot had to push through a film of oil, no new shoot was formed.

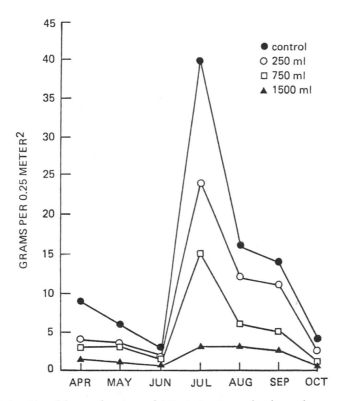

Figure 7-1. Monthly production of Mississippi marsh plants from repeatedly clipped quadrat after exposure to a single spill of 250, 750, and 1,500 ml Empire Mix crude oil per 0.25-m^2 quadrat in terms of dry biomass during spring and summer. (Natural growing period is April through July.) Periodic regression analyses showed that the 750- and 1,500-ml plots are significantly different from the control plot ($a = 0.05$); the 250-ml plot is not statistically significant from control. The maximum standard errors for each set of monthly samples are April, 0.92; May, 0.95; June, 0.42; July, 4.63; August, 6.5; September, 4.65; October, 0.70. *Source: After De la Cruz, A. A., C. T. Hackney, and B. Rajanna, 1981, Some effects of crude oil on a Juncus tidal marsh, Elisha Mitchell Sci. Soc. J. **97**:14–28, by permission.*

Table 7-2. Influence of crude oil on above-ground biomass, new shoots, and stem density of *S. alterniflora* in a Louisiana salt marsh

Crude Oil (l/m²)	Above-Ground Biomass (g/m²) 23 Sept. 1976	Above-Ground Biomass (g/m²) 16 Sept. 1977	New Shoots/m² 18 April 1977	Stem density/m² 16 Sept. 1977
0	2,000 ± 213	1,001 ± 133	116 ± 25	205 ± 30
1	1,908 ± 300	822 ± 72	102 ± 13	199 ± 19
2	2,015 ± 153	1,161 ± 277	111 ± 10	215 ± 21
4	1,819 ± 265	935 ± 110	101 ± 10	219 ± 2
8	1,832 ± 153	991 ± 162	98 ± 19	197 ± 20
LSD 0-05 Value	316	236	22	28

Source: From De Laune, R. D., W. H. Patrick, Jr., and R. J. Buresh, 1979, Effect of crude oil on a Louisiana *Spartina alterniflora* salt marsh, *Environ. Pollut.* **20**(1):21-31, by permission.

While Lytle (1975) and Bender et al. (1977) reported marked reductions in biomass and De Laune, Patrick, and Buresh (1979) recorded no significant changes in biomass of *S. alterniflora* following a heavy oiling, Baker (1971) observed a substantial enhancement of *Puccinellia maritima* biomass after the vegetation had been oiled with large amounts of Kuwait crude (Table 7-3). Baker noted that oiling can produce significant increases in shoot length and/or shoot numbers and dry weight for *P. maritima* as well as *Festuca rubra* and *Agrostis stolonifera*. One explanation may be the presence of growth-regulating compounds along with nutrients in the oil or available nutrients from oil-killed organisms.

While a single heavy oiling may not have an appreciable effect on vegetation, a number of such oilings are often damaging. Using Empire Mix and Saudi Arabian crude in a Mississippi *Juncus roemerianus* marsh, de la Cruz, Hackney, and Rajanna (1981) noted that single low levels of exposure to crude had only initial impact on productivity. In comparison to a steady increase in the number of culms in the control, there was an initial decrease in culms after one or two applications of oil, followed by an increase. With 4, 6, 8, and 10 doses of crude at monthly intervals, there was a drastic reduction in culms (Table 7-4). Correspondingly, the greater the number of oil applications, the slower the recovery in the number of culms and also biomass. After one year the quadrats that received low-level spills (0.5 to 1.2 l/m²) were fully recovered with biomass similar to the controls. Within two years, only the heaviest spills (3.6 to 6.0 l/m²) still contained 50% less plant biomass than the control. All plots had fully recovered by the third year.

Earlier, Nelson-Smith (1972) observed that chronic oil pollution usually produced insidious effects such as a lowering of the marsh surface through reduced or negative accretion rates caused by the killing of

Table 7-3.   Increase of dry weight of *Puccinellia maritima* following treatment with Kuwait atmospheric residue. Treated 23 April 1970; harvested 10 June 1970

Dosage	Mean dry wt, g/25 = cm quadrat[a]
Unoiled	5.4 ± 0.8
4 l/m^2	7.8 ± 1.4
8 l/m^2	11.7 ± 0.7

Source: From Baker, J. M., 1971, Studies on salt marsh communities, in *The Ecological Effects of Oil Pollution on Littoral Communities*, E. B. Cowell, ed., Institute of Petroleum, London, pp. 16-101, by permission.
[a]95% confidence limits.

vegetation. Dicks (1976) described two phases resulting from the chronic discharge of refinery effluents into Fawley marsh bordering Southampton Water in southern England. In 1950 the area was covered with a flourishing *S. anglica* community. During the 1951-1970 period, large areas of vegetation were killed and reduced to bare mud. Then the denuded area entered a recolonization phase and all the main marsh species became reestablished in various areas of the bare mud. The initial colonizers were *Salicornia* spp. and *Suaeda maritima* followed by *Aster tripolium* and *Halimione portulacoides*, with *Spartina* showing the least spread. This successional sequence appeared to be different from the typical sequence in nearby normal marshes. In this particular instance *Aster* and *Halimione* preceded *Spartina*, which normally follows *Salicornia* and *Suaeda*. Dicks suggested that the appearance of *Aster* and *Halimione* before *Spartina* was more the result of factors influencing the spread of the plants rather than a successional factor such as attainment of a suitable mud level. As pointed out earlier (Dalby, 1969; Baker, 1971), perennials are better able to survive than annuals, but annuals are opportunistic. *Salicornia, Suaeda,* and *Aster* are annuals that spread rapidly, whereas *Spartina* spreads by slower vegetative means and very poorly by seed germination. *Halimione* spreads by both seeds and vegetative means. In this particular Fawley marsh, the former *Spartina* marsh may not return and *Aster, Halimione, Suaeda,* and *Salicornia* will remain dominant as determined by seed distribution and seedling success. The pattern of recolonization may be the result of reduced oil spillage, improvements in effluent quality, and/or reduction in effluent volume. While milder winters may have helped enhance plant growth, Dicks (1976) believed that oil discharges have been reduced. This opinion was based on the idea that *Salicornia*, which is very sensitive to oil on the marsh surface, had expanded its distribution.

To determine the effect of repeated oilings, Baker (1973) oiled experimental plots 2, 4, 8, and 12 times at monthly intervals on three sites at Glamorgan, Wales. Recovery from up to four oilings was generally good, but considerable change resulted from 8 and 12 oilings (Figure 7-2).

Table 7-4. Monthly number of live culms in square-meter quadrats following initial clippings of a *Juncus roemarianus* marsh in Mississippi in January 1975 and varying frequency of simulated spills of 600 ml crude oil

No. of Spills (vol. Oil/Quadrat)	No. of Culms[a] before Spill	No. of Culms per Quadrat Following Spills[a]									
		Feb.	Mar.	Apr.	May	Jun.	July	Aug.	Sept.	Oct.	Nov.
0 (control)	244	235	311	315	334	336	349	388	375	343	388
1 (600 ml EMO)[b]	161	122	80	35	30	38	45	50	64	65	81
1 (600 ml SAO)[c]	192	125	109	121	118	132	159	191	190	207	230
2 (1.21 SAO)	198	197	110	103	97	94	142	186	182	198	242
4 (2.41 SAO)	208	150	101	82	65	58	61	80	82	80	89
6 (3.61 SAO)	174	100	68	65	52	35	23	19	11	12	11
8 (4.81 SAO)	178	129	101	97	62	36	37	18	73	9	9
10 (6.01 SAO)	201	119	101	110	75	38	26	12	9	12	10

Source: From De la Cruz, A. A., C. T. Hackney, and B. Rajanna, 1981, Some effects of crude oil on a *Juncus* tidal marsh, *Elisha Mitchell Sci. Soc. J.* **97**(1):14–28, by permission.

[a]Culms means all above-ground material, that is, *Juncus* leaves and stems of associated grasses.

[b]EMO = Empire Mix oil.

[c]SAO = Saudi Arabian oil.

Changes in species dominance or exposure of bare mud persisted into 1972, four years after the experiment was initiated. The more heavily oiled *S. anglica* areas recovered nicely, mainly through vegetative recolonization from untreated areas. In contrast, in the mid marsh, *Puccinellia maritima* had made hardly any recovery on the plots oiled 8 and 12 times. Such plots were bare except for patches of *Spergularia media, Armeria maritima, Triglochin maritima, Glaux maritima,* and *Salicornia* spp. In the upper marsh, after four years, *Juncus maritimus* continued to show a marked reduction. No bare mud was exposed, however, because of the dense mat of dying *Juncus* stems and coverage by the rapid invasion of the creeping stems of *Agrostis stolonifera.*

Salt marsh plants have displayed a wide range of susceptibility to typical crude oils. Therophytes (e.g., *Salicornia*) and chamaephytes (e.g., *Halimiones portulacoides*) are more susceptible than hemicryptophytes and geophytes. Baker (1979) recognized various tolerance groups: group I, very susceptible (*S. maritima, Salicornia* spp.); group II, susceptible (*H. portulacoides, J. maritimus*); group III, intermediate (*S. anglica, P. maritima, Festuca rubra*); group IV, resistant (*A. stolonifera, A. maritima, Plantago maritima, T. maritima*); group V, very resistant (*Oenanthe lachenalii*). This last species is not an important member of British salt marsh vegetation (Chapman, 1960, Baker, 1979).

Levasseur and Jory (1982) studied the process of reestablishment of vegetative cover following the Amoco Cadiz spill of 16 March 1978 on the northwest coast of France. At some sites, the destruction of the vegetation was total. These areas remained sterile, and thus a natural reestablishment of vegetation was not considered likely. Successful revegetation occurred after the area was planted, however, indicating that the germination phase had been inhibited. These plants trapped sediments, which in turn allowed seeds, brought in by the tide, to become established, which enhanced species diversity. Such diversity would not have occurred without the experimental plantings. In sites of natural colonization, a similar situation occurred among the layers of therophytes (annuals).

When Levasseur and Jory (1982) compared the current state of the vegetation with the vegetation immediately after the spill, they noted that the revegetation occurred in numerous places by means of a spatial redistribution of species. Such redistribution was attributed to two factors. First, the surviving plants, initially resistant, did not have the capabilities of vegetative extension sufficient to revegetate the denuded areas, whereas other species, although originally sensitive to the oil and the clean-up perturbations, were able to perform this function in secondary colonization. This accounted for the differences observed between the original and subsequent composition of flora at the site. Second, species that were completely resistant or partially resistant became sensitive to the chronic pollution to which the marsh had been subjected. As their populations declined, other species, which had been confined to the outside of the densest clones, were able to spread inward. Two such species, *Puccinellia maritima* and *H. portulacoides*, covered the surface of the soil by means of stolons, thus circumventing the below-ground stems or rhizomes, which remained long after the death of the plants.

Mode of Action of Oil.   When working with experimental oil spills in a *Juncus* marsh, de la Cruz, Hackney, and Rajanna (1981) observed a high level of oil residue in plant tissues three months after exposure to a single heavy dosage. The residue was reduced after six months, and none remained after nine months. In contrast, very little or no residue was detected three months after applications of lesser amounts of oil. However, oil residue levels had increased in plant tissues by 6 months and traces

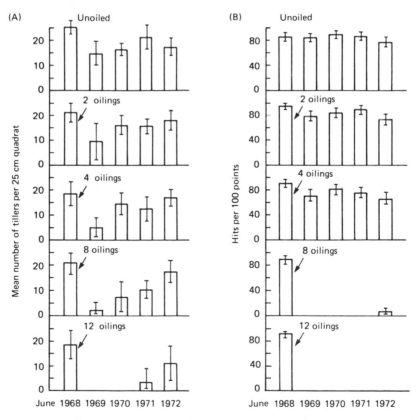

Figure 7-2.   Effects of successive oil sprayings on *(A) Spartina anglica* at Crofty, *(B) Puccinellia maritima* at Weobley Castle, and *(C) Juncus maritimus* and *(D) Agrostis stolonifera* at Llanrhidian, Wales with 95% confidence limits. *Source:*

were still evident after 12 months. Below-ground plant tissues showed traces of oil only in the surface layers and none below the 10-cm depth. De la Cruz, Hackney, and Rajanna were of the opinion that oil incorporation in marsh plants tended to be instantaneous after an acute spill, probably due to the lipophilic nature of the plant. The delayed uptake under low-level application suggested absorption and internal mobilization.

Nelson-Smith (1972) commented that weathered oil acts mechanically by smothering. Ranwell (1968) observed that mortality in marsh vegetation is highest when fresh oil adheres to actively growing vegetation. Baker (1970) noted that viscosity and surface tension influence the rate at which an oil spreads over and penetrates into a plant. Baker also perceived that the toxicity of oils varied according to the content of low-boiling compounds, unsaturated compounds, aromatics, and acids. Environmental conditions affect the extent of toxicity. If oil is ap-

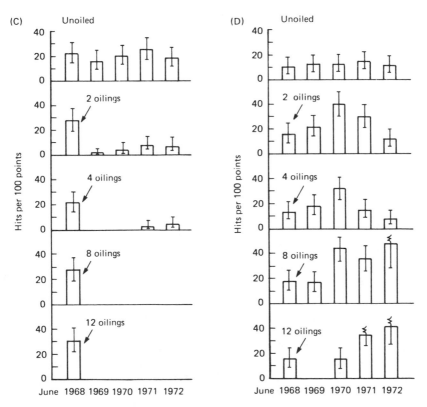

After Baker, J. M., 1973, Recovery of salt marsh vegetation from successive oil spillages, Environ. Pollut. **4:**223–230, *by permission.*

plied on a sunny day when the stomata are open, it can kill plants. When plants are exposed at night, the stomata are closed and the plants are not affected.

The oil appears to act by physically interfering with gas exchange. It also impedes transpiration by blocking stomata. The rate at which oil penetrates into the plant, and to what extent, depends on the type of oil, the plant species, the part of the plant initially oiled, the thickness of the cuticle, and the number of stomata.

Once in the plant, oils travel through the intercellular spaces, and, to a lesser degree, through the vascular system. The penetration of hydrocarbon molecules damages all membranes, causing the contents to leak and allowing oil to enter the cells. Respiration rates are variable, and any rate increase may be the result of mitochondrial damage. Oils also reduce photosynthesis by disrupting the chloroplasts; the amount of reduction depends on the type and amount of oil and the plant species. Another means of inhibition may be caused by accumulation of photosynthetic end products brought about by inhibition of outward translocation from the leaf. The oil's physical interference probably inhibits translocation (Baker 1970, 1971).

Flowering can be appreciably diminished if plants are oiled when the flower buds are forming. Flowers, if oiled, rarely produce seeds (Baker, 1971). Baker (1970, 1971) has inferred that germination may be inhibited by oil entering the seed and killing the embryo or by blocking the entry of oxygen and water. In 1979, however, Baker stated that seeds are not affected by oil. This point needs to be clarified. Quoting others, Baker (1971) reported that low concentrations of heavy oil inhibit germination, as do high concentrations of lighter oils, which can easily penetrate the seed cover.

Oil spills may have a lethal, inhibitory, or stimulatory effect—or even no apparent effect—on marsh vegetation. At the same time, the vegetation can serve as a trap, holding the oil as it comes ashore (Ranwell, 1968; Dalby, 1969; Stebbings, 1970; Nelson-Smith, 1972; Dibner, 1978). Dalby (1969) observed that marshes may be heavily damaged through smothering by large amounts of oiled vegetation, which have trapped oil at the initial oil stranding and then float to a new site. However, the toxic effects of the oil would probably be reduced by weathering.

Dibner (1978) suggested ways of handling trapped oil. His recommendations for clean-up were directed primarily at the more viscous and less toxic crude oils. Initial clean-up should consist of low-impact methods. Wherever possible, natural flushing should be allowed to clean the plants. Those that remain heavily oiled should be treated in such a way that their internal tissues are exposed to the atmosphere to prevent suffocation. This is usually done by cutting or burning. The success of cutting for reducing long-term plant damage depends on such factors as the biology of the contaminated species, the elapsed time between contamination and cutting, the season when cutting occurs, and the character of the oil. Cutting soon after oiling is usually beneficial, reducing long-term damage despite the trampling that occurs. Trampling does, however, enhance the chances of erosion of the marsh surface, especially in high-tidal energy areas such as the creek banks.

Sediments and Microbial and Meiofaunal Populations

Most oil has been observed to be adsorbed on the dead plant tissue and the component of the soil surface (DeLaune, Patrick, and Buresh 1979; Milan and Whelan, 1979). The amounts of aromatics, alkanes, and cycloalkanes adsorbed are large compared to those adsorbed at an uncontaminated site. When the grass dies, it is either incorporated into the sediment or enters the food chain in the form of detritus. Microbial activity breaks down the alkanes in the sediments, while the aromatics and cycloalkanes are more resistant to metabolic breakdown. In this way the sediments accumulate the latter two in greater quantities than that of the more labile alkanes. The aromatics and cycloalkanes can be released back into the water column through various sediment-reworking processes, such as waves, tidal action, bioturbation, and human activity (Milan and Whelan, 1979).

De la Cruz, Hackney, and Rajanna (1981) noted that the persistence of adsorbed oil on *Juncus roemerianus* mats reduced plant decomposition by 52%. They noted that traces of oil found in the below-ground plant tissues were limited to the surface layers and that there was some horizontal movement in the first 10 cm. In contrast, in another Mississippi marsh, Lytle (1975) observed a rapid movement of crude oil into the deeper sediments, 42 cm in 18 days. No change in the aliphatic hydrocarbons was observed. Later samples showed a gradual degradation of the crude oil, with the loss only of the lower-molecular-weight hydrocarbons after 12 months. Lee et al. (1981) found that the amounts of oil remained high in the sediments of a Georgia marsh for the first 45 days after an experimental oiling with No. 5 fuel oil. During the next 100 days, there was a rapid decline, and they estimated the half-life of the oil in the sediments to be 100 days. Such decreases in oil concentrations were attributed to weathering, which included evaporation, biodegradation, and photochemical oxidation.

As observed earlier and as Baker (1971) pointed out, oil can directly affect the soil as it penetrates the substrate. Baker observed that the use of emulsifiers facilitates the penetration of oil. She also noted that plants

Table 7-5.   Effect of a layer of crude oil on the overlying water upon the release of nutrients from the sediments of a Louisiana marsh into the overlying water after 28 days

	Concentration in Overlying Water ($\mu g/ml$)	
Nutrient	No Oil Layer	Oil Layer
Fe^{2+}	<0.1	2.3
Mn^{2+}	<0.1	2.7
$NH_4 - N$	<0.1	24.6

Source: From De Laune, R. D., W. H. Patrick, Jr., and R. J. Buresh, 1979, Effect of crude oil on a Louisiana *Spartina alterniflora* salt marsh, *Environ. Pollut.* **20**(1):21-31, by permission.

do not put out adventitious roots in oiled soils but do so either above or below the oiled layer.

Oil also affects soil indirectly by preventing the downward diffusion of oxygen into the roots. Normally, because of such gaseous diffusion, *Spartina* and other vegetation can live in anaerobic soils. Oiled stems and leaves will reduce or prevent such diffusion, causing an increase of toxic reduced ions (Baker, 1971).

De Laune, Patrick, and Buresh (1979) observed another indirect effect. In unstirred sediments, the lack of oxygen due to the oil barrier on the water surface caused the release of iron, manganese, and ammonium ions from the sediments to the water column. This resulted in sharp chemical changes between the sediments and the overlying water (Table 7-5).

Several studies have attempted to assess the effect of oil pollution on the organic carbon content of marsh sediments. Whelan, Ishmael, and Bishop (1976) compared oil fields in Louisiana to adjoining natural marshes to determine the effects of long-term chronic low-level petroleum influxes. They noted that the molecular distribution of alkane hydrocarbons was essentially the same in the control sites as it was in the oiled marshes. Surface sediments in the oil fields and control sites demonstrated little difference in molecular distribution of the indigenous hydrocarbons. No significant difference was observed in the amount of extractable organic matter or the amounts of hydrocarbons between oil fields and control sites (Table 7-6).

Whelan, Ishmael, and Bishop (1976) reported the evidence of microbial degradation of petroleum hydrocarbons. The Carbon 17 (C17)-to-pristane ratios in the oil field sediments was found to be significantly lower than that in the sediments of the control marshes. Bacterial processes seem to discriminate against branched-chain alkanes that are more abundant in petroleum than most biological lipids. In this way residues of branched-chain hydrocarbons such as pristane appear in sediments where selective

Table 7-6. The concentrations of dissolved organic carbon in the interstitial waters of the Leeville and Bully Camp oil fields of southern Louisiana and adjoining pristine marshes

Site	Concentration (mg C/l)	
	Average	*Range*
Freshwater natural marsh	42 ± 3	23-59
Freshwater oiled marsh	60 ± 4	30-102
Saltwater natural marsh	18 ± 3	4-42
Saltwater oiled marsh	37 ± 3	10-59

Source: After Whelan, T., III, J. T. Ishmael, and W. S. Bishop, 1976, Long term chemical effects of petroleum in South Louisiana wetlands. I. Organic carbon in sediments and waters, *Mar. Pollut. Bull.* 7:150-155.

bacterial degradation has partially removed straight-chain molecules. The high levels of dissolved organic carbon (DOC) in oil field marsh sediments may result from microbial degradation of petroleum into lower-molecular-weight organic compounds that are more soluble in water. Another explanation suggested by Whelan, Ishmael, and Bishop (1976) may be the direct solution of petroleum within the sediment sequence. However, due to the C17-to-pristane ratios and changes in microbial populations, microbial degradation is more important than the slower physical dissolution.

Lee et al. (1981) also found evidence of microbial degradation. This occurred more rapidly in oiled sediments (35 ng/g sediment per day) than in clean sediments (5 ng/g sediment per day) of the Georgia marsh site. Although Whelan, Ishmael, and Bishop (1976) found no appreciable difference in DOC between natural and oiled marshes, Hood et al. (1975) found significant differences in the concentrations of hydrocarbons between a pristine Louisiana marsh and an adjacent oiled marsh. The averages for the pristine and oiled marsh were 0.1835 mg/g and 0.5456 mg/g of dry sediment, respectively. While there were significant differences, the variability within sample periods was considerable. The ratio of hydrocarbon levels to total lipids within the two environments provided a more consistent and significant indicator of hydrocarbons.

Although Hood et al. (1975) found the difference between the bacterial biomasses at the two sites to be significant only at the 50% level, they recorded a highly significant (99%) difference between the two sites for the hydrocarbonoclastic bacteria to total bacteria ratio; this appeared to be a more consistent and valid indicator than the absolute number of hydrocarbonoclastic bacteria (Table 7-7). A regression analysis revealed a high correlation between concentrations of hydrocarbons and the ratio of hydrocarbonoclastic to total bacteria ($r = 0.87$), and between the relative

Table 7-7.   Ratio (expressed as percentage) of hydrocarbonoclastic bacteria to total heterotrophic aerobic bacteria in pristine and oil field salt marsh sediments of southern Louisiana[a]

Sample Period, 1973–1974	Pristine Marsh	Oil Field Marsh
June	20.5	16.1
August	1.8	9.4
October	7.6	35.9
December	2.5	7.0
February	1.0	8.6
April	0.01	11.2
June	0.1	6.6
Average	4.8	13.5

Source: From Hood, M. A., W. S. Bishop, Jr., F. W. Bishop, S. P. Meyers, and T. Whelan III, 1975, Microbial indicators of oil-rich salt marsh sediments, *Appl. Microbiol.* **30:**982–987, by permission.
[a]90% level of confidence.

amounts of hydrocarbons (ratio of hydrocarbon levels to extractable lipids) and the ratio of hydrocarbonoclastic to total bacteria ($r = 0.77$).

The average relative abundance of hydrocarbonoclastic and chromogenic bacteria as well as the ratio of different colony-forming units (CFUs) to total CFUs were significantly different between the two environments. Sediments from the oil field marsh showed a significantly (98% level) lower concentration of pigmented bacterial types than sediments from the pristine marsh. The number of different CFUs was significantly higher (90% level) in the oiled marsh than in the pristine marsh (Figure 7-3). The microbial diversity index for the oil field marsh was significantly higher (98% level) than for the pristine marsh (Table 7-8).

Using both fresh and artifically weathered Southern Louisiana crude oil, Kator and Herwig (1977) found that aerobic heterotrophic bacteria were the dominant autochthonous bacterial populations assayed by viable count. The mean numbers were 5.3×10^8, 8.6×10^8, and 4.2×10^8 CFUs per gram of wet sediment for unweathered oil, weathered oil, and control plots, respectively. The petroleum-degrading bacteria increased rapidly in both oiled plots in a matter of days, with a significant difference between the oiled plots and the control. The mean numbers of petroleum-degrading bacteria in the unweathered oiled plot, weathered oiled plot, and control were 3.6×10^6, 6.2×10^6, and 1.5×10^6 CFUs per gram of wet sediment, respectively. The proportion of petroleum-degrading to heterotrophic bacteria was 0.04% in the control and rose to 0.7 and 1.4% for the unweathered and weathered oiled plots, respectively.

A computer analysis by Kator and Herwig (1977) indicated that the petroleum-degrading bacteria shared a greater degree of similarity with each other than with the heterotrophs. Based on bacterial cell mass, conversion efficiency of hydrocarbons to all carbon, and the amount of carbon available in spilled oil, the volume of oil added could readily account for the observed duration of enrichment in petroleum-degrading bacteria. Kator and Herwig also observed that the weathered oil tended to support greater levels of petroleum-degrading bacteria than the unweathered oil. They surmised that such a reaction was due to the greater loss of unweathered oil from the marsh as a result of its differential volatilization and greater mobility.

In addition to changes in bacterial biomass, there are modifications in microbial ability to fix nitrogen on chronically oil-polluted marsh surfaces. Thomson and Webb (1984) used acetylene reduction activity (ARA) as a measure of the nitrogen-fixing ability in each control and oil-treated plot

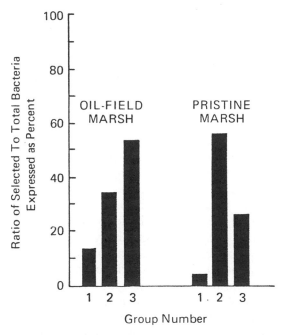

Figure 7-3. Relative abundance of bacterial groups in oil field and pristine marsh sediments from Louisiana. Group 1, ratio of hydrocarbonoclastic to total bacteria; group 2, ratio of chromogenic to total bacteria; group 3, ratio of different CFU to total CFU. *Source: After Hood, M. A., W. S. Bishop, Jr., F. W. Bishop, S. P. Meyers, and T. Whelan III, 1975, Microbial indicators of oil-rich salt marsh sediments, Appl. Microbiol.* **30:**982–987, by permission.

Table 7-8. Bacterial diversity index of pristine and oil field salt marsh sediments in southern Louisiana[a]

Sample Period, 1973–1974	Pristine Marsh	Oil Field Marsh
August	3.48	4.12
October	3.18	3.48
December	4.05	4.42
February	3.61	4.51
April	3.71	4.62
June	3.75	4.81

Source: From Hood, M. A., W. S. Bishop, Jr., F. W. Bishop, S. P. Meyers, and T. Whelan III, 1975, Microbial indicators of oil-rich salt marsh sediments, *Appl. Microbiol.* **30:**982–987, by permission.

Diversity index $= - \Sigma (N_i/N) (\log_2 N_i - \log_2 N)$, where N is the number of total colony units, and N_i is the number of individual units within the ith colony type.

[a]98% confidence level.

in a Virginia tidal marsh, although rates varied greatly within zones and from week to week. Seasonal patterns of ARA for treated and untreated marshes differed, particularly in late summer. Peaks of activity in control zones were observed during January, July, and early fall. In contrast, the highest rates in the experimental plots occurred in midspring and midsummer. Evidence suggested that the heterotrophic bacteria were the main contributors of nitrogen fixation rather than the filamentous blue-green algae.

The annual acetylene reduction activity (ARA) on the upper mud flat and *Spartina alterniflora* edge (zone A) for the oiled plots was considerably lower (0.11 ± 0.54 nmol/gm dry weight/hr) than for the control plots (0.32 ± 0.56 nmol). The open mud areas showed no signs of ARA. The mean annual values for the upper *S. alterniflora* (zone B) and *Juncus roemerianus* (zone C) were very similar for both the controls (zone B, 0.21 ± 0.39; zone C, 0.24 ± 0.32 nmol/gm dry wt/hr and for the oiled plots (zone B, 0.91 ± 1.35; zone C, 1.0 ± 0.53 nmol/gm dry wt/hr). Variation in zone C was less for both control and oiled plots and ARA in the oiled plots was much higher in both zones in contrast to the controls. The uppermost area of *J. roemerianus*, *Spartina patens*, and *Distichlis spicata* (zone D) showed no difference between oiled (0.58 ± 0.74) and control plots (0.73 ± 0.82 nmol/gm dry wt/hr). Rates throughout the year were similar to those of the *J. roemerianus* plots (zone C).

The considerable variation in nitrogen-fixation values within each zone over short periods was due, in part, to the patchiness of sediment composition, variation in tidal inundation, and differences in abundance of rhizomes and microflora among plots. There were similar acetylene reduction rates in sediment areas covered by filamentous green algae in both treated and control marshes. Thus, chronic oil pollution was considered to have no apparent effect on sediment-surface fixation rates.

The reduction of rates in the oiled plots of zone A may have resulted from the toxic effects of oil accumulation and from the increase in unconsolidated sediments due to plant mortalities. The rates of oiled plots in zones B, C, and D, in contrast to the depressed rates of zone A, were higher than the control rates during May, July, August, and September, especially for zones B and C. For comparison, the average rates were as follows: zone B oil, 53.6 versus control, 4.5 (μmol) $C_2H_4/m^2/hr$ and zone C oil, 51.2 versus control, 9.0 μmol C_2H_4. Such significant differences in average rates suggested an enhancement of ARA potential in zones B and C during the spring and summer due to chronic oil pollution and at higher temperatures. Thomson and Webb (1984) postulated that hydrocarbon-oxidizing bacterial populations, sustained by oil accumulation in treated transects in spring and through the summer, may have produced a greater amount of suitable carbon substrates for nitrogen fixers than would normally occur in the marsh. Such increased substrates would support greater nitrogen-fixation rates during the warmer months when depleted natural carbon substrates would normally limit the extent of nitrogen fixation. They suggested, however, that the estimated destruction of marsh vegetation stems, rhizomes, and roots, where much of the nitrogen fixation takes place, may reduce total marsh nitrogen fixation to a degree that would offset the increased contribution due to the greater supply of oxidizable substrates from chronic oil pollution.

Not only are bacterial populations modified by oil additions, but Meyers et al. (1973) also reported that oil contamination in the Barataria Bay area of southeastern Louisiana significantly altered the composition of the yeast community (Table 7-9). It was suggested that the water-soluble and volatile components of the oil may influence such a pattern. There was also evidence of a shift toward an asexual hydrocarbonoclastic flora. In addition, the evidence suggested a retarded cellulose degradation brought on by the volatiles in the oil, which inhibited the cellobiose-utilizing species, such as *Pichia spartinae*. Such a phenomenon could affect the production of a microbial food source for herbivores.

Meyers et al. (1973) observed a great enhancement of a number of yeast species in the presence of crude oil (Table 7-9). Certain yeast species, such as *Candida tropicalis* and *Endomycopsis lipolytica*, which are normally associated with chronically oiled habitats, displayed rates of oxygen uptake twice that of the most active indigenous species (*Pichia ohmeri*).

These various data from Meyers et al. (1973), Hood et al. (1975), and Kator and Herwig (1977) support the view that each marsh environment is composed of a distinctly unique microbial community structure. There

Table 7-9. Yeast populations in Barataria Bay, Louisiana, marshland sediments before and after one-year controlled enrichment with oil

	Percent of Total Population	
Species	Before	After
Pichia spartinae	15-40	<10
P. saitoi	20-30	<10
Kluyveromyces drosophilarum	10-25	<10
P. ohmeri	<10	20-30
Trichosporon sp.	<10	15-30
Rhodotorula sp.	<10	20-30
Cryptococcus sp.	<15	<10
Sporobolomyces sp.	<15	<10
Mean population[a]	7,800	17,400

Source: From Meyers, S. P., D. G. Ahearn, S. Crow, and N. Berner, 1973, The impact of oil on microbial marshland ecosystems, in *The Microbial Degradation of Oil Pollutants*, D. G. Ahearn and S. P. Meyers, eds., Publ. No. LSU OSG-73-01, Center for Wetland Resources, Louisiana State University, Baton Rouge.

[a]Based on the number of colony-forming units (CFUs)/cm^3 sediment, 72 samples analyzed quarterly.

is a shift from a cellulolytic type of bacterial community based on cellulose to one based on hydrocarbons. It has been suggested that such a shift may reflect a system that contains a greater variety of microbial habitats. Under these circumstances, the levels of hydrocarbons in such an oil field marsh may represent a nutrient enrichment where less resistant carbon may be limiting (Hood et al. 1975).

The disruption and alteration of cellulose (and chitin) can substantially alter the basis of the food web. According to Myers et al. (1973), organisms with the dispersant properties and enzymatic capacities for rapid attack on hydrocarbons are rare. In the absence of such rapid biodegradation, it is reasonable to expect that the physical coating of oil over microbial substrates will block sites for enzymatic attack on detritus. Following volatilization of the oil, the residue will also induce anaerobic conditions, which will not only affect the microbial community but undoubtedly alter the meiofaunal populations.

One study of meiofauna suggests that oil contamination has no obvious or pronounced effect. Fleeger and Chandler (1983) applied South Louisiana crude to plots of creek-bank levee *Spartina alterniflora.* Meiofauna samples were taken 1 to 3 hours before spraying the crude oil and again at 2, 5, 10, 20, 30, 60, 95, and 144 days after application. The meiofauna was dominated by nematodes and copepods. There were seasonal changes in species composition and in the relative abundance of the copepod fauna. Considerable variation in density was observed from collection to collection among most of the taxa. The introduction of crude oil did not cause any apparent decline in the densities of any meiofaunal groups. Higher densities of nematodes and copepods were attained from 5 to 60 days after the oil application. Fleeger and Chandler found this particularly surprising, as earlier investigators had observed extensive declines in the copepod populations following heavy oil applications. They suggested that the observed copepod increases may have resulted from increases in oil-degrading microbial populations (See Meyers et al., 1973; Kator and Herwig, 1977). The expansion in copepod numbers was caused by significant increases in *Enhydrosoma woodini*.

Species diversity values and evenness were very similar in both oiled and control plots. Although three rare species disappeared from the oiled plots shortly after oiling, there were no genera oil-induced fatalities and no significant declines in populations. What differences there were resulted from the change in relative abundance caused by the increase in *E. woodini*. This difference persisted until day 144, when the density of copepods was significantly lower. The community structure displayed a short-term early reduction in species and a longer increase in density followed by a decline. On the whole, Fleeger and Chandler (1983) observed that the meiofauna must have a high tolerance to hydrocarbon stress and low oxygen levels since oil remains in the marsh sediments and degrades slowly. This may not be too surprising, as marsh sediments have low oxygen levels and high carbon content. It would be interesting to see whether the population densities were restored following the decline on day 144.

Macro Invertebrates

General Effects.   Invertebrates respond in a variety of ways to oil spills, depending on the nature of the oil, when it contaminates, and the species affected. Lee et al. (1981) found three responses to a November experimental heavy oil spill of No. 5 fuel oil in a Georgia marsh: increase, decrease, and no change. Immediately following the spill there was an influx of the mud snail, *Ilyanassa obsoleta*, in the oiled site, presumably to feed on the dead animals created by the spill. By the following spring, the density of mud snails in oiled areas decreased to less than 1 snail per square meter, while control site densities increased to $33/m^2$. Juvenile snails were found in the control site but not in the oiled area. The number of periwinkles, *Littorina irrorata*, decreased in the oiled area to 2 animals/m^2 but increased from 3 to 16/m^2 in the control site. Five months after the spill, periwinkle density increased to 16/m^2, due to recolonization by juveniles. Lee et al. noted no change in the densities or the biomass of *Uca pugnax*, *Geukensia demissa*, and *Crassostrea virginica* after the spill.

Table 7-10. Number of species and species diversity index from oiled and control stations in Chedbucto Bay, Nova Scotia

	No. of Species (Diversity Index[a])	
	Oiled	*Control*
Sedimentary shores		
Station 2	13 (0.04)	17 (0.10)
Station 4	9 (0.04)	13 (0.05)
Rocky shores		
Station 1	29 (0.56) (0.30)	30 (0.26) (0.76)
Station 3	23 (0.34)	33 (0.52)

Source: From Thomas, M., 1978, Comparison of oiled and unoiled intertidal communities in Chedbucto Bay, Nova Scotia, *Canada Fish Res. Board J.* **35**(5):707-716, by permission.

[a]Shannon-Weiner diversity index, based on abundance as a measure of importance.

Thomas (1978) carried out a comprehensive study of a spill of Bunker C oil in February 1970 in Chedbucto Bay, on the south coast of Nova Scotia. The spill caused heavy mortality of the soft-shelled clam *Mya arenaria* in the subtidal area where the oil cover was extensive, but recovery was consistent. In general, Thomas found no significant difference in the distribution of intertidal species between oiled and nonoiled sites. However, there was a very consistent difference in species diversity, as shown by the numbers of species in oiled versus control sites (Table 7-10). While typically there is a marked difference between oiled and control sites immediately after a spill, the difference at Chedbucto Bay persisted for six years even though the shores were essentially free of oil. The overall difference between oiled and control sites was highly significant but no one level, group of levels, or stations showed significant differences. Thomas found that diversity indices were not useful due to variable results, so he suggested biomass as an effective comparative measure of species importance (Table 7-11). The data showed that floral biomass (algae and flowering plants) was significantly lower at the oiled sites. Among the fauna, the differences were generally less noticeable.

Specifically, Thomas found significantly larger populations of three gastropods, *Littorina obtusata*, *L. saxatilis*, and *Thais lapillus*, at the control sites. In contrast, the opposite trend was observed for *Mytilus edulis*, *Littorina vincta*, and *Gammarus oceanicus*. The periwinkle *Littorina littorea* was equally abundant throughout but showed significant length, weight, and length-to-weight ratio differences between oiled and control sites. After recovering from the initial heavy mortality, *Mya arenaria* became equally abundant throughout. However, it was significantly heavier and longer at the control sites while the equally abundant *L.*

Table 7-11. Abundance and biomass data for Chedbucto Bay, Nova Scotia, study stations

	Station 1		Station 2		Station 3		Station 4	
	Oiled	*Control*	*Oiled*	*Control*	*Oiled*	*Control*	*Oiled*	*Control*
Fauna								
Individuals/m²	14,776	1,963	17	157	144	1,136	8	103
Fresh biomass (g/m²)	59	58	13	17	67	3	5	190
Decalcified dry biomass (g/m²)	11.9	10.3	2.7	4.0	9.0	0.4	0.9	17.1
Ash-free biomass (g/m²)	8.0	7.8	2.3	2.3	6.2	0.4	0.7	9.6
Flora								
Fresh biomass (g/m²)	2,684	6,498	337	2,578	710	4,941	1,862	3,542
Dry biomass (g/m²)	615	1,787	69	455	143	1,089	315	600
Ash-free dry biomass (g/m²)	437	1,453	44	359	109	852	276	443

Source: From Thomas, M., 1978, Comparison of oiled and nonoiled intertidal communities in Chedbucto Bay, Nova Scotia, *Canada Fish. Res. Board J.* **35**(5):707–716, by permission.

Table 7-12. Length and weight data and population density for *Littorina littorea* and *Mya arenaria* collected from oiled and control stations in Chedbucto Bay, Nova Scotia

	Mean Length (cm)	Mean Weight (g)	No./m²
Littorina littorea			
Overall oiled	1.64	1.6	284.7
Overall control	1.41	1.1	568.0
Mya arenaria			
Overall oiled	2.76	3.2	126
Overall control	3.34	7.3	119

Source: After Thomas, M., 1978, Comparison of oiled and nonoiled intertidal communities in Chedbucto Bay, Nova Scotia, *Canada Fish. Res. Board J.* **35**(5):707-716, by permission.

littorea was significantly longer and heavier at the oiled sites (Table 7-12). Yet both displayed a slower increase in weight per unit length at the oiled sites than at the control locations.

After six years, sediments from the oiled sites still contained high concentrations of oil—up to 2.5% at a lagoonal site at high-tide level. Oil concentrations in animals were also higher at the oiled sites, but not significantly so. Wherever oil concentrations were particularly high, there continued to be above-normal mortalities among clams (*Mya*).

Upon completion of his studies, encompassing the organisms living in subtidal and intertidal rocky and sedimentary areas, Thomas (1978) concluded that Bunker C oil was clearly implicated in the mortality of several dominant and important species in these habitats.

Bender et al. (1977) studied the effects of experimental applications of fresh and artifically weathered South Louisiana crude on a York River, Virginia, marsh. They reported that numbers of benthic animals—including nereid polychaete worms, insect larvae, and amphipods—declined after both kinds of oiling. For example, a tremendous increase of amphipods in the control plots at the 20th week after oiling was not observed in the oiled plots. By the 39th week, however, numbers of amphipods were similar in both oiled plots and control plots (Figure 7-4). *Melampus bidentatus*, the most common species, showed initial declines in the weathered oil plots, but subsequent numbers became consistent with those of the control (Bender et al., 1977).

A spill of No. 2 fuel oil in September 1969 (Krebs and Burns, 1977, 1978) and another in October 1974 (Hampson and Moul, 1978) in Buzzards Bay, Massachusetts, produced visible mortalities of benthic invertebrates, which occurred immediately and extended outward to a depth of 2 to 2.5 meters. The ribbed mussel, *Geukensia demissa*, appeared to be one of the few organisms that successfully recovered from the latter spill. For months after the spill only empty valves were found. Two and three years after the spill, however, counts showed that the oiled sites in Winsor Cove, Buzzards Bay, had 3.4 times the density of ribbed mussels found at the control site at Chappaquoit marsh. The distribution pattern was similar in both areas, with most individuals situated in the mid- to upper marsh (Hampson and Moul, 1978).

The interstitial fauna was greatly reduced in Winsor Cove, with only 21

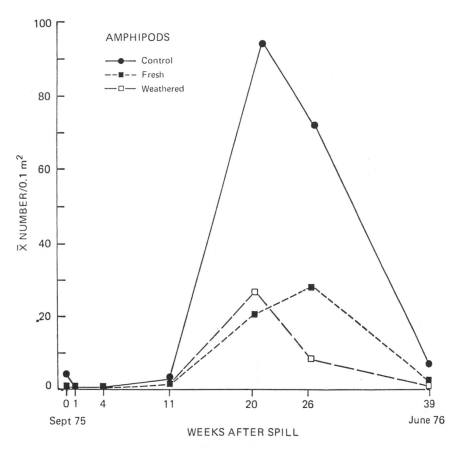

Figure 7-4. Amphipod population along transects through each enclosure of a Virginia marsh for a 39-week period. *Source: After Bender, M. E., E. A. Shearls, R. P. Ayres, C. Hershner, and R. J. Huggett, 1977, Ecological Effect of Experimental Oil Spills on Eastern Coastal Plain Estuarine Ecosystems, 1977 Oil Spill Conference Proceedings, American Petroleum Institute Publ. 4284, Washington, D.C., pp. 505–509, by permission.*

specimens recorded from four cores, in contrast to 261 individuals in two cores at Chappaquoit. Hampson and Moul (1978) found a high concentration of petroleum hydrocarbons in the peats at Winsor Cove. Hampson and Moul believed that the Winsor Cove marsh, like Chedbucto Bay (Thomas, 1978), acted like a sponge and, due to tidal oscillations and the uptake by the sediments of large quantities of oil, suffered repeatedly from the single spill. The slow chronic discharge of oil from the sediments caused a continuous stress on plant regeneration and animal repopulation. As Thomas (1978) pointed out, such changes in biomass abundance and distributions can have profound changes in energy-flow patterns, which in turn have broad ecological effects.

Chronic Pollution.   Thomas (1978) observed that oil concentration in animals was higher at contaminated sites but not significantly so. Lee (1977) also noted that animals from areas receiving low but chronic petroleum inputs did not always display a markedly higher total hydrocarbon content relative to animals from cleaner areas. However, the hydrocarbon fraction of organisms exposed to petroleum display an unresolved complex mixture (UCM) often referred to as an unresolved envelop. While the uptake of complex hydrocarbon mixtures by estuarine shellfish appears to be fairly inefficient, tissue concentrations can become high even when the concentration in the water is low (Stegeman, 1974). In reviewing the literature, Lee (1977) noted that mussels have been found to concentrate aromatic hydrocarbons by a factor of 10,000. Petroleum is absorbed from the water, food, or sediments. Milan and Whelan (1979) used three components of crude oil-saturated alkanes, aromatics, and cycloalkanes—as chemical parameters to characterize the relative petroleum enrichment in various estuarine and marsh organisms: killifish (*Fundulus grandis*), grass shrimp (*Palaemonetes* sp.), ribbed mussels (*Geukensia demissa*), oysters (*Crassostrea virginica*), and marsh periwinkles (*Littorina irrorata*); see Table 7-13. The enrichment factor was determined by dividing the concentration in the particular Louisiana oil field organism by the average concentration in the species at the two control sites.

According to Milan and Whelan (1979), benthic organisms such as periwinkles, mussels, and oysters displayed the greatest enrichment of all petroleum components. As filter feeders they are exposed to both adsorbed and soluble hydrocarbons in the water column and, being benthic in habitat, they are further exposed to contamination by aromatics and UCM that are released from the sediments. Based on the variety of petroleum hydrocarbons that can be taken up by benthic organisms, the aromatics and cycloalkane hydrocarbons appeared to Milan and Whelan to be the most persistent in the wake of chronic petroleum exposure. Although the grass shrimp occupies an intermediate position

Table 7-13. Enrichment factors for alkanes, aromatic hydrocarbons and the unresoved complex mixture (UCM) for various species taken from study sites in the Leeville oil field, Louisiana

Organism	Total Alkanes $C = 15$ to $C = 25$	UCM^a	Aromatics $310\,nm^b$	$365\,nm^c$
Oysters	4.50	3.48	4.85	5.28
Mussels	2.58	9.56	9.11	5.71
Grass shrimp	2.22	12.27	4.35	9.71
Grass	23.89	185.61	326.27	774.69
Periwinkle	2.32	6.62	12.11	14.67
Average, all fish	0.78	6.14	1.87	2.96

Source: After Milan, C. S., and T. Whelan III, 1979, Accumulation of petroleum hydrocarbons in a salt marsh ecosystem exposed to a steady state oil input, in *3rd Coastal Marsh Estuary Management Symposium Proceedings*, J. W. Day, Jr., D. D. Culley, Jr., R. E. Turner, and A. J. Mumphrey, eds., Louisiana State University, Baton Rouge, pp. 65-87, by permission.

[a]UCM - an array of normal, branched and cycloalkanes common to oil residues that cannot be resolved using available gas chromatography.

[b]Florescence at 310 nm results from alkyl-substituted single- and double-ringed aromatic hydrocarbons.

[c]Emission at 365 nm results from higher-molecular-weight, substituted three- and four-ringed aromatics.

between the killifish and the benthic organisms, its high enrichment values can be explained by the fact that it feeds on detritus, which adsorbs large amounts of petroleum hydrocarbons. The low alkane enrichment in killifish may result from the relative insolubility of alkanes and resulting minimal uptake across the gills. Alkanes adsorbed to detritus would not be ingested, since detritus is not used as food. In addition, fish are reported to be able to discriminate against petroleum-derived alkanes in their food. Alkanes can also be metabolized in fish and thus not accumulate. In contrast, aromatics and UCM accumulate because they can be absorbed across the gills and have a slower rate of metabolism than the alkanes (Milan and Whelan, 1979).

Milan and Whelan suggested a flow pattern for the fate of discharged oil in a salt marsh ecosystem (Figure 7-5). A surface slick is either partially adsorbed by particulate matter on the stems and roots of marsh vegetation and exposed sediments, or partially dissolved in the water column. Of the three components of crude oil that Milan and Whelan examined, the alkane hydrocarbons were considered relatively innocuous to biological systems since they are the least soluble and appear to be readily metabolized. For this reason, their overall enrichment in each organism examined was the lowest of the three components. The polar polynuclear aromatics, which displayed a 500% enrichment on the surface of the oiled vegetation, appeared to be only a physical phenomenon at the surface of the plant rather than a biochemical uptake at the cellular level. The sediments become enriched in cycloalkanes and aromatics relative to the more labile alkanes. As noted earlier, the marsh vegetation appeared to be the major adsorption site for the spilled oil (Table 7-13).

In another study, Lake and Hershner (1977) examined the identities and changes in concentration of petroleum hydrocarbons and petrosulfur compounds in ribbed mussels (*Geukensia demissa*) and oysters (*Crassostrea virginica*) subjected to simulated chronic exposure through weekly dosings of No. 2 fuel oil from 28 February to 14 August 1975. Animals were collected for examination 2, 6, and 15 weeks after dosing ceased. The concentration of the aromatic fraction decreased more rapidly than the saturate concentration in both the mussel and the oyster (Figure 7-6). The rate of decrease of the aromatics was initially greater for the mussel than for the oyster, while the decrease of the saturates fraction displayed a more steady decline. The concentration of aromatics two weeks after

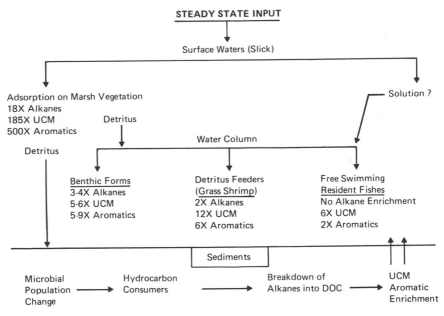

Figure 7-5. Proposed mechanism for the fate of oil in a marsh. *Source: After Milan, C. S., and T. Whelan III, 1979, Accumulation of petroleum hydrocarbons in a salt marsh ecosystem exposed to a steady state oil input, in 3rd Coastal Marsh Estuary Management Symposium Proceedings, J. W. Day, Jr., D. D. Culley, Jr., R. E. Turner, and A. J. Mumphrey, eds., Louisiana State University, Baton Rouge, pp. 65–87, by permission.*

dosage ceased was slightly more than three times higher in the mussel than in the oyster. Both mollusks showed a parallel magnitude of decrease in concentration of the petrosulfur compounds as compared to that of the aromatics.

Both species exhibited an accumulation of aromatic hydrocarbons at the beginning of the recovery period relative to the saturated hydrocarbons (as compared to the dosing oil). Both mollusks had lost a large portion of their accumulated petroleum hydrocarbons and petrosulfur compounds by 15 weeks after dosing ceased. In addition, both species displayed a more rapid rate of loss of aromatics than saturates. Such a loss could be explained, in part, by the greater water solubility of aromatics versus the saturated hydrocarbons. The aromatics of the fuel oil, being more soluble, would be rapidly lost from the marsh and would be less available for recontamination. The higher-molecular-weight petrosulfur compounds found in the mollusks were retained for longer periods. Lake and Hershner (1977) observed that the petro-sulfur compounds were depurated from the mussel and the oyster at similar rates as the aromatics.

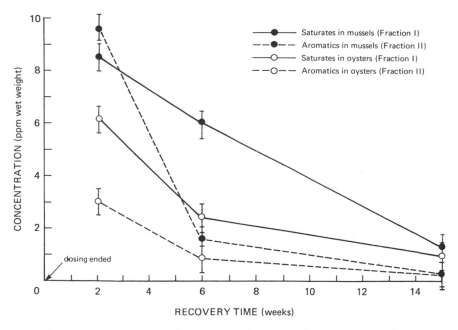

Figure 7-6. Concentrations of saturated and aromatic hydrocarbon fractions in mussels and oysters. *Source: After Lake, J. L., and C. Hershner, 1977, Petroleum Sulfur-Containing Compounds and Aromatic Hydrocarbons in the Marine Mollusks* Modiolus demissus *and* Crassostrea virginica, *1977, Oil Spill Conference Proceedings, American Petroleum Institute Publ. 4284, Washington, D.C., pp. 627–632, by permission.*

As Stegeman (1974) pointed out, the initial rate of uptake by mollusks is related to the concentration in the water; both uptake and disposal rates must determine the net accumulation during exposure. The rate of disposal appears to be a function of a given tissue concentration of hydrocarbons, although factors such as lipid character and hydrocarbon concentration in the water do modify the relationship. According to Stegeman, superimposed on the general pattern of hydrocarbon accumulation and disposal is the changing composition of oil in the tissues, not only in terms of total aromatic content but the altered proportions of individual aromatic and aliphatic compounds present.

Among the mollusks, such as the oyster, it is apparent that the various classes of petroleum hydrocarbons and individual compounds behave in a chemically distinct manner. In terms of potential biological effect, the lower-molecular-weight aromatics must be considered as the most significant. Not only are they toxic but they have a biological half-life longer than other hydrocarbons in shellfish. There is also the possibility of persistent histological changes, and it is likely that cellular defense mechanisms and susceptibility to pathogens are affected (Stegeman, 1974).

Long-Term Effects.   While a number of authors (Thomas, 1978; Hampson and Moul, 1978; Baker, 1979) have described the extended times for recovery of marsh vegetation and invertebrates following an oil spill, very few have portrayed the long-term effects on particular invertebrate species.

After the September 1969 oil spill in Buzzards Bay, Massachusetts, fiddler crabs that survived displayed locomotor impairment. Krebs and Burns (1977, 1978) found that this damage persisted for four years and was most obvious at lower temperatures, just after emergence and just before winter dormancy. The escape response more than doubled at 15°C for crabs ingesting oiled sediments (4.5 ± 0.5 seconds before and 10.2 ± 2.3 seconds after five days of feeding), while those tested at 25°C showed no significant difference in escape time. It is apparent from Krebs and Burns' observations that long-term exposures of sublethal concentrations lead to immobilization with enhanced opportunities to be preyed upon.

Population densities were reduced wherever sediment oil levels exceeded 200 ppm. The greatest reductions coincided with the highest oil concentrations. Concentrations of weathered fuel oil greater than 1,000 ppm were directly toxic to adults, whereas those of 100 to 200 ppm were toxic to over-wintering juveniles. Burrow construction was found to be abnormal in moderately to heavily oiled sediments (Krebs and Burns, 1977). The crabs absorbed oil through food and through respiration and lost it through exchange with water passing over the gills, by excretion after possible metabolism, or by storage in fat cells (Burns and Teal, 1979).

Recovery was still incomplete seven years after this relatively small spill and was highly correlated with the disappearance of the naphthalene fraction of the aromatics. By 1970-1971, all parent naphthalene compounds were gone from the sediments, but substituted naphthalenes were still in high concentrations. By 1972-1973, the substituted naphthalenes were still in high enough concentrations to prevent recruitment. By 1976 and 1977, these toxic compounds were at low enough levels so that the fiddler crab population was recovering by recruitment; increases in density were observed in both years. Recovery appeared to be complete, with oil concentrations below 100 ppm. Each year considerable numbers of juvenile crabs settled out, with the highest densities observed at the less oiled sites (Krebs and Burns, 1977, 1978).

The number of females was markedly reduced. At the control marsh (Sippewisset), females comprised 40.8 ± 2.4% while at the contaminated sites at Wild Harbor, females made up only 17.5 ± 5.4%. By 1973 the low-oil site recorded 43.5 ± 5.3% females, but the heavily oiled station had increased to 28.4 ± 4.7% females. Differential migration or mortality could account for the observed differences.

Krebs and Burns (1977, 1978) suggested several factors that could account for the observed effects of contaminated sediments on fiddler crabs. The uptake and concentration of tissue hydrocarbons could affect the molting process. Since the crabs remain in their burrow after molting, they could be exposed to oiled sediments at a very sensitive stage. Juveniles could be affected more because they molt more frequently than adults. In addition, heavy winter mortalities could result from direct exposure to contaminated sediments. Under the anoxic conditions of the marsh muds, the toxic effect of the oils would persist for a longer time (Krebs and Burns, 1977).

In a simulated chronic pollution situation, Laughlin, Young, and Neff (1978) continuously exposed immature mud crab (*Rhithropanopeus harrisii*) larvae for six months after hatching to the water-soluble fraction (WSF) of No. 2 fuel oil. They found the zoeal stages to be most sensitive. A 20% WSF (0.36 ppm total naphthalenes, 1.26 ppm total hydrocarbons) was acutely toxic, with the first zoeal stage being the most sensitive. The combined duration of the four zoeal stages was significantly increased by increasing WSF exposure concentrations.

The megalopa and crab stages were not particularly sensitive to continued exposure. However, mean duration of the megalopa and first crab stages was significantly affected by oil exposure. Individuals that survived the highest exposure concentrations as larvae appeared to grow larger during crab stages so that at the end of six months, comparably staged crabs were equal to or larger than both control crabs and those exposed to low WSF concentrations. There was no difference in stage distributions or sex ratios after six months of exposure to WSF concentrations. Laughlin, Young, and Neff (1978) found a marked recovery from the effects of chronic sublethal exposure to petroleum hydrocarbons. They observed that the most pronounced effect of oil pollution on this mud crab species may be on larval recruitment into the adult population. They also suggested that such a life-cycle bioassay could be used to discern the chronic and accumulative effects of a toxicant that cannot be detected by a 96-hour bioassay.

Effects on Metabolism.   Burns and Teal (1979), by suggesting that marine organisms may dispose of absorbed petroleum hydrocarbons through excretion or storage in fat cells, have implied that metabolic processes are involved.

Heitz et al. (1974) found that oil does not kill immediately by poisoning enzyme systems. Its immediate effects are physical, probably because a coating of oil disrupts the gaseous exchange across the gills. Although lack of obvious oil effects would suggest that oil does not enter the animals during acute exposures, various analyses showed the presence of varied groups of hydrocarbons in the tissues. It was evident that oil was entering even though the available oil in the water column was being diluted. The subtle cellular effects—such as membrane permeability changes, fatty infiltration of the liver, or modification of subcellular organelles—that might be indicative of damage require extended exposure periods. Heitz et al. noted that most of the enzymes affected were related to carbohydrate metabolism.

Burns (1976a) set out to determine whether fiddler crabs can oxidize foreign hydrocarbons, to determine if higher levels of these enzymes were induced or selected for in populations of crabs living in oil-contaminated areas, and whether the metabolic rate was fast enough to be an effective means of clearing body tissues of contaminating hydrocarbons and thus affect the survival of mud fiddler crabs (*Uca pugnax*) in a heavily polluted area such as Wild Harbor, Buzzards Bay, Massachussetts.

The metabolic enzymes responsible for the oxidation of foreign compounds, including hydrocarbons, are termed mixed-function oxidases (MFOs). Burns found *in vitro* MFO activities in crab tissue to be very low—close to the limits of detection. Further, the *in vivo* rates of naphthalene oxidation were so low that the calculated clearance time exceeded the life span of the crab. This means that *Uca pugnax* living in oiled sediments incorporated oil into their body tissues. Tissue hydrocarbon levels reached 280 ppm and persisted for four years at the Wild Harbor site (Krebs and Burns, 1977). An average total gravimetric amount of 242 ppm was determined for the Wild Harbor site, and the total hydrocarbon load for crabs in a clean environment was calculated to be 9.8 ppm (Burns, 1976a). Hydrocarbons from the clean site were derived from biogenic sources, whereas petroleum hydrocarbons in the contaminated habitat completely masked the biogenic hydrocarbons. Petroleum will persist for long periods in the marsh muds because of the anoxic conditions. For this reason the crabs were continuously exposed to oil hydrocarbons, and the total body burden of oil found in the crabs represented the maximum amount the crabs could absorb and survive.

While Burns (1976*a*) demonstrated that crabs have the microsomal mixed-function oxidase system for handling foreign hydrocarbons, the rate of oxidation was very low. There was no difference between crabs from clean and oiled marsh, so there was no enhancement in the system to accommodate to the polluted condition. The crabs apparently did not have the physiological ability to significantly increase their rate of enzymatic oxidation of foreign hydrocarbons, either through enzyme induction or through genetic selection.

Gilfillan (1973, 1975) has reported the effects of crude oil and salinity stress on the carbon budget of *Mytilus edulis* and *Geukensia demissa*. While crude oil may not be acutely toxic, small amounts of oil (1 to 10% of solution) markedly reduced the amount of carbon available for reproduction and growth.

At 31‰, a small amount of oil (1%) caused a sharp reduction in net carbon flux by decreasing assimilation and increasing respiration. At 21‰, the effects of salinity stress on metabolism were such that the net carbon flux was always negative. A 1% oil extract decreased the net carbon intake even further by increasing respiration. The assimilation ratio was so low that the increased gross carbon intake was offset by increased respiration. At 11‰, the salinity stress was very great. The presence of any oil was enough to stop feeding and assimilation completely (Fig. 7-7). The impact on *Geukensia* was reported to be greater than that on *Mytilus* (Gilfillan, 1975).

Fishes

General Effects.   The effect of petroleum hydrocarbons on fishes appears to vary as much as on invertebrates. Lytle (1975), in her experimental oiling with Empire Mix crude in a Mississippi salt marsh, found that the usual visible signs of a fish kill were absent, but mortalities must have occurred since seining showed a particularly marked decrease in the numbers of menhaden (*Brevoortia tyrannus*). When Bender et al. (1977) applied both fresh and artificially weathered South Louisiana crude to experimental plots in a mesohaline marsh off the York River in Virginia, they reported the highest mortalities among *Fundulus heteroclitus* in the weathered oil plots immediately after oiling, and all *Fundulus* were dead by nine days. No *Fundulus* died in the fresh oil plots during this time. Only a few (14 out of 200) died after the ninth day. The marsh organisms and the sediments rapidly adsorbed the weathered oil. Because of this

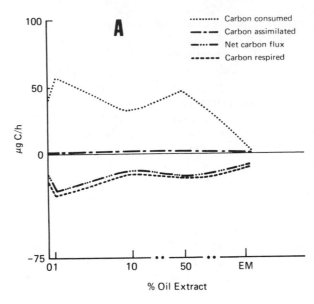

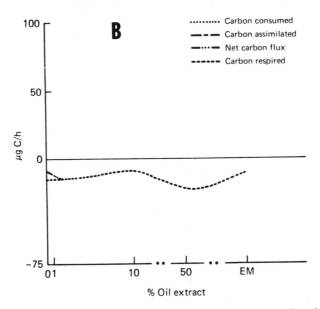

Figure 7-7.   Effects of crude oil extract on carbon budgets calculated for 100-mg mussels held at 21‰ *(A)* and 11‰ *(B)* under summer conditions (15°C, 215 μg C/l). Note changes in scale on *X* axis. *Source: After Gilfillan, E. S., 1975, Decrease of net carbon flux in two species of mussels caused by extracts of crude oil, Mar. Biol.* **29:***53–57, by permission.*

and its greater viscosity, the weathered oil was available to interact with organisms (Bender et al., 1977). Despite reduced gaseous exchange, various components of petroleum are taken up across the gills and are usually found in the liver and gall bladder. Those taken in by food ingestion are typically found in the stomach in addition to the gall bladder and liver (Heitz et al., 1974). Discharge is by means of the urine and feces (Lee, 1977), and it seems that an equilibrium may be established across the gills (Burns and Teal, 1979). Presumably, if the fish can get into clean water, depuration can be rapid. Lee (1977) stated that all tissues were usually cleansed in 7 to 14 days. Burns and Teal (1979) reported that the presence of hydrocarbons in *F. heteroclitus* after the 1969 oil spill gradually decreased until, by 1974, the amount of hydrocarbons was indistinguishable from that in the controls. Milan and Whelan's studies (1979) indicated that fishes such as *Fundulus grandis* are not as vulnerable to some groups of hydrocarbons as benthic organisms (see Table 7-13 and accompanying text).

What happens to fishes when subjected to concentrations of petroleum hydrocarbon that are greater than low-level chronic exposure levels and that kill, although not immediately? Dixit and Anderson (1977) prepared a 100% water-soluble fraction of No. 2 fuel oil. The ensuing solution, prepared by stirring one part of the oil with nine parts of Instant Ocean at 20‰ for 20 hours, contained approximately 7 ppm total dissolved hydrocarbons and 2 ppm naphthalenes. On exposure, *Fundulus similis* became hyperactive. This was followed by general disorientation and successive stages of distress, terminating in death at stage VI. Naphthalenes accumulated rapidly in a short period; the greatest concentrations were in the gall bladder (66,704 ppm), heart (9,714 ppm), liver (4,481 ppm), and brain (2,387 ppm) when the fish were in stage III (swimming upside down at the surface). When Dixit and Anderson placed stage V fish (slow opercular movement with fish on the bottom) in clean water, there was a gradual loss of naphthalenes from the body tissues with concentrations below detection level after 336 hours in clean water. This superb ability to recover is presumably the result of efficient detoxification mechanisms.

Foreign Compound Metabolism. "Cytochrome P-450 is a generic name given to a family of hemoproteins which exhibit Soret-absorption maxima at or near 450 nm in the CO-bound reduced state and which are involved in foreign-compound metabolism" (Stegeman, 1978). Biotransformations of a great variety of substrates are catalyzed by cytochrome P-450 or mixed-function oxidase (MFO) systems in fish—ranging from endogenous compounds such as steroid hormones to foreign compounds such as aromatic hydrocarbons and chlorinated hydrocarbons—and thus are transformed into oxidized metabolites. Such metabolites can then be discharged by diffusion across membranes or conjugated with serum components and excreted. In this way the system serves as a means of detoxification and depuration (Burns, 1976b; Stegeman, 1978).

Levels of hepatic cytochrome P-450 and the catalytic functions benzo [a] pyrene hydroxylase and aminopyrine demethylase were significantly greater in populations of *F. heteroclitus* sampled from contaminated marshes at Wild Harbor, West Falmouth, Massachusetts, than in the same species in nearby uncontaminated marshes. According to Stegeman, the higher benzo [a] pyrene hydroxylase activity suggested that levels of this MFO can be linked to environmental contamination. Stegeman was puzzled by the high level of animopyrene demethylase activity in fish from the contaminated Wild Harbor marshes and also Little Sippewissett, one of the marshes considered to be uncontaminated. This discrepancy may be partially explained by the findings of Burns (1976b) (Table 7-14). Although higher levels of aldrin epoxidation and cytochrome P-450 were evident in fishes taken from the site of the West Falmouth oil spill and from marshes (Sippewissett) subjected to sewage sludge containing pesticides, the results for cytochrome P-450 were not consistent. Burns suggested that cytochrome P-450 may not be a good parameter for comparison. Both she and Stegeman, however, believed that elevated levels of MFO activity in fish can be attributed to environmental contamination by petroleum hydrocarbons.

Effect on the Ecosystem and Food Chains

Considerable effort has been expended to examine the impact of oiling on the various species of tidal marsh vegetation and the fauna, but little evidence has been gathered of the impact of petroleum contamination on the marsh ecosystem. Baker (1979) found little long-term damage to perennial marsh vegetation regardless of the season. The first impact was a decline or die-back, with a subsequent highly significant growth stimulation. Bender et al. (1977) observed the same pattern for oiled phytoplankton blooms. Michael, Van Raalte, and Brown (1975) and others have pointed out that the persistence of oil in the sediments has a profound influence on the numbers of species as well as the density of individuals. In time, the difference in numbers of species and individuals becomes less distinct between oiled and noncontaminated marsh sites, yet the secondary production of the intertidal area can remain significantly reduced for years after the oil spill. Milan and Whelan (1979) have illustrated that the position occupied by aquatic organisms in the water column as well as the method of feeding and type of food ingested can have a material impact on the magnitude of petroleum enrichment of marsh organisms.

Table 7-14. Rates of aldrin epoxidation and levels of cytochrome P-450 in populations of *Fundulus heteroclitus* collected from different Massachusetts environments

	n Moles Dieldrin Formed ± SD[a] *mg mic. Protein min.*	*pm Cyt. P-450 mg mic. Protein*
Oil-polluted area	0.64 ± 0.037	322
West Falmouth	0.54 ± 0.075	437
	0.75 ± 0.080	350
	0.55 ± 0.022	342
Pesticide-contaminated area, Sippewissett	0.69 ± 0.103	404
Clean area, Cuttyhunk Island	0.25 ± 0.081	249
Clean area, Barnstable Harbor	0.39 ± 0.052	363
Clean area, Sippewissett	0.39 ± 0.018	251

Source: From Burns, K. A., 1976, Microsomal mixed function oxidases in an estuarine fish, *Fundulus heteroclitus*, and their induction as a result of environmental contamination, *Comp. Biochem. Physiol.* **53B**:443-446, by permisssion.
[a]Standard deviation of three determinations.

As Teal (1977) observed, because of their high solubility in lipids, hydrocarbons should be readily absorbed, along with lipids, through the guts of the animals. Thus food web transfer must occur. As noted earlier, depuration is an important process that influences the levels available for transport through the food web. If a food organism actively rids itself of pollutants, it will be a poor source of them for its predators. Long retention times have important implications for food web transport of hydrocarbons. Food web transport to fishes would seem to be largely a matter of uptake and accumulation of hydrocarbons from the environment by food organisms and of the transport and availability of food in different parts of the environment. Teal viewed assimilation efficiencies as important in the acquisition and storage of hydrocarbons. He also presumed that the accumulation of hydrocarbons by way of food web transport appears to be of much more importance than accumulation by means of transfer across the gills in the respiratory process.

Levasseur and Jory (1982) considered the vitality of the tidal marsh ecosystem is due more to its capacity for recovery via colonizations or direct implantations, when they are possible, than to the uncertain and generally long-term resistance of other species. There is, however, a fundamental subtlety between the reaction vis-à-vis an exceptional but finite perturbation, and a disturbance that becomes chronic and has not been integrated in the past, for example, by means of a particular selection of a species.

EFFECTS OF PETROLEUM FRACTIONS, SEASON, AGE OF OIL, AND SURFACTANTS

Petroleum Fractions

The toxic effects of petroleum hydrocarbons on tidal marsh plants and animals depend on a number of factors, including the source of the crude oil, the degree to which it has been refined, and the proportions of the various hydrocarbon components making up a refined oil. It is equally important to determine whether it acts in a physical way or interacts at the biochemical level in the cellular metabolism of an organism. The effects can also be species-specific.

Baker (1971) observed that, while low concentrations of heavy oils inhibited seed germination, higher concentrations of lighter oils were better able to penetrate the seed cover. Milan and Whelan (1979) reported that polar polynuclear aromatics acted primarily as a physical phenomenon at the plant surface and not as a biochemical uptake at the cellular level. Baker (1970) has suggested that the high-boiling oils have molecules too large to penetrate plant tissue and that the volatile oils may evaporate before they affect the plant. Viscosity can also influence the rate at which oil spreads over and penetrates a plant.

A number of investigators have commented on the increased toxicity associated with the water-soluble, volatile, low-boiling point, low-molecular-weight, unsaturated compounds, especially if they are rich in aromatic hydrocarbons. The naphtha and kerosene fractions are particularly toxic (Baker, 1970). Laughlin, Young, and Neff (1978) found the zoeal stages of the mud crab (*Rhithropanopeus harrisii*) to be particularly sensitive to naphthalenes. Stegeman, (1974) observed that the lower-molecular-weight aromatics are not only toxic to shellfish but have a biological half-life longer than other hydrocarbons, bringing about the possibility of persistent histological changes. Milan and Whelan (1979) found the alkane hydrocarbons to be relatively innocuous to biological systems, the least soluble, and readily metabolized.

Burns and Teal (1979) reported that the longest-lasting residue in the sediments consisted of the higher-molecular-weight aromatics, the naphthenoaromatics and naphthenes. The others had disappeared through dilution and evaporation. Furthermore, they found persistent levels of naphthalenes and other aromatics in animal tissues such as those of fiddler crabs. Teal, Burns, and Farrington (1978) noted that, while the lighter aromatics are responsible for most of the immediate and toxic effects, animals such as fiddler crabs would be in continuous contact with the heavier aromatics even in the absolute concentrations were low in the sediments. The effects of such concentrations may be masked by the lighter aromatics. It is not known to what extent animals take up heavy aromatics. That they do so was clearly suggested by the abnormal behavior and reduced survival of fiddler crabs years after an oil spill, as reported by Krebs and Burns (1977). Their observations lend support to the conclusion reached by Teal, Burns, and Farrington (1978) that the heavier aromatics in No. 2 fuel oil, the highly saturated naphthalenes, and the phenanthrenes are the compounds that could have adverse effects for periods that may be measured in decades.

Anderson et al. (1974a) have examined the water-soluble extracts of crude and refined oils and their toxicity on estuarine crustaceans and fishes. Two crude oils were tested, South Louisiana and Kuwait, and two refined oils, No. 2 and Bunker C residual oil. The water-soluble fractions (WSFs) of the crude oils had higher total oil-hydrocarbon concentrations and were richer in light-aliphatic and single-ring aromatics than were the WSFs of the refined oils. The WSFs of the refined oils contained significantly higher concentrations of naphthalenes than did the crudes. The hydrocarbon composition of the aqueous phase of oil-in-water dispersions (OWDs) closely resembled that of the parent oils. There was a rapid (80 to 90%) loss of the aqueous hydrocarbons from the OWDs in 24 hours. Alkanes disappeared from the dispersions more rapidly than the aromatics.

The WSFs and OWDs of the crude oils were considerably less toxic than those of the refined oils. This was true for three crustaceans and three fishes tested to determine median tolerance limits (TLMs), defined as the concentrations of oil causing 50% mortality in the time stated. Anderson et al. (1974a) suggested that the oil concentrations encountered in the tests were probably much greater than any level that could be expected in the sea, even during an oil spill. The 24-hour test on the three fish species resulted in TLMs ranging from 6,610 to more than 80,000 ppm OWDs of the crude oil. With the exception of the mysid (*Mysidopsis almyra*), the test organisms had 24-hour TLM values of 1,000 ppm or greater of OWDs for both crude oils. In the mysid, the TLM was 165 ppm for the Louisiana crude and 72 for the Kuwait crude.

Overall, the six test species can be ranked according to increasing sensitivity to oil from the least to the most sensitive: *Cyprinodon variegatus, Menidia beryllina, Fundulus similis, Panaeus aztecus* post larvae, *Palaemonetes pugio*, and *Mysidopsis almyra*. Anderson et al., (1974a), however, reported considerable variability. *Cyprinodon* was considerably more tolerant to the OWDs of the two crudes than were *Menidia* and *Fundulus*. *Cyprinodon* and *Menidia* were essentially equally sensitive to the OWDs of No. 2 fuel oil, whereas *Fundulus* was very sensitive. Both *Cyprinodon* and *Fundulus* were quite tolerant to the WSFs of the crude oils; *Menidia* was somewhat more so. *Menidia* and *Fundulus* were equally sensitive to the WSFs of both No. 2 fuel oil and Bunker C. *Cyprinodon* was somewhat more tolerant to the WSFs of the two refined oils but, like the other fish, more sensitive to the WSF of Bunker C than to that of No. 2 fuel oil. Kuwait WSFs and OWDs were significantly more toxic to *Mysidopsis* than were those of South Louisiana crude. There was no significant difference between the Bunker C and No. 2 fuel oil WSFs for *Mysidopsis* and *Palaemonetes*. The WSF of Bunker C was more toxic to *Penaeus* than that of No. 2 fuel oil.

When considering the potential impacts of spills of different oils on the marine community, Anderson et al. (1974a) concluded that the amount of oil per unit of water volume was the greatest cause of mortality. They also suggested that confinement in a relatively small body of water of the toxic and dispersible fuel oil might allow aqueous hydrocarbon concentrations to reach toxic levels more rapidly than volatilization and weathering would remove the more toxic aromatics.

Anderson et al. (1974a) reported a species-specific response to petroleum hydrocarbons. Additional research (Anderson et al., 1974b) has extended this perception. The sheepshead minnow (*Cyprinodon variegatus*) showed a respiratory response that increased somewhat in intensity as the exposure concentration was increased. The response of the fish to WSFs of South Louisiana and Kuwait crude oils, No. 2 fuel oil, and Bunker C residual oil varied with respect to concentration required to induce a significant change in the respiratory rate, the direction of change (stimulation or suppression), or magnitude of respiratory response. The shrimps *Panaeus aztecus* and *Palaemonetes pugio* showed slight depressions in respiratory rate during and immediately after exposure to the WSFs of the various oils. In most cases, the magnitude of response was greatest at the lowest exposure concentration. Anderson et al. (1974a), as well as Dixit and Anderson (1977) and Lee (1977), demonstrated that marsh organisms such as *Palaemonetes* can cleanse their tissues of hydrocarbons, raising their respiratory rate in three days to a level approaching the pre-exposure control rate. The fishes' respiratory rate also returned to normal shortly after they were returned to clean water. Anderson et al. (1974a) concluded that the nature and magnitude of respiratory response to sublethal concentrations of oil was species-dependent and also dependent on the hydrocarbon composition and concentration of the exposure water. The response was also transitory and reversible.

Season, Age of Oil, and Surfactants

A tidal marsh gives the appearance of the greatest damage when an oil spill occurs in the winter, yet that is when it may be the least affected.

Even relatively fresh oil can be trapped on dead standing vegetation without causing a significant kill of vegetation. Plants are most susceptible to fresh oil and even weathered oil during the growing season. During spring and summer, oiling can inhibit seed germination and damage newly formed seedlings, which are especially vulnerable. Oil contamination will materially reduce flowering of such plants as *Juncus, Festuca rubra, Plantago maritima,* and *Spartina anglica* (or *S. alterniflora*) if the plants are oiled as the flower buds develop. Such oiled flowers seldom produce seeds. It appears that marshes have the best chance for recovery when the spill occurs in January (Ranwell 1968; Cowell and Baker 1969; Baker, 1971, 1979; Nelson-Smith 1972; Hershner and Moore, 1977).

Fresh crude oil and the various refined products are more toxic than weathered crude oil on a per-volume basis. (Baker, 1971; Bender et al. 1977; Krebs and Burns, 1977; Hampson and Moul, 1978). Stebbings (1970) reported that salt marshes in France recovered from heavy oil contamination with only slight floral changes. The oil spill had been at sea for 14 to 18 days before coming ashore, and most of the toxic materials had been lost. When it did come ashore, the weathered oil acted as an impervious layer that inhibited gaseous exchange. Apparently a few hours at sea can make an appreciable difference in the level of toxicity (Cowell, 1969). Ranwell (1968) and Cowell (1969) reported that the marsh vegetation suffered little damage when weathered oil came ashore on the Cornwall coast of England after the Torrey Canyon spill. Yet Cowell described severe damage to Pembrokeshire, Wales, marshes following a crude oil spill that came ashore in January on a spring tide and a northerly wind. It appears that the sooner the oil comes ashore, the greater the damage, even for crude oil spilled in winter.

Petroleum of normal consistency tends not to penetrate muddy or sandy shores unless it is emulsified by chemical treatment or by wave action (Nelson-Smith, 1972). Emulsifiers can facilitate the penetration of oils into the marsh sediments (Baker, 1971). Surfactants greatly enhance the damage done by oils. This was especially true for the early emulsifiers since they had high concentrations of aromatics. It was difficult to assess the effect of the oils since the surfactants were so much more damaging (Cowell, 1969; Baker, 1979). Ranwell (1968) stated that there was little point in using emulsifiers on oil-contaminated vegetation since they would kill the plants if the oil had not already done so. Nelson-Smith (1972) expressed the view that emulsifiers should be used with great care because they spread the oil film when it should be confined. Cowell (1969) warned that any treatment by surfactants could have severe adverse effects on reclamation sites where *Spartina* is used to stabilize and bind the substrate, because of the lethal effects on the plants and the sediment-binding properties of the root systems.

SYNTHESIS

The outcome of various spills that have occurred in tidal marshes, as well as experimental spills, have produced a variety of results ranging from the specific to the ambiguous and to the contradictory. Some generalizations can be made, however.

Oil spills may have a lethal, inhibitory, stimulatory, or even no apparent effect on marsh vegetation. Marsh plants can be relegated to various categories of resistance, ranging as follows: group I, very sensitive (*Suaeda maritima, Salicornia*); group II, sensitive (*Halimione portulacoides, Juncus maritimus*); group III, intermediate (*Spartina anglica, Puccinellia maritima, Festuca rubra*); group IV, resistant (*Agrostis stolonifera, Armeria maritima, Plantago maritima, Triglochin maritima*); and group V, very resistant (*Oenanthe lachenalii*) (Baker, 1979).

Damage is most evident where oil persists for weeks or months after the spill, and the damage generally is less acute farther from the initial zone of contact. The oil will be redistributed with the ebb and flow of the tide except where it has been trapped by vegetation. Such subsequent redistributions tend to have less severe impacts on the vegetation. Perennials will survive better than annuals because new growth can occur from underground vegetative systems. Perennials like *Spartina* will revegetate a denuded area by growth of underground rhizomes originating from neighboring uncontaminated sources. Annuals return because they are opportunistic species adapted to occupying sites that change frequently. They repopulate a decimated area by seed germination. However, seed germination can be inhibited or prohibited by heavy oils, which impair the movement of water or oxygen through the seed cover. Light oils can diffuse through the seed cover and kill the seed embryo. Should an oil spill occur after seed germination has taken place, the new seedlings are especially vulnerable.

Depending on the intensity and duration of an oil spill, primary production will either drop off for a time or be terminated until the oil level in the affected area has been reduced to a level that permits revegetation. Due to the differential rates of revegetation by seeding or vegetative means, the plant species present before oiling may be replaced by faster-growing, more aggressive species with a consequential change in floral composition and perhaps production. Whereas many scientists have recorded a reduction in productivity, others have noted a stimulatory effect. Not only did the plants increase in biomass but they also took on a deeper green color. This suggests that the oils themselves had nutritive properties or that nutrients were released from the dead and dying vegetation affected by the oil.

Production can be influenced not only by the intensity and duration of the oiling, but by the frequency at which the tides redistribute the oil and by the number of new spills to which a particular plot of vegetation is subjected. There is usually an inverse relationship between the number of spills and the magnitude of production. A single heavy oiling may not have an impact, but a number of such oilings can have a pronounced effect. The time for recovery is considerably extended with an increase in the number of oilings.

Oil acts by physically coating the plants and thus preventing gaseous exchange, and inhibiting transpiration by blocking the stomata. Once the oil penetrates the plants, it travels primarily through the intercellular spaces and, to a lesser extent, through the vascular system. There is physical disruption of cellular content as well as biochemical desolation. Respiration and photosynthetic processes are impaired or destroyed.

Studies of oil penetration into sediments have produced differing results. In some cases penetration has been slow, in others rapid. The fact that oil can affect sediments directly has been illustrated by the lack of adventitious roots in an oiled area where plants had put out roots either above or below the despoiled layer. It has also been demonstrated that oil indirectly affects the soil by inhibiting oxygen diffusion, with a resulting increase in toxic reduced ions. The proportions of the various hydrocarbon constituents have changed with time due to physical dilution, volatilization, and microbial action. Microbial degradation of petroleum hydrocarbons has been associated with the concomitant enhancement of particular groups of bacteria and their biomass. Such activity can substantially alter the food web. However, one study has indicated that meiofaunal populations were not materially changed.

Generally, oil spills have led to high mortality rates for macro-invertebrates. Numbers of individuals have been greatly reduced and there have been significant differences in species diversity between clean and oiled marshes. While some recovery has been evident within a few months, differences have persisted for years after the spill. In some instances, species diversity has not been as revealing as the differences in biomass between an oiled and natural site. Just as with plants, there have been specific differences in the reactions of various animal species in terms of initial survival and subsequent recruitment. In one study, the numbers of *Littorina obtusata* and *L. saxatilis* were depressed, while *L. vincta, Mytilus edulis,* and *Gammarus oceanicus* increased in population in the same oiled site. Growth in size and weight also demonstrated species differences between contaminated and pristine situations.

Numbers of individuals and levels of recruitment have usually been inversely related to the amount of oil retained in the sediments. Through physical dilution and differential evaporation, proportions of hydrocarbons have varied in the sediments; this in turn has been reflected in the quality and quantity of hydrocarbon loads found in the animals' tissues. These hydrocarbons are acquired by diffusion across the gills and by ingestion of food. The magnitude of hydrocarbon acquisition can be attributed to the habitat occupied by the invertebrates and fish as well as to their feeding habits. Proportions of these hydrocarbons within the body change with each animal's differential ability to metabolize the various hydrocarbon components. Some invertebrates such as the mussel and oyster are capable of accumulating large amounts of these hydrocarbons even though the levels dissolved in the water are very low. Invertebrates and fish can depurate these oil hydrocarbons by diffusion across the gills, excrete them, store them in fats, or metabolize them to a less toxic material. The length of time to cleanse the body varies with the species. It may take weeks for a shellfish or days for a fish like *Fundulus*. The rate will be determined by the quantity held in the tissues as well as the nature of the hydrocarbon and water temperature.

Several of the marsh fauna have enzyme systems that can be enhanced in the presence of petroleum hydrocarbons, which in turn can hasten the metabolism of the oil. Species of *Fundulus* apparently have this ability. In contrast, fiddler crabs possess low levels of these mixed-function oxidases, and the enzymes are not stimulated in the presence of the petroleum hydrocarbons. Sublethal levels of hydrocarbons have been responsible for impaired locomotion, behavior, and molting in fiddler and mud crabs, as well as for impaired respiration, food uptake, and assimilation in *Mytilus* and *Geukensia*.

The degree of toxicity depends on the nature of the petroleum product. Fresh crude oil and refined products are more toxic than weathered crude oil. The various crude oils have different levels of toxicity. Higher toxicity is associated with lighter aromatic components and diminishes as these aromatics evaporate from the oil or water solution. Petroleum hydrocarbons are more toxic during the active growing season, which usually coincides with the warm portion of the year. The more the oil has weathered, the less toxic it usually is.

The use of surfactants to emulsify the oil and thus hasten its removal should be discontinued, since surfactants are more toxic than the oils. Probably the most effective treatment is to allow the tidal flushing to remove the contaminating oil gradually. The lighter refined oils affect the flora, fauna, and sediments so rapidly that probably little can be done to prevent damage. With the heavy crude oils, it is possible to remove the oil and oiled vegetation by cutting, burning, or both. However, trampling and burning may be as harmful as the physical smothering or toxic effects of the oil.

A perusal of the literature reveals that relatively few organisms associated with the tidal marsh have been carefully examined for the impacts of petroleum hydrocarbon contamination. Most study periods have been a few weeks or months, a few studies have extended over a couple of years.

Teal, Burns, and Farrington (1978) have suggested that the impacts may extend over decades. Sanders et al. (1980) succinctly explained the need for further study:

> Most necessary are carefully conducted, quantitative, long-term studies, especially those designated to detect physiological and behavioral damage, of the effects of oil spills on all levels of the marine trophic structure. Mathematical techniques, especially diversity indices, must be used with comprehension and care. Only through such studies can society appreciate the true price paid for undramatic, pervasive, ever-spreading, chronic pollution which disrupts and alters increasingly great reaches of natural habitats.

PART II

Legal Concerns
and
Management

Chapter 8

Legal Aspects

Chapter 1 portrayed the value of tidal marshes through their contributions to the coastal environment. It also discussed current uses and activities that may prove deleterious to functions that make the marsh so valuable to society and the economy. A controversy has arisen over private versus public uses of the tidal marsh: Many owners of marshlands believe they have the prerogative to do whatever they please with their own property, but the general public also has an interest in the best use of that same property. Until very recently, the tidal wetlands have been treated as a commons where, in the words of Hardin (1968), "each man is locked into a system that compels him to increase his herd without limit—in a world that is limited . . . each [man] pursuing his own best interest in a society that believes in the freedom of the commons." Hardin believed that "freedom in a commons brings ruin to all." As the human population has increased, the commons has had to be abandoned in one aspect after another. It has become increasingly evident that we can no longer treat the tidal wetlands as a commons. Each expanded use by one interest has resulted in the infringement of another's personal liberty. The varying perceptions of tidal marsh values and uses has engendered conflicts that are difficult to resolve.

The philosophy that the public has little or no right to exercise interest, concern, or control over what individuals or businesses do with land or other resources in their possession is being seriously eroded by the conservation principles now evolving. It has been pointed out that individuals and businesses own land only because the sovereign states allow it and only as long as their use of it does not seriously interfere with similar rights of their neighbors (Hawkes, 1966; Sax, 1971).

The impacts of newly created tidal wetlands legislation can be felt throughout the coastal states of the United States. Such legislation has affected tax bases, employment in the construction industries, and the health of marine industries. It has resulted in the development of new coastal zone plans to replace the traditional designs. Priorities have been modified: cost effectiveness in now tempered by the need for environmental impact mitigation. Housing, highways, and boating facilities are the three areas most affected. They must be developed in ways that are compatible with environmental constraints through proper planning and engineering (Greenman, 1978).

PUBLIC TRUST DOCTRINE: RIGHTS AND LIABILITIES

Among the legal problems encountered in tidal marsh management are the rights and liabilities of persons seeking to alter the natural condition of a marsh; boundaries of ownership interest within a marsh; and boundaries of the jurisdictions of government agencies having powers to regulate filling, dredging, or other activities within the marsh (Briscoe, 1979).

For the concept of the public trust to be useful in developing a comprehensive legal approach to resource management problems, it must meet three criteria: it must contain some perception of the legal right of the general public; it must be enforceable against the government; and it must be capable of an interpretation consistent with contemporary concerns for environmental quality (Sax, 1970).

History

Both common law and civil law are applicable to the tidelands of the United States. The common law, which originated in English law (developed around the Magna Charta), is based in part on customary usages and in part on common sense. It is a body of judicial rulings said to be derived from "common custom of the realm." It is unwritten law: judge-made law or case law. Civil law has its antecedents in Roman law and is based on an emphasis of statutes and on codes of law. Basically it is entirely stated in a written code.

By the feudal period, the emphasis on public ownership of waterways and tidal areas, as expressed in Roman civil law, had gradually given way to private ownership. The signing of the Magna Charta, which was in part a reaction to the proliferation of private ownership (by the sovereign) and the accompanying increase in public inconvenience, can be seen as the event that started the pendulum swinging back to protect the public's interest, especially in areas of navigation and fisheries (Drayton, 1970). Nevertheless, because our modern laws are derived from both Roman civil and English common law, they contain many doctrinal inconsistencies and confusing aspects, and at the same time a core of rights pertaining to tidal areas (Drayton, 1970; Sax, 1970; Smith and Sammons, 1974). These ambiguities are compounded by the existence of two judiciary and legislative systems: federal and state (Shalowitz, 1962; Salsbury, 1970).

Under early English common law, a riparian subject could own the beds of both fresh and tidal waters to the extent that they were of value to him. The reign of Elizabeth I saw a significant change: the courts began to accept the theory that the crown owned the beds including the foreshore ("land that lies between the high and low water marks and that is alternately wet and dry according to the flow of the tide" [Salsbury, 1970]). Since these lands were incapable of ordinary or private occupations, cultivation or improvement, the title of such lands belonged to the monarch, who could not grant them to others. They were held by the sovereign as the representative of the people and subject to the public right (*jus publicum*) of navigation and fishing. On the other hand, the sovereign also retained the rights and privileges accorded ownership of private property (*jus privatum*), including the power of deposition. The states succeeded the English ruler as sovereign and the concept of sovereign ownership of the tidelands and related public trust doctrine became part of American law (Haueisen, 1974).

As a result of this dichotomy of rights, the present-day state may be subject to certain limitations and use and disposal of such lands (Shalowitz, 1962; Salsbury, 1970). On one hand, the state has all of the rights and privileges accorded ownership of private property (*jus privatum*) including the ability to dispose of land as it sees fit. On the other hand, there are certain public rights (*jus publicum*) which are part of the establishment and acknowledgment of sovereignty and thus put certain restraints on the state. These rights are the public's, and the state cannot destroy, impair, or surrender them. If the right to use tidal waters and the land beneath them is part of this *jus publicum*, the state may not grant a property right in, or authorize use of such tidal waters. From this restraint on the legislative plenary powers springs the public trust doctrine. The public trust doctrine provides a foundation for granting any citizen the standing to challenge any administrative decision granting permission to use or alienate state wetlands. It enables an individual—a shareholder in the *jus publicum*—to have a concrete interest in a state's wetlands (Salsbury, 1970; Echeverria and Linky, 1978).

State ownership in most cases extends landward to the line of mean high tide, including marsh lands and shallows. In navigable inland waters, ownership usually extends to the mean high-water mark. Although federal law has determined the extent of submerged lands that each state acquired upon its admission to the union, the subsequent disposition of such lands is a matter of state law (Schoenbaum, 1972). With the adoption of the Constitution and the formation of the federal government, the latter succeeded to such rights as the states chose to surrender. Any power not specifically identified in the Constitution remained with the individual states, subject to the public rights of navigation and fishing (Shalowitz, 1962). To determine the extent of any state's ownership of submerged lands, it is necessary to explore the law of that particular state from the time it became a state to the present (Schoenbaum, 1972). Each state has addressed the matter of riparian rights according to its own views of justice and policy: some retain title, others consider the tidelands as connected to the upland, and still others have granted their use to individuals, independent of the ownership of the uplands.

The individual states as sovereigns are free to convey public trust lands, and to define the extent of public rights in such lands, but they cannot abdicate their trust over such property. It has been generally accepted that the grantee of the state cannot obtain a better title than the grantor and that private persons obtain and hold such lands subject to the trust. The title of the private owner is thus severely restricted in the use of the property; it must be compatible with the rights of the public and cannot violate the trust. What constitutes a violation depends on the facts of the particular case and the extent of the public trust according to state law (Schoenbaum, 1972).

There have been three types of grants to private ownership from the sovereign: those from the Lord Proprietors; those given by the Crown itself; and, since the American Revolution, grants from individual states. The states have absolute title to submerged lands and most have prima facie title (presumed title) to tidelands (between mean high water and mean low water). Each state can determine the disposition of these lands. In some states, grants to private individuals give title to the land to the low-water mark. On the other hand, many states have forbidden further sale of state tidelands or submerged lands. In some instances certain public rights of use have been preserved under a "public trust" concept (Haueisen, 1974; Hershman, 1977).

The public trust doctrine provides the state with a strong constitutional basis for new or amended coastal legislation. While the public trust regulations of tidelands have become codified in most states, they can be subjected to limited reinterpretation. Therefore, this public trust doctrine, representing a flexible source of authority and regulation, can serve an important role in implementing a state's coastal program. Since every state already has public trust authority, either in common law or statutory form, or both, each state should implement its coastal management program through decisions grounded in and developed from traditional notions of the public trust (Echeverria and Linky, 1978).

Scope

The public trust doctrine, as it exists today, has two aspects. The first pertains to the title ownership of the property in question, and the second deals with the public interest regarding protection and preservation of the water and land use. The title aspect of the doctrine has ancient roots, whereas the use aspect is a relatively new facet of modern society (Porro, 1983).

The reaction of private ownership which resulted in the Magna Charta expanded the scope of citizen's easement rights in waterways and tidal areas. The public trust theory of tidal and navigable waters held that the public had certain important rights on the foreshore that superseded any conflicting private rights, including those claimed by the sovereign. The sovereign was acknowledged as trustee for these public rights but could not appropriate them for his own use (Drayton, 1970; Haueisen, 1974). Since that time, there has been a steady expansion of interest in easements as a consequence of increasing competition and conflict in the uses of tidal resources. The doctrinal trend toward the recognition of easements and common ownership in these tidal resources has tended to lag behind the conflicting demands for such resources. As more interests are threatened, new public concerns are created and/or rediscovered. The more easements there are, the less any one of them can be absolute, and the courts can no longer depend on rigid formulas to resolve conflicts. Drayton (1970) has suggested that perhaps the day will soon come when common law citizens will have as many rights in the foreshore as those enjoyed by the Roman citizens.

At the time of the Magna Charta and subsequently, the scope of public rights was restricted to the issues of navigation and fishing. The separate states and, in some cases, private owners are subject to the paramount right of control by the federal government for navigation and commerce (Haueisen, 1974). In recent years other interests have been incorporated. The California Supreme Court, for example, has asserted that the more important aspects of public rights in privately held trust land include the preservation of these lands in their natural state for the enhancement of wildlife as well as for their intrinsic aesthetic beauty (Schoenbaum, 1972).

The gradual shift from *jus privatum* to *jus publicum* provides clues to indicate how traditional tideland rights are being adapted to meet the objectives of modern coastal zone management. In the past, public trust in some states has been restricted solely to navigational and fishing interests with no control over private manipulation of the tidelands. Current thinking favors the expansion of public rights by increasing the number of public interest uses to include recreation, conservation, hunting, gathering seaweed, and bathing (Commission on Marine Science, Engineering and Resources, 1969; Maloney and Ausness, 1974; Echeverria and Linky, 1978). It is evident that the scope of state and federal control over navigable water belongs to the public. Private owners may use their land only in a way that does not cause harm to the public (Dawson, 1978). The federal government maintains easements in the foreshore for national defense, flood control, electric power generation, and international affairs in addition to the conventional uses of navigation, fishing, and commerce (Haueisen, 1974).

Even though the state owns the beds of navigable waters, the private riparian landowner is deemed to possess certain rights by virtue of his proximity to the water. The principle is well established in common law the riparian owner can claim any land adjacent to the water that has been added by accretion or by reliction (exposure by subsiding). Thus the riparian owners are assured of continuing access to the water. In Maryland, for example, the various state statutory provisions have caused difficulties in defining and circumscribing the riparian rights. Such difficulties along with increased value of coastal water front property and more efficient means of filling, have caused some riparian owners to engage in wetland reclamation. This in turn raises the question of whether the riparian owner has the right to reclamation adjacent to his property. Due to the uncertainties of the law, many land titles are clouded. Such uncertainties might enable the riparian owner to gain title to accretions formed by natural or artificial means. The Maryland Wetlands Statute, however, conforms more to the common law than the previous statutory law, in that it entitles the riparian owner to natural accretion only. Artificial accretion is eliminated (Salsbury, 1970).

The Taking Question

"Taking" involves a conflict between two valid and equally important issues: the need for a livable environment and the importance of private property rights (Bosselman, Callies, and Banta, 1973). Taking is the formal condemnation of physical confiscation of property by the government. A taking may also occur when some governmental regulation causes a direct and immediate interference with the use or value of the property (Salsbury, 1970; Metzgar, 1973). The Fifth Amendment of the U.S. Constitution, in conjunction with the due process clause of the Fourteenth Amendment, places a restraint on the power of eminent domain for both the federal and state governments: the taking of private property by a state or federal agency for public use without just compensation violates the Fourteenth Amendment. Most state constitutions contain similar provisions. The problem of taking becomes complicated when the valid exercises of police power for the good of the majority creates hardship for one or more individuals although no actual taking occurs. Should not these citizens be paid a just compensation for their loss? Should this loss be treated as a taking of property even if no formal expropriation occurs? Once this determination has been made, how many dollars comprise the "just compensation" (Michelman, 1967)?

In what turned out to be a watershed case dealing with the taking issue, Supreme Court Justice Oliver Wendell Holmes, in *Pennsylvania Coal Co.* v. *Mahon*, stated the test that became the basis for countless future decisions: "The general rule at least is that, while property may be regulated to a certain extent, if regulation goes too far it will be recognized as a taking" (Bosselman, Callies, and Banta, 1973).

How is it that regulation (police powers) may be construed as a taking? This was not the intent of the Magna Charta, which stated that "no free man shall be deprived of his freehold—unless by the lawful judgement of his peers and by the law of the land." Nor was it so stated in U.S. Constitution ("nor shall private property be taken for public use without just compensation") While the use of the land was regulated throughout English and American history, it was not until Justice Holmes's decision at the turn of the twentieth century that excessive regulation could be equated to a taking. The distinction between regulation and a taking is a matter of degree rather than kind. Compensation was generally provided for physical takings of developed property while regulations of land were enforced without any compensation to the landowner in the early days of the United States or in England. A change in interpretation began to take place in the latter part of the nineteenth century, culminating in the Holmes decision, wherein a diminution of property values becomes a taking when it reaches a certain magnitude (Bosselman, Callies, and Banta, 1973).

There has been a great deal of effort expended by legal scholars and others to distinguish between takings, which require compensation, and the exercise of police powers, which may not. In recent years, interest in environmental quality has generated property-regulating attempts that actually or potentially clash with the constitutional taking provision. The freedom that has been given private resource users to degrade natural resources may be attributed in large measure to a limited comprehension of property rights. The traditional view of property rights has focused solely on activities occurring within the physical boundaries of the user's property. Sax (1971) has advocated recognition of the interrelationships among various uses of apparently unrelated pieces of property. He proposed that, once property is seen as an interdependent network of competing uses rather than as a number of independent and isolated entities, property rights and the law of takings are open for modification.

According to the dominant view, when private parties incur economic loss as a result of government managerial activity, the activity may be considered a taking. In addition, where losses are incurred as a result of the government's action as a mediator in the competition among various nongovernmental property owners, such losses need not be compensated as a constitutional right (Sax, 1964). On the basis of the views expressed by Sax (1971), much of what was formerly considered a taking issue might better be viewed as an application of police power to justify what has been called "public rights."

At the present time, the takings laws are concerned with four criteria: diminution of value; invasion whereby government has formally taken possession or title; the noxious use test, which deems certain activities socially undesirable; and cause of the harm test, which determines whether an activity causes harm to a neighbor or the public. According to present perceptions of takings law (the lessening of value theory), the criterion for recognizing a particular economic injury that follows from government action is the extent of economic loss. The question is whether, and to what extent, the owner's ability to profit from the piece of property in question has been impaired. If it has, the government is said to have taken and the owner is entitled to compensation. Such a sentiment is tied to an assumption that the right to compensation can be determined by examining the economic effects that occur solely within the physical boundaries of a property.

Sax (1971) deemed it inappropriate to find a taking has occurred simply because the government's intercession has curtailed the owner's former use of the property within his boundaries. He felt the restriction may instead depict a resolution of conflicting claims in order to protect and maintain the uses of other parcels of property within their boundaries.

It is apparent from known environmental parameters that there is a marked complexity in the use of natural resources. If we are to deal in a sensible fashion with the use of resources, we must focus attention on the nature and degree to which the consequences of any use are dispersed across property, state, and even national boundaries. Sax (1971) went on to say that the law relating to property rights and takings ought to reflect such a perception.

Sax's view would recognize diffusely held claims as public rights, entitled to equal consideration in legislative or judicial resolution of conflicting claims to the common resource base, without regard to the manner in which they are held. Competition in the use of wetlands is an excellent example of this complexity of claims. Marine organisms that breed along the shallow wetland shoreline require that such a habitat remain intact. Wetland owners, by modifying their property, could have far-reaching effects on those who derive benefit from the ocean resource. On the other hand, those whose interests depend on the stability of the marine environment for a livelihood may force the wetland owners to restrict the use of their rightful property.

At present, most courts have found that reasonable regulations imposed on the wetlands do not constitute a taking. Regulations that deprive the owner of all reasonable use of the property are the only ones that constitute a taking and that must be compensated by public purchase of the lands to ensure their preservation. Such a view has brought forth the proposition that a wetland owner who wants to impose a restriction on the use of the oceans to promote activities on his or her lands ought to be compelled to buy that right. Wetlands cases have not been handled in this fashion because the ocean is not owned as private property, but by the public at large. We have a traditional inability to recognize public rights: while the public's interest is very great, the interest of each individual is very small. According to Sax (1971), the penalty for ignoring the cumulative right is that each person with an interest in the use of the marine resource is treated as an intruder and is required to pay for the protection of his or her interest. The claims of right to use resources ought not to be discriminated against simply because they are held in one conventional form of ownership rather than another.

Those cases finding a taking allege that, when the government restricts the use of private property, the public has acquired something to which it did not previously have a right. While preventing total loss to the particular owner, it usually interposes the loss on diffusely held interests such as those dependent on the wetland resources disrupted by filling and dredging.

The constitutional takings provision, it is assumed, guarantees compensation when government restrains the profit-making capacity of private property owners in favor of a more general public claim. In so doing, recognition of extant public rights is being denied. The prevailing view of compensation law has a practical effect on resource allocation: the prospect of having to pay compensation is a constraint on government regulation of private property. Such compelled compensation may deter legislators from imposing such a restriction.

Sax (1971) emphasized that what is being proposed does not obliterate the distinctions between private properties. Rather, it points out that the simplistic way in which that distinction has been made under existing property law, attending solely to physical boundaries of property, is insufficient. It does not make less valid a demand for compensation when the government restricts uses that do not have spillover effects. Sax would put competing resource users in a position of equality when their demands are in conflict and when their uses would involve some spillover on the neighbors or the public. In such cases, and in such cases only, there is a conflict in which neither is *a priori* entitled to prevail, because neither claimant has any more right to impose on his neighbor than his neighbor does on him. Only in such situations may private use be curtailed by the government without triggering the taking clause. The most obvious type of spillover occurs when the use of one's land results in the physical restriction of the uses of other land. A second type of spillover effect involves the use of a common resource to which another landowner has an equal right. The wetland that serves as a breeding ground and nursery for the adjacent coastal waters should be viewed as a common resource with conflicting demands between the ocean users and the wetland owner. A visual prospect is also a common resource. If the landscape, as a visual prospect, is not confined to a single tract of land, no single landowner is entitled to dominate it. A third type of spillover concerns the use of property that affects the health or well-being of others, including wildlife. Regardless of the severity of the loss, any use of property that has spillover effects as identified here may be constitutionally restrained without any compensation being required; each of the competing interests that would be adversely affected by such uses has, *a priori*, an equal right to be free of such burdens. Where spillovers do not occur, takeovers must be compensated (Sax, 1971). In summary, Sax has stated that the goal of a system that regulates property rights should be the maximization of the output of the entire resource base upon which competing claims of right are dependent, rather than maintenance of the profitability of individual parcels of property.

It is evident from Holmes's decision (Bosselman, Callies, and Banta, 1973) that economic profit can play an important role in the taking question. Since the time of that decision, many courts have weighed the public benefits of the regulation against the magnitude of loss of property values. Because the Supreme Court lost interest in the taking question for a long period after the Holmes decision, it has been taken up by the lower federal courts and the state courts. The result has been a wide range in the interpretation of the taking issue, on a case-by-case basis. In general, the courts tend to uphold well-thought-out regulations. They appear to prefer regulations that control uses of land that were treated as "nuisances" under the traditional common law. There does not seem to be any consistent pattern involving the diminution theory, wherein the property values are reduced by a regulation and the courts deem the regulation to be constitutional. There is a strong tendency by the courts to approve land use regulations if the purpose of the regulation is statewide or regional rather than local. The courts also show a marked preference for regulations having broad, multipurpose goals (Bosselman, Callies, and Banta, 1973).

Harwood (1978), in relating the outcome of a New York Court of Appeals case, observed that the only substantial difference between an overly harsh land use regulation and the actual taking of property is that "the restriction leaves the owner subject to the burden of payment of taxation while outright confiscation would relieve him of that burden" (*Avenue Bay Construction Co.* v. *Thatcher* [1938]).

Much the same view was expressed by Salsbury (1970), who commented that the rules and regulations may result in an unconstitutional taking if the landowner has been denied the practical use of his property. Such an action would deprive him of the use of his land yet would still burden him with the need to pay taxes. Michelman (1967) believed that a court assigned to differentiate among impacts that are and are not takings is essentially engaged in deciding when the government may execute public programs while leaving associated costs disproportionately concentrated on one or a few persons. Harwood (1978) went on to say that the courts have been critical of a government that restricts land use yet imposes taxes as if no restrictions existed. The courts have reacted favorably to a reduction in tax assessment in line with restrictions of land use. This reflects a modification of Holmes's view (Bosselman, Callies, and Banta, 1973), in that reduced profitability should reflect reduced economic value. Conversely, maintaining high taxes on wetlands implies that those lands should be developed and may actually compel the owners to develop in order to meet the costs of owning and maintaining the land. This would thus negate legislative stipulations that are part of various wetland protection statutes. One might presume that long-term environmental and economic harm to society justifies restrictions on development. Although failure to reflect land use restrictions in tax assessments should not be considered a taking, reduced assessments can act as an incentive for wetland protection by removing the economic pressures to develop land in order to meet high tax burdens. Reduced tax assessments would reflect the use value of the lands, not their prior fair market value (Harwood, 1978).

The legal approaches to the protection of wetlands are the exercise of eminent domain, acquisition, zoning ordinances, and the use of police power (Metzgar, 1973; Hershman, 1977; Dawson, 1978). A state's power to restrict the use of privately owned land is an aspect of its police power, and a state may reasonably restrict such use without compensation only for the promotion of health, safety, morals, or general community welfare. Even so, if the restriction is too severe, it could be declared a taking without compensation. The state thus has the choice of taking by eminent domain and paying compensation or enacting less restrictive regulations.

Zoning for purely aesthetic purposes may not constitute a valid exercise of the police power. As of 1973, Metzgar reported that only two states (New York and Oregon) have held zoning for aesthetic purposes to be a valid exercise of police power. Dawson (1978) thought that zoning ordinances in wetlands should be concerned primarily with protecting human health and safety. He felt that other environmental factors, including aesthetic values and statements to preserve wetlands in their natural state, should be avoided. However, a zoning ordinance that tends to promote an aesthetic purpose will be upheld if it also serves to promote public health, safety, or welfare. Aesthetic purposes are also upheld if they protect property values in the community. Of interest in this regard is a 1978 U.S. Supreme Court case, *Penn Central Transportation Company et al.* v. *City of New York* (438 U.S. 104), in which the New York City Landmark Act was upheld against an argument that it was a taking because it restricted alterations to Grand Central Station. Protection of property values is considered a matter of public welfare (Metzgar, 1973).

Banta (1978) has identified three key points associated with the issue of taking and wetlands: property, procedure, and effect.

1. In wetlands, public rights coexist with private ownerships. The public may fail to defend their rights actively and private uses may be valid. Where private-use rights have been created in public trust land, the public trust may have to be reasserted after the passage of time or changes in the statutes or conditions of use. Legal argument over the terms and conditions of competing public interest must precede any constitutional taking claim. In this way it can be easier to sidestep the narrower taking argument.
2. The individual without a permit has in effect not applied, and as a result he does not yet have a taking claim. The courts will seldom consider such a claim unless all administrative procedures have been exhausted. The essential procedural requirement is a fair evaluation of the proposed use or development that does not preclude all alternatives.
3. Some will argue that economic loss has been incurred because of a regulation that restricted or precluded the use of a wetland resource; thus such a regulation constitutes a taking. Value loss may not define the constitutionality of such a regulation, however.

A permit program that allows a number of use options as long as environmental standards are observed would not deny all practical use and would thus not overstep the constitutional limit. A question may arise when no practical use of a wetland resource is allowed. The best way to consider the practical use of a resource is to examine the public purpose of the regulation and to weigh the purpose against the burden imposed on the private property owner (Banta, 1978).

Dawson (1978) believed that zoning ordinances should list a maximum of permitted uses. Reportedly the courts are more sympathetic to partial restrictions of land use than to prohibitions that deprive the landowner of all value. The ordinance must contain a permit system to counteract complaints that local procedures deny the due process of law because they do not conform to federal and state administrative procedures. Dawson expressed the opinion that, while statewide land use laws are subject to political pressures (as is local zoning), the federal political arena is larger and thus from an environmental point of view a better forum for debate. Dawson also held the belief that control through local zoning will not be fully effective where the zoning body controls only a small portion of the relevant land.

A key to the federal environmental perspective is the National Environmental Policy Act of 1969 (NEPA) (Banta and Nauman, 1978). In addition, a salient point in any discussion of the taking issue is the nature and character of the permit program administered by the Corps of Engineers, known as Section 404 of the Federal Water Pollution Control Act (FWPCA) Amendments of 1972 (Banta, 1978). Authority of the corps's regulatory powers is based primarily on sections of the River and Harbor Act of 1899, Section 404 of the FWPCA, and Section 103 of the Marine Protection, Research and Sanctuaries Act of 1972. Section 103 is concerned with a permit program to regulate the ocean dumping of dredged material. The process of deciding what development in wetlands is in the public interest and which locations and designs are least destructive is the subject of contemporary dredge-and-fill permitting. Clearly, the environmental focus is new to the permit process (Banta and Nauman, 1978).

The federal government's focus on protection of wetlands has been directed at pollution control and preservation of migratory bird nesting and resting areas. Its efforts at water pollution control have been embodied in the Rivers and Harbors Act of 1899, the Oil Pollution Act of 1924, the Water Pollution Control Act of 1948, the 1956 amendments to the 1948 act, the Federal Water Pollution Control Act (FWPCA) Amendments of 1961, the Federal Water Quality Act of 1965, the Federal Clean Water Restoration Act of 1966, the Water Quality Improvement Act of 1970, and the Federal Water Pollution Control Act of 1972. Federal legislation enacted to protect migratory waterfowl has included the Migratory Bird Treaty Act of 1918, the Migratory Bird Conservation Act of 1929, the Migratory Bird Hunting Stamp Act of 1934, the Federal Aid in Wildlife Restoration Act of 1937, and the Accelerated Wetlands Acquisition Act of 1961. With the passage of the Coastal Zone Management Act of 1972, the federal government recognized that the coastal zone represents a distinct natural resource whose management is of national importance (Haueisen, 1974; Echeverria and Linky, 1978). In addition, the various coastal states have passed legislation protecting their coastal wetlands (Haueisen, 1974).

The River and Harbor Act of 1899 was enacted to protect navigation and the navigable capacity of the nation's waters. This was the case until 1968, when the Corps of Engineers published a list of factors besides navigation that could be considered in review of permit applications: fish and wildlife, conservation and pollution, aesthetics, ecology, and general public interest. The 1968 change in policy identified this as a "public interest review" related to a national concern for environmental values. A further revision in 1970 made it clear that permits were required for any work commenced landward of an established harbor line and that such permits would get a full public interest review. In 1972 the "navigable waters" definition was enlarged to include all waters now, in the past, or susceptible to be used for transport of commerce, as well as all waters subject to the ebb and flow of the tide. The landward limit of the jurisdiction was established as the ordinary high-water mark for fresh water; the shoreward limit of tidal water was the mean high-water mark. Final revisions were made in 1974 to the permit regulations for various reasons, including adoption of a wetlands policy that would protect them from undue destruction and identifying criteria that would be considered in evaluating permits (Chastaen, 1978; McCormick, 1978).

Congress enacted the FWPCA amendments with the announced purpose of restoring and maintaining the chemical, physical, and biological integrity of the nation's waters. Section 404 established a permit program to regulate the discharge of polluted materials, including dredge spoil. In 1974, revisions restricted Section 404 to the mean high-water mark and to the navigable waters, but this restriction was considered to limiting. Concern was expressed over the need to regulate the entire aquatic system, including all wetlands, rather than aquatic areas arbitrarily distinguished by the mean high-water mark. As a result of these concerns, the Corps of Engineers' definition of navigable waters was expanded to include coastal waters, wetlands, mud flats, freshwater streams, rivers susceptible to transport and their tributaries, and so on (Chastaen, 1978).

Because of this expanded coverage and work load, the Corps of Engineers created a permit program, which involves local, state, and federal agencies (Roe, 1976; Chastaen, 1978). Roe proposed a reform of the three multipermit requirements calling for a one-procedure mechanism: all applications for environmental protection and natural resource use permits would be subjected to a process involving one public notice, one public hearing, one environmental impact statement, one final decision, and one appellate review process. Roe believed that such a procedure would relieve the work load by replacing the various ordinances dealing with the permit process. On the other hand, Dawson (1978) expressed concern about the emphasis on streamlining or establishing the so-called one-stop-shop permit process. Dawson's concern was that such a procedure might be designed to inhibit public input and administrative or judicial review.

Mitigation is another facit of the permit process. The environmental quality of coastal development is usually treated as a question of design, location, construction, and operation. Mitigation is that part of this process that is concerned with the beneficial consequences for the environment and does not directly serve as a proposed project's functional purpose—it is any additional work recommended to restore or enhance an ecosystem and improve the ecosystem's carrying capacity. It creates difficult problems in the administrative decision-making process, and thus can become the last ounce of environmental quality that can be injected into a project within legally and politically acceptable limits. In so doing, mitigation can become a matter of negotiation.

THE BOUNDARY QUESTION

Where does the beach begin, and to what extent is this a legal question? This is a query that Corker (1966) posed when discussing the boundary issue. In the case of *Hughes* v. *State of Washington*, the Washington Supreme Court decided that the boundary between the upland and tideland is the fixed vegetation line that existed when Washington became a state in 1889: "the line of ordinary tide," or "the line which the water impresses on the soil by covering it for sufficient periods to deprive the soil of vegetation." In contrast, earlier in the same case, the court of appeals had determined the boundary to be the line of mean high tide established by the "average elevation of all high tides as observed at a location through a complete cycle of 18.6 years" and to be located "where that unchanging elevation meets the shore." This earlier decision was based on the U.S. Supreme Court decision of 1935 in *Borax Consolidated, Ltd.*, v. *Los Angeles*, in which the mean high tide was defined by the Coast and Geodetic Survey, and not by the vegetation line. Corker believed that the fixed boundary line defined by the Washington Supreme Court would invariably be inland of a mean high-tide line and the horizontal distance between the two lines could be substantial, so that the private landowner might be deprived of considerable land holdings as the state acquired more land. At present it could be extremely difficult to ascertain the ordinary high-tide line or line of vegetation existing at some earlier date, such as the time of entry to statehood.

This case not only illustrates the concerned about the boundary issue—where it is and how it is defined—but also introduces the question of who owns any land accretions. A third point, also raised by Corker (1966), is the fundamental issue concerning the extent to which state or federal laws provide the answers.

Resolution of these questions is of prime importance. There are tremendous competing interests and uses striving to take possession and title to tracts that are inundated and overflowed periodically by the tides. Such activity results from a well-known American trait: the desire to convert previously empty land to valuable realty. Thus land prices have been forced upward and title questions affecting ownership are becoming increasingly prevalent and important. On the one side is the protection of public interests and the ability to regulate and direct land use. On the other hand is the long-standing respect for private property rights and the constitutional protection of the concept of due process. The basic premise is that the sovereign state is interested in all tidelands. The problems are to define tidelands and to locate the boundary separating private from state holdings (Porro, 1970; Hershman, 1977). While questions of whether a salt marsh belongs to the land or the sea, whether underlying peat is part of the bottom or the marsh, and whether the marsh is flooded to a given depth twice or only once a day may be academic, they become critical when ownership and control of the marshes is at issue (Hawkes, 1966). In addition, inherent in the management of this coastal resource is the need to designate boundaries of ownership or regulatory jurisdiction, or both (Teleky, 1978).

Since Corker's (1966) article, Hershman (1977) has provided us with some insights about the extent to which state and federal laws provide answers. It is well established in the common law of some states that the line of distinction between private and public interests is a line at ordinary high water. In some states, this line of demarcation has shifted from the mean high-tide to the mean low-tide datum (Porro, 1970; Porro and Teleky, 1972; Hershman, 1977). Submerged lands waterward of the "ordinary low-water mark" are never available for private ownership. Swamp and overflowed lands may be sold to private parties and are free to any public trust for navigation. Briscoe (1979) presented the view that the purchaser of tidelands owns the soil subject to an easement for the public for the uses of navigation and commerce, via the public trust doctrine. In most jurisdictions, however, the state owns the tidelands and beds under navigable waters, holding then under the same doctrine (Porro and Teleky, 1972; Schoenbaum, 1972; Metzgar, 1973; Maloney and Ausness, 1974).

The coastal zone comprises many overlapping jurisdictions—private, federal, state, local—and each involves separate issues. The rights of riparian or littoral properties in the soil below high-water mark are governed by the laws of the various states, subject to the powers granted to the federal government for regulating and improving navigation. The extent of such riparian rights is a matter governed by the statutes and court decisions of the various states (Shalowitz, 1962).

Since early in the history of the United States, the Supreme Court has ruled that the states own the tidelands and submerged lands beneath the navigable waters within the states. In 1947 the Court ruled that the federal government owned the submerged lands seaward of the low-water mark and outside any inland waters. Subsequently, Congress passed the Submerged Lands Act of 1953, which allows the states to extend their control up to 3 geographic miles along the Atlantic and Pacific coasts. States bordering the Gulf of Mexico control potentially 10.6 miles, or 3 marine leagues, from the shore, and those bordering the Great Lakes control the area to the international boundary (Hershman, 1977).

Hershman (1977) cautioned that in reviewing jurisdictional boundaries for government management, it is important that they be geographically defined with reference to charts and maps (to the limits of the state's jurisdiction) or designated by reference to specific subjects, either of which he considered to be legally valid. Such jurisdiction may apply irrespective of ownership (within constitutional limits). The most efficient way to determine jurisdiction is to review ownership and resources. The longer the list of resources in the vicinity (salt-tolerant vegetation, endangered species, periodically submerged land, fisheries, etc.), the greater the likelihood of state or federal jurisdiction in addition to the traditional local building and setback controls (Hershman, 1977).

The second of Corker's (1966) concerns, simple accretion and erosion in the creation or loss of wetlands, is not considered a real problem. The creation of new land by accretion shifts title from the state to the private property owner. Conversely, erosion shifts title to the state. The greater problem is presented by artificial changes that fall into two categories: private changes, such as land fills; and public changes, such as highway systems, mosquito ditching, drainage plans, dredging, and digging subsurface wells. These activities not only cause direct and immediate movement of soil, but also have an impact on erosion and accretion (Porro and Teleky 1972; Maloney and Ausness, 1974). In addition, they tend to increase the value of coastal waterfront property, thus inducing riparian owners to engage in wetland reclamation. This has created concerns about whether the riparian owner has the right to reclamation adjacent to his property (Salsbury, 1970). According to Maloney and Ausness (1974), however, there is no change in title boundaries with sudden additions or losses of soil. The landowner may not intentionally add to his property by accretion or reliction.

The title dilemma of tidal lands arises from old English common law, which holds that title to the foreshore belonged to the sovereign while upland property was privately owned. All lands covered by the "flux and reflux of the sea at ordinary tides" were considered part of the foreshore. Therefore, the ordinary high-water mark constituted the landward limit of the foreshore, and ordinary low-water mark formed the seaward limit. More important, the ordinary high-water mark identified the seaward limit of the upland. Its utility was reduced as a boundary due to the uncertainty of the meaning of "ordinary tide." English courts, since the 1854 *Attorney General* v. *Chambers* case, have considered the ordinary high-water mark to be "the line of the medium high tide between the springs and the neaps." American courts have generally followed the definition of high tide put forth in *Borax Consolidated, Ltd.* v. *City of Los Angeles* case and upheld in the Supreme Court, wherein the Court adopted the mean high-tide standard and the survey methods described in U.S. Coast and Geodetic Survey publications (Maloney and Ausness, 1974). The law is basically simple: it is the proof of location that is the challenge (Porro, 1970; Porro and Weidener, 1978; Teleky, 1978).

Many U.S. jurisdictions follow the English rule—Alabama, Alaska, California, Connecticut, Florida, Maryland, Mississippi, New Jersey, New York, North Carolina, Oregon, Rhode Island, South Carolina, and Washington. Some states have departed from the common law position. Massachusetts and Maine, for example, recognize the low-water line in accordance with a colonial ordinance. Delaware, Georgia, New Hampshire, Pennsylvania, and Virginia also use the low-water line. Texas recognized the English position with respect to common law grants, but uses the line of higher high tides when Spanish or Mexican grants are involved. Louisiana has adopted the civil law boundary of the line of the highest winter tide. In Hawaii the upland owner has title to the upper reaches of the wash of the waves (Maloney and Ausness, 1974).

As originally conceived, title did not technically repose in ownership, but in an incorporeal hereditament (an intangible right) in the nature of an easement recognizing the right of fisheries, navigation, and the need for the water course as a common public way. Thus the sovereign did not own outright, but held such water courses in trust for free public use. This did not extend to the surrounding marshlands. Since, however, by English common law the sovereign was considered to be the only source of title for all lands in the kingdom, the soil between high and low water would have been included.

In the United States the distinction between corporeal and incorporeal hereditary rights has disappeared. However, the state cannot convey to any citizen the public rights of either navigation or fisheries. The incorporeal rights are held in public trust for all (Porro, 1970). At the same time, landowners whose property borders on the ocean or a navigable water course have certain riparian or littoral rights. These rights depend on contact with the water and not on ownership of the submerged lands beneath the water. They cannot be impaired by the state without compensation. These landowners share with the public the right to fish, navigate, swim, bath, and so forth, subject to certain regulations imposed by the state. Their property is also subject to accretion, reliction, avulsion, and erosion (Maloney and Ausness, 1974).

Some guidelines must be established to determine when and where private interests should give way to public interests. The fundamental point of real property jurisprudence is to divide interests in various parcels of real estate by boundary. A line is normally established on some visible surface. In the marsh the boundary is determined by the tide and, because of the variability of this determinant, such a boundary is ambiguous and ambulatory. (Shalowitz, 1962; Porro, 1970; Maloney and Ausness, 1974; Teleky, 1978).

Private ownership interests have been and are striving to secure documented recorded title while the government has been and is attempting to reestablish its responsibility to protect public interests or trust in the property involved. Many states have actively sought enforcement of the sovereign interest and are in this way bringing about a direct confrontation with record title holders. Thus there is a real need to define and locate this "invisible boundary" using whatever data and resources at hand to help solve coastal problems (Porro, 1970; Hull, 1978).

The mean high tide, which has been equated with the "ordinary high water mark," refers to the intersection of a tidal plane with the shore and has no relation to a physical mark or a vegetation line. Such an approach is justified as spring tide occur at the same regularity as neap tides and, since one is appreciably above a medium plane and the other is below the medium, they cancel each other out. From a technical point of view, it is easier to obtain a plane of mean high water that includes all tides than to calculate a plane that excludes spring and neap tides (Maloney and Ausness, 1974).

Establishing tidal boundaries involves two engineering aspects: a vertical one predicted on the basis of the height of the tide during its rise and fall, establishing a tidal plane or datum such as mean high water, and a horizontal one related to the line where the tidal plane intersects the shore to form the tidal boundary desired, such as the mean high-water mark and the mean low-water mark. The first measure is derived from tidal observations and, based on long-term observations, it is for all practical purposes a permanent one. The second depends on the first, but it is also affected by natural processes such as erosion, accretion, and artificial changes. Such a water boundary, determined by tidal definition, is thus not a fixed, visible mark on the ground but represents a condition at the water's edge during a particular instant of the tidal cycle (Shalowitz, 1962).

Borax Consolidated, Ltd. v. *City of Los Angeles* was a landmark case in the law of tidal boundaries. The Supreme Court accepted the U.S. Coast and Geodetic Survey definition that "mean high water at any place is the average height of all the high waters at that place over a considerable period of time and from theoretical considerations of an astronomical character there should be a periodic variation in the rise of water above sea level having a period of 18.6 years." To ascertain the mean high-tide line with requisite certainty in fixing the boundary of valuable tidelands, an average of 18.6 years should be determined as near as possible (Shalowitz, 1962). Such a period represents a tidal epoch and includes the Metonic cycle of 235 lunations, which includes the 18.6-year cycle for regression of the moon's nodes and other astronomic variables (Porro and Weidener, 1978). Very few stations have sufficient records, however, and extrapolation of coastal data into estuaries can lead to grave errors of demarcation. A few courts have ruled that the full tidal cycle of 18.6 years be used when possible, but that a "considerable or reasonable period" would be an adequate substitute. Since tidal lines change with time, most state and federal laws require the legal boundaries to conform to such a gradually changing line (Hershman, 1977).

Provost (1976) noted that the mean annual high-water line has a seasonal component. If the tides reach their marsh-building limits on a seasonal basis, the upper edge of the marsh has to be related to a correspondingly seasonal tidal datum. Both Provost and Maloney and Ausness (1974) commented on a Florida case where the court favored a landward mean high-water line (or "winter line") over a seasonal mean high-water line (or "summer line"). Provost reasoned that the courts are thus taking into account the ambulatory nature of the shoreline and that precedence exists for jurisdictional boundaries that take account of seasonal realities in tidal phenomena.

Consistent elevational differences are reported to exist between the upper limit of tidal marshes (ULM is the median point within the marsh-upland transition zone) and the tidal datum of mean high water (MHW) from Chesapeake Bay. These ULM-MHW differences were reported to fall into two groups, distinguishing saline and freshwater tidal marshes. For the saline marshes, the group average of the ULM elevation was 0.95 feet above MHW; for freshwater marshes, the average ULM elevation was 0.59 feet above MHW (Boon, Boule, and Silberhorn, 1977). Based on 20-year tidal records in the Chesapeake, the ULM elevation designated for saline marshes would be exceeded by approximately 10% of the high tides in the course of an average year. The freshwater ULM elevation would be exceeded by approximately 20% of the high tides in an average year.

Weather can have a greater-than-average effect on tides in shallow, broad embayments. Local wind and pressure effects do not alter the tidal datums (MHW, MLW), but they do cause a large variance in observed water levels above and below their mean elevations. The ULM elevation in such embayments was found to be between 0.3 and 0.5 feet higher in relation to MHW than the average ULM elevation determined for saline marshes in this particular study, apparently in response to greater tidal immersion (Boon, Boule, and Silberhorn, 1977).

Several authors have expressed the view that there is a relationship between marsh vegetation and its vigor and the mean high-tide line (Anderson and Wobber, 1973; Bartlett et al., 1976; Brown, 1978). Brown recognized an upper wetland boundary in New York and New Jersey marshes, which represented the landward extent of tidal inundation. In New Jersey, a biological high water line was identified using plant species to indicate the approximate line of mean high water. Because of the extremely low relief within freshwater wetlands and the sharp topographic break separating wetland from upland, the biological high water and upper wetland boundary lines were often coincidentally drawn. In the saline marshes, due to differential sediment deposition, there may be considerable marsh expanse between these two lines. Brown (1978) concluded that, in such saline wetlands, the upper wetland boundary can be economically and accurately delineated by using plant species as indicators, as determined from aerial photos. New York and New Jersey have used this technique to claim control over wetlands seaward of the upper wetland boundary.

Based on their work in Georgia, Fornes and Reimold (1973) suggested that the biological species border may be as valid as the use of elevation (mean high water) to establish a line between state-owned marshland and privately owned upland. They did express caution that, in the firmer marshes, the border is between various species whereas, in the softer substrate of other marshes, the variation is between higher- and lower-vigor plant growth of the same species (e.g., *Spartina alterniflora*). They asserted that the distinction between color variations on a color infrared transparency are as accurate as surveying a line, less expensive, and faster.

In contrast, Lagna (1975), Porro and Weidener (1978), and Teleky (1978) did not consider a biological high-water line to be a viable determinant in establishing tidal boundaries. They recognized that the use of vegetation with its relation to biological and physical data in addition to infrared photography, both black-and-white and color, had some success in establishing a demarcation line. However, they considered the establishment of the mean high-tide line by vegetative analyses to be uncertain. They believed that neither species distribution nor plant vigor exhibit a consistent relationship to mean high water. Thus the upper margin of *S.*

alterniflora should not be equated to MHW since it may occur below or above MHW. If the former, the area of publicly owned wetlands would be reduced. Correspondingly, if the transition is above MHW, the private landowner would be deprived of land holdings.

After reviewing the results of much litigation, Porro and Weidener (1978) concluded that biological mapping as applied to boundaries is not valid beyond a general delineation of the coastal zone. They were of the opinion that the establishment of the mean high-water line is the purview of the professional land surveyor and that such an individual will require specialized education and experience to delimit this boundary properly. They also cautioned that great care must be taken in surveying in a MHW tide line because the difference of 0.1 foot in elevation could mean a very considerable difference on the horizontal in the amount of marsh lost or gained.

A tidal datum offers a distinct border that can be incorporated into a wetland definition but only as one of several criteria. Others would include reduction in the number of marsh plants, presence of salt marsh peat at the surface, a change in growth form from grass to shrub, and the establishment of an upper margin to determine an elevation that would include most of the highest tides (Lagna, 1975). The Delaware Wetlands Act of 1973 defines a tidal wetland as all the land up to two feet above the local MHW, and includes a list of plant species considered to be a typical flora of a tidal wetland. In Virginia, the Wetlands Act defines tidal wetlands as all land lying between and contiguous to mean low water and to an elevation above mean low water equal to a factor 1.5 times the mean tide range at the site of the proposed project, and upon which is growing one or more of some 35 forms of marsh vegetation (Anderson, Garten, and Smolen, 1974).

Porro and Weidener (1978) concluded that the only acceptable demarcation of a tidal boundary is the accurate determination of a local tidal datum coupled with conventional surveying techniques. They went on to say that the world of science, with its objectivity, has much to contribute while the world of law must strive to establish legal guidelines and principles that are technically rooted. Only by such a combination can the necessary legal stability required for title ownership in the tidal wetlands be achieved.

Porro and Teleky (1972) proposed a quasi-judicial solution using a combination of historical and scientific data. Wetland areas could initially be classified as state-owned, privately-owned, or controversial according to technical and scientific criteria. State-owned wetlands would be areas that are naturally and clearly situated below the mean high-water line and that have satisfied the criteria for a low marsh. Conversely, privately-owned marshes would be wetlands clearly above the mean high-water line that meet the criteria for high marsh. Controversy, of course, would arise over wetlands that do not fall clearly into either category.

A factor-percentage system was recommended by Porro and Teleky for wetlands where conclusive proofs are either unavailable or too expensive to obtain. A list of scientific, technical, and historical criteria would be assembled. Each item would be given a numerical value (factor points) depending on its conclusiveness and reliability. To evaluate the relative strength or weakness of either the state's or the record owner's claim, a percentage would be calculated, based on the ratio of the factor points favorable to the contestant's claim divided by the total number of factor points applicable to the land. If the factor-percentage representing the strength of the record owner's claim is above a designated percentage (e.g., 50%), the owner would have clear title to the land by paying to the state an amount equal to the state's factor-percentage of the unimproved market value of the property. Conversely, if the claim of the record owner is below the designated percentage, the state would have the right to obtain clear title to the land by paying the record owner an amount equal to his factor-percentage of the unimproved market value of the property.

Chapter 9

Management Concepts and the Future

A tidal marsh can be characterized in a variety of ways. Specific symbols denote its presence on a map and provide an approximation of its size. It can be detected on a photograph by the pattern of drainage creeks and/or ditches. It can be identified on color and false color photographs through a distinctive color signature. It is distinguished by hydrophytic plants and hydric soils, both of which are dominated by the ebb and flow of the tides. The upper limit is marked by a change from predominantly hydrophytic vegetation, much of which is salt-tolerant, to mainly mesophytic or xerophytic vegetation, and a change from predominantly saturated hydric soils to nonhydric, nonsaturated soil. The lower limit is identified by the extreme reaches of the low, low spring tides (Cowardin et al., 1979).

Much of this intertidal habitat has been subjected to some form of human use over the centuries. Some of this exploitation has generated conflicts and some has been abusive. Sidney Lanier in his poems — *Hymns of the Marshes* (Lanier, 1981) — during the latter part of the last century, touched on the calamities that can befall a marsh but, in a soaring flow of words, brought forth the beauty and serenity of the tidal marsh. More recently, Anne Simon presented a gloomy assessment of the marsh's future in her book *The Thin Edge* (1978): "Wherever we turn on the coast we confront the awful destruction of its magnificent natural system. We can no longer escape the results of years of short-sighted use but must, for the first time ever, witness the dying coast and wonder if we can still save it. Knowing what we know makes ours the crucial generation." Human exploitation of this intertidal landscape has brought us to the point when the use or abuse of all wetlands—even those that are considered unproductive—must be guarded (Horwitz, 1978). There is increasing agreement with the concerns of Ketchum (1972) that we cannot survive without coming to terms with our natural surroundings. Kusler (1978) and Costle (1979), among others, have noted that we are beginning to perceive the value of these ecosystems and are identifying procedures for protecting existing values.

Environmentalism is now generally viewed as practical and constructive. There has been a gradual and positive change of attitude among all parties involved, including the scientist, environmentalist, politician, lawyer and businessman. As Chapman (1931), E. P. Odum (1971), and others have pointed out, the words *economy* and *ecology* are derived from the same Greek root: *oikos*, meaning "house." Economy is the management of the house, and ecology is the study of the house. The ecologist must study the habitat to determine how the system works. The manager must use this information to develop environmentally sound management practices.

Gabrielson (1941), discussing wildlife management, described conservation as the restoration and future wise use of renewable resources. He identified three concepts that apply equally well to tidal marsh conservation: (1) soil, water, wildlife, and upland conservation are only parts of one inseparable program; (2) tidal marsh wildlife must have an environment suited to its needs if it is to survive; and (3) any use that is made of the living resource must be limited to not more than the annual increase if the essential seed stock is to be continually available. E. P. Odum (1971) saw the aim of conservation as twofold: "to insure the preservation of a quality environment that considers aesthetic and recreational as well as product needs" and "to insure a continuous yield of useful plants, animals, and materials by establishing a balanced cycle of harvest and renewal."

Leopold (1939) developed a thesis that conservation can be brought about by the judicious use of management concepts. One concept is preservation, where nothing is done and nature is allowed to take its course. For the most part, however, management involves the exercise of some level of manipulation and control. Good control is achieved through the coordination of science and use, and the purpose of management is to explore the possibilities of such coordination. Leopold pointed out more than four decades ago that marshes can be maintained or restored by the creative use of the very tools that have disrupted or destroyed them.

Tidal marsh management is built on the firm foundation of a continually expanding body of knowledge concerning relationships between tidal marsh organisms and the physical-chemical components of the marsh environment. In light of our present knowledge, marsh management can deal only with a very limited number of species in a particular marsh habitat. With continuing effort, the much-needed techniques of general ecological management will gradually evolve. In its present state, such management is in part an effort to apply the data that are now available, always with the awareness that existing tools, methods, and processes may have to be discarded as new and better information becomes available. However, tidal marsh management must involve more than the acquisition and interpretation of scientific facts and the response to economic pressures; It must recognize those that touch the human spirit.

VALUES AND PRIORITIES

Humans have used tidal marshes in ways that have not, in general, been based on informed understanding or consideration for the resources they contain. Until recently, people had not been thoroughly aware of the full range of values of these resources. Trappers appreciated the monetary value of muskrat pelts, construction personnel were aware of the value of the gravel that could be mined from below the marsh sediments, developers understood the value of wetlands for home development, and hunters derived satisfaction from the recreational harvesting of waterfowl. Prior to the National Environmental Policy Act (NEPA) of 1969, there had been one national objective for dealing with marshlands: economic development. Since then, coequal national objectives have been recognized: economic development and environmental quality. Thus, we are becoming aware of the nonmonetary assets of marshlands, assets identified by the public trust doctrine but long ignored or sacrificed. These include such basics as the landscape and the diversity of life forms, which had been jeopardized by human exploitation and habitat destruction (Jahn, 1981). Beeftink (1977b) suggested that conservation is not so much a question of ecological knowledge as of ethics, ideas, and cooperation in the world of human beings.

Reppert et al. (1979) identified two main categories of wetland characteristics: primary functions and cultural values. Primary functions comprise: biological production, general and specialized habitat for terrestrial and aquatic species, aquatic study areas, sanctuaries and refuges, hydrologic support functions, shoreline protection, storm and flood water storage, natural groundwater recharge, and water purification. Cultural values include socioeconomic and other socially discernable topics: commercial and recreational fisheries, renewable resources and agriculture, recreation, aesthetics, and other special values.

Whether economically or culturally perceived, the wetland assets are those manifestations of biological and physical functional relations that comprise a wetland. Analyses of economic and cultural values can serve to confirm or further reinforce the evaluation of wetlands based on their natural characteristics. In some instances, these values could carry much more weight in an evaluation of wetlands than would the inherent biological and physical functions (Reppert et al., 1979). Traditionally, aesthetic considerations have received short measure in the calculation of benefit-cost ratios and other economic considerations, partially because of the real difficulty in assessing these qualities and partially because of a technological point of view that is geared to physical benefits (Carls, 1979).

In evaluating the less tangible sociocultural assets of wetlands, Reimold, Phillips, and Hardisky (1980) believed that it is necessary to ask what benefits wetland systems offer the biosphere. These sociocultural values are generally removed from the economic realm and involve higher human aspirations. They can be categorized as aesthetic, recreational, and educational. Along with the concepts of preservation and sound ecological management, an appreciation of these values will provide the best way to perpetuate our wetland heritage and maintain an ecologically balanced biosphere (Niering, 1979). Reimold, Phillips, and Hardisky (1980) suggested that the aesthetic appreciation of wetlands is essentially a sensual one and that, to understand and evaluate them, we need to observe them over time. Such aesthetic perceptions of wetlands can be achieved through the medium of the painter and the photographer, and through literature, music, and the natural sounds of nature (Niering, 1979; Reimold, Phillips, and Hardisky, 1980).

Because the quest to establish worth is usually based on the monetary standard, value determinations often fail to evaluate intangible attributes of wetlands, such as beauty and purity. There is no common denominator in the assessment of cultural, visual, and aesthetic values with those of basic life support for such things as fisheries or wetland grazing. These various aesthetic components are attributable to the inherent presence of the undisturbed wetlands. While all these aesthetic components have worth, none can be assessed adequately in the present economic marketing structure (Reimold, Phillips, and Hardisky, 1980). Only the observer's mental and physical perceptions can dictate the final value determination.

Another sociocultural asset is recreation. Recreational values form a continuum from those that are consumptive or destructive to those that are purely nonconsumptive. Reimold, Phillips, and Hardisky (1980) admonished that it was important to make this distinction when wetland resources are used for public pleasure. An area that has aesthetic appeal attracts people and, in so doing, may become abused, thus reducing or destroying its aesthetic appeal. Even areas that are well managed and able to maintain mass appeal have little or no value for those who seek the solitude of the wetlands (Reimold, Phillips, and Hardisky, 1980).

The methodology for measuring aesthetic quality in the environment and the aesthetic assets of people who participate in outdoor recreation is at a relatively immature stage of development (Carls, 1979; Reimold, Phillips, and Hardisky, 1980). One attempt to compute recreational resource values of tidal marshes is to determine the money spent by waterfowl hunters, bird watchers, campers, boaters, and so on. However, Reimold, Phillips, and Hardisky (1980) suggested that such procedures are probably misleading. In spite of a growing public awareness of environmental quality, intensified population pressures can destroy the resource. Coastal resource managers, as well as the users of coastal resources, have an ethical responsibility to protect the aesthetic qualities associated with the landscape and the recreational experience along with other, more tangible aspects of the tidal marsh environment. Carls (1979) believed that such a challenge can be met, given time and a modicum of good taste and common sense, based on the interactions and methodologies developed in both the environmental and social sciences. As Niering (1979) and Reimold, Phillips, and Hardisky (1980) pointed out, education of citizens is essential for the continued conservation of the wetlands.

A number of workers (Walker, 1973; Queen, 1977; Carls, 1979; Niering, 1979; Jahn, 1981) have suggested that calculations of marsh value need to emphasize the natural characteristics and processes that recent ecological studies have brought to light. According to Queen (1977), these include biological production (such as primary producers and the various levels and kinds of consumers), aquaculture, waste-water assimilation, erosion control, flood control, and nitrogen cycling.

The important question for Queen (1977) was not "what are the uses of marshes in a natural state?" but "how should marshes be used?" Are uses to be related to natural characteristics of marshes, or should marsh property owners be allowed to alter them freely for residential, commercial, or industrial uses? At least four recognizable factors contribute to a lack of agreement on these two questions. (1) Many of the economic benefits that are derived from natural marshes do not accrue to marsh owners (owners normally do not profit from fish catches). (2) Scientific information concerned with many marsh processes and characteristics is limited. (3) There are considerable differences of opinion regarding the value to humans of even those processes and characteristics that are based on extensive scientific information. (4) Benefit-cost analyses that are routinely done for goods in the marketplace do not relate to common-property features such as marsh traits and processes. While it may be desirable to precisely quantify and assign monetary values to impacts on wetlands, current technology does not allow evaluators to be that definitive (Queen, 1977; Hansen et al. 1980).

Schamberger and Kumpf (1980) have proposed a method to quantitatively assess the value of habitat to fish and wildlife: Habitat Evaluation Procedures (HEP). Specifically, habitat values must be established within the perspective of three general value systems: the ability of the habitat to provide a resource based on the size of the area, resources present, and probable changes in these resources; economic data based on some measure of the dollar value of the resources; and the relative importance, including legal protection, that society places on the resources. The HEP system presumes that habitat value can be quantified, that habitat suitability for a particular animal species can be determined by evaluating the physical and chemical parameters of the habitat, and that its quantity and quality are directly related to animal populations.

There have been other attempts to assess wetland resource values in monetary terms. H. T. Odum (1971) suggested an evaluation based on energy flow in the marsh. Pope and Gosselink (1973) took a "component" approach. They assigned a monetary value to each marsh use for example, biological production, aquaculture, and waste assimilation. They then summed these individual values to obtain a total marsh value. This approach has been criticized by many, including Shabman and Batie (1978, 1980), who pointed out that wetlands have been developed for industrial, commercial, or residential sites in response to price incentives in the marketplace. However, there is no marketplace for ecological services such as fish and wildlife habitat, sediment trapping, or waste assimilation because neither the buyer nor the seller considers the value of such services. As a result, the market price of tidal marshes will not reflect the worth of these ecological services. In addition, there will be no recognition value of services that are forgone when the marsh is developed. Markets for ecological services of natural environments fail to exist or do not function according to certain economic criteria. Thus the observed market prices for tidal wetlands will not reflect the total value of the services they provide.

Up until now this discussion has focused on the evaluation of the natural characteristics of tidal marshes. The second part of Queen's (1977) question, which related to human exploitation of tidal marshes, is of equal importance. Darnell (1979) identified naturalness of the marsh and the magnitude of disturbance as well as values and the kinds of impacts among the variables with which environmental management must deal. He suggested that the values that one places on environmental impacts are determined by background and education, specific environmental experience and knowledge, perception of alternate uses to which the habitat may be subjected, and the scarcity of the environmental resource. Therefore the ranking of such impact values would be a personal matter. These environmental impacts will represent a significant modification of human values that are normally thought to be associated with nature. Such a definition would require the assignment of a series of agreed-upon values, which would in turn identify a set of management goals. According to Darnell, there would also be a recognition of the concept of significant modification. Hence, a basis for judging values, risks, and levels of acceptability would be established. In this way human use would be measured against established standards.

In the assessment of human impacts, primary or physical modification can generally be expressed in quantitative terms and the predictability of models designed for such evaluation can be high. However, the margin of error appreciably increases as we move from the physical to the biological. While generalizations about tidal marsh functions may be reasonably well established, site-specific factors are very important in determining response patterns. Methods and data developed at one locality may have limited transferability.

A consequence of physical modification is the degradation, even loss, of tidal wetlands. This in turn causes the loss of species, which results in reduced genetic diversity. Only the hardy species, the "biological weeds," would persist. As a consequence, future generations would lose the benefit of the evolutionary development of our wildlife heritage. Because of these impacts, recreational, aesthetic, and even possibly human health values could be placed in danger. Unfortunately, the biological results of such impacts are not readily discernible and are less easy to measure than the direct dollar increase resulting from physical modification of marshlands (Darnell, 1979).

Activities that threaten to destroy wetlands are overvalued in the marketplace but the natural characteristics, recreational uses, and aesthetic qualities of marshes are undervalued (Walker, 1973; Niering, 1979; Reimold, Phillips, and Hardisky, 1980; Shabman and Batie, 1980). Since wetlands are perceived as property in common, any action by one individual will have an impact on others. When this occurs, resource management is necessary; it is usually supervised by the political administrative systems of government. At the same time, to allocate productive natural resources properly, an evaluation system needs to be established, and because there is no marketplace for most wetland values—and therefore no generally accepted measure of value—those interested in wetlands must turn to the political marketplace to determine the value of the wetland resource. Therefore the management and preservation of wetlands becomes a political issue as well as one with economic and ecological consequences (Walker, 1973). Clark (1979) presented a similar view when he stated that the values that society wants to preserve through marshland conservation are determined by public policies. He believed that such policies should be based on scientific principles.

Kusler (1978) remarked that awareness of the natural functions of wetlands is growing and that such functions are of national, regional, statewide, and local significance. Niering (1970) drew attention to the dilemma of the coastal wetlands, pointing out conflicts at all levels in the political hierarchy. He suggested that the assignment of responsibility for formulating a wetlands policy cannot be delegated to the state or local authorities since wetlands cross political boundaries. In a similar approach, Kusler (1978) voiced a widespread skepticism about wetland regulation at the local level due to a lack of expertise, pro-development perspectives, and inadequate geographical scope. This may also be true at the national level.

Several writers, including Niering (1970), Ketchum (1972), and Kusler (1978), have called attention to the hierarchial arrangement of the political organization as it deals with coastal wetlands. Odum (1979) suggested that there is evidence that wetland values can be arranged in a hierarchy that parallels a geographical hierarchy of local, regional, national, and global levels. Such an order is also chronological, in that the first to be recognized are the population-level values.

The possibility of wetlands that might play a significant role in atmospheric stability and the maintenance of global life-support systems is just beginning to be recognized. The values of fish and wildlife were the first to be recognized and accepted by the public. Over the years fishery values have been dominant in coastal marshlands. Such values have carried enough weight in the past to promote preservation in the absence of strong economic pressure. As land prices rise, however, there must be a parallel rise in the intrinsic values of the wetlands to justify preservation. Many tidal marshlands have their greatest value at the state or regional level rather than at the local level and should be dealt with politically and economically at that level. A small patch of wetland, when considered as an isolated ecosystem, will have reduced value and will have a small chance in competition with other land uses. If it can be shown to be part of a larger system, its chances for preservation will be greater (Odum, 1979).

It is apparent that those concerned with the preservation and conservation of tidal wetlands need to identify and categorize the various kinds of assets associated with wetland resources. There is a continuing need to give recognition to nonmonetary as well as monetary values. There must be continuing efforts to refine techniques for appraising these various assets so that a total worth can be ascertained for the wetland. Only then can management of this intertidal resource be truly effective. As Stearns (1978) pointed out, management requires direction or purpose solidly based on merit to be influential. Nonmonetary values also place limits on the extent of alteration permissible. In addition, the Coastal Zone Management Act of 1972 indicates that decisions in the coastal zone are to be reached only after equal treatment is given to ecological, cultural, historical, and aesthetic values as well as to the need for economic development (Hershman, 1975). In practice there has not been an equal treatment.

MANAGEMENT CONCEPTS

Principles and Objectives

Clark (1974) considered vegetated tidelands (salt marshes and mangroves) to be vital or preservation areas—those portions of the ecosystem of such critical importance and high value that they are to be preserved intact and protected from harmful outside forces. These areas should be encompassed within an area of environmental concern, that is, a region such as an estuary in which human activity must be controlled but not necessarily prohibited. He considered estuaries and tidal marshes up to the storm-tide line to be part of the coastal waters province. Special management considerations are required to preserve the tidal marsh intact as a vital area. One aspect of management must be the control of adverse land use practices in the flood plain and adjacent high ground, since the quality and quantity of freshwater input has a profound influence on the wetlands. The Coastal Zone Management Act was enacted to provide that sort of management: to protect the coastal waters and adjacent lands, the use of which has a direct and significant impact on the coastal waters. The greater the development of coastal areas, the greater the need to preserve tidal marshes.

As a part of his discussion of vital areas and areas of environmental concern, Clark (1974) suggested a system of three use categories, which he called the PCU concept: preservation, conservation, and utilization. The preservation category would encompass the vital areas where no development would be suitable; conservation, all areas where carefully controlled manipulation would be possible; and utilization, areas of reduced ecological, recreational, and public importance that would be suitable for exploitation with a modicum of control. Conservation areas would serve as the buffers between preservation and development areas.

According to Beeftink (1977), the conservation of salt marsh biota requires both external aspects of management, to deal primarily with protection, and internal aspects of management, to address regulation. External human influences can emanate from the sea, the land, and the air—for example, pollution or the introduction of exotic species. Protection from air or sea pollution is difficult, as it requires cleaning up the estuary or coastal system. Discharges from the land are usually more restricted and can be controlled by storage or purification. However, nonpoint discharges can be difficult to identify and eliminate, and are often far more significant than recognized point sources of discharge. In contrast, internal influences are usually as mild as waterfowl hunting or plant gathering but can be as severe as land reclamation, salt panning, or gravel mining. Beeftink believed, however, that the marsh can absorb all but the most disruptive influences.

Leopold (1939) and Chabreck (1976), among others, considered tidal marsh management to be a manipulative process with two key components: regulation of water level and regulation of salinity. Other management techniques include planting, burning, creation of artificial potholes, and control of undesirable species. For a successful conservation plan, however, specific management goals should be developed from a combination of wetland tolerances to stress and societal needs, values, and conflicts (Livingstone and Loucks, 1979; Bryan, 1982).

Ranwell (1975) identified four broad aims of management (Figure 9-1). The first concerns the preservation of the flora and fauna, and identifies the space in which the natural physiographic processes operate to create such habitats. A second aim is to gather information through research, with sufficient control over human use and disturbance, in an area large enough to prevent edge effects from influencing results. Third is education of the public, including field trips into the resource area conducted in such a way that disturbance would be minimized. The fourth aim is the maintenance of sustained yields regardless of the level of exploitation.

Gray (1977) and Weller (1978) designated a more specific set of tidal marsh management objectives: to maintain or promote high species richness; to maintain some specific floral or faunal status quo; to preserve, increase, or introduce desirable species; to preserve natural assemblages of plants and animals as a "museum of types"; to maintain high productivity of characteristic fauna and flora whether for harvest, enjoyment, or natural biological processes; and to establish experimental studies aimed at enhancing management decisions. Thus one of the goals of tidal wetland conservation is the establishment and enhancement of a wetland ethic that recognizes the multiplicity of functions of these wetlands (Niering, 1978a, 1979; Stearns, 1978), to produce a system that is attractive to a variety of interests (Weller, 1978). Such systems management requires an understanding of the needs of resident biota, the effect that the dynamics of the system has on them, and the wisest use of natural processes to benefit the resident wildlife (Weller, 1978).

The concept of multiple land use began to develop with the growing demands of outdoor recreation. MacNamara (1957) observed that land use was based on broad interpretations of land classification and conservation along with careful evaluation of existing potentials for the various uses. Effective land use should be correlated with existing ecological conditions to produce a state of harmony between humans and the land. If the policy of multiple land use is to advance, managers must be aware of the broad picture, an ecosystem perspective, particularly as it applies to natural resources in relation to human needs (MacNamara, 1957) and the maintenance of the gene pool.

Ketchum (1972) identified three stages in the process of dealing with the coastal zone: exclusive use, displaceable use, and multiple use. Exclusive use (only one use, i.e., fish harvest) of earlier years is now beset by numerous other interests. Displaceable use (one use displacing another, i.e., gravel mining replacing harvest of hay) has modified sites irrevocably. The generation of the multiple-use concept results from the consideration of use compatibility. It requires an effective management plan to identify the kinds of interrelationships of uses, and recognizes the constraints they impose on each other. Hershman (1975) stressed the interdependence among the varied uses of the coastal zone. Conflicts arise where compatible or multiple uses exceed the carrying capacity of the environment, or begin to interfere with one another. However, many such conflicts can be avoided by thorough advanced planning.

To achieve any of these management aims and objectives requires a

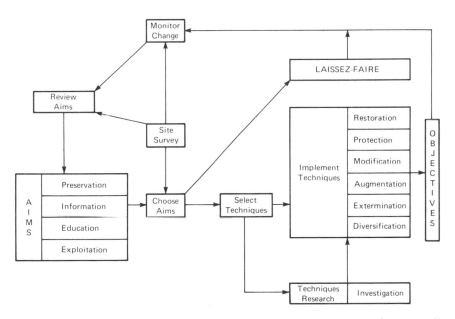

Figure 9-1.   Options available for tidal marsh management. *Source: After Ranwell, D. S., 1975, Management of salt-marsh and coastal dune vegetation, in Estuarine Research, vol. 2, L. E. Cronin, ed., Academic Press, New York, pp. 471–483, by permission.*

site survey of resources, and an effective means to monitor subsequent change so as to provide feedback to management (Ranwell, 1975; Niering, 1978a; Bryan, 1982). Bryan (1982) also suggested a user inventory to determine the characteristics of the various constituencies using the resource: their needs, purposes, and impacts. Just as the multiplicity of tidal marsh uses has generated conflicts, so do conflicts develop among management objectives within the same tract of land; as a result, some objectives become unattainable (Gray, 1977). Disagreements regarding the issue of manipulation are most likely to occur where artificial and aesthetically questionable systems are used. Most common is the conflict between management-oriented groups with different goals, or among those attempting to make decisions on the basis of insufficient knowledge of the subject (Weller, 1978). Thus priorities need to be established. With more extensive tracts of marsh, it is, of course, possible to achieve more objectives among the various competing interests. However, it is also apparent, as Gray (1977) pointed out, that marsh management is still very much an experimental effort; we know very little about the consequences that a particular management program might have on a particular ecosystem.

To implement any objectives of management, Ranwell (1975) identified six options open to the manager: (1) protection to prevent degradation; (2) restoration to repair degradation; (3) modification of the habitat to change the population balance; (4) augmentation by introduction of desirable species; (5) extermination of undesirable species; and (6) diversification through the creation of new habitat (Figure 9-1). Ranwell suggested that these options are not mutually exclusive. For example, diversification can be enhanced by allowing or restricting grazing, and water levels can be manipulated at the same time that other modifications are being made to the habitat. Not only can the use of dredged material encourage desirable species, but it can create a new habitat (augmentation and diversification). The extermination of *Phragmites* by the judicious use of herbicides or water control could be carried out for the express purpose of enhancing desirable species (extermination and augmentation).

From a broader perspective, Tiner (1984) identified 12 governmental options and 6 options open to the private citizen to slow or halt wetland losses and to improve the quality of the remaining tidal and freshwater wetlands.

Government Options:

1. Develop a consistent national policy to protect wetlands of national significance.
2. Strengthen federal, state and local wetlands protection.

3. Ensure proper implementation of existing laws and policies through adequate staffing, surveillance and enforcement.
4. Remove government subsidies which encourage wetland drainage.
5. Provide tax and other incentives to private landowners and industry to encourage wetland preservation and remove existing tax benefits which encourage wetland destruction.
6. Increase wetland acquisition in selected areas.
7. Improve wetland management of federal and state-owned lands.
8. Scrutinize cost-benefit analyses and justifications for flood control projects that involve channelization of wetlands and water courses.
9. Increase the number of marsh creation and restoration projects, especially to mitigate for unavoidable wetland losses by government-sponsored water resources projects.
10. Complete the National Wetlands Inventory, monitor wetland changes and periodically update these results in problem areas.
11. Increase public awareness of wetland values and the status of wetlands through various media.
12. Conduct research to increase our knowledge of wetland values and to identify ways of using wetlands that are least disruptive to their ecology.

Private Options:

1. Rather than drain or fill wetlands, seek compatible uses of those areas, e.g., timber harvest, waterfowl production, fur harvest, hay and forage, wild rice, hunting leases, etc.
2. Donate wetlands or funds to purchase wetlands to private and public conservation agencies for tax purposes.
3. Maintain wetlands as open space.
4. Work in concert with government agencies to educate the public on wetland values, etc.; private industry's expertise in marketing/advertising is particulary valuable.
5. Construct ponds in upland areas and manage for wetland and aquatic species.
6. Purchase federal and state duck stamps to support wetland acquisition.

As Clark (1974, 1979) and others have pointed out, the planning framework for a conservation program developed to protect and sustain a coastal ecosystem must be based on the interaction among accumulated ecological facts, management principles, and statements of public policy. In addition, it requires a system for evaluating and classifying areas of general sensitivity as well as particularly critical (vital) areas. Such a perspective is imperative where moving water is involved because a vital area can be disturbed by an impact imposed on the water column some distance from the vital area. By means of such a system of evaluation and classification, use allocations can be established. Water provides the essential connection between the land and sea elements of the coastal ecosystem. Thus water management, in its many aspects, is a primary consideration—including and beginning with the expansive coastal watershed.

Wetlands managers are faced with a variety of goals to accommodate the many specific and distinct kinds of interest in this resource. They must make decisions in relation to the manipulation, perpetuation, and use of the resource (Stearns, 1978; Schoning, 1984). As Gray (1977), Schoning (1984), and others have observed, it is imperative to have clearly stated objectives, developed in the public arena. The failure or lack of support for management plans is usually the result of unclear, imprecise, or unobtainable objectives. As Schoning emphasized, those involved must understand what the management program is attempting to achieve including why, how, and for how long. They must be aware that objectives may vary among plans, dictating new operational concepts with different biological impacts. Such decisions involve the maintenance of a functioning system for a specific goal. A functioning system implies a biotic community: an ecosystem (Stearns, 1978). However, it has been suggested that, to formulate successful wetlands management policies, one must be aware that critical decisions affecting natural resources are usually generated by the private marketplace and by the political process, not by science (Walker, 1973). Such policies should be formulated by a combination of scientists, engineers, planners, politicians, and voters.

Management decisions tie everything together. The correct decisions are not always clear and may depend on the decision makers, who may be the public, the management staff, a politician, a commission, or the courts. The management staff has the responsibility to provide what supporting data it has, incomplete as they may be, and to supply interpretation and meaning in clear, concise language. Managers also have the responsibility to qualify the information and make recommendations as necessary (Schoning, 1984); otherwise, conflicts will arise (Weller, 1978). Furthermore, it is well to remember Ranwell's (1975) admonition: "The urge to manage, to act, frequently takes precedence over clear thought about the aims, options, and feasibility of management." We can no longer afford to repent at leisure after hasty decisions.

Needs and Problems

It is the general belief that the management of tidal marshes should be directed at allowing the marsh to carry out its natural functions (Ketchum, 1972; Clark, 1974; Beeftink, 1977b; Provost, 1977; Queen, 1977; Kusler, 1978; Costle, 1979; Niering, 1979; Weller, 1979). Weller (1979), although he was discussing freshwater wetlands, stressed that "natural" methods of management—including water-level management, fire, and control of herbivores—are the cheapest and last the longest. He considered the use of blasting, bulldozers, ditching equipment, and the cutting of vegetation to be artificial management: more costly, less aesthetically appealing, and less apt to produce typical communities. On the other hand, Larsson (1969) and Cadwalladr and Morley (1974) advocated grazing (and/or mowing) in the marsh as good management for waterfowl and shore birds. Furthermore, judicious ditching and pool construction, through the use of ditching equipment, are key components of open marsh water management (see Chapter 3). Weller (1979) emphasized that management may be unnecessary and even detrimental to less common species. Yet management can also optimize conditions as well as conserve fauna. Provost (1977) warned that because the natural habitat is in equilibrium, any management scheme to promote one objective will have, almost certainly an adverse effect on some other resource or function of a marsh. As a result of this interdependence among the various marsh uses, the regulation of or demand for one use will put a demand on another function (Hershman, 1975). Provost noted that, until the mid-1960s, the resolution of environmental problems engendered by mosquito control was in the direction of satisfying wildlife interests—for example, waterfowl—with no concern about the overall functioning of a natural ecosystem. Such management plans were concerned with a particular interest and could not be classed as a natural treatment of a marsh. Beginning in the mid-1960s, the perception of the total role of tidal marshes, independent of any special interests, began to evolve (Provost, 1977).

The need for a holistic perspective to wetlands ecology and management has become increasingly apparent (Niering, 1970, 1978b; Ranwell, 1972; Odum and Skjei, 1974; Usher, 1977; Larsson, Loucks, and Clark, 1978; Cutler, 1979; Livingstone and Loucks, 1979). As Ranwell (1972) has pointed out, the human impact on tidal marshes has not generally been based on informed understanding or consideration for the resources they contain. For this reason, there is a need for long-term multidisciplinary work on basic wetland processes in a whole-system context if principles of reliable management are to be developed (Livingstone and Loucks, 1979). Comprehensive management requires long-term response forecasting, which must be based on understanding systems functions. Specific management goals should be developed from a combination of wetland tolerances to stress and societal needs and values (Beeftink, 1977b; Livingstone and Loucks, 1979). Ketchum (1972), Usher (1977), and Livingstone and Loucks (1979) stressed the importance of developing simulation models and systems analyses to ascertain the long-term consequences of use, and to have predictive value in the formulation of management decisions. Only when the various forms of management are integrated can a proper value be assigned for a tidal marsh (Ranwell, 1972). In spite of such desired predictability, however, Usher warned that the sea will ensure that complete precision will be impossible and that the manager must be knowledgeable about the ecology of catastrophes.

Clark (1974), Silberhorn (1978), and Niering (1979) pointed out the need for a conceptual understanding that would recognize that the upland, tidal marsh, mud flat, and estuary are interacting parts of a horizontally stratified system. The tidal mud flat has not received a great deal of attention, although its functional role in the marsh ecosystem is beginning to be understood (Coles, 1979). Since tidal mud flats are not legally protected in a number of states, more information is needed to make well-founded decisions, particularly with respect to maintenance and the disposal of dredged material (Silberhorn, 1978).

There is increasing evidence that a continuous disequilibrium, due to periodic physical disruption, is necessary for continued high levels of wetland productivity. For this reason, wetland management goals based on concepts of homeostasis and stability could be highly disruptive to the productivity of the wetland and adjacent systems. Walker (1973) suggested that stability is an inappropriate concept in understanding a tidal marsh, the very nature of which is characterized by a great variability, to which only a few species have adapted successfully. Livingstone and Loucks (1979) stated that it is important for research and management to consider short- and long-term fluctuations of key functions as well as "catastrophic" effects. Weller (1978), in his work on freshwater wetlands, considered stability to be detrimental for a marsh system. He suggested that marshes continually change, especially in unstable climates. He further stated (Weller, 1979) that animals' present uses of habitats are the result of evolutionary adaptations to commonly encountered habitats in specific geographic regions. Time, population pressures, and genetic adaptability have influenced the degree of plant and animal specializations in marshes. Weller went on to say that the adaptive nature of wetland animals can be an advantage in the development of any efforts for wetland restoration and management. In contrast, Chabreck (1976) believed that marshes subjected to severe tidal action and drastic salinity changes provide poor wildlife habitat. He suggested that the ideal coastal marsh management program for wildlife improvement should include procedures for reducing fluctuations in water level, salinity, rate of tidal exchange, and turbidity levels. Roman, Niering, and Warren (1984) have demonstrated that restrictions in tidal flow had a deleterious effect on Connecticut tidal marshes by encouraging the production of *Phragmites*. Beeftink (1977b), while stressing that tidal marshes are best suited for grazing and hay production in the Low Countries, urged that such marshes be managed to keep standing biomass low and stability high.

Recent legislative actions and government programs, as well as private activities, have greatly increased the need for dependable scientific information about wetlands. This requires coordination among technical disciplines as well as political entities to understand and enhance the important aspects of wetlands science. Cutler (1979) identified six basic missions of such science: (1) to define and characterize a wetland; (2) to collect, analyze, and interpret data about wetland ecosystems and their interaction with other ecosystems; (3) to use data derived from wetlands to devise natural resource programs; (4) to communicate results of research and program improvements to land managers; (5) to monitor changing conditions in wetlands and wetland programs; and (6) to blend technical knowledge with the aims of public and private land managers. To accomplish these missions, Larson, Loucks, and Clark (1978) proposed a series of near- and long-term projects. The near-term enterprises would include identification and delineation of major national and regional research questions, the establishment or enhancement of national and regional centers for the accumulation and exchange of information, and the review and evaluation of primary technical elements underlying national and international policy on wetland conservation. Long-term undertakings would include the following: continued basic research on the dynamics of natural wetland processes and functions, assessment of wetlands as units of the landscape, establishment of priorities for applied research on the impacts of various levels of wetland alteration, establishment of principles of wetland restoration, and advancement of the understanding of the social significance of wetlands, including economic, aesthetic, and historical values. Niering (1970, 1978a) called for the establishment of a national wetlands policy, stressing that this be done at the federal level since wetlands extend across political boundaries. He also stressed the importance of broadly trained advisors who could examine the total ecological system rather than individuals who looked only at specific problems (Niering, 1970). Cutler (1979) explained that the holistic view would consider the effects of change on all values, not just those associated with wildlife, insect control, aesthetics, and the like. Such a view would also evaluate the effects of making no change. In addition, the holistic approach would assure that decisions pertaining to wetlands would be made part of an overall land use plan. Weller (1979) discussed the need for a directed research program aimed at understanding the structure and function of wetland ecosystems. This would provide data to evaluate habitats for animals, to assess acquisition needs for the conservation of wetland forms, and to develop sound management strategies.

Ketchum (1972) very ably summarized the needs of wetlands management in his discussion of the coastal zone. To have an effective management plan, it is necessary to identify the kinds of interrelationships of uses, and recognize the constraints they impose on each other. Decisions about wetlands cannot be made without taking into account adjoining ecosystems and the broader geographic region.

We need to view the wetland as a natural system in order to utilize resources in harmony with the system. With a best-use objective in mind, wetland management will have three points of emphasis: developing and understanding the wetland as a system; using such knowledge to create a dynamic plan for its best use; and implementing and enforcing the plan. The functions of management within such a structure are based on the principles of allocation of resources, identification of priorities, and regulation, including the positive use of resources (Ketchum, 1972).

The most clearly defined management plans and objectives will not succeed unless the public understands the problem. Educational programs need to be fostered whereby the general public will be sensitized to the overall benefits of well-managed wetland systems. An informed community, aware of planning implications, will contribute to and evaluate developmental decisions and ensure wise management of a valuable resource (Stearns, 1978; Livingstone and Loucks, 1979; Healy, 1980; Schoning, 1984). Stearns (1978) asked, "What is good management?" Bryan (1982) answered with the following definition: " 'Good management' is giving people what they want to the extent that the resource can support it, substituting activities and settings for those who will tolerate it when there is a resource shortage, and offering a logical and consistent management rationale that the public can appreciate and understand — regardless of whether they get what they want." This requires that management supplement scientific expertise with social and ethical judgments (Beeftink, 1977*b*).

Such societal implications pose four sets of strictures for the wetlands manager: (1) Decisions must be made concerning the kind of environment society wants. Such decisions can be made only after society is educated, or else the process stands a good chance of failing. (2) It is necessary to understand the wetland ecosystem well enough to know how it can be manipulated without degradation, and to protect it from negative impacts. (3) There is need to recognize and use all the resources available for managing wetland ecosystems. (4) Finally, it is necessary to understand the absolute and conditional constraints under which the wetland management system must operate (Darnell, 1979). Absolute constraints to prevent species extinction and excessive loss of genetic material cannot be violated. Conditional constraints can be manipulated to some extent, and must include levels of acceptance of environmental degradation, and identify levels of research needed to establish an ecosystem response to manipulation and related value loss. Thus the elements of management operation include understanding the existing system, clearly defining the desired future state of the system, defining the acceptable limits of deviation from attaining this future state, recognizing the tools available for achieving the goal, and recognizing the two classes of constraints (absolute and conditional) (Darnell, 1979).

Hershman (1975) has assessed the situation by identifying the following factors: the interdependence of uses and the finiteness of the coastal zone; single-resource versus multiresource management; multiagency review within and between government levels; determination of the public will; and measurement of cumulative impacts and impacts beyond local significance.

Klose (1980) noted that during the early days after the passage of the National Environmental Policy Act of 1969 (NEPA) there was no clear definition of what constituted an impact, nor was there any guidance given as to how severe an effect would have to be in order to be considered important. Data were insufficient for assessment. According to Klose, however, much work has been done toward resolving problems associated with environmental impact assessment. Extensive data bases have been developed for environmental activities. There has been a shift toward the quantification of an ecosystem's natural services rather than assessments of specific components such as pounds of fish landed, waterfowl harvested, or man-days of recreation. Due to the complex nature of ecological systems, the greatest hurdle to the effective use of ecological impact data continues to be the inability to establish direct links between ecological effects and economic values. Further, the great variety of projects requiring impact assessment has made it more difficult to assess the effects quantitatively (Klose, 1980).

Present laws and programs covering the coastal area, including tidal wetlands, are not fully adequate to meet coastal resource problems (Hershman, 1975). The issuance of permits and enforcement are an integral portion of wetlands legislation. Enforcement practice must distinguish between detection of wetland developments that have evaded permit requirements and inspection of completed developments for compliance with permit conditions. According to Rosenbaum (1979) enforcement has been relatively neglected, emphasis has instead been given to development of use standards, field evaluations of ecological significance, and the processing of permits. Accordingly, he admonished policy makers and wetland scientist to devote more energy and time to the problem of enforcement. The scientist has the responsibility to provide sound and convincing technical information to support prosecution and restoration efforts. Enforcement policies must be carried out with a higher level of vigor and competence that is consistent throughout state and federal agencies.

To be effective, enforcement must ultimately rest on the affected public's acceptance of the necessity and legitimacy of public policy (see Chapter 8). Voluntary compliance based on an informed public's acceptance is far better than coerced compliance based on the deterrent effect of enforcement (Rosenbaum, 1979). The majority of the public appreciate the natural resource values of wetlands but have much less patience with the procedures of permit acquisition and the process of regulation. This is due, in part, to the lack of adequate explanation for such procedures. The public also questions the appropriateness of the various levels of governmental involvement, particularly at the federal level (Rosenbaum, 1979).

Ketchum (1972), however, expressed the view that the scope of the problems and the common resources identified require that government agencies manage the coastal zone, including the tidal wetlands. He identified a hierarchy of federal, state, and interstate groupings and local agencies that must have clearly defined responsibilities. Furthermore, authority must be delegated to the lowest level of government consistent with the scope of the problem. Passing decisions to state and federal levels can be impractical and wasteful of manpower. Bypassing the local level in matters of local concern can only generate conflict. One solution has been to establish guidelines at the state and federal level with more specific controls provided at the local level. The Coastal Zone Management Act of 1972 was such an example. On the whole, this act has been reasonably successful. Each state was allowed to establish guidelines that best suited its particular circumstances. States with strong local units opted to set up local programs, and those with less strong local units established statewide programs. The federal directive tended to force a consolidation toward a single management policy within each state. The act also enhanced communication between the various governmental agencies.

Ranwell (1979) identified four kinds of problems relating to the management of coastal systems common to both North America and Europe: (1) conflict between economic and environmental needs; (2) establishing common ground between administrators and ecologists (3) gathering and handling large amounts of data; and (4) translating results into field action. All four are effectively problems of communication between individuals, and the complicating hierarchy of governmental involvement. Ranwell specified three levels of involvement: individual, regional, and national.

The individual site, according to Ranwell (1979), is of local interest, consisting usually of one dominant coastal habitat. Use is governed by local socioeconomic and political factors. Management strategies are heavily weighted toward restoration and protection. Much of the conflict in planning and management results from disparities between different perceptions of problems among users with differing needs and motives.

Regional-level studies display three things relevant to planning effective management strategies: the need for extensive surveys to provide inventory information so that future changes can be measured; the need to develop computer techniques to handle the large volume of data; and the need to understand how the marsh system works. When working at the regional level, policy makers must take into account the boundaries between major habitats, since these units function within their own right but also interact with adjoining major habitats both physically and biologically. Strategies at the regional level of management require inventories for comparative purposes and awareness of the functional importance of boundaries, thresholds, and behavioral characteristics of both physical and biological components of the environment. Ranwell (1979) considered conceptual and mathematical models useful in the development of regional strategies.

At the national level, Ranwell (1979) stressed the need to consider a national survey of habitat resources, the problem of invasive species, and concerns about rare and endangered species.

The recognition of needs, identification of problems, and establishment of management strategies may be only partially effective if they are not periodically evaluated. Tippie (1980) suggested that the purpose of evaluation is to measure the effects of a program against the goals it set out to accomplish; this is a means of contributing to subsequent decision making about the program and improving future programming. Tippie identified four steps in evaluation: defining program goals; formulating measurable evaluation criteria; collecting and organizing data; and evaluating results. Once a plan is established, the mechanisms of implementation are set in motion. The evaluation process measures the outcomes against the objectives. Such feedback should lead to more effective management.

A SYNTHESIS WITH SUGGESTIONS FOR THE FUTURE

An important determination of tidal marsh management is the size of the marsh in question. Marshes with extensive acreage should be treated from a holistic perspective. Ecotonal boundaries of expansive marshes will comprise only a small portion of the total area, so that these transition zones and their adjoining ecosystems will have little direct influence. Correspondingly, the smaller the tidal marsh, the greater will be the influence of the boundary zone or "edge effect." Very small marshes may be diminishing due to expansion or alteration of surrounding ecosystems. Often the best management for these small marshes is no management at all, allowing the natural progression to occur. An alternative would be to use the small marsh unit for an activity that will have other economic or social values. However, if it is possible that such a unit is the forerunner of a new marsh developed by rising sea level, the protection form of management should be encouraged.

Whatever the form management may take, it is imperative that information be acquired with a holistic perspective concerning the life history of each ecological community within the particular marsh system. Coastal ecological features directly related to the existence and persistence of the marsh—for example, meteorological and oceanographic factors as well as water and air quality—also need to be considered. Spatial and temporal variations in the marsh need to be identified and evaluated. These, in turn, need to be considered in any forecasts for future use of the area—not only for use of the specific marsh but also for use of the adjoining ecosystems. Such forecasts can be established only by determining the uses to which the marsh area will be subjected, and the number and kinds of users—plants and animals (including, but not limited to, humans).

Marsh management for the enhancement and maintenance of the resource is a sociological problem. It includes an assessment of the impacts on the various users as well as the economics of treating the resource as an industry. Whatever the management decisions, they must be based on a solid understanding and enhancement of the natural marsh system for the benefit of the resource. For them to be effective, however, there must be public support. This is most effective when the public is informed not only of the final decision but also of data collection and interpretation.

Management is made possible in part by legislation. One form such legislation can take is to decree management by date, by location, or by time. However, such management can be good only if the legislation has a sound scientific basis and rationale. If it is arbitrary and capricious, the courts are likely to overturn it. Legislation bestows order on marsh management. Legislation, in conjunction with the concept of the public trust doctrine, helps the riparian owner identify marshland boundaries. It allows management to enforce decisions by specifying criminal and civil penalties for transgressors. It may also prohibit certain forms of management. Before any legislation is enacted, an informed public must be given the opportunity to express relevant ecological, social, and economic concerns.

Marshland legislation should identify which activities are allowable and which are not. Such permit decisions must be based on scientific information and common sense. Permits should be limited to marine-oriented activities and allow the building of only those structures that must have a shoreline or marsh location. The amount of marshland to be altered must comprise a minimal portion of the total marsh area. The design and execution of any structure or activity must take into account the adverse impacts associated with restricting the ebb and flow of the tide, any fish spawning or migration, indigenous plant production, or other natural marsh functions, as well as future maintenance dredging needs.

Activities that might not be considered contrary to the public interest, and are thus permitted, include channel dredging essential for navigation and public health, selective excavations for mosquito control, public recreation (hunting, fishing, and trapping), enhancement of public access to water (catwalks and boat ramps), roadways placed on pilings rather than on filled causeways, erosion control, control of pests through the use of biodegradable substances, and marinas and commercial docks (where no upland site is available).

Activities that can be considered contrary to the public interest include fill for residential, commercial, and industrial sites, parking lots, and roadways; boat-storage sites; dump sites for waste or dredged material; dredging canals or ditches constructed solely to drain the marsh; construction of lagoons for waste treatment, cooling, or aquaculture; and structures that constitute an unreasonable obstruction to the view of adjoining landowners.

Lawsuits can play a very important role in the management of tidal marshes. For instance, they can bring about the repeal of arbitrary and capricious laws that are not based on an understanding of the natural functions of this ecosystem. The repeal of such laws can open marsh areas to scientific investigation and positive management procedures. Legal action also introduces science and technology into the law through expert testimony. Lawsuits also stress the need to translate scientific findings into a form the public can understand. Legal action also directs the public's attention to the identification, importance, and rights of the riparian owner, to the public trust doctrine, and to the tidal marsh itself.

The following ideas should be taken into account in future management programs for tidal wetlands:

1. A few well-designed laws are always better than many capricious or outdated pieces of legislation. They should provide coverage wide enough to address all needs. A national problem should be approached through a federal law. In contrast, a local problem requires a local law, but one written in such a way to preclude conflict at higher governmental levels.

2. It has been suggested that one national set of standards could be established for the management of all tidal marshes within the national boundaries. Such a concept would be applicable only in the broadest of views. Regional and local differences are already understood well enough to warrant consideration on a regional or case-by-case basis. While functions are generally known and general principles can be applied, the

specific processes are variable enough to put such a national set of standards in a dubious position. A more effective approach is regionalization, which allows the groupings of wetlands into similar biogeographic regions. This facilitates planning and resource management at the national and regional levels. However, it is only as effective as the degree of cooperation among the various governmental agencies.

3. As it is now, extensive marshes that span political boundaries cannot be treated as a unit because of disparate laws existing on either side of the political boundary. It may be better to operate such areas according to administrative rules rather than legislation. Guidelines for action would be established yet flexibility would be enhanced. Such actions could be appropriate throughout the governmental hierarchy. Regional problems could be overseen by the establishment of interstate compacts or commissions; at the international level, treaties would enable managers to operate from a holistic perspective.

4. Any marshland legislation should provide for issuing revocable licenses and permits. A time limit should be set on the duration of any such issuance, so that a review board could decide whether the license should be renewed or revoked. It would also be possible to establish state ownership with a lease-back option under a revocable license with or without fees. The creation of new marsh preserves should be an ongoing consideration, and should not be limited to situations involving threatened or endangered species. Care must be taken, though, that such a tract would be large enough to carry out its natural functions.

5. Tax incentives can be helpful. Property taxes can be set at the lowest rate as an incentive to leave the marsh undisturbed for a designated period. The tax rate would increase if the owner were to divide the marsh or reduce the acreage. Concerned taxpayers could be given the option of tax write-off for government-owned marsh preserves.

6. We need to give further consideration to the removal of federal insurance coverage for storm damage in disaster-prone areas. Until recently, homeowners (and others who invested in the intertidal area) could avoid any substantive loss because storm damage was covered by federal insurance. With the passage of the Coastal Barrier Islands Act of 1982, no new construction in selected areas — as designated by the Department of the Interior — of the shore zone of the Atlantic and Gulf coasts will be covered by federal storm damage insurance. However, only portions of the intertidal area are covered by this act, and it is not clear whether pre-existing structures, if damaged, would remain insurable when rebuilt. The elimination of federal insurance coverage would reduce the incentives to carry out dredge and fill operations and other activities designed to establish tourist-related facilities and summer homes in marshlands. A restriction on the number of times a pre-existing structure could be

rebuilt with federal insurance dollars could phase out such development without providing undue hardship to the owners.

7. Mitigation may also be a tool of management. Restoration or creation of a tidal marsh should be fostered when an existing marsh has been impaired or destroyed. However, it should not be undertaken only to justify the destruction of a wetland; rather, it should substitute for the unavoidable loss of a marsh, and at the same time enhance the estuarine system with which the marsh is associated.

8. One aspect of management might be the imposition of user fees. The free use of a common resource by the public is becoming less tenable. The perpetuation of a tidal marsh as an ecological entity and as a resource requires great expenditure of time, energy, and money. It seems appropriate, then, that those who wish to use the tidal marsh should bear at least some of the cost of management and maintenance.

9. Who should make the management decisions? It could be a court of law, some panel of experts, a private conservation organization, or some government agency. Any and all of these groups will need the expert advice of well-trained professionals who are knowledgeable about the ecological components that comprise the tidal marsh, who are cognizant of the laws governing such a habitat, who are aware of the economic pressures, and who can communicate with and have the support of a well-informed public. The final decision is up to the well-informed public.

References

Able, K. W., and M. Castagna, 1975, Aspects of an undescribed reproductive behavior in *Fundulus heteroclitus* (Pisces: Cyprinodontidae) from Virginia, *Chesapeake Sci.* **16**(4):282-284.

Able, K. W., J. K. Shisler, and C. W. Talbot, 1979, Preliminary survey of fishes utilizing New Jersey marshes altered for control of salt marsh mosquitos, *New Jersey Mosq. Control Assoc. Proc.* **66**:103-115.

Allan, P. F., 1950, Ecological basis for land use planning in Gulf Coast marshlands, *J. Soil and Water Conserv.* **5**(2):57-62, 85.

Alls, R. T., 1969, *Killifish Predation of Mosquitoes in Low Level Impounded Delaware Salt Marshes*, Master's thesis, University of Delaware, 73p.

Anderson, J. F., and F. R. Kneen, 1969, The temporary impoundment of salt marshes for the control of coastal deer flies, *Mosq. News* **29**(2):239-243.

Anderson, J. W., J. M. Neff, B. A. Cox, H. E. Tatem, and G. M. Hightower, 1974a, Characteristics of dispersions and water-soluble extracts of crude and refined oils and their toxicity on estuarine crustaceans and fish, *Mar. Biol.* **27**(1):75-88.

Anderson, J. W., J. M. Neff, B. A. Cox, H. E. Tatem, and G. M. Hightower, 1974b, The effects of oil on estuarine animals: toxicity, uptake and depuration, respiration, in *Pollution and Physiology of Marine Organisms*, F. J. Vernberg and W. B. Vernberg, eds., Academic Press, New York, pp. 285-310.

Anderson, R. D., D. Garten, and T. Smolen, 1974, *Legal Symposium on Wetlands: An Executive Summary*, Virginia Institute of Marine Science, Gloucester Point, 8p.

Anderson, R. R., V. Carter, and J. McGinness, 1973, Mapping southern Atlantic coastal wetlands, South Carolina-Georgia, using ERTS-1 imagery, in *Remote*

Sensing of Earth Resources, F. Shahrokhi, ed., University of Tennessee, Knoxville, pp. 1021-1028.

Anderson, R. R., and F. J. Wobber, 1973, Wetlands mapping in New Jersey, *Photogram. Eng.* **39**:353-358.

Atwater, B. F., S. G. Conard, J. N. Dowden, C. W. Hedel, R. L. MacDonald, and W. Savage, 1979, History, landforms, and vegetation of the estuary's tidal marshes, in *San Francisco Bay: The Urbanized Estuary*, T. J. Conomos, ed., American Association for the Advancement of Science, Pacific Division, San Francisco, pp. 347-385.

Aurand, D., 1968, *The Seasonal and Spatial Distribution of Nitrate and Nitrite in the Surface Waters of Two Delaware Marshes*, Master's thesis, University of Delaware, 140p.

Aurand, D., and F. C. Daiber, 1973, Nitrate and nitrite in the surface waters of two Delaware salt marshes, *Chesapeake Sci.* **14**(2):105-111.

Axtell, R. C., 1976, Horse flies and deer flies (Diptera: Tabanidae) in *Marine Insects*, L. Cheng, ed., North-Holland Publ. Co., Amsterdam, pp. 415-445.

Bailey, N. S., 1948, A mass collection and population technique for larvae of Tabanidae (Diptera), *Brooklyn Entomol. Soc. Bull.* **43**:22-29.

Baker, J. M., 1970, The effects of oils on plants, *Environ. Pollut.* **1**:27-44.

Baker, J. M., 1971, Studies on salt marsh communities, in *The Ecological Effects of Oil Pollution on Littoral Communities*, E. B. Cowell, ed., Institute of Petroleum, London, pp. 16-101.

Baker, J. M., 1973, Recovery of salt marsh vegetation from successive oil spillages, *Environ. Pollut.* **4**:223-230.

Baker, J. M., 1976, *Marine Ecology and Oil Pollution*, John Wiley & Sons, New York, 566p.

Baker, J. M., 1979, Responses of salt marsh vegetation to oil spills and refinery effluents, in *Ecological Processes in Coastal Environments*, R. L. Jeffries and A. J. Davy, eds., Blackwell Scientific Publ., Oxford, pp. 529-542.

Baldwin, W. P., 1968, Impoundments for waterfowl on South Atlantic and Gulf coastal marshes, in *Marsh and Estuary Management Symposium Proceedings*, J. D. Newsom, ed., Louisiana State University, Baton Rouge, pp. 127-133.

Balling, S. S., and V. H. Resh, 1982, Arthropod community response to mosquito control recirculation ditches in San Francisco Bay salt marshes, *Environ. Entomol.* **11**(4):801-808.

Balling, S. S., T. Stoehr, and V. H. Resh, 1980, The effects of mosquito control recirculation ditches on the fish community of a San Francisco Bay salt marsh, *California Fish and Game* **66**(1):25-34.

Banta, J. S., 1978, Wetlands and the taking issue, in *National Wetlands Protection Symposium Proceedings*, J. H. Montanari and J. A. Kusler, eds., Fish & Wildlife Serv. Biol. Serv. Prog. FWS/OBS-78/97, Washington, D.C., pp. 179-183.

Banta, J. S., and J. Nauman, 1978, Mitigation in federal dredge and fill permits, in *Coastal Zone '78*, vol. 2, Symposium on Technical, Environmental, Socioeconomic and Regulatory Aspects of Coastal Zone Management, American Society of Civil Engineers, New York, pp. 1316-1332.

Banus, M. D., I. Valiela, and J. M. Teal, 1975, Lead, zinc and cadmium budgets in experimentally enriched salt marsh ecosystems, *Estuarine Coast. Mar. Sci.* 3(4):421-430.

Barber, R. T., W. W. Kirby-Smith, and P. E. Parsley, 1979, Wetland alternations for agriculture, in *Wetland Functions and Values: The State of Our Understanding*, P. E. Greeson, J. R. Clark, and J. E. Clark, eds., American Water Resources Assoc., Minneapolis, Minn., pp. 642-651.

Bartlett, D. S., 1976, *Variability of Wetland Reflectance and Its Effect on Automatic Categorization of Satellite Imagery*, Master's thesis, University of Delaware, 108p.

Bartlett, D. S., 1979, *Spectral Reflectance of Tidal Wetland Plant Canopies and Implications for Remote Sensing*, Ph.D. Dissertation, University of Delaware, 239p.

Bartlett, D. S., and V. Klemas, 1979, *Assessment of Tidal Wetland Habitat and Productivity*, 13th International Symposium on Remote Sensing of Environment Proc., Ann Arbor, Mich., pp. 693-701.

Bartlett, D. S., and V. Klemas, 1980, Quantitative assessment of tidal wetlands using remote sensing, *Environ. Manage.* 4:337-345.

Bartlett, D. S., and V. Klemas, 1981, In situ spectral reflectance studies of tidal wetland grasses, *Photogram. Eng. Remote Sensing* 47:1695-1703.

Bartlett, D. S., V. Klemas, O. W. Crichton, and G. R. Davis, 1976, *Low-cost Aerial Photographic Inventory of Tidal Wetlands*, Final report for the Department of Natural Resources and Environmental Control, State of Delaware.

Bascand, L. D., 1968, *The Control of Spartina species*, 21st New Zealand Weed and Pest Control Conf. Proc., pp. 108-113.

Beeftink, W. G., 1975, The ecological significance of embankment and drainage with respect to the vegetation of the south-west Netherlands, *J. Ecol.* 63:423-458.

Beeftink, W. G., 1977a, The coastal salt marshes of western and northern Europe: an ecological and phytosociological approach, in *Wet Coastal Ecosystems*, V. J. Chapman, ed., Elsevier Scientific Publ. Co., Amsterdam, pp. 109-155.

Beeftink, W. G., 1977b, Salt-marshes, in *The Coastline*, R. S. K. Barnes, ed., John Wiley & Sons, London, pp. 93-121.

Beeman, O., and A. Benkendorf, 1978, Productive land use of dredged material areas, in *Coastal Zone '78*, vol. 2, Symposium on Technical, Environmental, Socioeconomic and Regulatory Aspects of Coastal Zone Management, American Society of Civil Engineers, New York, pp. 721-735.

Bender, M. E., and D. L. Correll, 1974, *The Use of Wetlands as Nutrient Removal Systems*, Chesapeake Research Consortium No. 29, VIMS Contrib. No. 624, Gloucester Point, Va., 12p.

Bender, M. E., E. A. Shearls, R. P. Ayres, C. Hershner, and R. J. Huggett, 1977, *Ecological Effects of Experimental Oil Spills on Eastern Coastal Plain Estuarine Ecosystems*, 1977 Oil Spill Conference Proceedings, American Petroleum Institute Publ. 4284, Washington, D.C., pp. 505-509.

Bent, A. C., 1929, Life histories of North American shore birds, *U.S. Natl. Mus. Bull.* 146:I-IX, 1-412.

Benton, A. R., S. L. Hatch, W. L. Kirk, R. M. Newman, W. W. Snell, and J. G.

Williams, 1977, *Monitoring of Texas Coastal Wetlands*, Texas A & M University, TR RSC-88, 101p.

Berstein, B. B., 1981, Ecology and economics: complex systems in changing environments. *Ann. Rev. Ecol. Syst.* 12:309-330.

Best, R. G., M. E. Wehde, and R. L. Linder, 1981, Spectral reflectance of hydrophytes, *Remote Sensing Environ.* 11:27-35.

Beynon, L. R., and E. B. Cowell, eds., 1974, *Ecological Aspects of Toxicity Testing of Oils and Dispersants*, John Wiley & Sons, New York, 149p.

Bongiorno, S. F., 1970, Nest-site selection by adult laughing gulls (*Larus atricilla*), *Anim. Behav.* 18:434-444.

Bonsteel, J. A., 1909, *Soils in the Vicinity of Savannah, Ga.: A Preliminary Report*, U.S. Dept. of Agric. Bur. of Soils Circ. No. 19, 19p.

Boon, J. D., M. E. Boule, and G. M. Silberhorn, 1977, *Delineation of Tidal Wetlands Boundaries in Lower Chesapeake Bay and Its Tributaries*, Spec. Rept. No. 140, Virginia Institute of Marine Science, Gloucester Point, 127pp.

Bosselman, F., D. Callies, and J. Banta, 1973, *The Taking Issue*, Council on Environmental Quality, Supt. of Documents, Stock No. 4111-00017, Washington, D.C., 329p.

Botkin, D. B., J. E. Estes, R. M. MacDonald, and M. V. Wilson, 1984, Studying the earth's vegetation from space, *Bioscience* 34:508-514.

Bourn, W. S., and C. Cottam, 1950, *Some Biological Effects of Ditching Tidewater Marshes*, Research Report 19, Fish and Wildlife Service, U.S. Dept. of Interior, Washington, D.C., 17p.

Boyce, J. S., 1976, Soil-plant relationships in dredged material marshes with particular reference to heavy metal and nutrient availability, in *Dredging and Its Environmental Effects*, P. A. Krenkal, J. Harrison, and J. C. Burdick III, eds., American Society of Civil Engineers, New York, pp. 496-511.

Boyes, D., and P. M. Capotosto, 1978, Two years of open marsh water management in Barrington, R. I., *New Jersey Mosq. Exterm. Assoc. Proc.* 65:76-83.

Bradbury, H. M., 1938, Mosquito control operations on tide marshes in Massachusetts and their effect on shore birds and waterfowl, *J. Wildl. Manage.* 2(2):49-52.

Briscoe, J., 1979, Legal problems of tidal marshes, in *San Francisco Bay: The Urbanized Estuary*, T. J. Conomos, ed., Pacific Division, American Association for the Advancement of Science, San Francisco, pp. 387-400.

Brown, W. W., 1978, Wetland mapping in New Jersey and New York, *Photogram. Eng. Remote Sensing* 44(3):303-314.

Bruder, K. W., 1980, The establishment of unified open marsh water management standards in New Jersey, *New Jersey Mosq. Control Assoc. Proc.* 67:72-76.

Bryan, H., 1982, A social science perspective for managing recreational conflict, in *Marine Recreational Fisheries*, R. H. Stroud, ed., 7th Annual Marine Recreational Fish. Symp. Proceedings, Sports Fish. Instit. Washington, D.C., pp. 15-22.

Buchner, G. E., 1979, Engineering aspects of strip land reclamation with special reference to the Wash, in *Estuarine and Coastal Land Reclamation and Water*

Storage, B. Knights and A. J. Phillips, eds., Saxon House, Farnborough, England, pp. 68-81.

Budd, J. T. C., and E. J. Milton, 1982, Remote sensing of salt marsh vegetation in the first four proposed Thematic Mapper bans, *Internat. J. Remote Sensing* **3**:147-161.

Burger, J., 1977, Nesting behavior of herring gulls: invasion into Spartina saltmarsh areas of New Jersey, *Condor* **79**:162-169.

Burger, J., and J. Shisler, 1978*a*, Nest-site selection of willets in a New Jersey salt marsh, *Wilson Bull.* **90**(4):599-607.

Burger, J., and J. Shisler, 1978*b*, The effects of ditching a salt marsh on colony and nest site selection by herring gulls *Larus argentatus*, *Am. Midl. Nat.* **100**(1):54-63.

Burger, J., J. Shisler, and F. Lesser, 1978, The effects of ditching saltmarshes on nesting birds. Compiled by W. Southern, Proceedings Colonial Water Bird Group. Publ. at Northern Illinois Univ., DeKalb, pp. 27-37.

Burns, K. A., 1976*a*, Hydrocarbon metabolism in the intertidal fiddler crab, *Uca pugnax*, *Mar. Biol.* **36**:5-11.

Burns, K. A., 1976*b*, Microsomal mixed function oxidases in an estuarine fish, *Fundulus heteroclitus*, and their induction as a result of environmental contamination, *Comp. Biochem. Physiol.* **53B**:443-446.

Burns, K. A., and J. M. Teal, 1979, The West Falmouth oil spill: hydrocarbons in the salt marsh ecosystem, *Estuarine Coast. Mar. Sci.* **8**(4):349-360.

Butera, M. K., 1978, *A Determination of the Optimum Time of Year for Remotely Classifying Marsh Vegetation from Landsat Multispectral Scanner Data*, NASA TM 58212, NSTL Station MS, 14p.

Butera, M. K., 1983, Remote sensing of wetlands, *Geosci. Remote Sensing Trans.* **GE21**:383-392.

Butera, M. K., J. A. Browder, and A. L. Frick, 1984, A preliminary report on the assessment of wetland productive capacity from a remote-sensing based model—a NASA/NMFS joint research project, *IEEE Geosci. Remote Sensing Trans.* **GE22**:502-511.

Butler, P. A., 1963, Commercial fishery investigations, Pesticides-Wildlife Studies, U.S. Fish and Wildlife Cir. 199, pp. 5-28.

Butler, P. A., 1966, Pesticides in the marine environment, in *Pesticides in the Environment and Their Effects on Wildlife*, N. W. Moore, ed., Suppl. *J. Appl. Ecol.* **3**:253-259.

Butler, P. A., A. J. Wilson, Jr., and A. J. Rick, 1960, Effects of Pesticides on Oysters, *Nat. Shellfish Assoc. Proc.* **51**:23-32.

Cadwalladr, D. A., and J. V. Morley, 1973, Sheep grazing preferences on a salting at Bridgwater Bay National Nature Reserve, Somerset, and their significance for wigeon (*Anas penelope* L.) conservation, *Br. Grassld. Soc. J.* **28**:235-242.

Cadwalladr, D. A., and J. V. Morley, 1974, Further experiments on the management of saltings pasture for wigeon (*Anas penelope* L.) conservation at Bridgwater Bay National Nature Reserve, Somerset, *J. Appl. Ecol.* **11**(2):461-466.

Cadwalladr, D. A., M. Owen, J. V. Morley, and R. S. Cook, 1972, Wigeon (*Anas penelope* L.) conservation and salting pasture management at Bridgwater Bay National Nature Reserve, Somerset, *J. Appl. Ecol.* 9(2):417-425.

Cairns, W. E., 1974, *The Macro-Invertebrate Fauna of the Cape Jourimain, New Brunswick Salt Marsh Complex*, Baccalaureate Honors thesis, Mount Allison University, Sackville, New Brunswick, 139p.

Cameron, H. L., 1950, The use of aerial photography in seaweed surveys, *Photogram. Eng.* 16:493-501.

Cammen, L. M., 1976, Microinvertebrates. Colonization of *Spartina* marshes artificially established on dredge spoil, *Estuarine Coast. Mar. Sci.* 4:357-372.

Cammen, L. M., E. D. Seneca, and B. J. Copeland, 1974, *Animal Colonization of Salt Marshes Artificially Established on Dredge Spoil*, University of North Carolina Sea Grant Program Publ. UNC-SG-74-15, Chapel Hill, N.C., 67p.

Campbell, B. C., and R. F. Denno, 1976, The effect of temephos and chlorpyrifos on the aquatic insect community of a New Jersey saltmarsh, *Environ. Entomol.* 5(3):477-483.

Carls, E. G., 1979, Coastal recreation: esthetics and ethics, *Coastal Zone Manage. J.* 5:119-130.

Carr, A., 1952, *Handbook of Turtles*, Comstock Publ. Co., Ithaca, N. Y., 542p.

Carter, V., 1978, Coastal Wetlands: Role of Remote Sensing, in *Coastal Zone '78*, Symposium on Technical Environment, Socioeconomic and Regulatory Aspects of Coastal Zone Management, Amer. Soc. Civil Eng., N. Y., pp. 1261-1283.

Carter, V., 1982, Applications of remote sensing to wetlands, in *Remote Sensing for Resource Management*, C. J. Johannsen and J. L. Sanders, eds., Soil Conservation Society of America, Ankeny, Ia., pp. 284-300.

Carter, V., and R. R. Anderson, 1972, *Interpretation of Wetlands Imagery Based on Spectral Reflectance Characteristics of Selected Plant Species*, 38th Annual Meeting, American Society of Photogrammetry Proc., Washington, D.C., pp. 580-595.

Carter, V., and J. Schubert, 1974, *Coastal Wetlands Analysis from ERTS MSS Digital Data and Field Spectral Measurements*, 9th International Symposium on Remote Sensing of Environment Proc., Environmental Research Inst., Ann Arbor, Mich, pp. 1241-1260.

Carter, V., D. L. Malone, and J. H. Burbank, 1979, Wetland classification and mapping in western Tennessee, *Photogram. Eng., Remote Sensing* 45:273-284.

Carter, V., M. K. Garrett, L. Shima, and P. Gammon, 1977, The Great Dismal swamp. Management of a hydrologic resource with the aid of remote sensing, *Water Resour. Bull.* 13:1-12.

Catts, E. P., Jr., 1957, *Mosquito Prevalence on Impounded and Ditched Salt Marshes, Assawoman Wildlife Area, Delaware, 1956*, Master's thesis, University of Delaware, 65p.

Catts, E. P., 1970, A canopy trap for collecting Tabanidae, *Mosq. News* 30(3): 472-474.

Catts, E. P., and E. J. Hansens, 1975, To build a better fly trap, *Delaware Conserv.* 19(1):20. Also Delaware Marine Advisory Services Publ. No. 8, Univ. Delaware Sea Grant Program, 5p.

Catts, E. P., Jr., F. H. Lesser, R. F. Darsie, Jr., O. Florschutz, and E. E. Tindall, 1963, *Wildlife Usage and Mosquito Production on Impounded Tidal Marshes in Delaware, 1956-1962*, 29th North American Wildlife Nat. Res. Conf. Trans, pp. 125-132.

Chabreck, R. H., 1963, Breeding habits of the Piedbilled grebe in an impounded coastal marsh in Louisiana, *Auk* 80(4):447-452.

Chabreck, R. H., 1968a, The Relation of Cattle and Cattle Grazing to Marsh Wildlife and Plants, *Southeast. Assoc. Game and Fish Comm. 22nd Ann. Conf. Proc.*, pp. 55-58.

Chabreck, R. H., 1968b, Wiers, plugs and artificial potholes for the management of wildlife in coastal marshes, in *Marsh and Estuary Management Symposium Proceedings*, J. D. Newsom, ed., Louisiana State University, Baton Rouge, pp. 178-192.

Chabreck, R. H., 1976, Management of wetlands for wildlife habitat improvement, in *Estuarine Processes*, vol. 1, M. Wiley, ed., Academic Press, New York, pp. 226-233.

Chabreck, R. H., and A. W. Palmisano, 1973, The effects of hurricane Camille on the marshes of the Mississippi River delta, *Ecology* 54(5):1118-1123.

Chapman, H. C., and F. Ferrigno, 1956, A three year study of mosquito breeding in natural and impounded salt marsh areas in New Jersey, *New Jersey Mosq. Exterm. Assoc. Proc.* 43:48-65.

Chapman, H. C., P. F. Springer, F. Ferrigno, and D. MacCreary, 1954, Studies on mosquito breeding in natural and impounded salt marsh areas in New Jersey and Delaware, *New Jersey Mosq. Exterm. Assoc. Proc.* 41:225-226.

Chapman, H. C., P. F. Springer, F. Ferrigno, and R. F. Darsie, Jr., 1955, Studies of mosquito breeding in natural and impounded salt marsh areas in New Jersey and Delaware in 1954, *New Jersey Mosq. Exterm. Assoc. Proc.* 42:92-94.

Chapman, R. N., 1931, *Animal Ecology*, McGraw-Hill, New York, 464p.

Chapman, V. J., 1937, A note on salt marshes of Nova Scotia, *Rhodora* 39:53-57.

Chapman, V. J., 1960, *Salt Marshes and Salt Deserts of the World*, Interscience Publ., New York, 392p.

Chapman, V. J., 1974, *Salt Marshes and Salt Deserts of the World*, 2nd suppl. reprint ed., Verlag Von J. Cramer, Bremerhaven, Germany.

Chapman, V. J., 1977, *Wet Coastal Ecosystems*, Elsevier Scientific Publ. Co., Amsterdam.

Chastaen, G., 1978, The Corps of Engineers Permit Program, in *Coastal Zone '78*, vol. 1, Symposium on Technical, Environmental, Socioeconomic and Regulatory Aspects of Coastal Zone Management, American Society of Civil Engineers, New York, pp. 539-552.

Cheng, L., ed., 1976, *Marine Insects*, North-Holland Publ. Co., Amsterdam, 581 pp.

Chidester, F. E., 1916, *A Biological Study of the More Important of the Fish Enemies of the Salt-Marsh Mosquitos*, New Jersey Agricultural Experiment Station Bull. 300, 16p.

Christiansen, M. E., J. D. Costlow, and R. J. Monroe, 1978, Effects of the insect growth regulator Dimilin (TH 6040) on larval development of two estuarine crabs, *Mar. Biol.* 50:29-36.

Christopher, S., and N. W. Bowden, 1957, Mosquito control in reservoirs by water level management, *Mosq. News* 17(4):273-277.

Clark, A. H., 1968, *Acadia: The Geography of Early Nova Scotia to 1760*, University of Wisconsin Press, Madison, Wis., 450p.

Clark, J. R., 1974, *Coastal Ecosystems: Ecological Considerations for Manage-ment of the Coastal Zone*, The Conservation Foundation, Washington, D.C., 178p.

Clark, J. R., 1979, Foreword, in *Wetland Functions and Values: The State of Our Understanding*, P. E. Greeson, J. R. Clark, and J. E. Clark, eds., American Water Resources Assoc., Minneapolis, Minn., pp. 1-3.

Clarke, J. L., 1938, Mosquito control as related to marsh conservation, *New Jersey Mosq. Exterm. Assoc. Proc.* 25:139-147.

Clymer, J. P., 1978, *The Distributions, Tropic Activities and Competetive Inter-actions of Three Salt Marsh Killifishes (Pisces: Cyprinodontidae)*, Ph.D. dissertation, Lehigh University, 281p.

Cochran, W. S., 1935, The relation of mosquito control to the muskrat industry on the salt marshes, *New Jersey Mosq. Exterm. Assoc. Proc.* 22:19-23.

Cochran, W. S., 1938, New developments in mosquito control in Delaware, *New Jersey Mosq. Exterm. Assoc. Proc.* 25:130-137.

Cole, R. A., 1978, *Habitat Development Field Investigations, Buttermilk Sound Marsh Development Site Atlantic Intracoastal Waterway, Georgia*, Sum-mary Report, U.S. Army Corps of Engineers Technical Rept. D-78-26, 34p.

Coles, S. M., 1979, Benthic microalgal populations on intertidal sediments and their role as precursors to salt marsh development, in *Ecological Processes in Coastal Environments*, R. L. Jeffries and A. J. Davy, eds., Blackwell Scien-tific Publ., Oxford, pp. 25-42.

Colwell, R. N., 1961, Some practical applications of multiband spectral recon-naissance, *Am. Sci.* 49:9-36.

Colwell, R. N., 1963, Basic matter and energy relationships involved in remote reconnaissance, *Photogram. Eng.* 29:761-799.

Colwell, R. N., 1967, Remote sensing as a means of determining ecological conditions, *Bioscience* 17:444-449.

Colwell, R. N., 1968, Remote sensing of natural resources, *Sci. Am.* 218:54-69.

Commission on Marine Science, Engineering and Resources, 1969, Developing law in the coastal zone, in *Science and Environment*, Supt. Doc. Washington, D.C., Chapter 8, pp. III-107-III-131.

Connell, W. A., 1940, Tidal inundation as a factor limiting distribution of *Aedes* spp. on a Delaware salt marsh, *New Jersey Mosq. Exterm. Assoc. Proc.* 27:166-177.

Corker, C., 1966, Where does the beach begin, and to what extent is this a federal question, *Washington Law Rev.* 42:33-118.

Corlett, J., and A. J. Gray, 1976, *The Wash Water Storage Scheme Feasibility Study. A Report on the Ecological Studies*, Natural Environ. Res. Council Publ. C. No. 15, Natural Environment Research Council, Alhambia House, London, 36p.

Cory, E. N., and S. L. Crosthwait, 1939, Some conservation and ecological aspects of mosquito control, *J. Econ. Entomol.* 32(2):213-215.

Costle, D. M., 1979, The national stake in wetlands, in *Wetland Functions and Values: The State of Our Understanding*, P. E. Greeson, J. R. Clark, and J. E. Clark, eds., American Water Resources Assoc., Minneapolis, Minn., pp. 7-10.

Cottam, C., 1938, The coordination of mosquito control with wildlife conservation, *New Jersey Mosq. Exterm. Assoc. Proc.* 25:217-227.

Cottam, C., W. S. Bourn, F. C. Bishop, L. L. Williams, Jr., and W. Vogt, 1938,

294 Conservation of Tidal Marshes

What's wrong with mosquito control? *North American Wildlife Conf. Trans.* 3:81-107.

Cowardin, L. M., and V. I. Meyers, 1974, Remote sensing for identification and classification of wetland vegetation, *J. Wildl. Manage.* 38:308-314.

Cowardin, L. M., V. Carter, F. C. Golet, and E. T. LaRoe, 1979, *Classification of Wetlands and Deepwater Habitats of the United States*, U.S. Dept. Interior FWS/OBS-79/31, Washington, D.C., 103p.

Cowell, E. B., 1969, The effects of oil pollution on salt marsh communities in Pembrokeshire and Cornwall, *J. Appl. Ecol.* 6:133-142.

Cowell, E. B., ed., 1971, *The Ecological Effects of Oil Pollution on Littoral Communities*, Institute of Petroleum, London, 250p.

Cowell, E. B., and J. M. Baker, 1969, Recovery of a salt marsh in Pembrokshire, Southwest Wales, from pollution by crude oil, *Biol. Conserv.* 1:291-295.

Crane, J., 1975, *Fiddler Crabs of the World: Oxypodidae: Genus Uca*, Princeton University Press, Princeton, N.J., 736p.

Croft, B. A., and A. W. A. Brown, 1975, Responses of arthropod natural enemies to insecticides, *Ann. Rev. Entomol.* 20:285-335.

Croker, R. A., and A. J. Wilson, 1965, Kinetics and effects of DDT in a tidal marsh ditch, *Amer. Fish. Soc. Trans.* 94(2):152-159.

Curran, P. J., 1980, *Multispectral Photographic Remote Sensing of Vegetation Amount and Productivity*, 14th International Symposium on Remote Sensing of Environment Proc., Ann Arbor, Mich., pp. 623-637.

Curran, P. J., 1982, Multispectral photographic remote sensing of green vegetation biomass and productivity, *Photogram. Eng. Remote Sensing* 48:243-250.

Curran, P. J., 1983, Multispectral remote sensing for the estimation of green leaf area index, *R. Soc. London Philos. Trans.*, ser. A, 309:257-270.

Cutler, M. R., 1979, The mission of wetland science, in *Wetland Functions and Values: The State of Our Understanding*, P. E. Greeson, J. R. Clark, and J. E. Clark, eds., American Water Resources Assoc., Minneapolis, Minn., pp. 11-15.

Daiber, F. C., 1977, Salt-marsh animals: distributions related to tidal flooding, salinity and vegetation, in *Wet Coastal Ecosystems*, V. J. Chapman, ed., Elsevier Scientific Publ. Co., Amsterdam, pp. 79-108.

Daiber, F. C., 1982, *Animals of the Tidal Marsh*, Van Nostrand Reinhold Co., New York, 422p.

Dalby, D. H., 1969, Some observations on oil pollution of salt marshes in Milford Haven, *Biol. Conserv.* 1:295-296.

Dalby, D. H., 1970, The salt marshes of Milford Haven, Pembrokeshire, *Field Stud.* 3(2):297-330.

Dalby, R., 1957, Problems of land reclamation. Salt marsh in the Wash, *Agr. Rev.* 2(11):31-37.

Darnell, R. M., 1967, The organic detritus problem, in *Estuaries*, G. H. Lauff, ed., Publ. No. 83, American Association for the Advancement of Science, Washington, D.C., pp. 374-375.

Darnell, R. M., 1978a, *Overview of major development impacts on wetlands*, in National Wetland Protection Symposium Fish & Wildlife Serv. Biol. Serv. Prog. Proc., J. H. Montanari and J. A. Kusler, eds., FWS/OBS-78/97, Washington, D.C., pp. 29-36.

Darnell, R. M., 1978*b*, Minimization of construction impacts on wetlands: dredge and fill, dams, dikes and channelization, in *National Wetland Protection Symposium Fish & Wildlife Serv. Biol. Serv. Prog. Proc.*, J. H. Montanari and J. A. Kusler, eds., FWS/OBS-78/97, Washington, D.C., pp. 29-36.

Darnell, R. M., 1979, Impact of human modification on the dynamics of wetland systems, in *Wetland Functions and Values: The State of Our Understanding*, P. E. Greeson, J. R. Clark, and J. E. Clark, eds., American Water Resources Assoc., Minneapolis, Minn., pp. 200-209.

Darnell, R. M., W. E. Pequegnat, B. M. James, F. J. Benson, and R. A. Defenbaugh, 1976, *Impacts of Construction Activities in Wetlands of the United States*, EPA-600/3-76-045, U.S. Environmental Protection Agency Ecol. Res. Serv. Washington, D.C., 393p.

Darsie, R. F., Jr., and P. F. Springer, 1957, *Three-year Investigation of Mosquito Breeding in Natural and Impounded Tidal Marshes in Delaware*, Univ. Delaware Agr. Exp. Sta. Bull. 320, 65p.

Dawson, A. D., 1978, Lessons from a wet state, in *National Wetland Protection Symposium Proceedings*, J. H. Montanari and J. A. Kusler, eds., Fish & Wildlife Serv. Biol. Serv. Prog. FWS/OBS-78-97, Washington, D.C., pp. 185-195.

Day, J. W., Jr., W. G. Smith, P. R. Wagner, and W. C. Stowe, 1973, Community structure and carbon budget of a salt marsh and shallow bay estuarine system in Louisiana, Publ. No. LSU-SG-72-04, Center for Wetlands Resources, Louisiana State University, Baton Rouge, 80p.

De la Cruz, A. A., and C. T. Hackney, 1980, *The Effects of Winter Fire and Harvest on the Vegetational Structure and Primary Productivity of Two Tidal Marsh Communities in Mississippi*, Miss.-Ala. Sea Grant Cons. MASGP-80-013, 115p.

De la Cruz, A. A., C. T. Hackney, and B. Rajanna, 1981, Some effects of crude oil on a *Juncus* tidal marsh, *Elisha Mitchell Sci. Soc. J.* 97(1):14-28.

De Laune, R. D., W. H. Patrick, Jr., and R. J. Buresh, 1979, Effect of crude oil on a Louisiana *Spartina alterniflora* salt marsh, *Environ. Pollut.* 20(1):21-31.

De Nekker, J., and K. D'Angremond, 1976, Dredged material: natural resource or national nuisance, in *Dredging and Its Environmental Effects*, P. A. Krenkel, J. Harrison, and J. C. Burdick III, eds., American Society of Civil Engineers, New York, pp. 866-881.

DeWitt, P., and F. C. Daiber, 1973, The hydrography of the Broadkill River estuary, Delaware, *Chesapeake Sci.* 14(1):28-40.

DeWitt, P, and F. C. Daiber, 1974, The hydrography of the Murderkill estuary, Delaware, *Chesapeake Sci.* 15(2):84-95.

Diaz, R. J., D. F. Boesch, J. L. Hauer, C. A. Stone, and K. Munson, 1978, Aquatic biology—benthos, in *Habitat Development Field Investigations, Windmill Point Marsh Development Site, James River, Virginia. Appendix D: Environmental Impacts of Marsh Development with Dredged Material: Botany, Soils, Aquatic Biology, and Wildlife*, U.S. Army Corps of Engineers Dredged Material Res. Prog. Tech. Rept. D-77-23, pp. 18-54.

Dibner, P. C., 1978, Response of a salt marsh to oil spill and cleanup, Interagency energy/environment. R & D program report, EPA-600/7-78-109, Washington, D.C., 52p.

Dicks, B., 1976, The effects of refinery effluents: the case history of a saltmarsh, in *Marine Ecology and Oil Pollution*, J. M. Baker, ed., John Wiley & Sons, New York, pp. 227-245.

Dixit, D., and J. W. Anderson, 1977, *Distribution of Naphthalenes with Exposed* Fundulus similis *and Correlations with Stress Behavior*, 1977 Oil Spill Conference Proceedings, American Petroleum Institute Publ. 4284, Washington, D.C., pp. 633-636.

Doiron, L. N., and R. T. Wilson, 1974, Remote sensing techniques for wildlife inventories in the coastal marsh—the muskrat, in *Remote Sensing of Earth Resources*, F. Shahrokhi, ed., University of Tennessee, Knoxville, pp. 685-696.

Dolan, T. J., S. E. Bayley, J. Zoltek, and A. J. Hermann, 1981, Phosphorus dynamics of a Florida freshwater marsh receiving treated waste water, *J. Appl. Ecol.* 18(1):205-219.

Dottavio, C. L., and F. D. Dottavio, 1984, Potential benefits of new satellite sensors to wetland mapping, *Photogram. Eng. Remote Sensing* 50:599-606.

Doumlele, D., and G. Silberhorn, 1978, Botanical studies, in *Habitat Development Field Investigations, Windmill Point Marsh Development Site, James River, Virginia. Appendix D: Environmental Impacts of Marsh Development with Dredged Material: Botany, Soils, Aquatic Biology, and Wildlife*, U.S. Army Corps of Engineers Dredged Material Res. Prog. Tech. Rept. D-77-23, pp. 79-88.

Doyle, F. J., 1978, The next decade of satellite remote sensing, *Photogram. Eng. Remote Sensing* 44:155-164.

Dozier, H. L., 1947, Salinity as a factor in Atlantic Coast tide water muskrat production, *North American Wildlife Conf. Trans.* 12:298-420.

Dozier, H. L., 1953, *Muskrat Production and Management*, Fish and Wildlife Service Circ. 18, U.S. Dept. of Interior, Washington, D.C., 42p.

Dozier, H. L., M. H. Markley, and L. M. Llewellyn, 1948, Muskrat Investigations on the Blackwater National Wildlife Refuge, Maryland, 1941-1945, *J. Wildl. Manage.* 12(2):177-190.

Drake, B. G., 1976, Season changes in reflectance and standing crop biomass in three salt marsh communities, *Plant Physiol.* 58:696-699.

Drayton, W., Jr., 1970, The public trust in tidal areas: a sometime submerged traditional doctrine, *Yale Law J.* 79:762-789.

Dredge Disposal Study San Francisco Bay and Estuary, 1976, Appendix K. Marshland Development U.S. Army Engr. Dist., San Francisco, Corps Engr. San Francisco, Calif. 61p., unpublished.

Drifmeyer, J. E., and W. E. Odum, 1975, Lead, zinc, and manganese in dredge-spoil pond ecosystems, *Environ. Conserv.* 2(1):39-45.

Durant, C. J., and R. J. Reimold, 1971, Effects of estuarine dredging of toxaphene-contaminated sediments in Terry Creek, Brunswick, Ga., 1971, *Pesticides Monitoring J.* 6(2)94-96.

Eaton, A. W. H., 1972, *The History of Kings County*, Mika Studio, Belleville, Ontario, pp. 12-15.

Echeverria, J., and E. J. Linky, 1978, Traditional public rights in tidelands and modern coastal zone management in *Coastal Zone '78*, vol. 3, Symposium on Technical, Environmental, Socioeconomic and Regulatory Aspects of Coastal

Zone Management, American Society of Civil Engineers, New York, pp. 1995-2012.

Ecological Study of the Amoco Cadiz Oil Spill, 1982, Rept. NOAA-CNEXO Joint Sci. Comm. U.S. Dept. of Commerce, National Oceanic and Atmospheric Administration and Centre National pour l'Exploitation des Oceans, 479p.

Egan, W. G., and M. E. Hair, 1971, *Automated Delineation of Wetlands in Photographic Remote Sensing*, 7th International Symposium on Remote Sensing of Environment Proc., Ann Arbor, Mich., pp. 2231-2251.

Eleuterius, L. N., and H. A. McClellan, 1976, Transplanting maritime plants to dredged material in Mississippi waters, in *Dredging and Its Environmental Effects*, P. A. Krenkel, J. Harrison, and J. C. Burdick III, eds., American Society of Civil Engineers, New York, pp. 900-918.

Enslin, W. R., and M. C. Sullivan, 1974, The use of color infared photography for wetlands assessment, in *Remote Sensing of Earth Resources*, F. Shahrokhi, ed., University of Tennessee, Knoxville, pp. 697-719.

Ernst-Dottavio, C. L., R. M. Hoffer, and R. P. Mroczynski, 1981, Spectral characteristics of wetland habitats, *Photogram. Eng. Remote Sensing* 47:223-227.

Errington, P. L., 1963, *Muskrat Populations*, Iowa State University Press, Ames, Ia., 665p.

Evans, J., 1970, *About Nutria and Their Control*, Fish and Wildlife Service Resource Publ. No. 86, U.S. Dept. of Interior, Washington, D.C., 65p.

Eyre, L. A., 1971, High altitude color photos, *Photogram. Eng.* 37:1149-1153.

Ferrigno, F., 1958, A Two-year Study of Mosquito Breeding in the Natural and Untouched Salt Marshes of Egg Island, *New Jersey Mosq. Exterm. Assoc. Proc.* 45:132-139.

Ferrigno, F., 1959, Further study on mosquito production on the newly acquired Cadwalader tract, *New Jersey Mosq. Exterm. Assoc. Proc.* 46:95-102.

Ferrigno, F., 1961, Variations in mosquito-wildlife associations on coastal marshes, *New Jersey Mosq. Exterm. Assoc. Proc.* 48:193-203.

Ferrigno, F., 1970, Preliminary effects of open marsh water management on the vegetation and organisms of the salt marsh, *New Jersey Mosq. Exterm. Assoc. Proc.* 57:79-94.

Ferrigno, F., 1976, Snow goose management, *New Jersey Outdoors* 3(5):22-24.

Ferrigno, F., and D. M. Jobbins, 1966, A summary of nine years of applied mosquito-wildlife research on Cumberland County, N. J. salt marshes, *New Jersey Mosq. Exterm. Assoc. Proc.* 53:97-112.

Ferrigno, F., and D. M. Jobbins, 1968, Open Marsh Water Management, *New Jersey Mosq. Exterm. Assoc. Proc.* 55:104-115.

Ferrigno, F., D. M. Jobbins, and M. P. Shinkle, 1967, Coordinated mosquito control and wildlife management for the Delaware Bay coastal marshes, *New Jersey Mosq. Exterm. Assoc. Proc.* 54:80-94.

Ferrigno, F., L. G. MacNamara, and D. M. Jobbins, 1969, Ecological approach for improved management of coastal meadowlands, *New Jersey Mosq. Exterm. Assoc. Proc.* 56:188-202.

Ferrigno, F., P. Slavin, and D. M. Jobbins, 1975, Salt marsh water management for mosquito control, *New Jersey Mosq. Control Assoc. Proc.* 62:30-38.

Fitzpatrick, G., and D. J. Sutherland, 1978, Effects of the organophosphorous insecticides temephos (Abate) and chlorpyrifos (Dursban) on populations of the salt marsh snail *Melampus bidentatus. Mar. Biol.* **46**:23-28.

Fleeger, J. W., and G. T. Chandler, 1983, Meiofauna responses to an experimental oil spill in a Louisiana salt marsh, *Mar. Ecol. Prog. Ser.* **11**:257-264.

Florschutz, O., Jr., 1959a, *Mosquito Production and Wildlife Usage in Natural, Ditched, and Impounded Tidal Marshes on Assawoman Wildlife Area, Delaware,* Master's thesis, University of Delaware, 94pp.

Florschutz, O., Jr., 1959b, Mosquito production and wildlife usage in impounded, ditched and unditched tidal marshes at Assawoman Wildlife Area, Delaware, *New Jersey Mosq. Exterm. Assoc. Proc.* **46**:103-111.

Floyd, K. W., and C. L. Newcombe, 1976, *Growth of Intertidal Marsh Plants on Dredge Material Substrate,* San Francisco Bay Marine Research Center, Richmond, Calif., 101p.

Fornes, A. O., and R. J. Reimold, 1973, *The Estuarine Environment: Location of Mean High Water—Its Engineering, Economic and Ecological Potential,* American Society Photogrammetry Proceedings, Fall Convention, Falls Church, Va., Part II, pp. 938-978.

Franz, D. R., 1963, Production and distribution of mosquito larvae on some New Jersey salt marsh impoundments, *New Jersey Mosq. Exterm. Assoc. Proc.* **50**:279-285.

Friedman, R. M., and C. B. DeWitt, 1979, Wetlands as carbon and nutrient reservoirs: a spatial, historical, and societal perspective, in *Wetland Functions and Values: The State of Our Understanding,* P. E. Greeson, J. R. Clark, and J. E. Clark, eds., American Water Resources Assoc., Minneapolis, Minn., pp. 175-185.

Fultz, T. O., Jr., 1978, Mosquito source reduction and present water management regulations in coastal Georgia, *New Jersey Mosq. Control Assoc. Proc.* **65**:36-39.

Gabrielson, I. N., 1941, *Wildlife Conservation,* Macmillan, New York, 250p.

Gallagher, J. L., 1975, Effect of ammonium nitrate pulse on the growth and elemental composition of natural stands of *Spartina alterniflora* and *Juncus roemarianus, Am. J. Bot.* **62**(6):644-648.

Gallagher, J. L., and R. J. Reimold, 1973, *Tidal Marsh Plant Distribution and Productivity Patterns from the Sea to Fresh Water-A Challenge in Resolution and Discrimination,* 4th Biennial Workshop on Aerial Color Photography in the Plant Sciences, University of Maine, Orono, pp. 165-183.

Gallagher, J. L., R. J. Reimold, and D. E. Thompson, 1972a, *Remote Sensing and Salt Marsh Productivity,* 38th Ann. Meeting Proc., American Society of Photogrammetry, Washington, D.C., pp. 338-348.

Gallagher, J. L., R. J. Reimold, and D. E. Thompson, 1972b, *A Comparison of Four Remote Sensing Media for Assessing Salt Marsh Productivity,* 8th International Symposium on Remote Sensing of Environment Proc., Ann Arbor, Mich., pp. 1287-1295.

Gallagher, J. L., R. J. Reimold, R. A. Linthurst, and W. J. Pfeiffer, 1980, Aerial production, mortality, and mineral accumulation-export dynamics in *Spartina alterniflora* and *Juncus roemarianus* plant stands in a Georgia salt marsh, *Ecology* **61**(2):303-312.

Gammon, P. T., and V. Carter, 1979, Vegetation mapping with seasonal color infared photographs, *Photogram. Eng. Remote Sensing* **45**:87-97.

Ganong, W. F., 1903, The vegetation of the Bay of Fundy salt and diked marshes: an ecological study, *Bot. Gaz.* **36**:161-186, 280-302, 349-367, 429-455.

Garbisch, E. W., Jr., 1977, *Recent and Planned Marsh Establishment Work throughout the Contiguous United States.* A Survey and Basic Guidelines, U.S. Army Corps Eng. Dredged Material Res. Prog. Contract Rept. D-77-3, 42p.

Garbisch, E. W., Jr., 1978, Wetland rehabilitation, in *National Wetland Protection Symposium Proceedings*, J. H. Montanari and J. A. Kusler, eds., Fish & Wildlife Serv. Biol. Serv. Prog. FWS/OBS-78/97, Washington, D.C., pp. 217-219.

Garbisch, E. W., P. B. Woller, W. J., Bostian, and R. J. McCallum, 1975, Biotic techniques for shore stabilization, in *Estuarine Research*, vol. 2, L. E. Cronin, ed., Academic Press, New York, pp. 405-426.

Garren, K. H., 1943, Effects of fire on vegetation of the southeastern United States, *Bot. Rev.* **9**:617-654.

Garrett, M. K., and V. Carter, 1977, *Contribution of Remote Sensing to Habitat Evaluation and Management in a Highly Altered Ecosystem*, 42nd North American Wildlife and Natural Resources Conf. Trans., Wildlife Management Inst., Washington, D.C., pp. 56-65.

Gausman, H. W., 1974, Leaf reflectance of near-infared, *Photogram. Eng.* **40**:183-191.

Gausman, H. W., W. A. Allen, and A. Cardenas, 1969, Reflectance of cotton leaves and their structure, *Remote Sensing Environ.* **1**:19-22.

Gibbons, E., 1962, *Stalking the Wild Asparagus*, D. McKay Co., New York.

Gilfillan, E. S., 1973, *Effects of Seawater Extracts of Crude Oil on Carbon Budgets in Two Species of Mussels*, Joint Conference on Prevention and Control of Oil Spills Proceedings, American Petroleum Institute, Washington, D.C., pp. 691-695.

Gilfillan, E. S., 1975, Decrease of net carbon flux in two species of mussels caused by extracts of crude oil, *Mar. Biol.* **29**:53-57.

Gillham, M. E., 1955, Ecology of the Pembrokeshire Islands. III. The effect of grazing on the vegetation, *J. Ecol.* **43**(1):172-206.

Gilmer, D. S., E. A. Work, J. E. Colwell, and D. L. Rebel, 1980, Enumeration of prairie wetlands with Landsat and aircraft data, *Photogram. Eng. and Remote Sensing* **46**:631-634.

Glue, D. E., 1971, Salt marsh reclamation stages and their associated bird life, *Bird Study* **18**(4):187-198.

Grant, R. R., Jr., and R. Patrick, 1970, Tinicum Marsh as a water purifier, in *Two Studies of Tinicum Marsh*, Conservation Foundation, pp. 105-123.

Gray, A. J., 1970, The colonization of estuaries following barrage building, in *The Flora of a Changing Britain*, F. H. Perring, ed., E. W. Classey, Hampton, England, pp. 63-72.

Gray, A. J., 1972, The ecology of Morecambe Bay. V. The salt marshes of Morecambe Bay, *J. Appl. Ecol.* **9**:207-220.

Gray, A. J., 1976, The Ouse washes and the Wash, in *Nature in Norfolk, A Heritage in Trust*, Norfolk Naturalist's Trust, eds., Jarrold & Son, Norwich, England, pp. 123-129.

Gray, A. J., 1977, Reclaimed land, in *The Coastline*, R. S. K. Barnes, ed., John Wiley & Sons, London, pp. 253-270.

Gray, A. J., 1979, The ecological implications of estuarine and coastal land reclamation, in *Estuarine and Coastal Land Reclamation and Water Storage*, B. Knights and A. J. Phillips, eds., Saxon House, Farnborough, England, pp. 177-194.

Gray, A. J., and P. Adam, 1974, The reclamation history of Morecambe Bay, *Nature Lancs.* 4:13-20.

Gray, A. J., and R. G. A. Bunce, 1972, The ecology of Morecambe Bay. VI. Soils and vegetation of the salt marshes: a multivariate approach, *J. Appl. Ecol.* 9(1):231-232.

Gray, A. J., and R. Scott, 1975, *Genecology of Salt Marsh Plants*, Ann. Rept. 1974, Institute of Terrestial Ecology Natural Environment Research Council, Her Majesty's Stationary Office, London, pp. 35-36.

Gray, A. J., and R. Scott, 1977, Ecology of Morecambe Bay. VII. The distribution of *Puccinellia maritima*, *Festuca rubra* and *Agrostis stolonifera* in the salt marshes, *J. Appl., Ecol.* 14:229-241.

Gray, A. J., R. J. Parsell, and R. Scott, 1979, The genetic structure of plant populations in relation to the development of salt marshes, in *Ecological Processes in Coastal Environments*, R. L. Jeffries and A. J. Davy, eds., Blackwell Scientific Publ., Oxford, pp. 43-64.

Greenhalgh, M. E., 1971, The breeding bird communities of Lancashire salt marshes, *Bird Study* 18:199-212.

Greenhalgh, M. E., 1974, Population growth and breeding success in a salt marsh. Common Tern Colony, *Naturalist* 931:121-127.

Greenman, A. B., 1978, Impact of wetlands laws on development in New York State, in *Coastal Zone '78*, vol. 2, Symposium on Technical, Environmental, Socioeconomic and Regulatory Aspects of Coastal Zone Management, American Society of Civil Engineers, New York, pp. 1182-1187.

Greeson, P. E., J. R. Clark, and Judith E. Clark, 1979, *Wetland Functions and Values: The State of Our Understanding*, American Water Resources Assoc., Minneapolis, 674p.

Griffith, R. E., 1940, Waterfowl Management of Atlantic Coast Refuges, *North American Wildlife Conf. Trans.* 5:373-377.

Gundlach, E. R., and M. O. Hayes, 1978, Vulnerability of coastal environments to oil spill impacts, *Mar. Tech. Soc. J.* 12:18-27.

Gunter, G., and L. N. Eleuterius, 1971, Some effects of hurricanes on the terrestrial biota, with special reference to Camille, *Gulf Res. Repts.* 3(2):283-289.

Guss, P., 1972, *Tidelands Management Mapping for the Coastal Plains Region*, Coastal Mapping Symposium Proc., American Society of Photogrammetry, Washington, D.C., pp. 243-262.

Hagmann, L. E., 1953, Biology of *Mansonia pertubans* (Walker), *New Jersey Mosq. Exterm. Assoc. Proc.* 40:141-147.

Haines, E. B., 1976a, Relation between the stable carbon isotope composition of fiddler crabs, plants, and soils in a salt marsh, *Limnol. Oceanogr.* 21(6): 880-883.

Haines, E. B., 1976b, Stable carbon isotope ratios in the biota, soils, and tidal water of a Georgia salt marsh, *Estuarine Coastal Mar. Sci.* 4(6):609-616.

Haines, E. B., 1978, The origins of detritus in Georgia salt marsh estuaries, *Oikos* 29(2):254-260.

Haines, E. B., 1979, Interactions between Georgia salt marshes and coastal waters: a changing paradigm, in *Ecological Processes in Coastal and Marine Systems*, R. J. Livingston, ed., Marine Science, vol. 10, Plenum Press, New York, pp. 35-46.

Hampson, G. R., and E. T. Moul, 1978, No. 2 fuel oil spill in Bourne, Massachusetts: immediate assessment of the effects on marine invertebrates and a 3-year study of growth and recovery of a salt marsh, *Canada Fish. Res. Board J.* 35:731-744.

Hansen, D. J., 1969, Avoidance of pesticides by untrained sheepshead minnows, *Amer. Fish. Soc. Trans.* 98(3):426-429.

Hansen, J. A., F. H. Lesser, R. W. Lombardi, J. K. Shisler, and P. Slavin, 1976, The economics of marsh water management, *New Jersey Mosq. Exterm. Assoc. Proc.* 63:77-81.

Hansen, W. J., S. E. Richardson, R. T. Reppert, and G. E. Galloway, 1980, Wetlands' values—contributions to environmental quality or to national economic development? in *Estuarine Perspectives*, V. S. Kennedy ed., Academic Press, New York, pp. 17-29.

Hansens, E. J., 1949, The biting fly problem in New Jersey resorts and its relation to mosquito control, *New Jersey Mosq. Exterm. Assoc. Proc.* 36:126-130.

Hanson, H. C., 1951, Characteristics of some grassland, marsh and other plant communities in Western Alaska, *Ecol. Monogr.* 21(4):317-375.

Hardin, G., 1968, The tragedy of the commons, *Science* 162:1243-1248.

Hardisky, M. A., 1979, Marsh restoration on dredged material Buttermilk Sound, Georgia, 1978, in *6th Annual Conference on Wetlands Restoration and Creation Proceedings*, D. P. Cole, ed., Environmental Studies Center, Hillsborough Community College, Tampa, Fla., pp. 143-173.

Hardisky, M. A., 1983, *Remote Sensing of Aboveground Biomass and Annual New Arial Primary Productivity in Tidal Wetlands*, Ph.D. dissertation, University of Delaware, 252p.

Hardisky, M. A., and V. Klemas, 1985, *Remote Sensing of Coastal Wetlands Biomass Using Thematic Mapper Wavebands*, in Landsat-4 Science Characterization Early Results Symp., National Aeronautics and Space Administration Publ. 2355, vol. 4, NASA Goddard SFC, Greenbelt, Md., pp. 251-269.

Hardisky, M. A., V. Klemas, and F. C. Daiber, 1983, Remote sensing salt marsh biomass and stress detection, in *Advances in Space Research*, vol. 2, COSPAR, Pergamon Press, London, pp. 219-229.

Hardisky, M. A., V. Klemas, and R. M. Smart, 1983, The influence of soil salinity, growth form and leaf moisture on the spectral radiance of *Spartina alterniflora* canopies, *Photogram. Eng. Remote Sensing* 49:77-83.

Hardisky, M. A., R. M. Smart, and V. Klemas, 1983, Seasonal spectral characteristics and aboveground biomass of the tidal marsh plant; *Spartina alterniflora, Photogram. Eng. Remote Sensing* 49:85-92.

Hardisky, M. A., F. C. Daiber, C. T. Roman, and V. Klemas, 1984, Remote sensing of biomass and annual net aerial primary productivity of a salt marsh, *Remote Sensing Environ.* 16:91-106.

Hardy, J. D., Jr., 1978, *Development of Fishes of the mid-Atlantic Bight: An Atlas of Egg, Larval and Juvenile Stages*, vol. 2, *Anguillidae through*

Syngnathidae, Fish and Wildlife Service, Biol. Serv. Prog., FWS/OBS-78-12, Washington, D.C., pp. 141-216.

Harrington, R. W., and W. L. Bidlingmayer, 1958, Effects of Dieldrin on fish and invertebrates of a salt marsh, *J. Wildl. Manage.* 22(1):76-82.

Harrington, R. W., Jr., and E. S. Harrington, 1961, Food selection among fishes invading a high subtropical salt marsh: from onset of flooding through the progress of a mosquito brood, *Ecology* 42(4):646-666.

Harrington, R. W., Jr., and E. S. Harrington, 1982, Effects on fishes and their forage organisms of impounding a Florida saltmarsh to prevent breeding by salt marsh mosquitos, *Mar. Sci. Bull.* 32(2):523-531.

Harrison, F. J., Jr., 1970, *The Use of Low Level Impoundments for the Control of the Salt-marsh Mosquito*, Aedes sollicitans (*Walker*), Master's thesis, University of Delaware, 66p.

Harvey, M. J., 1973, Salt marshes of the maritimes, *Nature Canada* 2(2):22-26.

Harwood, C. C., 1978, Wetlands, taxation and the taking issue, in *National Wetland Protection Symposium Proceedings*, J. H. Montanari and J. A. Kusler, eds., Fish & Wildlife Serv. Biol. Serv. Prog. FWS/OBS-78/97, Washington, D.C., pp. 185-195.

Haslam, S. M., 1968, The Biology of Reed (*Phragmites communis*) in Relation to Its Control, 9th British Weed Control Conf. Proc., pp. 392-397.

Haslam, S. M., 1969, *The Reed: A Study of Phragmites communis Trin. in Relation to Its Cultivation and Harvesting in East Anglia for the Thatching Industry*, Norfolk Reed Growers Assoc. vol. 1.

Haslam, S. M., 1972, Biological flora of the British Isles, *Phragmites communis* Trin., *J. Ecol.* 60:585-610.

Hatcher, A. I., 1977, *Aspects of Carbon and Nitrogen Cycling in a Spartina Dominated Salt Marsh on the Northumberland Strait, Nova Scotia: And the Effects of Impoundment*, Master's thesis, Dalhousie University, 110p.

Haueisen, A. J., 1974, An examination of legislation for the protection of the wetlands of the Atlantic and Gulf Coast states, *Gulf Res. Repts.* 4(3):233-263.

Hawkes, A. L., 1966, Coastal wetlands—Problems and opportunities, *North American Wildlife Conf. Trans.* 31:59-77.

Headlee, T. J., 1915, *The Mosquitos of New Jersey and Their Control*, New Jersey Agric. Exp. Sta. Bull. 276, 135p.

Headlee, T. J., 1939, Relation of mosquito control to wildlife, *New Jersey Mosq. Exterm. Assoc. Proc.* 26:5-12.

Healy, W. B., 1980, A New Zealand research programme to assist community management of an estuary, in *Estuarine Perspectives*, V. S. Kennedy, ed., Academic Press, New York, pp. 59-65.

Heinle, D. R., and D. A. Flemer, 1976, Flows of materials from poorly flooded tidal marshes and an estuary, *Mar. Biol.* 35(4):359-373.

Heitz, J. R., L. Lewes, J. Chambers, and J. D. Yarbrough, 1974, The acute effects of empire mix crude oil on enzymes in oysters, shrimp and mullet, in *Pollution and Physiology of Marine Organisms*, F. J. Vernberg, and W. B. Vernberg, eds., Academic Press, New York, pp. 311-328.

Herke, W. H., 1968, Weirs, potholes and fishery management, in *Marsh and Estuary Management Symposium Proceedings*, J. D. Newsom, ed., Louisiana State University, Baton Rouge, pp. 193-211.

Herke, W. H., 1979, Some effects of semi-impoundment on coastal Louisiana fish and crustacean nursery usage, in *3rd Coastal Marsh and Estuary Management Symposium Proceedings*, J. W. Day., Jr., D. D. Culley, Jr., R. E. Turner, and A. J. Mumphrey, Jr., eds., Louisiana State University, Baton Rouge, pp. 325-346.

Hershman, M. J., 1975, Coastal zone management: accommodating competing coastal uses, in Coastal Resources Geoscience and Man, H. J. Walker, ed., **12:**109-115.

Hershman, M. J., 1977, Boundaries, ownership, and jurisdictional limits in the coastal zone, in *Coastal Ecosystem Management*, J. R. Clark, ed., John Wiley & Sons, New York, pp. 581-587.

Hershman, M. J., and A. A. Ruotsala, 1978, Implementing environmental mitigation policies, in *Coastal Zone '78*, vol. 2, Symposium on Technical, Environmental, Socioeconomic and Regulatory Aspects of Coastal Zone Management, American Society of Civil Engineers, New York, pp. 1333-1345.

Hershner, C., and K. Moore, 1977, *Effects of the Chesapeake Bay Oil Spill on Salt Marshes of the Lower Bay*, 1977 Oil Spill Conference Proceedings, American Petroleum Institute Publ. 4284, Washington, D.C., pp. 529-533.

Hilliard, S. B., 1975, The tidewater rice plantation: an ingenious adaptation to nature, *Coastal Resources Geoscience and Man*, H. J. Walker, ed., vol. 12, pp. 57-66.

Hindley, E., and J. H. G. Smith, 1957, Spectrophotometric analysis of foliage of some British Columbia conifers, *Photogram. Eng.* **23:**894-895.

Hocking, A., 1978, *Prince Edward Island*, The Canadian Series. McGraw-Hill Ryerson Ltd. Toronto, 64 pp.

Hoffpauer, C. M., 1968, Burning for Coastal Marsh Management, in *Marsh and Estuary Management Symposium Proceedings*, J. D. Newsom, ed., Louisiana State University, Baton Rouge, pp. 134-139.

Hood, M. A., W. S. Bishop, Jr., F. W. Bishop, S. P. Meyers, and T. Whelan, III, 1975, Microbial indicators of oil-rich salt marsh sediments, *Appl. Microbiol.* **30:**982-987.

Horwitz, E. L., 1978, *Our Nation's Wetlands*, an interagency task force report, Council on Environmental Quality, Washington, D.C., 70p.

Hoskins, W. M., and H. T. Gordon, 1956, Arthropod resistance to chemicals, *Ann. Rev. Entomol.* **1:**89-122.

Howard, R., D. G. Rhodes, and J. W. Simmers, 1978, *A Review of the Biology and Potential Control Techniques for* Phragmites australis, U.S. Army Corps of Engineers, Vicksburg, Miss., Environmental Laboratory, Waterways Experiment Station, Internal Working Document D-78-26, 80p.

Howe, L., 1981, Ditching the pesky mosquito, *Smithsonian News Service Release*, August 1981, Smithsonian Institution, Washington, D.C., 4p.

Howland, W. G., 1980, Multispectral aerial photography for wetland vegetation mapping, *Photogram. Eng. Remote Sensing* **48:**87-99.

Hull, W. V., 1978, The significance of tidal datums to coastal zone management in *Coastal Zone '78*, vol. 2, Symposium on Technical, Environmental, Socioeconomic and Regulatory Aspects of Coastal Zone Management, American Society of Civil Engineers, New York, pp. 965-971.

Hulten, E., 1964, *The Circumpolar Plants. I. Vascular Cryptogams, Conifers,*

Monocotyledons, Sv. Vet. Akad. Handl. Band 8. Nr. 5, Almquist & Wiksell, Stockholm, 280p.

Hulten, E., 1971, *The Circumpolar Plants. II. Dicotyledons*, Sv. Vet. Akad. Handl. Band 13. Nr. 1, Almquist & Wiksell, Stockholm, 463p.

Hunt, L. J., 1979, Principles of Marsh Establishment, in *6th Annual Conference on Wetlands Restoration and Creation Proceedings*, D. P. Cole., ed., Environmental Studies Center, Hillsborough Community College, Tampa, Fla., pp. 127-142.

Hurd, L. E., G. W. Smedes, and T. A. Dean, 1979, An ecological study of a natural population of diamondback terrapin (*Malaclemys t. terrapin*) in a Delaware salt marsh, *Estuaries* 2:28-33.

Husak, S., 1973, Destructive control of stands of *Phragmites communis* and *Typha angustifolia* and its effects on shoot production followed for three seasons, in *Littoral of the Nesyt Fishpond*, J. Kvet ed., Ceskoslovenska Akademie Ved. Studie CSAV, Prague, pp. 89-91.

Ives, R. L., 1939, Infrared photography as an aid in ecological surveys, *Ecology* **20**:433-439.

Jackson, C. I., and J. W. Maxwell, 1971, *Landowners and Land Use in the Tantramar Area, New Brunswick*, Joint publ Canada Land Inventory, Dept. Regional Economic Expansion, CLI Rept. No. 9, and the Policy Research and Coordination Branch, Dept. of Energy, Mines and Resources, Geographical Paper No. 47, 1971, Information Canada, Ottawa, 37p.

Jahn, L. R., 1981, Resource management: challenge of the eighties, *Water Spectrum* **13**(3):1-8.

Jamnback, H., and W. J. Wall, 1959, *The Common Salt Marsh Tabanidae of Long Island, New York*, New York State Museum Bull. 375, 77p.

Jensen, A., 1980, Seasonal changes in near infrared reflectance ratio and standing crop biomass in a salt marsh community dominated by *Halimione portulacoides* (L.) Aellen. *New Phytol.* **86**:57-67.

Jensen, H. A., and R. N. Colwell, 1949, Panchromatic versus infrared minus blue aerial photography for forestry purposes in California, *Photogram. Eng.* **15**:201-223.

Jensen, P. A., and J. M. Tyrawski, 1978, Wetlands and water quality, in *Coastal Zone '78*, vol. 2, Symposium on Technical, Environmental, Socioeconomic and Regulatory Aspects of Coastal Zone Management, American Society of Civil Engineers, New York, pp. 1145-1164.

Jéquel, N., and D. Rouve, 1983, *Marais, Vasieres, Estuaires*, Quest-France, Rennes, France, 64p.

Jerling, L., 1983, Composition and viability of the seed bank along a successional gradient on a Baltic sea shore meadow, *Holarctic Ecol.* **6**(2):150-156.

Jerling, L., and M. Andersson, 1982, Effects of selective grazing by cattle on the reproduction of *Plantago maritima*, Holarctic Ecol. **5**:405-411.

Johnson, D. W., 1967, *The New England-Acadian Shore Line*, Hafner, N. Y., 608p.

Johnson, D. W., 1968, Pesticides and fish—a review of selected literature, *Amer. Fish. Soc. Trans.* **97**(4):398-424.

Johnson, L. E., and W. V. McGuinness, Jr., 1975, *Guidelines for Material Placement in Marsh Creation*, U.S. Army Corps of Engineers Dredge Material Res. Prog. Contract Rept. D-75-2, 189p. plus appendices.

Jordan, C. F., 1969, Derivation of leaf area index from quality of light on the forest floor, *Ecology* 50:663-666.

Kadlec, R. H., 1978, Wetland for tertiary treatment, in *Wetland Functions and Values: The State of Our Understanding*, P. E. Greeson, J. R. Clark, and J. E. Clark, eds., American Water Resources Assoc., Minneapolis, Minn., pp. 490-504.

Kadlec, R. H., and J. A. Kadlec, 1978, Wetlands and water quality, in *Wetland Functions and Values: The State of Our Understanding*, P. E. Greeson, J. R. Clark, and J. E. Clark, eds., American Water Resources Assoc., Minneapolis, Minn., pp. 436-456.

Kalber, F. A., Jr., 1959, A hypothesis on the role of tidemarshes in estuarine productivity, *Estuarine Bull.* 4(1):3, 14-15.

Kale, H. W., II, 1964, Food of the long-billed marsh wren, *Talmatodytes palustris griseus* in the salt marshes of Sapelo Island, Georgia, *The Oriole* 29(4):47-66.

Kat, P. 1978, *The Functional Morphology and Ecology of Cyrenoidea Floridana Dall (Bivalva: Cyrenoididae)*, Master's thesis, University of Delaware.

Kator, H., and R. Herwig, 1977, *Microbial Responses after Two Experimental Oil Spills in an Eastern Coastal Plain Estuarine Ecosystem*, 1977 Oil Spill Conference Proceedings, American Petroleum Institute Publ. 4284, Washington, D.C., pp. 517-522.

Katz, L. M., 1975, *Laboratory Studies on Diet, Growth and Energy Requirements of* Fundulus heteroclitus (*Linnaeus*), Ph.D. dissertation, University of Delaware, 80p.

Katz, M., 1961, Acute toxicity of some organic insecticides to three species of salmonids and to the three spine stickleback, *Amer. Fish Soc. Trans.* 90(3):264-268.

Keefe, C. W., 1972, Marsh production: a summary of the literature, *Contrib. Mar. Sci., Univ. Texas* 16:163-181.

Kestner, F. J. T., 1962, The old coastline of the Wash, *Geogr. J.* 128:457-478.

Kestner, F. J. T., 1972, The effects of water conservation works on the regime of Morecambe Bay, *Geogr. J.* 138:178-208.

Kestner, F. J. T., 1975, The loose boundary regime of the Wash, *Geogr. J.* 141:388-414.

Ketchum, B. H., ed., 1972, *The Waters Edge: Critical Problems of the Coastal Zone*, MIT Press, Cambridge, Mass., 393p.

Klemas, V., F. C. Daiber, D. S. Bartlett, O. Crichton, and A. O. Fornes, 1974, Inventory of Delaware's wetlands, *Photogram. Eng.* 40:433-439.

Klemas, V., F. C. Daiber, D. S. Bartlett, and R. H. Rogers, 1975, Coastal zone classification from satellite imagery, *Photogram. Eng. Remote Sensing* 41:499-513.

Klose, P. N., 1980, Quantification of environmental impacts in the coastal zone, in *Estuarine Perspectives*, V. S. Kennedy, ed., Academic Press, New York, pp. 27-35.

Kneib, R. T., and A. E. Stiven, 1978, Growth, reproduction, and feeding of *Fundulus heteroclitus* (L.) on a North Carolina salt marsh, *J. Exp. Mar. Biol. Ecol.* 31(2):121-140.

Knights, B., and A. J. Phillips, eds., 1979, *Estuarine and Coastal Land Reclamation and Water Storage*, Saxon House, Farnborough, England, 247p.

Kozlowski, T. T., and C. E. Ahlgren, eds., 1974, *Fire and Ecosystems*, Academic Press, New York.

Krebs, C. T., and K. A. Burns, 1977, Long-term effects of an oil spill on populations of the salt-marsh crab *Uca pugnax, Science* 197:484-487.

Krebs, C. T., and K. A. Burns, 1978, Long-term effects of an oil spill on populations of the salt-marsh crab *Uca pugnax, Canada Fish. Res. Board J.* 35(5):684-649.

Kruczynski, W. L., R. T. Huffman, and M. K. Vincent, 1978, *Habitat Development Field Investigations, Apalachicola Bay Marsh Development Site, Apalachicola Bay, Florida.* Summary Report, U.S. Army Corps of Engineers Dredged Material Res. Prog. Tech. Rept. D-78-32, 39p.

Kuenzler, E. J., and H. L. Marshall, 1973, *Effects of Mosquito Control Ditching on Estuarine Ecosystems*, Water Resources Research Institute, Univ. North Carolina Rept. No. 81, 83p.

Kusler, J. A., 1978, Summary: future directions, in *National Wetland Protection Symposium Proceedings*, J. H. Montanari and J. A. Kusler, eds., Fish & Wildl. Serv. Biol. Serv. Prog. FWS/OBS-78/97, Washington, D.C., pp. 251-255.

Kvet, J., 1973, *Littoral of the Nesyt Fishpond*, Ceskoslovenska Akademie Ved. Studie CSAV, Prague, 172p.

Lagna, L., 1975, *The Relationship of* Spartina alterniflora *to Mean High Water*, New York Sea Grant Institute NYSSGP-RS-75-002, 48p.

Lake, J. L., and C. Hershner, 1977, *Petroleum Sulfur-Containing Compounds and Aromatic Hydrocarbons in the Marine Mollusks* Modiolus demissus *and* Crassostrea virginica, 1977 Oil Spill Conference Proceedings, American Petroleum Institute Publ. 4284, pp. 627-632.

Landers, J. L., A. S. Johnson, P. H. Morgan, and W. P. Baldwin, 1976, Duck foods in managed tidal impoundments in South Carolina, *J. Wildl. Manage.* 40:721-728.

Lanier, M. D., 1981, *Poems of Sidney Lanier*, University of Georgia Press, Athens, 272p.

LaRoe, E. T., 1978, Mitigation: a concept for wetland restoration, in *National Wetland Protection Symposium Proceedings*, J. H. Montanari and J. A. Kusler, eds., Fish & Wildl. Serv. Biol. Serv. Prog. FWS/OBS-78/97, Washington, D.C., pp. 221-224.

Larson, J. S., O. Loucks, and J. Clark, 1978, Program and priorities for wetland research developed by the National Wetlands Technical Council, in *National Wetland Protection Symposium Proceedings*, J. H. Montanari and J. A. Kusler, eds., Fish & Wildl. Serv. Biol. Serv. Prog. FWS/OBS-78/97, Washington, D.C., pp. 243-244.

Larsson, T., 1969, Land use and bird fauna on shores in southern Sweden, *Oikos* 20:136-155.

Larsson, T., 1976, Composition and density of the bird fauna in Swedish shore meadows, *Ornis Scand.* 7(1):1-12.

LaSalle, R. N., and K. L. Knight, 1974, *Effects of Salt Marsh Impoundments on Mosquito Populations*, Water Resources Research Institute Univ. North Carolina Rept. No. 92, 85p.

Laughlin, R. B., Jr., L. G. L. Young, and J. M. Neff, 1978, A long-term study of the effects of water-soluble fractions of No. 2 fuel oil on the survival, development rate, and growth of the mud crab *Rhithropanopeus harrisii*, *Mar. Biol.* 47:87-95.

Lawson, D. T., 1975, *No Heir to Take Its Place*, The Rice Museum, Georgetown, S.C., 32p.

Lay, D. W., and T. O'Neil, 1942, Muskrats on the Texas coast, *J. Wildl. Manage.* 6(4):301-312.

Lee, R. F., 1977, Accumulation and turnover of petroleum hydrocarbons in marine organisms, in *Fate and Effects of Petroleum Hydrocarbons in Marine Organisms and Ecosystems*, D. A. Wolfe, ed., Pergamon Press, New York, pp. 60-70.

Lee, R. F., B. Dornseif, F. Gonsoulin, K. Tenore, and R. Hanson, 1981, Fate and effects of a heavy fuel oil spill on a Georgia salt marsh, *Mar. Environ. Res.* 5:125-143.

Lent, C. M., 1969, Adaptations of the ribbed mussel, *Modiolus demissus* (Dillwyn) to the intertidal habitat, *Am. Zool.* 9:283-292.

Leopold, A., 1939, *Game Management*, Charles Scribner's Sons, New York, 481p.

Lesser, C. R., 1975, *Some Effects of Grid Systems Mosquito Control Ditching on Salt Marsh Biota in Delaware*, Master's thesis, University of Delaware, 24p.

Lesser, C. R., and D. E. Saveikis, 1979, *A Study of the Impacts of a Mosquito Control Integrated Pest Management Program on Selected Parameters of the Ecology of Chesapeake Bay High Marsh Communities in Maryland*, Final Report, EPA Grant No. X003147-01, Maryland Department of Agriculture, Plant Industries and Pest Management, Mosquito Control, 194p.

Lesser, C. R., R. M. Altman, and L. F. George, 1978, Open marsh water management in Maryland, *New Jersey Mosq. Exterm. Assoc. Proc.* 65:41-46.

Lesser, C. R., F. J. Murphy, and R. W. Lake, 1976, Some effects of the grid system mosquito control ditching on salt marsh biota in Delaware, *Mosq. News* 36(1):69-77.

Lesser, F. H., 1965, *Some Environmental Considerations of Impounded Tidal Marshes on Mosquito and Waterbird Prevalence, Little Creek Wildlife Area, Delaware*, Master's thesis, University of Delaware, 121p.

Levasseur, J. E., and M. L. Jory, 1982, Retablissement Naturel d'Une Vegetation de Marais Maritimes Alterée par les Hydrocarbures de l'Amoco-Cadiz: Modalites et Tendances, in *Ecological Study of the Amoco Cadiz Oil Spill*, Rept. NOAA-CNEXO Joint Sci. Comm., U.S. Dept. Commerce, National Oceanic and Atmospheric Administration and Centre National Pour L'Exploitation des Oceans, pp. 329-362.

Livingstone, R. J., and O. L. Loucks, 1979, Productivity, trophic interactions, and food-web relationships in wetlands and associated systems, in *Wetland Functions and Values: The State of Our Understanding*, P. E. Greeson, J. R. Clark, and J. E. Clark, eds., American Water Resources Assoc., Minneapolis, Minn., pp. 101-119.

Lorio, W. J., M. R. Capeyya, and O. H. Dakin, 1979, Aquatic ecological parameters associated with salt marsh mosquito ditch systems, Southeast Association Assoc. Fish & Wildlife Agencies Ann. Conf. Proc. 33:484-494.

Lunz, J. D., R. J. Diaz, and R. A. Cole, 1978, *Upland and Wetland Habitat*

Development with Dredged Material: Ecological Considerations, U.S. Army Corps of Engineers Dredged Material Res. Prog. Tech. Rept. DS-78-15, 50p.

Lynch, J. J., 1941, The place of burning in management of the Gulf Coast Wildlife refuges, *J. Wildl. Manage.* 5(4):454-457.

Lynch, J. J., T. O'Neil, and D. W. Lay, 1947, Management significance of damage by geese and muskrats to Gulf Coast marshes, *J. Wildl. Manage.* 11:50-76.

Lyon, J. G., 1979a, *Remote Sensing Analyses of Coastal Wetlands Characteristics: The St. Clair Flats, Michigan*, 13th International Symposium on Remote Sensing of the Environment Proceedings, Ann Arbor, Mich., pp. 1117-1129.

Lyon, J. G., 1979b, *An Analysis of Vegetation Communities in the Lower Columbia River Basin*, Michigan Sea Grant. MICH U-SG-79-311, Ann Arbor, Mich., 7p.

Lytle, J. S., 1975, *Fate and Effects of Crude Oil on an Estuarine Pond, 1975 Conference for the Prevention and Control of Oil Pollution Proceedings*, American Petroleum Institute, Washington, D.C., pp. 595-600.

MacConnell, W., and W. Niedzwiedz, 1979, Remote sensing the White River in Vermont, *Photogram. Eng. Remote Sensing* 45:1393-1399.

MacCreary, D., 1940, *Report on the Tabanidae of Delaware*, Univ. Delaware Agric. Exp. Sta. Bull. 226, 41p.

MacInnis, A. R. G., 1979, *Waterfowl Utilization of Two Coastal Marshes at Cape Jourimain, New Brunswick*, Master's thesis, Acadia University, Wolfville, N.S., 161p.

MacLeod, H., and B. MacDonald, 1976, *Edible Wild Plants of Nova Scotia*, Nova Scotia Museum, Halifax, N.S.

MacNamara, L. G., 1949, Salt-marsh development at Tuckahoe, New Jersey, *North Am. Wildl. Conf. Trans.* 14:100-117.

MacNamara, L. G., 1952, Needs for additional research on mosquito control from the standpoint of fish and game management, *New Jersey Mosq. Exterm. Assoc. Proc.* 39:111-116.

MacNamara, L. G., 1953, The production and conservation of wildlife in relation to mosquito control of state owned lands in New Jersey, *New Jersey Mosq. Exterm. Assoc. Proc.* 40:74-79.

MacNamara, L. G., 1957, Multiple use of our lands, especially marshland, *New Jersey Mosq. Exterm. Assoc. Proc.* 44:103-106.

Malone, M., 1976, Vegetation succession in newly flooded impoundments at Shepody and Tintamarre National Wildlife Areas in 1976, Canadian Wildlife Service, Sackville, N.B., unpublished report, 14p.

Maloney, F. E., and R. C. Ausness, 1974, The use and legal significance of the mean high water line in coastal boundary mapping, *North Carolina Law Rev.* 53:185-273.

Mangold, R. E., 1962, The role of low-level dike salt impoundments in mosquito control and wildlife utilization, *New Jersey Mosq. Exterm. Assoc. Proc.* 49:117-120.

Marshall, D. E., 1970, Characteristics of *Spartina* marsh which is receiving treated municipal sewage wastes, in *Studies of Marine Estuarine Ecosystems Developing with Treated Sewage Wastes*, H. T. Odum and A. F. Chestnut, eds., University of North Carolina Institute of Marine Science Annual Report 1969-1970, pp. 317-359.

Marshall, J. T., Jr., 1948, Ecologic races of song sparrows in the San Francisco Bay region. I. Habitat and abundance, *Condor* 50:193-215.

Mason, C. F., and R. J. Bryant, 1975, Production, nutrient content and decomposition of *Phragmites communis* Trin. and *Typha angustifolia* L., *J. Ecol.* 63(1):71-95.

Masry, S. E., and S. MacRitchie, 1980, Different considerations in coastal mapping, *Photogram. Eng. Remote Sensing* 46:521-528.

Maxwell, E. L., 1976, A remote rangeland analysis system, *J. Range Manage.* 29:66-73.

McCormick, J., 1970, The natural features of Tinicum Marsh, with particular emphasis on the vegetation, in *Two Studies of Tinicum Marsh. Delaware and Philadelphia Counties, Pennsylvania*, The Conservation Foundation, 104p.

McCormick, J., 1978, Ecology and the regulation of freshwater wetlands, in *Freshwater Wetlands*, R. E. Good, D. F. Whigham, and R. L. Simpson, eds., Academic Press, New York, pp. 341-355.

McEwen, R. B., W. J. Kosco, and V. Carter, 1976, Coastal wetland mapping, *Photogram. Eng. Remote Sensing* 42:221-232.

McKenzie, M. D., J. V. Miglarese, B. S. Anderson, and L. A. Barcley, eds., 1980, *Ecological Characterization of the Sea Island Coastal Region of South Carolina and Georgia. Vol. II Socioeconomic features of the Characterization Area*, Fish and Wildlife Serv. Biol. Serv. Prog. FWS/OBS-79/41, Washington, D.C., pp. 72-78, 186-206.

McMahan, E. A., R. L. Knight, and A. R. Camp, 1972, A comparison of microarthropod populations in sewage-exposed, and sewage-free *Spartina* salt marshes, *Environ. Entomol.* 1:244-252.

Means, T. H., 1903, *Reclamation of Salt Marsh Lands*, U.S. Dept. Agric. Bur. Soils Circ. 8, Washington, D.C., 10p.

Meany, R. A., I. Valiela, and J. M. Teal, 1976, Growth, abundance and distribution of larval tabanids in experimentally fertilized plots on a Massachusetts salt marsh, *J. Appl. Ecol.* 13(2):323-332.

Mendelssohn, I., 1979, Nitrogen metabolism in the height forms of *Spartina alterniflora* in North Carolina, *Ecology* 60(3):574-584.

Metzgar, R. G., 1973, *Wetlands in Maryland*, Maryland Dept. State Planning Publ. No. 157, Baltimore, pp. xiv-1-xiv-15.

Meyers, S. P., D. G. Ahearn, S. Crow, and N. Berner, 1973, The impact of oil on microbial marshland ecosystems, in *The Microbial Degradation of Oil Pollutants*, D. G. Ahearn and S. P. Meyers, eds., Publ. No. LSU OSG-73-01, Center for Wetland Resources, Louisiana State University, Baton Rouge.

Michael, A. D., C. R. Van Raalte, and L. S. Brown, 1975, *Long-term Effects of an Oil Spill at West Falmouth, Massachusetts*, 1975 Conference for the Prevention and Control of Oil Pollution Proceedings, American Petroleum Institute, Washington, D.C., pp. 573-582.

Michelman, F. I., 1967, Property, utility and fairness: comments on the ethical foundations of "Just Compensation" law, *Harvard Law Rev.* 80:1165-1258.

Milan, C. S., and T. Whelan, III, 1979, Accumulation of petroleum hydrocarbons in a salt marsh ecosystem exposed to a steady state oil input, in *3rd Coastal Marsh Estuary Management Symposium Proceedings*, J. W. Day, Jr., D. D. Culley, Jr., R. E. Turner, and A. J. Mumphrey, eds., Louisiana State University, Baton Rouge, pp. 65-87.

Miller, D. C., 1961, The feeding mechanisms of fiddler crabs with ecological considerations of feeding adaptations, *Zoology* **46**(8):89-101.

Miller, K. G., and D. Maurer, 1973, Distribution of the fiddler crabs, *Uca pugnax* and *Uca minax*, in relation to salinity in Delaware rivers, *Chesapeake Sci.* **14**(3):219-221.

Miller, W. R., and R. E. Egler, 1950, Vegetation of the Wequetequork-Pawcatuck tidal marshes, Connecticut, *Ecol. Monogr.* **20**:143-172.

Møller, H. S., 1975, Danish salt-marsh communities of breeding birds in relation to different types of management, *Ornis Scand.* **6**(2):125-133.

Montanari, J. H., and J. A. Kusler, eds., 1978, *National Wetland Protection Symposium Proc., Fish & Wildlife Serv. Biol. Serv. Prog.* FWS/OBS-78/97, Washington, D.C., 255p.

Mook, J. H., and J. Van Der Toorn, 1982, The influence of environmental factors and management on stands of *Phragmites australis*. II Effects on yield and its relationships with shoot density. *J. Appl. Ecol.* **19**(2):501-517.

Moore, N. W., 1967, A synopsis of the pesticide problem, *Adv. Ecol. Res.* **4**:75-129.

Morantz, D. L., 1976, *Productivity and Export from a Marsh with a 15 m Tidal Range, and the Effect of Impoundment of Selected Areas*, Master's thesis, Dalhousie University, 77p.

Morgan, M. H., 1961, *Annual Angiosperm Production on a Salt Marsh*, Master's thesis, University of Delaware, 34p.

National Academy of Science, 1976, *Pest Control: An Assessment of Present and Alternative Technologies*, vol. 5, *Pest Control and Public Health*, National Academy of Science, Washington, D.C., 282p.

Neely, W. W., 1962, Saline soils and brackish waters in management of wildlife fish and shrimp, *North Am. Wildl. Conf. Trans.* **27**:321-334.

Neff, J. M., and J. W. Anderson, 1981, *Response of Marine Animals to Petroleum and Specific Petroleum Hydrocarbons*, Applied Science Publ. Ltd., London, 177p.

Nelson-Smith, A., 1972, Effects of the oil industry on shore life in estuaries, *R. Soc. London Proc.*, ser. B, **180**:487-496.

Nesbit, D. M., 1885, *Tidal Marshes of the United States*, U.S. Dept. Agric. Misc. Spec. Rept. No. 7, 244p.

Newcombe, C. L., and C. R. Pride, 1975, The establishment of intertidal marsh plants on dredge material substrate, San Francisco Bay Marine Research Center, Richmond, Cal., 152p., unpublished.

Nicol, E. A., 1936, The ecology of a salt marsh, *J. Mar. Biol. Assoc. U.K.* **20**:203-261.

Niering, W. A., 1970, The dilemma of the coastal wetlands: conflict of local, national, and world priorities, in *The Environmental Crisis*, H. W. Helfrich, Jr., ed., Yale University Press, New Haven, Conn., pp. 143-156.

Niering, W. A., 1978a, Wetland values, in *National Wetland Protection Symposium Proceedings*, J. H. Montanari and J. A. Kusler, eds., Fish & Wildl. Serv. Biol. Serv. Prog. FWS/OBS-78/97, Washington, D.C., pp. 7-8.

Niering, W. A., 1978b, Some research priorities, in *National Wetland Protection Symposium Proceedings*, J. H. Montanari and J. A. Kusler, eds., Fish & Wildl. Serv. Biol. Serv. Prog. FWS/OBS-78/97, Washington, D.C., pp. 245-246.

Niering, W. A., 1979, Our wetland heritage: historic, artistic, and future perspectives, in *Wetland Functions and Values: The State of Our Understanding*, P. E. Greeson, J. R. Clark, and J. E. Clark, eds., American Water Resources Assoc., Minneapolis, Minn., pp. 505-522.

Niering, W. A., and R. S. Warren, 1980, Vegetation patterns and processes in New England salt marshes, *Bioscience* 30(5):301-307.

Nixon, S. W., and C. A. Oviatt, 1973, Ecology of a New England salt marsh, *Ecol. Monogr.* 43(4):463-498.

Nixon, S. W., C. A. Oviatt, J. Garber, and V. Lee, 1976, Diel metabolism and nutrient dynamics in a salt marsh embayment, *Ecology* 57(4):740-750.

Nordhagen, R., 1954, Studies on the vegetation of salt and brackish marshes in Finmark (Norway), *Vegetatio* 5-6:381-394.

Norgaard, R. B., 1976, The economics of improving pesticide use, *Ann. Rev. Entomol.* 21:45-60.

O'Brien, R. D., 1967, *Insecticides Action and Metabolism*, Academic Press, New York, 332p.

Odum, E. P., 1961, The role of tidal marshes in estuarine production, *N. Y. State Conserv.* 16:12-15, 35.

Odum, E. P., 1971, *Fundamentals of Ecology*, 3rd ed., W. B. Saunders, Philadelphia, Pa., 574p.

Odum, E. P., 1979, The value of wetlands: a hierarchial approach, in P. E. Greeson, J. R. Clark, and J. E. Clark, eds., *Wetland Functions and Values: The State of Our Understanding*, American Water Resources Assoc., Minneapolis, Minn., pp. 16-25.

Odum, E. P., and A. A. de la Cruz, 1967, Particulate organic detritus in a Georgia salt marsh-estuarine ecosystem, in *Estuaries*, G. H. Lauff, ed., Publ. 83, American Association for the Advancement of Science, Washington, D.C., pp. 383-388.

Odum, E. P., and A. E. Smalley, 1959, Comparison of population energy flow of a herbivorous and a deposit feeding invertebrate in a salt marsh ecosystem, *Natl. Acad. Sci. (USA) Proc.* 45:617-622.

Odum, H. T., 1971, *Environment, Power and Society*, Wiley-Interscience, New York, 331p.

Odum, H. T., 1978, Value of wetlands as domestic ecosystems, in *National Wetland Protection Symposium Proceedings*, Fish & Wildlife Serv. Biol. Serv. Prog., J. H. Montanari and J. A. Kusler, eds., FWS/OBS-78/97, Washington, D.C., pp. 9-18.

Odum, W. E., and S. S. Skjei, 1974, The issues of wetlands preservation and management: a second view, *Coastal Zone Manage. J.* 1(2):151-163.

Oliver, F. W., 1913, Some remarks on Blakeney Point, Norfolk, *J. Ecol.* 1(1):4-15.

312   Conservation of Tidal Marshes

Olkowski, W., 1966, *Biological Studies of Salt Marsh Tabanids in Delaware*, Master's thesis, University of Delaware, 116p.

Olson, C. E., and R. E. Good, 1962, Seasonal changes in light reflectance from forest vegetation, *Photogram. Eng.* 28:107-114.

O'Neil, T., 1949, *The Muskrat in the Louisiana Coastal Marshes*, Louisiana Dept. Wildlife and Fish, Baton Rouge, 152p.

Oney, J., 1954, *Final Report: Clapper Rail Survey and Investigation Study*, Georgia Game and Fish Commission, Atlanta, 50p.

Owen, M., 1971, The selection of feeding site by white-fronted geese in winter, *J. Appl. Ecol.* 8(3):905-917.

Owen, M., 1972a, Some factors affecting food intake and selection in white-fronted geese, *J. Anim. Ecol.* 41:79-92.

Owen, M., 1972b, Movements and feeding ecology of white-fronted geese at the New Grounds, Slimbridge, *J. Appl. Ecol.* 9:385-398.

Owen, M., 1973a, The management of grassland areas for wintering geese, *Wildfowl* 24:123-130.

Owen, M., 1973b, The winter feeding ecology of wigeon at Bridgwater Bay, Somerset, *Ibis* 115(2):227-243.

Owen, M., 1975, Cutting and fertilizing grassland for winter goose management, *J. Wildl. Manage.* 39:163-167.

Pearson, R. L., L. D. Miller, and C. J. Tucker, 1976, Hand-held spectral radiometer to estimate gramineous biomass, *Appl. Opt.* 15:416-418.

Pearson, R. L., C. J. Tucker, and L. D. Miller, 1976, Spectral mapping of short grass prairie biomass, *Photogram. Eng. Remote Sensing* 42:317-323.

Pechuman, L. L., 1972, *The horse flies and deer flies of New York (Diptera, Tabanidae)*. Search:Agriculture, Cornell Univer. Exp. Sta. 2(5), 72p.

Pechuman, L. L., D. W. Webb, and H. J. Teskey, 1983, *The Diptera, or True Flies of Illinois. 1. Tabanidae*, Illinois Natural History Survey Bull., vol. 33, article 1, 121p.

Penfound, W. T., and E. S. Hathaway, 1938, Plant communities of the marsh lands of southeastern Louisiana, *Ecol. Monogr.* 8(1):1-56.

Penfound, W. T., and J. D. Schneidau, 1945, The relation of land reclamation to aquatic wildlife resources in southeastern Louisiana, *North Am. Wildl. Conf. Trans.* 10:308-318.

Penny, M. E., and H. H. Gordon, 1975, *Remote sensing of wetlands in Virginia*, 10th International Symposium on Remote Sensing of Environment Proceedings, Ann Arbor, Mich., pp. 495-503.

Perkins, C. J., 1968, Controlled burning in the management of muskrats and waterfowl in Louisiana coastal marshes, Ann. Tall Timbers Fire Ecol. Conf. Proc. vol. 8, Tall Timbers Research Station, Tallahassee, pp. 269-280.

Pestrong, R., 1969, Multiband photos for a tidal marsh, Photogram. Eng. 35:453-470.

Pfeiffer, W. J., R. A. Linthurst, and J. L. Gallagher, 1973, *Photographic imagery and spectral properties of salt marsh vegetation as indicators of canopy characteristics*, Fall Convention, American Society of Photogrammetry Proc., Falls Church, Va., pp. 1004-1015.

Phleger, F. B., 1970, Foraminifera populations and marine marsh processes, *Limnol. Oceanogr.* 15:522-534.

Pickral, J. C., and W. E. Odum, 1977, Benthic detritus in a salt marsh tidal creek, in *Estuarine Processes*, vol. 2, M. Wiley, ed., Academic Press, New York, pp. 280-292.

Plapp, F. W., 1976, Biochemical genetics of insecticide resistance, *Ann. Rev. Entomol.* 21:179-197.

Pope, R. M., and J. G. Gosselink, 1973, A tool for use in making land management decisions involving tidal marsh land, *Coastal Zone Manage. J.* 1(1):65-74.

Porro, A. A., Jr., 1970, Invisible boundary—Private and sovereign marshland interests, *Nat. Resour. Lawyer* 3(3):512-520.

Porro, A. A., Jr., 1983, Legal prospectives—Coastal zone and the public trust, *Coast. Soc. Bull.* 7(2):14-15.

Porro, A. A., Jr., and L. S. Teleky, 1972, Marshland title dilemma: a tidal phenomenon, *Seton Hall Law Rev.* 3(2):323-348.

Porro, A. A., Jr., and J. P. Weidener, 1978, *The Mean High Water Line: Biological vs. Conventional Methods. The New Jersey Experience*, paper presented at the 1978 ACSM-ASP Annual Spring Convention, Feb. 26-March 4, 1978, Washington, D.C.

Post, W., 1974, Functional analysis of space-related behavior in the seaside sparrow, *Ecology* 55(3):564-574.

Pough, R. H., 1961, Valuable vistas: a way to protect them, *Connecticut Arboretum Bull.* 12:28-30.

Price, M. H., 1938, New developments in mosquito control in Rhode Island, *New Jersey Mosq. Exterm. Assoc. Proc.* 25:111-115.

Prinslow, T. E., I. Valiela, and J. M. Teal, 1974, The effect of detritus and ration size on the growth of *Fundulua heteroclitus* (L.), *J. Exp. Mar. Biol. Ecol.* 16(1):1-10.

Provost, M. W., 1948, Marsh-blasting as a wildlife management technique, *J. Wildl. Manage.* 12(4):350-387.

Provost, M. W., 1968, Managing impounded salt marsh for mosquito control and estuarine resource conservation, in *Marsh and Estuary Management Symposium Proceedings*, J. D. Newsom, ed., Louisiana State University, Baton Rouge, pp. 163-171.

Provost, M. W., 1969, Ecological Control of Salt Marsh Mosquitos with Side Benefits to Birds, *Tall Timbers Conf. on Ecol. Animal Control by Habitat Management Proc.*, vol. 1, Tall Timbers Research Station, Tallahassee, Fla., pp. 193-206.

Provost, M. W., 1974, Salt Marsh Management in Florida, *Tall Timbers Conf. on Ecol. Animal Control by Habitat Management Proc.*, Tall Timbers Research Station, Tallahassee, Fla., vol. 5, pp. 5-17.

Provost, M. W., 1976, Tidal datum planes circumscribing salt marshes, *Bull. Mar. Sci.* 26(4):558-563.

Provost, M. W., 1977, Source reduction in salt marsh mosquito control: past and future, *Mosq. News* 37:689-698.

Queen, W. H., 1977, Human uses of salt marshes, in *Wet Coastal Ecosystems*, V. J. Chapman, ed., Elsevier Scientific Publ. Co., Amsterdam, pp. 363-368.

Race, M. S., and D. R. Christie, 1982, Coastal zone development: mitigation, marsh creation, and decision making, *Environ. Manage.* 6(4):317-328.

Ranwell, D. S., 1960, Newborough Warren, Anglesey. III. Changes in the vegetation on parts of the dune system after the loss of rabbits by myxomatosis, *J. Ecol.* 48(2):385-395.

Ranwell, D. S., 1961, *Spartina* salt marshes in southern England. I. The effects of sheep grazing at the upper limits of *Spartina* marsh in Bridgwater Bay, *J. Ecol.* 49(2):325-340.

Ranwell, D. S., 1967, World resources of *Spartina townsendii (sensu lato)* and economic use of *Spartina* marshland, *J. Appl. Ecol.* 4:239-256.

Ranwell, D. S., 1968, Extent of damage to coastal habitats due to the Torrey Canyon incident, in *The Biological Effects of Oil Pollution on Littoral Communities*, J. D. Carthy and D. R. Arthur, eds., Field Studies Council, London, pp. 39-47.

Ranwell, D. S., 1972, *Ecology of Salt Marshes and Sand Dunes*, Chapman and Hall, London, 258p.

Ranwell, D. S., 1975, Management of salt-marsh and coastal dune vegetation, in *Estuarine Research*, vol. 2, L. E. Cronin, ed., Academic Press, New York, pp. 471-483.

Ranwell, D. S., 1979, Strategies for the management of coastal systems, in *Ecological Processes in Coastal Environments*, R. L. Jeffries and A. J. Davy, eds., Blackwell Scientific Publ., Oxford, pp. 515-527.

Ranwell, D. S., and B. M. Downing, 1959, Brent goose (*Branta bernicla* L.) winter feeding pattern and *Zostera* resources at Scolt Head Island, Norfolk, *Anim. Behav.* 7:42-56.

Ranwell, D. S., and B. M. Downing, 1960, The use of Dalapon and substituted urea herbicides for control of seed-bearing *Spartina* (cord grass) in inter-tidal zones of estuarine marsh, *Weeds* 8(1):78-88.

Reed, A., and G. Moisan, 1971, The *Spartina* tidal marshes of the St. Lawrence estuary and their importance to aquatic birds, *Naturaliste Canadien* 98:905-922.

Reed, A., and A. D. Smith, 1972, Man and Waterfowl in Tidal Shorelines of Eastern Canada, in *Coastal Zone. Proceedings of a Seminar at Bedford Institute of Oceanography, Dartmouth, N.S.*, compiled by Atlantic Unit, Water Management Service, Dept. of Environment, Ottawa, Canada, pp. 151-155.

Reimold, R. J., 1968, *Evidence for Dissolved Phosphorus Hypereutrophication in Various Types of Manipulated Salt Marshes of Delaware*, Ph.D. dissertation, University of Delaware, 169p.

Reimold, R. J., 1974, *Toxaphene Interactions in Estuarine Ecosystems*, Georgia Marine Science Center Tech. Rept. Ser. No. 74-6, 80p.

Reimold, R. J., 1978, Coastal alternative dredged material rehabilitation, in *Coastal Zone '78*, vol. 2, Symposium on Technical, Environmental, Socioeconomic and Regulatory Aspects of Coastal Zone Management, American Society of Civil Engineers, New York, pp. 736-744.

Reimold, R. J., and C. J. Durant, 1972, *Survey of Toxaphene Levels in Georgia Estuaries*, Georgia Marine Science Center Tech. Rept. Ser. No. 72-2, 51p.

Reimold, R. J., J. L. Gallagher, and D. E. Thompson, 1972, *Coastal Mapping with Remote Sensors*, Coast Mapping Symposium Proceedings, American Society of Photogrammetry, Washington, D.C., pp. 99-112.

Reimold, R. J., J. L. Gallagher, and D. E. Thompson, 1973, Remote sensing of tidal marsh, *Photogram. Eng.* **39**:477-488.

Reimold, R. J., M. A. Hardisky, and P. C. Adams, 1978*a*, Habitat Development Field Investigations, Buttermilk Sound Marsh Development Site, Atlantic Intracoastal Waterway, Georgia, Appendix A: Propagation of Marsh Plants and Post Propagation Monitoring, U.S. Army Corps of Engineers Dredged Material Res. Prog. Tech. Rept. D-78-26, 223p.

Reimold, R. J., M. A. Hardisky, and P. C. Adams, 1978*b*, *The Effects of Smothering a* Spartina alterniflora *Salt Marsh with Dredged Material*, U.S. Army Corps of Engineers Dredged Material Res. Prog. Tech. Rept. D-78-38, 114p.

Reimold, R. J., R. A. Linthurst, and P. L. Wolf, 1975, Effects of grazing on a salt marsh, *Biol. Conserv.* **8**:105-125.

Reimold, R. J., J. H. Phillips, and M. A. Hardisky, 1980, Sociocultural values of wetlands, in *Estuarine Perspectives*, V. S. Kennedy, ed., Academic Press, New York, pp. 79-89.

Reinert, S. E., F. C. Golet, and W. R. DeRagon, 1981, Avian use of ditched and unditched salt marshes in southeastern New England: a preliminary report, *Northeast. Mosq. Control Assoc. Proc.* vol. 27, 23p.

Reppert, R. T., W. Sigleo, E. Stakhiv, L. Messman, and C. Myers, 1979, *Wetland Values: Concepts and Methods for Wetlands Evaluation*, Institute for Water Resources Research Rept. 79-R1, U.S. Army Corps of Engineers, Fort Belvoir, Va., 109p.

Retson, G. C., 1966, Marshland farming in the Sackville area of New Brunswick, *Can. Farm. Econ.* **1**(3):20-26.

Rio, D. F., 1970, A laboratory study of the effects of Abate and Malathion on the fiddler crab, *New Jersey Mosq. Exterm. Assoc. Proc.* **57**:99-102.

Ripper, W. E., 1956, Effect of pesticides on balance of arthropod populations, *Ann. Rev., Entomol.* **1**:403-438.

Ristich, S. S., S. W. Frederick, and E. H. Buckley, 1976, Transplantation of *Typha* and the distribution of vegetation and algae in a reclaimed estuarine marsh, *Torrey Bot. Club Bull.* **103**(4):157-164.

Rockel, E. G., 1969, Marsh physiography: influence on distribution of intertidal organisms, *New Jersey Mosq. Exterm. Assoc. Proc.* **56**:102-115.

Rockel, E. G., and E. J. Hansens, 1970, Distribution of larval horseflies and deerflies (Diptera: Tabanidae) of a New Jersey salt marsh, *Entomol. Soc. Am. Ann.* **63**:681-684.

Roe, C. B., Jr., 1976, Wetlands: where developers and regulatory programs meet, *Real Property, Probate and Trust J.* **11**(4):701-710.

Rogers, A. J., 1962, Effects of impounding and filling on the production of sand flies (*Culicoides*) in Florida salt marshes, J. Econ. Entomol. **55**:521-527.

Roman, C. T., 1978, *Tidal Restriction: Its Impact on the Vegetation of Six Connecticut Coastal Marshes*, Master's thesis, Connecticut College, 178p.

Roman, C. T., 1981, *Detrital Exchange Processes of a Delaware Salt Marsh*, Ph.D. dissertation, University of Delaware, 144p.

Roman, C. T., W. A. Niering, and R. S. Warren, 1984, Salt marsh vegetation change in response to tidal restriction, *Environ. Manage.* **8**(2):141-150.

Rosenbaum, N., 1979, Enforcing wetlands regulations, in *Wetland Functions and Values: The State of Our Understanding*, P. E. Greeson, J. R. Clark, and J. E. Clark, eds., American Water Resources Assoc., Minneapolis, Minn., pp. 43-49.

Rouse, J. W., R. H. Hass, J. A. Schell, and D. W. Deering, 1973, *Monitoring vegetation systems in the Great Plains with ERTS*, 3rd Earth Resources Tech. Satellite-1 Symposium, NASA, Washington, D.C., pp. 309-317.

Rowan, W., 1913, Note on the food plants of rabbits on Blakeney Point, Norfolk, *J. Ecol.* 1(4):273-274.

Ruber, E., and R. E. Murray, 1978, Some ideas about coastal management from production and export studies on a Massachusetts salt marsh, *New Jersey Mosq. Exterm. Assoc. Proc.* 65:51-58.

Rudd, R. L., 1964, *Pesticides and the Living Landscape*, University of Wisconsin Press, Madison, 320p.

Ruesink, W. G., 1976, Status of the systems approach to pest management, *Ann. Rev. Entomol.* 21:27-44.

Russell, O., and F. J. Wobber, 1972, Aerial multiband wetlands mapping, *Photogram. Eng.* 38:1188-1189.

Russell-Hunter, W. D., M. L. Apley, and R. D. Hunter, 1972, Early life history of *Melampus* and the significance of semilunar synchrony, *Biol. Bull.* 143(3):623-656.

Ryther, J. H., T. A. DeBusk, M. D. Hanisak, and L. D. Williams, 1978, Fresh water macrophytes for energy and waste water treatment, in *Wetland Functions and Values: The State of Our Understanding*, P. E. Greeson, J. R. Clark, and J. E. Clark, eds., American Water Resources Assoc., Minneapolis, Minn., pp. 652-660.

Salley, A. S., ed., 1967, *Narratives of Early Carolina, 1650-1708*, Barnes and Noble, New York, 69p.

Salsbury, S. M., 1970, Maryland's wetlands: the legal quagmire, *Maryland Law Rev.* 30(3):240-266.

Sanders, H. L., J. F. Grassle, G. R. Hampson, L. S. Morse, S. Garner-Price, and C. C. Jones, 1980, Anatomy of an oil spill: long-term effects from the grounding of the barge Florida off West Falmouth, Massachusetts, *J. Mar. Res.* 38:265-380.

Sanders, J. E., and C. W. Ellis, 1961, Geological aspects of Connecticut's coastal marshes, *Connecticut Arboretum Bull.* 12:16-20.

Sax, J. L., 1964, Takings and the police power, *Yale Law J.* 74:36-76.

Sax, J. L., 1970, The public trust doctrine in natural resource law: effective judicial intervention, *Michigan Law Rev.* 68:471-566.

Sax, J. L., 1971, Takings, private property and public rights, *Yale Law J.* 81(2):149-186.

Scarpace, F. L., R. W. Kiefer, S. L. Wynn, B. K. Quirk, and G. A. Friedericks, 1975, *Quantitative photo-interpretation for wetland mapping*, 41st Annual Meeting Proceedings, American Society of Photogrammetry, Washington, D.C., pp. 750-771.

Schamberger, M. L., and H. E. Kumpf, 1980, Wetlands and wildlife values: a practical field approach to quantifying habitat values, in *Estuarine Perspectives*, V. S. Kennedy, ed., Academic Press, New York, pp. 37-46.

Schneider, W. J., 1966, Water resources in the Everglades, *Photogram. Eng.* 32:958-965.

Schneider, W. J., 1968, Color photographs for water resources, *Photogram. Eng.* 34:257-262.

Schoenbaum, T. J., 1972, Public rights and coastal zone management, *North Carolina Law Rev.* 51:1-30.

Schoning, R. W., 1984, Some impacts of resource data use in fisheries management, *J. Fish. Mgmt.* 4(1):1-8.

Schulte, O. W., 1951, The use of panchromatic, infrared and color aerial photography in the study of plant distributions, *Photogram. Eng.* 17:688-714.

Seal, W. P., 1910, Fishes in their relation to the mosquito problem, *Bur. Fish. Bull.* 28:833-838.

Seher, J. S., and P. T. Tueller, 1973, Color aerial photos for marshland, *Photogram. Eng.* 39:489-499.

Seidel, K., 1971, Macrophytes as functional elements in the environment of man, *Hydrobiology* 12:121-130.

Seneca, E. D., 1974, Stabilization of coastal dredge spoil with Spartina alterniflora, in *Ecology of Halophytes*, R. J. Reimold and W. H. Queen, eds., Academic Press, New York, pp. 525-530.

Seneca, E. D., W. W. Woodhouse, and S. W. Broome, 1975, Salt-water marsh creation, in *Estuarine Research*, vol. 2, L. E. Cronin, ed., Academic Press, New York, pp. 427-438.

Seneca, E. D., S. W. Broome, W. W. Woodhouse, L. M. Cammen, and J. T. Lyon, III, 1976, Establishing *Spartina alterniflora* marsh in North Carolina, *Environ. Conserv.* 3(3):185-188.

Shabman, L. A., and S. S. Batie, 1978, Economic value of national coastal wetlands: a critique, *Coastal Zone Mgmt. J.* 4(3):231-247.

Shabman, L. A., and S. S. Batie, 1980, Estimating the economic value of coastal wetlands: conceptual issues and research needs, in *Estuarine Perspectives*, V. S. Kennedy, ed., Academic Press, New York, pp. 3-15.

Shalowitz, A. L., 1962, 1964, *Shore and Sea Boundaries*, U.S. Dept. of Commerce Publ. 10-1, U.S. Government Printing Office, Washington, D.C., vol. 1, 420pp; vol. 2, 749pp.

Shanholtzer, G. F., 1974, Relationship of vertebrates to salt-marsh plants, in *Ecology of Halophytes*, R. J. Reimold and W. H. Queens, eds., Academic Press, New York, pp. 463-474.

Shaw, S. P., and W. F. Crissey, 1955, Wetlands and the management of water fowl, in *Water. The Yearbook of Agriculture 1955*, U.S. Dept. Agriculture, Washington, D.C., pp. 604-614.

Shay, J. R., 1967, Remote sensing for agricultural purposes, *Bioscience* 17:450-451.

Shima, L. J., R. R. Anderson, and V. Carter, 1976, The use of aerial color infrared photography in mapping the vegetation of a freshwater marsh, *Chesapeake Sci.* 17:74-85.

Shisler, J. K., 1973, Pioneer plants on spoil piles associated with mosquito ditching, *New Jersey Mosq. Exterm. Assoc. Proc.* **60**:135-141.

Shisler, J. K., 1978a, Water management methods being utilized in coastal marshes to control mosquito populations, *New Jersey Mosq. Control Assoc. Proc.* **65**:59-66.

Shisler, J. K., 1978b, The efficiency of water management in coastal areas, *New Jersey Mosq. Control Assoc. Proc.* **65**:196-198.

Shisler, J. K., 1979, The effect of water management on coastal productivity in New Jersey, *Florida Anti-Mosq. Assoc. Proc.* **50**:37-40.

Shisler, J. K., and D. M. Jobbins, 1975, Aspects of biological productivity in mosquito ditched salt marshes, *New Jersey Mosq. Control Assoc. Proc.* **62**:48-49.

Shisler, J. K., and D. M. Jobbins, 1977a, Salt marsh productivity as effected by the selective ditching technique, open marsh water management, *Mosq. News* **37**:631-636.

Shisler, J. K., and D. M. Jobbins, 1977b, Tidal variations in the movement of organic carbon in New Jersey salt marshes, *Mar. Biol.* **40**(2):127-134.

Shisler, J. K., and F. H. Lesser, 1979, Early succession in a low-level salt marsh impoundment, *Florida Anti-Mosq. Assoc. Proc.* **50**:40-43.

Shisler, J. K., and T. L. Schulze, 1976, Some aspects of open marsh water management procedures on clapper rail production, *Northeast. Fish & Wildl. Conf. Proc.* **33**:101-104.

Shisler, J. K., F. H. Lesser, B. Gooley, J. Hansen, and P. Slavin, 1978, Practical application of the rotary ditcher in pond construction, *Mosq. News* **38**:112-115.

Shoemaker, W. E., 1964, A biological control for *Aedes sollicitans* and the resulting effect upon wildlife, *New Jersey Mosq. Exterm. Assoc. Proc.* **51**:93-97.

Silberhorn, G. M., 1976, *Tidal Wetland Plants of Virginia*, Educational Series 19, Virginia Institute of Marine Science, Gloucester Point, 86p.

Silberhorn, G. M., 1978, Research priorities: coastal mud flats and tidal freshwater wetlands, in *National Wetland Protection Symposium Proceedings*, J. H. Montanari and J. A. Kusler, eds., Fish. & Wildl. Serv. Biol. Serv. Prog. FWS/OBS-78/97, Washington, D.C., pp. 251-255.

Simon, A. W., 1978, *The Thin Edge*, Harper and Row, New York.

Sinclair, T. R., R. M. Hoffer, and M. M. Schreiber, 1971, Reflectance and internal structure of leaves from several crops during a growing season, *Agron. J.* **63**:864-868.

Singh, P. B., and K. Nathan, 1965, Hydraulic studies of drainage ditches under tidal influence, *Am. Soc. Agric. Eng. Trans.* **8**:460-463, 469.

Slavin, P. T., R. E. Good, and E. R. Squiers, 1975, Effects of three mosquito larviciding oils on production of salt marsh *Spartina* grasses, *Bull. Environ. Contam. and Toxicol.* **13**(5):534-536.

Slavin, P., J. Shisler, and F. Ferrigno, 1978, Current status of tidal restoration of salt hay impoundments for mosquito control in Cumberland County, New Jersey, *New Jersey Mosq. Exterm. Assoc. Proc.* **65**:214-216.

Smart, R. M., and J. W. Barko, 1980, Nitrogen nutrition and salinity tolerance of *Distichlis spicata* and *Spartina alterniflora*, *Ecology* **61**(3):630-638.

Smith, A. D., 1967, *Waterfowl Habitat, Productivity and Management at Missaquash Marsh, Nova Scotia*, Master's thesis, Acadia University, Wolfville, N.S., 121p.

Smith, D. H., 1968, *Wildlife prevalence on Low Level Impoundments Used for Mosquito Control in Delaware, 1965-1967*, Master's thesis, University of Delaware.

Smith, H. K., 1976, Habitat development on dredged material, in *Dredging and Its Environmental Effects*, P. A. Krendel, J. Harrison, and J. C. Burdick III, eds., American Society of Civil Engineers, New York, pp. 856-865.

Smith, H. K., 1978a, *An Introduction to Habitat Development on Dredged Material*, U.S. Army Corps of Engineers Dredged Material Res. Prog. Tech. Rept. DS-78-19, 37p.

Smith, H. K., 1978b, Habitat development: an alternative method of dredged material disposal, in *Coastal Zone '78*, vol. 2, Symposium on Technical, Environmental, Socioeconomic and Regulatory Aspects of Coastal Zone Management, American Society of Civil Engineers, New York, pp. 795-803.

Smith, J. B., 1902, *The Salt-Marsh Mosquito. Culex sollicitans Wlk.*, New Jersey Agricultural Experimental Station Spec. Bull., 10p.

Smith, J. B., 1904, *The Common Mosquitoes of New Jersey*, New Jersey Agricultural Experimental Station Bull. 171, 40p.

Smith, J. B., 1907, *The New Jersey Salt Marsh and Its Improvement*, New Jersey Agricultural Experimental Station Bull. 207, 24p.

Smith, J. O., and J. L. Sammons, 1974, Public rights in Georgia's tidelands, *Georgia Law Rev.* 9(1):79-114.

Smith, T. J., III, 1983, Alteration of salt marsh plant community composition by grazing snow geese, *Holartic Ecol.* 6(2):204-210.

Smith, T. J., III, and W. E. Odum, 1981, The effects of grazing by snow geese on coastal salt marshes, *Ecology* 62:98-106.

Sperling, J., 1982, America's vanishing wetlands, *Natl. Fisherman* 63(5 and 6):14-15, 26-27.

Springer, P. F., 1964, Wildlife management concepts compatible with mosquito suppression, *Mosq. News* 24(1):50-55.

Springer, P. F., and R. F. Darsie, Jr., 1956, Studies on mosquito breeding in natural and impounded coastal salt marshes in Delaware during 1955, *New Jersey Mosq. Exterm. Assoc. Proc.* 43:74-79.

Spurr, S. H., 1949, Films and filters for forest aerial photography, *Photogram. Eng.* 15:473-481.

Spurr, S. H., and C. T. Brown, 1946, Specifications for aerial photographs used in forest management, *Photogram. Eng.* 12:131-141.

Stearns, F., 1978, Management potential: summary and recommendations, in *Freshwater Wetlands*, R. E. Good, D. F. Whigham, and R. L. Simpson, eds., Academic Press, New York, pp. 357-363.

Stearns, L. A., and M. W. Goodwin, 1941, Notes on the winter feeding of the muskrat in Delaware, *J. Wildl. Manage.* 5(1):1-12.

Stearns, L. A., D. MacCreary, and F. C. Daigh, 1939, Water and plant requirements of the muskrat on a Delaware tide water marsh, *New Jersey Mosq. Exterm. Assoc. Proc.* 26:212-221.

Stearns, L. A., D. MacCreary, and F. C. Daigh, 1940, *Effects of Ditching on the Muskrat Population of a Delaware Tide Water Marsh*, Delaware Univ. Agr. Exp. Sta. Bull. 225, 55p.

Stebbings, R. E., 1970, Recovery of salt marsh in Brittany sixteen months after heavy pollution by oil, *Environ. Pollut.* 1:163-167.

Steenis, J. H., N. G. Wilder, H. P. Cofer, and R. A. Beck, 1954, *The Marshes of Delaware, Their Improvement and Preservation*, Delaware Bd. Game and Fish Comm., Pittman-Robertson Bull. 2, 42p.

Steers, J. A., 1969, *Coasts and Beaches*, Oliver and Boyd, London, 136p.

Stegeman, J. J., 1974, Hydrocarbons in shellfish chronically exposed to low levels of fuel oil, in *Pollution and Physiology of Marine Organisms*, F. J. Vernberg and W. B. Vernberg, eds., Academic Press, New York, pp. 329-347.

Stegeman, J. J., 1978, Influence of environmental contamination on cytochrome P-450 mixed-function oxygenases in fish: implications for recovery in the Wild Harbor marsh, *Canada Fish. Res. Board J.* 35(5):668-674.

Steindorsson, S., 1954, The coastline vegetation at Gasar in Eyjafjordur, in the north of Iceland, *Mytt Mag. Bot.* 3:203-212.

Steindorsson, S., 1975, Studies on the mire-vegetation of Iceland, *Visindafelag Islendinga* 41, Reykjavik, pp. 131-138.

Stevenson, J. C., ed., 1978, Recovery potential of oiled marine Northern environments, *Canada Fish. Res. Board J.* 35(5):499-795.

Steward, K. K., and W. H. Ornes, 1975, Assessing a marsh environment for waste water renovation, *Water Pollut. Control Fed. J.* 47(7):1880-1891.

Stewart, R. E., 1951, Clapper rail populations of the Middle Atlantic states, *North Am. Wildl. Conf. Trans.* 16:421-430.

Stewart, R. E., 1962, *Waterfowl Populations in the Upper Chesapeake Regions*, U.S. Fish & Wildlife Serv. Spec. Rept., Wildl. 65, 208p.

Stewart, W. R., V. Carter, and P. D. Brooks, 1980, Inland (non-tidal) wetland mapping, *Photogram. Eng. Remote Sensing* 46:617-628.

Stewart, N. E., R. E. Milleman, and W. P. Breese, 1967, Acute toxicity of the insecticide Sevin and its hydrolytic product 1-naphthol to some marine organisms, *Am. Fish. Soc. Trans.* 96(1):25-30.

Stone, J. H., L. M. Bahr, Jr., and J. W. Day, Jr., 1978, Effects of canals on freshwater marshes in coastal Louisiana and implications for management, in *Freshwater Wetlands*, R. E. Good, D. F. Whigham, and R. L. Simpson, eds., Academic Press, New York, pp. 299-320.

Stroud, L. M., and A. W. Cooper, 1968, *Color-Infrared Aerial Photographic Interpretation and Net Primary Productivity of Regularly Flooded North Carolina Salt Marsh*, University of North Carolina Water Resources Research Institute No. 14, 86p.

Sullivan, M. J., 1976, Long-term effects of manipulating light intensity and nutrient enrichment on the structure of a salt marsh diatom community, *J. Phycol.* 12(2):205-210.

Sullivan, M. J., 1979, *Effects of Ammonia Enrichment and High Light Intensity on a Salt Marsh Diatom Community*, Water Resources Research Institute, Mississippi State University, Project No. A-124-MISS, 53p.

Sullivan, M. J., and F. C. Daiber, 1974, Response in production of cord grass, *Spartina alterniflora*, to inorganic nitrogen and phosphorus fertilizer, *Chesapeake Sci.* 15(2):121-123.

Sullivan, M. J., and F. C. Daiber, 1975, Light, nitrogen and phosphorus limitation of edaphic algae in a Delaware salt marsh, *J. Exp. Mar. Biol. Ecol.* 18(1):79-88.

Synthesis of Research Results, 1978, *Wetland Habitat Development with Dredged Material: Engineering and Plant Propagation*, U.S. Army Corps of Engineers Dredged Material Res. Prog. Tech. Rept. DS-78-16, 107p., tables and appendices.

Talbot, C. W., K. W. Able, J. K. Shisler, and D. Coorey, 1980, Seasonal variation in the composition of fresh and brackish water fishes of New Jersey mosquito control impoundments, *New Jersey Mosq. Control Assoc. Proc.* 67:50-63.

Taylor, M. H., L. DiMichele, and G. J. Leach, 1977, Egg stranding in the life cycle of the mummichog *Fundulus heteroclitus, Copeia* 1977:397-399.

Taylor, M. H., G. J. Leach, L. DiMichele, W. H. Levitan, and W. F. Jacob, 1979, Lunar spawning cycle in the mummichog *Fundulus heteroclitus* (Pisces: Cyprinodontidae), *Copeia* 1979(2):291-297.

Teal, J. M., 1962, Energy flow in the salt marsh ecosystem of Georgia, *Ecology* 43(4):614-624.

Teal, J. M., 1977, Food chain transfer of hydrocarbons, in *Fate and Effects of Petroleum Hydrocarbons in Marine Organisms and Ecosystems*, D. A. Wolfe, ed., Pergamon Press, New York, pp. 71-77.

Teal, J. M., K. Burns, and J. Farrington, 1978, Analyses of aromatic hydrocarbons in intertidal sediments resulting from two spills of No. 2 fuel oil in Buzzards Bay, Massachusetts, *Canada Fish. Res. Board J.* 35(5):510-520.

Teleky, L. S., 1978, Are the cries of Hermes being heard in the wetlands? in *Coastal Zone '78*, vol. 3, Symposium on Technical, Environmental, Socioeconomic and Regulatory Aspects of Coastal Zone Management, American Society of Civil Engineers, New York, pp. 2026-2035.

Thomas, J. R., C. L. Wiegand, and V. I. Meyers, 1967, Reflectance of cotton leaves and its relation to yield, *Agron. J.* 59:551-554.

Thomas, M., 1978, Comparison of oiled and unoiled intertidal communities in Chedbucto Bay, Nova Scotia, *Canada Fish. Res. Board J.* 35(5):707-716.

Thompson, D. C., J. E. Ragsdale, R. J. Reimold, and J. L. Gallagher, 1973, Seasonal aspects of remote sensing coastal resources, in *Remote Sensing of Earth Resources*, F. Shahrokhi, ed., University of Tennessee, Knoxville, pp. 1201-1249.

Thomson, A. D., and K. L. Webb, 1984, The effect of chronic oil pollution on salt-marsh nitrogen fixation (acetylene reduction), *Estuaries* 7(1):2-11.

Tindall, E. E., 1961, A two year study of mosquito breeding and wildlife usage in Little Creek impounded salt marsh, Little Creek Wildlife area, Delaware, 1959-1960, *New Jersey Mosq. Exterm. Assoc. Proc.* 48:100-105.

Tiner, R. W., Jr., 1984, *Wetlands of the United States: Current Status and Recent Trends*, National Wetlands Inventory, Fish and Wildlife Service, U.S. Dept. of Interior, Washington, D.C., 59p.

Tippie, V. K., 1980, Evaluating the effectiveness of coastal zone management, in *Estuarine Perspectives*, V. S. Kennedy ed., Academic Press, New York, pp. 47-57.

Travis, B. V., G. H. Bradley, and W. C. McDuffie, 1954, The effect of ditching on a salt marsh vegetation in Florida, *New Jersey Mosq. Exterm. Assoc. Proc.* 41:235-244.

Tripp, M. R., 1974, Effects of organophosphate pesticides on adult oysters (*Crassostrea virginica*), in *Pollution and Physiology of Marine Organisms*, F. J. Vernberg and W. B. Vernberg, eds., Academic Press, New York, pp. 225-236.

Tucker, C. J., 1978, A comparison of satellite sensor bands for vegetation monitoring, *Photogram. Eng. Remote Sensing* 44:1369-1380.

Tucker, C. J., 1979, Red and photographic infrared linear combinations for monitoring vegetation, *Remote Sensing Environ.* 8:127-150.

Tucker, C. J., J. H. Elgin, Jr., J. E. McMurtrey III, 1979, Temporal measurements of corn and soybean crops, *Photogram. Eng. Remote Sensing* 45:643-653.

Tucker, C. J., J. H. Elgin, Jr., J. E. McMurtrey, III, and C. J. Fan, 1979, Monitoring corn and soybean crop development with hand-held radiometer spectral data, *Remote Sensing Environ.* 8:237-248.

Tucker, C. J., J. H. Elgin, Jr., and J. E. McMurtrey III, 1980, Relationship of crop radiance to alfalfa agronomic values, *Internat. J. Remote Sensing* 1:69-75.

Tucker, C. J., B. N. Holben, J. H. Elgin, Jr., and J. E. McMurtrey III, 1980, Relationship of spectral data to grain yield variation, *Photogram. Eng. Remote Sensing* 46:657-666.

Tucker, C. J., B. N. Holben, J. H. Elgin, Jr., and J. E. McMurtrey III, 1981, Remote sensing of total dry-matter accumulation in winter wheat, *Remote Sensing Environ.* 11:171-189.

Tucker, C. J., L. D. Miller, and R. L. Pearson, 1973, Measurement of the combined effect of green biomass, chlorophyll and leaf water on canopy spectroreflectance of the shortgrass prairie, in *Remote Sensing of Earth Resources*, F. Shahrokhi, ed., University of Tennessee, Knoxville, pp. 601-627.

Turner, R. E., J. W. Day, Jr., M. Meo, P. M. Payonk, J. H. Stone, T. B. Ford, and W. G. Smith, 1976, Aspects of land-treated waste applications in Louisiana wetlands, in *National Symposium on Freshwater Wetlands and Sewage Effluent Disposal Proceedings*, D. L. Tilton, R. H. Kadlec, and C. J. Richardson, eds., Ann Arbor, Mich., pp. 147-167.

Tyler, G., 1967, On the effect of phosphorus and nitrogen, supplied to Baltic shore-meadow vegetation, *Bot. Notiser* 120:433-447.

Tyrawski, J., 1977, *A Study of the Common Reedgrass* (Phragmites communis *Trin.*) *in the Coastal Zone of Delaware*, Master's thesis, University of Delaware, 164p.

Urner, C. A., 1935, Relation of mosquito control in New Jersey to bird life of the salt marshes, *New Jersey Mosq. Exterm. Assoc. Proc.* 22:130-136.

Usher, M. B., 1977, Coastline management: some general comments on management plans and visitor surveys, in *The Coastline*, R. S. K. Barnes, ed., John Wiley & Sons, London, pp. 291-311.

Valiela, I., and J. M. Teal, 1974, Nutrient limitation in salt marsh vegetation, in *Ecology of Halophytes*, R. J. Reimold and W. H. Queen, eds., Academic Press, New York, pp. 547-563.

Valiela, I., M. D. Banus, and J. M. Teal, 1974, Response of salt marsh bivalves to enrichment with metal-containing sewage sludge and retention of lead, zinc and cadmium by marsh sediments, *Environ. Pollut.* **7**:149-157.

Valiela, I., J. M. Teal, and N. Y. Persson, 1976, Production and dynamics of experimentally enriched salt marsh vegetation: below ground biomass, *Limnol. Oceanogr.* **21**(2):245-252.

Valiela, I., J. M. Teal, and W. J. Sass, 1973, Nutrient retention in salt marsh plots experimentally fertilized with sewage sludge, *Estuarine Coast. Mar. Sci.* **1**:261-269.

Valiela, I., J. M. Teal, and W. J. Sass, 1975, Production and dynamics of salt marsh vegetation and effect of sewage contamination. I. Biomass, production and species composition, *J. Appl. Ecol.* **12**:973-982.

Valiela, I., S. Vince, and J. M. Teal, 1976, Assimilation of sewage by wetlands, in *Estuarine Processes*, vol. 1, M. Wiley, ed., Academic Press, New York, pp. 234-253.

Van Der Toorn, J., and J. H. Mook, 1982, The influence of environmental factors and management on stands of *Phragmites australis*. I. Effects of burning, frost and insect damage on shoot density and shoot size, *J. Appl. Ecol.* **19**(2):477-499.

Van Zoost, J. R., 1969, *The Ecology and Waterfowl Utilization of the John Lusby National Wildlife Area*, Master's thesis, Acadia University, Wolfville, N.S., 183p.

Vernberg, F. J., and W. B. Vernberg, eds., 1974, *Pollution and Physiology of Marine Organisms*, Academic Press, New York, 492p.

Viosca, P., Jr., 1928, Louisiana wetlands, *Ecology* **9**:216-229.

Vogl, R. L., 1973, Effects of fire on the plants and animals of a Florida wetland, *Am. Midl. Nat.* **89**:334-347.

Walker, R. A., 1973, Wetlands preservation and management on Chesapeake Bay: the role of science in natural resource policy, *Coastal Zone Manage. J.* **1**(1):75-101.

Wall, W. J., Jr., and O. W. Doane, Jr., 1960, A preliminary study of the blood-sucking Diptera on Cape Cod, Massachusetts, *Mosq. News* **20**:39-44.

Wallentinus, H. G., 1973, Above-ground primary production of a *Juncetum gerardi* on a Baltic sea-shore meadow, *Oikos* **24**:200-219.

Ward, D. V., and D. A. Busch, 1976, Effects of Temefos, an Organophosphorus Insecticide, on Survival and Escape Behavior of the Marsh Fiddler Crab *Uca Pugnax, Oikos* **27**:331-335.

Warren, G. M., 1911, *Tidal Marshes and Their Reclamation* U.S. Dept. Agriculture Exp. Sta. Bull. 240, pp. 1-99.

Webb, J. W., J. D. Dodd, B. W. Cain, W. R. Leavens, L. R. Hossner, C. Lindau, R. R. Stickney, and H. Williamson, 1978, *Habitat Development Field Investigations, Bolivar Peninsula Marsh and Upland Habitat Development Site, Galveston Bay, Texas*, U.S. Army Corps Engineers Dredged Material Res. Prog. Tech. Rept. D-78-15, 521p.

Weisberg, S. B., 1981, *Food Availability and Utilization by the Mummichog Fundulus heteroclitus (L.)*, Ph.D. dissertation, University of Delaware, 109p.

Weisberg, S. B., and V. A. Lotrich, 1982, Ingestion, egestion, excretion, growth, and conversion efficiency for the mummichog, *Fundulus heteroclitus* (L.), *Exp. Mar. Biol. Ecol. J.* **62**:237-249.

Weisberg, S. B., R. Whalen, and V. A. Lotrich, 1981, Tidal and diurnal influence on food consumption of a salt marsh killifish *Fundulus heteroclitus, Mar. Biol.* **61**:243-246.

Weller, M. W., 1978, Management of freshwater marshes for wildlife, in *Freshwater Wetlands*, R. E. Good, D. F. Whigham, and R. L. Simpson, eds., Academic Press, New York, pp. 267-284.

Weller, M. W., 1979, Wetland habitats, in *Wetland Functions and Values: The State of Our Understanding*, P. E. Greeson, J. R. Clark, and J. E. Clark, eds., American Water Resources Assoc., Minneapolis, Minn., pp. 210-234.

Wetzel, R. and S. Powers, 1978, Soils analysis, in *Habitat Development Field Investigations, Windmill Point Marsh Development Site, James River, Virginia.* Appendix D: Environmental Impacts of Marsh Development with Dredged Material: Botany, Soils, Aquatic Biology, and Wildlife, U.S. Army Corps of Engineers Dredged Material Res. Prog. Tech. Rept. D-77-23, pp. 103-119.

Whelan, T., III, J. T. Ishmael, and W. S. Bishop, Jr., 1976, Long term chemical effects of petroleum in South Louisiana wetlands. I. Organic carbon in sediments and waters, *Mar. Pollut. Bull.* **7**:150-155.

Whigham, D. F., and R. L. Simpson, 1976, The potential use of freshwater tidal marshes in the management of water quality in the Delaware River, in *Biological Control of Water Pollution*, J. Toubier and R. W. Pierson, Jr., eds., University of Pennsylvania Press, Philadelphia.

Whigham, D. F., J. O'Neill, and M. McWethy, 1980, *The Effect of Open Marsh Water Management on the Ecology of Chesapeake Bay High Marsh Vegetation*, Progress Report and Budget Request for FY81, Chesapeake Bay Center for Environmental Studies, Smithsonian Institution, Edgewater, Md., 187p.

White, D. J. B., 1961, Some observations on the vegetation of Blakeney Point, Norfolk, following the disappearance of the rabbits, *J. Ecol.* **49**(1):113-118.

Whitman, W. R., 1974, *The Response of Macro-invertebrates to Experimental Marsh Management*, Ph.D. dissertation, University of Maine, 114p.

Wicker, K. M., and K. J. Meyer-Arendt, 1982, Utilization of remote sensing in wetland management, in *Pecora VII Symposium Proceedings*, B. F. Richason, ed., American Society Photogrammetry, Washington, D.C., pp. 217-229.

Wilkinson, R. N., 1967, *Toxicity of Some Organophosphate Insecticides to Salt Marsh Killifish and Crustaceans*, Master's thesis, University of Delaware, 44p.

Williams, R. E., 1955, Development and improvement of coastal marsh ranges, in *Water. The Yearbook of Agriculture 1955*, U.S. Dept. of Agriculture, Washington, D.C., pp. 444-450.

Windom, H. L., 1975, Heavy metal fluxes through salt-marsh estuaries, in *Estuarine Research*, vol. 1, L. E. Cronin, ed., Academic Press, New York, pp. 137-152.

Windom, H. L., 1976, *Geochemical Interactions of Heavy Metals in Southeastern Salt Marsh Environments*, Ecol. Res. Ser. EPA-600/376-023, Washington, D.C., 36p.

Windom, H. L., 1977, *Ability of Salt Marshes to Remove Nutrients and Heavy Metals from Dredged Material Disposal Area Effluents*, U.S. Army Corps of Engineers Dredged Material Res. Prog. Tech Rept. D-77-37, 43p.

Windom, H., W. Gardner, J. Stephens, and F. Taylor, 1976, The role of methylmercury production in the transfer of mercury in a salt marsh ecosystem, *Estuarine Coast. Mar. Sci.* 4(5):579-583.

Wobber, F. J., and R. R. Anderson, 1972, *Operational Wetlands Mapping Using Multiband Aerial Photography*, Coastal Mapping Symposium Proceedings, American Society of Photogrammetry, Washington, D.C., pp. 95-97.

Woodhouse, W. W., Jr., E. D. Seneca, and S. W. Broome, 1972, *Marsh Building with Dredge Spoil in North Carolina*, North Carolina State Univ. Agric. Exp. Sta. Bull. 445, 28p.

Woodhouse, W. W., Jr., E. D. Seneca, and S. W. Broome, 1974, *Propagation of Spartina alterniflora for Substrate Stabilization and Salt Marsh Development*, Technical Memo 46, U.S. Army Corps of Engineers Coastal Engineering Research Center, Ft. Belvoir, Va., 155p.

Woodhouse, W. W., Jr., E. D. Seneca, and W. S. Broome, 1976, *Propagation and Use of Spartina alterniflora for Shoreline Erosion Abatement*, Technical Rept. 76-2, U.S. Army Corps of Engineers Coastal Engineering Research Center, Ft. Belvoir, Va., 72p.

Woodwell, G. M., and D. E. Whitney, 1977, Flax Pond ecosystem study: exchanges of phosphorus between a salt marsh and the coastal waters of Long Island Sound, *Mar. Biol.* 41(1):1-6.

Woolfenden, G. E., 1956, Comparative breeding behavior of *Ammospiza caudacuta* and *A. maritima*, *Kansas Univ. Mus. Nat Hist. Publ.* 10:47-75.

Work, E. A., and D. S. Gilmer, 1976, Utilization of satellite data for inventorying prairie ponds and lakes, *Photogram. Eng. Remote Sensing* 42:685-694.

Worsham, A. D., R. F. Soots, and J. F. Parnell, 1974, Herbicides for vegetation management in restoring dredge islands as nesting sites for coastal nesting birds, *South. Weed Sci. Soc. Proc.* 27:298.

Wright, H. A., and A. W. Bailey, 1982, *Fire Ecology*, John Wiley & Sons, New York, 501p.

Wright, J. O., 1907, *Reclamation of Tidal Lands*, U.S. Dept. Agriculture Ofc. Exp. Sta. Rept. 1906, pp. 373-397.

Yapp, R. H., 1923, *Spartina townsendii* on the Dovey salt marshes: a correction, *J. Ecol.* 11:102.

Ydenberg, R. C., and H. H. Th. Prins, 1981, Spring grazing and the manipulation of food quality by barnacle geese, *J. Appl. Ecol.* 18(2):443-453.

Zedler, J. B., 1984, *Salt Marsh Restoration: A Guide Book for Southern California*, California Sea Grant Report No. T-CSGCP-009, 46p.

Zetka, E. F., 1982, Coastal zone management information needs: Potential Landsat applications, in *Remote Sensing for Resource Management*, C. J. Johannsen and J. L. Sanders, eds., Soil Conservation Society of America, Ankeny, Ia., pp. 111-122.

Author Index

Able, K. W., 91, 112, 114
Adam, P., 57, 61, 64
Adams, P. C., 24, 148, 152, 155, 159, 163, 168, 175
Ahearn, D. G., 209
Ahlgren, C. E., 36
Allan, P. F., 1
Allen, W. A., 52
Alls, R. T., 91
Altman, R. M., 104
Anderson, B. S., 62, 72, 79, 83, 86
Anderson, J. F., 89
Anderson, J. W., 190, 225, 229, 230
Anderson, R. D., 259
Anderson, R. R., 50, 52, 258
Andersson, M., 27
Apley, M. L., 3
Atwater, B. F., 8, 75
Aurand, D., 79
Ausness, R. C., 243, 253, 256
Axtell, R. C., 189
Ayres, R. P., 193, 196, 214, 223, 225, 231

Bahr, L. M., 116
Bailey, A. W., 36
Bailey, N. S., 98
Baker, J. M., 190, 191, 192, 197, 201, 220, 226, 231
Baldwin, W. P., 79, 86
Balling, S. S., 99
Banta, J. S., 149, 150
Banus, M. D., 129, 132
Barber, R. T., 59
Barclay, L. A., 62, 72, 79, 83, 86
Barko, J. W., 5
Bartlett, D. S., 49, 52, 53, 258
Bascand, L. D., 44
Batie, S. S., 66
Bayley, S. E., 121, 125, 129, 135
Beck, R. A., 42, 86, 87
Beeftink, W. G., 1, 7, 11, 14, 47, 59, 263, 269, 274, 278
Beeman, O., 140
Bender, M. E., 121, 129, 134, 193, 196, 214, 223, 225, 231
Benkendorf, A., 140
Benson, F. J., 8
Bent, A. C., 4
Benton, A. R., 50
Berner, N., 209
Best, R. G., 53
Baynon, L. R., 190

Bidlingmayer, W. L., 183
Bishop, F. W., 205, 209
Bishop, W. S., Jr., 204, 205, 209
Boesch, D. F., 173
Bongiorno, S. F., 5
Bonsteel, J. A., 62
Boon, J. D., 257
Bosselman, F., 243, 247
Bostian, W. J., 147
Botkin, D. B., 55
Boule, M. E., 257
Bourn, W. S., 96, 99
Bowden, N. W., 78
Boyce, J. S., 147
Boyes, D., 104
Bradbury, H. M., 92, 96
Bradley, G. H., 96
Breese, W. P., 183
Briscoe, J., 239, 253
Brooks, P. D., 50
Broome, S. W., 121, 125, 135, 144, 148, 150, 152, 154, 155, 156, 161, 167, 175
Browder, J. A., 53
Brown, A. W. A., 184
Brown, C. T., 48
Brown, L. S., 226
Brown, W. W., 50, 258
Bruder, K. W., 104
Bryan, H., 270, 272
Bryant, R. J., 42
Buchner, G. E., 56, 67
Buckley, E. H., 153, 155
Budd, J. T. C., 53
Bunce, R. G. A., 2, 61, 165
Burbank, J. H., 50
Buresh, R. J., 194, 196, 203
Burger, J., 5, 100, 104, 114, 115
Burns, K. A., 214, 220, 222, 225, 226, 228, 229, 235
Busch, D. A., 182
Butera, M. K., 52, 53
Butler, P. A., 178, 182, 183

Cadwalladr, D. A., 5, 15, 22, 27, 31, 275
Cairns, W. E., 85, 89
Callies, D., 243, 247
Cameron, H. L., 48
Cammen, L. M., 150, 165, 167, 168, 173, 175
Camp, A. R., 132
Campbell, B. C., 182

Capeyya, M. R., 100
Capotosto, P. M., 104
Cardenas, R., 52
Carls, E. G., 264
Carr, A., 4
Carter, V., 49, 50, 51, 52, 261
Castagna, M., 114
Catts, E. P., Jr., 76, 78, 88, 92, 98, 189
Chabreck, R. H., 5, 76, 92, 270, 276
Chambers, J., 222
Chandler, G. T., 210
Chapman, H. C., 78, 88, 89
Chapman, R. N., 262
Chapman, V. J., 1, 13, 199
Chastaen, G., 251
Cheng, L., 5
Chidester, F. E., 103
Christiansen, M. E., 183
Christie, D. R., 176
Christopher, S., 78
Clark, A. H., 7, 61, 64
Clark, J. E., 10
Clark, J. R., 6, 10, 267, 274
Clarke, J. L., 76, 101
Clymer, J. P., 113
Cochran, W. S., 96, 101
Cofer, H. P. 42, 86, 87
Cole, R. A., 141, 146, 175
Coles, S. M., 60, 276
Colwell, R. N., 48
Conard, S. G., 8, 75
Connell, W. A., 68, 98, 103
Cook, R. S., 5, 22
Cooper, A. W., 49
Copeland, B. J., 165, 167, 168
Corker, C., 252
Corlett, J., 60, 61
Correll, D. L., 121, 129, 134
Cory, E. N., 97
Costle, D. M., 262, 274
Costlow, J. D., 183
Cottam, C., 77, 78, 96, 97, 99, 101
Cowardin, L. M., 50, 261
Cowell, E. B., 190, 191, 192, 231
Cox, B. A., 229
Crane, J., 3
Crichton, O. W., 49, 258
Crissey, W. F., 75
Croft, B. A., 184
Croker, R. A., 182
Crow, S., 209
Curran, P. J., 53
Cutler, M. R., 275

Daiber, F. C., 3, 5, 49, 52, 54, 79, 99, 118, 121
Daigh, F. C., 16, 95, 98
Dakin, O. H., 100

Dalby, D. H., 14, 191, 197, 202
Dalby, R., 57, 61, 96
D'Angremond, K., 140, 167
Darnell, R. M., 6, 8, 9, 49, 141, 266, 278
Darsie, R. F., Jr., 68, 76, 78, 84, 88, 89, 91, 92
Davis, G. R., 258
Dawson, A. D., 243, 248, 252
Day, J. W., Jr., 116, 120, 123, 127, 162
Dean, T. A., 5
DeBusk, T. A., 134
Deering, D. W., 54
Defenbaugh, R. A., 8
De la Cruz, A. A., 38, 194, 200, 203
De Laune, R. D., 194, 196, 203
De Nekker, J., 140, 167
DeRagon, W. R., 100
DeWitt, C. B., 10
DeWitt, P., 3
Diaz, R. J., 141, 146, 173
Dibner, P. C., 192, 202
Dicks, B., 197
DiMichele, L., 5, 114
Dixit, D., 225, 230
Doane, O. W., Jr., 98
Doiron. L. N., 50
Dolan, T. J., 121, 125, 129, 135
Dornseif, B., 203, 211
Dottavio, C. L., 53
Dottavio, F. D., 53
Doumlele, D., 154, 165, 168
Dowden, J. N., 8, 75
Downing, B. M., 23, 28, 29, 44, 45
Doyle, F. J., 55
Dozier, H. L., 3, 8, 34
Drake, B. G., 53
Drayton, W., Jr., 240
Drifmeyer, J. E., 167
Durant, C. J., 166

Eaton, A. W. H., 64
Echeverria, J., 240, 243, 251
Egan, W. G., 50
Egler, R. E., 3
Eleuterius, L. N., 5, 140, 144
Elgin, J. H., Jr., 54
Ellis, C. W., 8
Enslin, W. R., 50
Ernst-Dottavio, C. L., 53
Errington, P. L., 8, 34
Evans, J., 8
Eyre, L. A., 51

Fan, C. J., 54
Farrington, J., 228, 235
Ferrigno, F., 16, 33, 68, 69, 75, 97, 100, 101, 103, 104, 112, 115
Fitzpatrick, G., 182

Fleeger, J. W., 210
Flemer, D. A., 4
Florio, A., 47
Florschutz, O., Jr., 76, 78, 84, 88, 92, 98
Floyd, K. W., 152, 156, 159, 163, 168
Ford, T. B., 120, 123, 127, 162
Fornes, A. O., 49, 158
Franz, D. R., 88
Fredrick, S. W., 153, 155
Friedman, R. M., 10
Friedericks, G. A., 49
Fultz, T. O., Jr., 103, 112

Gabrielson, I. N., 262
Gallagher, J. L., 5, 49, 50, 51, 52, 118, 122
Galloway, G. E., 266
Gammon, P. T., 50, 52
Ganong, W. F., 3, 57, 62, 67, 83, 96
Garber, J., 5
Garbisch, E. W., Jr., 147
Gardner, W., 129
Garrett, M. K., 52
Garten, D., 259
Gausman, H. W., 52
George, L. F., 104
Gibbons, E., 14
Gilfillan, E. S., 223
Gillham, M. E., 22, 28, 31
Gilmer, D. S., 52
Glue, D. E., 69
Golet, F. C., 100, 261
Gonsoulin, F., 203, 211
Good, R. E., 48, 193
Goodwin, M. W., 16
Gooley, B., 103
Gordon, H. H., 51
Gordon, H. T., 181
Gosselink, J. G., 266
Grant, R. R., Jr., 133
Gray, A. J., 2, 8, 14, 15, 16, 22, 23, 34, 56, 57, 61, 64, 96, 165, 270, 274
Greenhalgh, M. E., 5, 35, 69
Greenman, A. B., 239
Greeson, P. W., 10
Griffith, R. E., 32, 33
Gundlach, E. R., 193
Gunter, G., 5
Guss, P., 49

Hackney, C. T., 38, 194, 200, 203
Hagmann, L. E., 89
Haines, E. B., 4, 141
Hair, M. E., 50
Hampson, G. R., 193, 214, 220, 231
Hanisak, M. D., 134
Hansen, D., 183
Hansen, J. A., 103

Hansen, W. J., 266
Hansens, E. J., 97, 98
Hanson, H. C., 3
Hanson, R., 203, 211
Hardin, G., 238
Hardisky, M. A., 24, 51, 54, 148, 152, 154, 155, 159, 160, 163, 168, 175, 264, 267
Hardy, J. D., Jr., 4
Harrington, E. S., 91
Harrington, R. W., Jr., 91, 183
Harrison, F. J., Jr., 85
Harvey, M. J., 7, 14, 61, 64
Harwood, C. C., 248
Haslam, S. M., 29, 37, 42, 46
Hass, R. H., 54
Hatcher, A., 4, 84
Haueisen, A. J., 49, 241, 251
Hauer, J. L., 173
Hawkes, A. L., 5, 7, 79, 239, 253
Headlee, T. J., 96, 103
Healy, W. B., 278
Hedel, C. W., 8, 75
Heinle, D. R., 4
Heitz, J. R., 222
Herke, W. H., 92
Hermann, A. J., 121, 125, 129, 135
Hershman, M. J., 176, 241, 248, 253, 257, 269, 271, 275, 279
Hershner, C., 192, 193, 196, 214, 218, 219, 223, 225, 231
Herwig, R., 209
Hightower, G. M., 229
Hilliard, S. B., 72
Hindley, E., 48
Hocking, A., 7, 64
Hoffer, R. M., 52, 53
Hoffpauer, C. M., 36, 41
Holben, B. N., 54
Holmes, O. W., 244
Hood, M. A., 205, 209
Horwitz, E. L., 262
Hoskins, W. M., 181
Howard, R., 43
Howe, L., 105
Howland, W. G., 49
Huffman, R. T., 142, 149
Huggett, R. J., 193, 196, 214, 223, 224, 231
Hull, W. V., 256
Hulten, E., 3
Hunt, L. J., 146
Hunter, R. D., 3
Hurd, L. E., 5
Husak, S., 43

Ishmael, J. T., 204
Ives, R. L., 48

Jackson, C. I., 62, 65, 75, 79
Jacob, W. F., 114
Jahn, L. R., 263
James, B. M., 8
Jamnback, H., 189
Jensen, A., 53
Jensen, H. A., 48
Jensen, P. A., 136
Jéquel, N., 59
Jerling, L., 27, 29, 43
Jobbins, D. M., 69, 75, 97, 101, 103, 104,
    111, 112, 115
Johnson, A. S., 79, 86
Johnson, D. W., 3, 178
Johnson, L. E., 142, 147
Jordan, C. F., 52
Jory, M. L., 199, 227

Kadlec, J. A., 117, 137
Kadlec, R. H., 117, 134, 137
Kalber, F. A., Jr., 6
Kale, H. W., II, 5
Kat, P., 3
Kator, H., 209
Katz, L. M., 113
Katz, M., 183
Keefe, C. W., 4
Kestner, F. J. T., 59, 75
Ketchum, B. H., 8, 262, 268, 271, 274,
    277, 280
Kiefer, R. W., 49
Kirby-Smith, W. W., 59
Klemas, V., 49, 51, 52, 53, 54, 258
Klose, P. N., 279
Kneen, F. R., 89
Kneib, R. T., 5, 113
Knight, K. L., 84, 88
Knight, R. L., 132
Knights, B., 56
Kozlowski, T. T., 36
Krebs, C. T., 214, 220, 229
Kruczynski, W. L., 142, 149
Kuenzler, E. J., 97
Kumpf, H. E., 266
Kusler, J. A., 10, 262, 268, 274
Kvet, J., 42

LaRoe, E. T., 261
La Roe, T. T., 141
Lagna, L., 258
Lake, J. L., 218, 219
Lake, R. W., 99
Landers, J. L., 79, 86
Lanier, M. D., 261
Larson, J. S., 275
Larsson, T., 14, 34, 275
LaSalle, R. N., 84, 88
Laughlin, R. B., Jr., 221, 228

Lawson, D. T., 72, 73
Lay, D. W., 16, 32, 38
Leach, G. J., 5, 114
Lee, R. F., 203, 211, 216, 225, 230
Lee, V., 5
Lent, C. M., 3
Leopold, 262, 270
Lesser, C. R., 91, 99, 104
Lesser, F. H., 76, 78, 88, 92, 103
Levasseur, J. E., 199, 227
Levitan, W. H., 114
Lewes, L., 222
Linder, R. L., 53
Linky, E. J., 240, 243, 251
Linthurst, R. J., 5, 24, 30, 36, 52, 141
Livingstone, R. J., 270, 275, 278
Lombardi, R. W., 103
Lorio, W. J., 100
Lotrich, V. A., 113
Loucks, O., 270, 275, 278
Lunz, J. D., 141, 146
Lynch, J. J., 16, 32, 37, 38, 41
Lyon, J. G., 52
Lyon, J. T., 150, 167, 175
Lytle, J. S., 193, 196, 203

McCallum, R. J., 147
McClellan, H. A., 140, 144
MacConnell, W., 50
McCormick, J., 67, 251
MacCreary, D., 16, 95, 98
MacDonald, B., 14
MacDonald, R. L., 8, 75
McDuffie, W. C., 96
McEwen, R. B., 51
McGinness, J., 52
McGuiness, W. V., Jr., 142, 147
MacInnis, A. R. G., 93
McKenzie, M. D., 62, 72, 73, 76, 79, 83,
    86
McLeod, H., 14
McMahan, E. A., 132
McMurtrey, J. E., III, 54
MacNamara, L. G., 75, 76, 87, 92, 101,
    270
MacRitchie, S., 51
McWethy, M., 105
Malone, M., 84
Maloney, F. E., 243, 253, 256
Mangold, R. E., 85, 91, 94
Marshall, D. E., 52, 118, 122, 132
Marshall, J. T., Jr., 5
Mason, C. F., 42
Masry, S. E., 51
Maurer, D., 3
Maxwell, E. L., 54
Maxwell, J. W., 62, 65, 75, 79
Means, T. H., 66, 95

Meany, R. A., 132
Mendelssohn, I., 5
Meo, M., 120, 123, 127, 162
Meredith, W. H., 105, 111
Messman, L., 5, 263
Metzgar, R. G., 243, 238, 253
Meyer-Arendt, K. J., 51
Meyers, S. P., 205, 209
Meyers, V. I., 52
Michael, A. D., 226
Michelman, F. I., 248
Miglarese, J. V., 62, 72, 79, 83, 86
Milan, C. S., 203, 216, 226
Miller, D. C., 3
Miller, K. G., 3
Miller, L. D., 52, 53
Miller, W. R., 3
Milleman, R. E., 183
Milton, E. J., 53
Moisan, G., 5, 14, 61, 64
Møller, H. S., 14, 34, 70
Monroe, R. J., 183
Montanari, J. H., 10
Mook, J. H., 43
Moore, K., 192, 231
Moore, N. W., 181, 184
Morantz, D. L., 82
Morgan, M. H., 4
Morgan, P. H., 79, 86
Morley, J. V., 5, 15, 22, 27, 31, 275
Moul, E. T., 193, 214, 220, 231
Mroczynski, R. P., 53
Munson, K., 173
Murray, R. E., 83
Myers, C., 5, 263

Nathan, K., 95
Nauman, J., 250
Neeley, W. W., 41, 100
Neff, J. M., 190, 221, 228, 229
Nelson-Smith, A., 196, 201, 231
Nesbit, D. M., 72, 73
Newcombe, C. L., 151, 152, 156, 159,
    163, 168
Nicol, E. A., 3
Niedzwiedz, W., 50
Niering, W. A., 2, 5, 8, 10, 70, 265, 268,
    272, 276, 277
Nixon, S. W., 4, 5
Nordhagen, R., 3
Norgaard, R. B., 186

O'Brien, R. D., 180
O'Neil, T., 16, 32, 38, 41
O'Neill, J., 105
Odum, E. P., 4, 6, 141, 262, 268
Odum, H. T., 5, 10, 117, 139, 266
Odum, W. E., 5, 33, 167, 275

Oliver, F. W., 31
Olkowski, W., 89
Olson, C. E., 48
Oney, J., 5, 100, 115
Ornes, W. H., 127, 135
Oviatt, C. A., 4, 5
Owen, M., 5, 15, 22, 25, 28, 31, 36

Palmisano, A. W., 5
Parsell, R. J., 22
Parsley, P. E., 59
Patrick, R., 133
Patrick, W. H., Jr., 194, 196, 203
Payonk, P. M., 120, 123, 127, 162
Pearson, R. L., 52, 53
Pechuman, L. L., 188, 189
Penfound, W. T., 3, 36, 41, 67, 74, 79
Penny, M. E., 51
Pequegnat, W. E., 8
Perkins, C. J., 37, 41
Persson, N. Y., 118, 123
Pfeiffer, W. J., 5, 52
Phleger, F. B., 3
Phillips, A. J., 56
Phillips, J. H., 264, 267
Pickral, J. C., 5
Plapp, F. W., 181, 184
Pope, R. M., 266
Porro, A. A. Jr., 242, 253, 255, 258, 259
Post, W., 4, 100
Pough, R. H., 7
Powers, S., 165, 168
Price, M. H., 77, 78, 101
Pride, C. R., 151, 156, 163
Prins, H. H. Th., 28
Prinslow, T. E., 113
Provost, M. W., 6, 76, 83, 92, 99, 103,
    186, 257, 274

Queen, W. H., 265, 274
Quirk, B. K., 49

Race, M. S., 176
Ragsdale, J. E., 51
Rajanna, B., 194, 200, 203
Ranwell, D. S., 1, 13, 17, 22, 23, 28, 29,
    31, 44, 45 202, 231 272, 275, 280
Reed, A., 5, 14, 61, 64
Reimold, R. J., 5, 24, 30, 36, 49, 50, 51,
    82, 140, 141, 148, 152, 154, 155, 159,
    163, 166, 168, 175, 258, 264, 267
Reinert, S. E., 100
Reppert, R. T., 5, 263, 266
Resh, V. H., 99, 100, 112
Retson, G. C., 65
Rhodes, D. G., 43
Richardson, S. E., 266
Rio, D. F., 182, 183

Ripper, W. E., 184
Ristich, S. S., 153, 155
Rockel, E. G., 97, 100
Roe, C. B., Jr., 251
Rogers, A. J., 89
Rogers, R. H., 52
Roman, C. T., 5, 43, 54, 69, 70, 130, 276
Rosenbaum, N., 279
Rouse, J. W., 54
Rouve, D., 59
Rowan, W., 31
Ruber, E., 83
Rudd, R. L., 178
Ruesink, W. G., 185
Ruotsala, A. A., 176
Russell, O., 49
Russell-Hunter, W. D., 3
Ryther, J. H., 134

Salley, A. S., 72
Salsbury, S. M., 240, 243, 248, 254
Sammons, J. L., 240
Sanders, J. E., 8
Sass, W. J., 123, 129, 133
Savage, W., 8, 75
Saveikis, D. E., 91, 104
Sax, J. L., 239, 245
Scarpace, F. L., 49
Schamberger, M. L., 266
Schell, J. A., 54
Schneidau, J. D., 67, 74, 79
Schneider, W. J., 50
Schoenbaum, T. J., 241, 253
Schoning, R. W., 274, 278
Schreiber, M. M., 52
Schubert, J., 52
Schulte, O. W., 48
Scott, R., 15, 16, 22, 34
Seal, W. P., 103
Seher, J. S., 50
Seidel, K., 136
Seneca, E. D., 148, 150, 152, 154, 155,
    165, 167, 168, 175
Shabman, L. A., 266
Shaler, 66
Shalowitz, A. L., 240, 254
Shanholtzer, G. F., 24
Shaw, S. P., 75
Shay, J. R., 48
Shearls, E. A., 193, 196, 214, 223, 225,
    231
Shima, L. J., 50, 52
Shinkle, M. P., 75, 101
Shisler, J. K., 68, 75, 76, 83, 91, 97, 100,
    103, 104, 111, 112, 114, 115
Shoemaker, W. E., 85, 88, 91, 94
Sigleo, W., 5, 263
Silberhorn, G. M., 42, 154, 165, 168, 257,
    276

Simmers, J. W., 43
Simon, A. W., 261
Simpson, R. L., 133
Sinclair, T. R., 52
Singh, P. B., 95
Skjei, S. S., 275
Slavin, P. T., 68, 75, 103, 193
Smalley, A. E., 4
Smart, R. M., 5, 54
Smedes, G. W., 5
Smith, A. D., 62, 64
Smith, D. H., 85, 92
Smith, H. K., 142
Smith, J. B., 5, 68, 86, 95, 98, 102, 178
Smith, J. H. G., 48
Smith, J. O., 240
Smith, T. J., III, 33
Smith, W. G., 120, 123, 127, 162
Smolen, T., 259
Sperling, J., 116
Springer, P. F., 68, 78, 84, 88, 89, 91, 94,
    101
Spurr, S. H., 48
Squiers, E. R., 193
Stakhiv, E., 5, 263
Stearns, F., 268, 270, 274, 278
Stearns, L. A., 16, 95, 98, 101, 106
Stebbings, R. E., 192, 202, 231
Steenis, J. H., 42, 86, 87
Steers, J. A., 2
Stegeman, J. J., 216, 220, 226
Steindorsson, S., 3, 15
Stephens, J., 129
Stevenson, J. C., 190
Steward, K. K., 127, 135
Stewart, N. E., 183
Stewart, R. E., 3, 97, 100, 115
Stewart, W. R., 50
Stiven, A. E., 5, 113
Stoehr, T., 100, 112
Stone, C. A., 173
Stone, J. H., 116, 120, 123, 127, 162
Stroud, L. M., 49
Sullivan, M. C., 50
Sullivan, M. J., 118, 121, 123, 133
Sutherland, D. J., 182

Talbot, 91, 112
Tatem, H. E., 229
Taylor, F., 129
Taylor, M. H., 5, 114
Teal, J. M., 4, 113, 117, 118, 123, 129,
    132, 133, 136, 220, 225, 227, 228,
    235
Teleky, L. S., 253, 258, 259
Tenore, K., 203, 211
Teskey, H. J., 189
Thomas, J. R., 52
Thomas, M., 212, 216, 220

Thompson, D. C., 51
Thompson, D. E., 49, 50
Thomson, A. D., 207
Tindall, E. E., 76, 84, 88, 92
Tiner, R. W., Jr., 51, 272
Tippie, V. K., 281
Travis, B. V., 96
Tripp, M. R., 180
Tucker, C. J., 52, 53, 54
Tueller, P. T., 50
Turner, R. E., 120, 123, 127, 162
Tyler, G., 118, 121, 125
Tyrawski, J., 42, 136

Urner, C. A., 96, 100
Usher, M. B., 275

Valiela, I., 113, 117, 118, 123, 129, 132,
    133, 136
Van Der Toorn, J., 43
Van Raalte, C. R., 226
Van Zoost, J. R., 75, 79
Vernberg, F. J., 190
Vernberg, W. B., 190
Vincent, M. K., 142, 149
Vogl, R. L., 40

Walker, R. A., 267, 274
Wall, W. J., Jr., 98, 189
Wallentinus, H. G., 29
Ward, D. V., 182
Warren, G. M., 7, 57, 62, 66, 83, 96
Warren, R. S., 2, 8, 70, 276
Webb, D. W., 189
Webb, J. W., 150, 153, 163, 168, 175
Webb, K. L., 207
Wehde, M. W., 53
Weidener, J. P., 255, 258
Weisberg, S. B., 113
Weller, M. W., 270, 274, 277

Wetzel, R., 165, 168
Whalen, R., 113
Whelan, T., III, 203, 204, 205, 209, 216,
    226
Whigham, D. F., 105, 133
White, D. J. B., 31
Whitman, W. R., 76
Whitney, D. E., 4
Whittendale, T., 47
Wicker, K. M., 51
Wiegand, C. L., 52
Wilder, N. G., 42, 86, 87
Wilkinson, R. N., 180
Williams, L. D., 134
Williams, R. E., 14, 16
Wilson, A. J., 182
Wilson, R. T., 50
Windom, H. L., 129, 167
Wobber, F. J., 49, 50, 258
Wolf, P. L., 24, 30, 36, 141
Woller, p. B., 147
Woodhouse, W. W., Jr., 121, 125, 135,
    144, 148, 150, 152, 155, 156, 161,
    167, 175
Woodwell, G. M., 4
Woolfenden, G. E., 4
Work, E. A., 52
Wright, H. A., 36
Wright, J. O., 7, 57, 95
Wynn, S. L., 49

Yapp, R. H., 17
Yarbrough, J. D., 222
Ydenberg, R. C., 28
Young, L. G. L., 221, 228

Zedler, J. B., 140
Zetka, E. F., 52
Zoltek, J., 121, 125, 129, 135

Scientific Name Index

Acnida cannabina, 73
Aedes cantator, 98
Aedes sollicitans, 88, 98, 106, 187
Aedes taeniorhynchus, 187
Agropyron pungens, 191
Agropyron repens, 84
Agrostis scabra, 85
Agrostis stolonifera, 16, 22, 25, 29, 196, 199
Alisma triviale, 85
Alnus serrulata, 154
Amaranthus canabinus, 46, 73, 87, 149, 154, 156
Ammospiza caudacuta, 4, 94
Ammospiza maritima, 4, 94
Anas acuta, 93
Anas americana, 92
Anas crecca carolinensis, 93
Anas discors, 93
Anas penelope, 22
Anas rubripes, 69, 93, 100
Anas strepera, 93
Anchoa, 92
Anchoa mitchilli, 4
Anopheles bradleyi, 88
Anser albifrons, 22, 27
Anthoxantum odoratum, 16
Arctium minus, 23
Armeria maritima, 191, 199
Artemisia maritima, 191
Arum masculatum, 23
Asclepsias incarnata, 97
Aster novi-belgii, 97
Aster subulatus, 96
Aster tripolium, 16, 24, 28, 191, 197
Atriplex hastata, 16, 18
Aythya, 93

Baccharis, 85, 110
Baccharis halimifolia, 3, 42, 74, 96
Bacillus thuringiensis, 188
Batrachium fluitans, 16
Beta vulgaris maritima, 24
Bidens, 86, 154
Bidens frondosa, 85
Bidens trichosperma, 97
Borrichia frutescens, 154, 159, 160, 162, 176
Botaurus lentiginosus, 100
Branta bernicla, 28
Branta canadensis, 32

Branta leucopsis, 28
Brevoortia, 92
Brevoortia tyrannus, 223

Calamagrostis canadensis, 84, 90
Calamagrostis neglecta, 15
Calidris alpina, 34
Callinectes sapidus, 180
Candida tropicalis, 209
Carex lasiocarpa, 85, 90
Carex Lyngbyei, 15
Carex nigra, 16
Carex otrubae, 24
Carex paleacea, 84
Catoptrophorus semipalmatus, 4, 100, 114
Cephalanthus occidentalis, 42
Chaoborus, 90
Chelydra serpentina, 91
Chen caerulescens, 16, 32
Chrysops, 98
Chrysops fuliginosus, 89, 132
Circus cyaneus, 93
Cladium jamaicense, 127, 135
Cladophora, 87
Cochlearia, 191
Cochlearia officinalis, 16
Coquillettidia perturbans, 88
Crassostrea virginica, 4, 132, 211, 216
Cryptococcus, 210
Culex, 90
Culex salinarius, 88, 98
Culex sollicitans, 95
Cyathura polita, 171, 173
Cyprinodon variegatus, 91, 113, 229
Cyrenoidea floridana, 3

Dendroica dominica, 94
Deschampsia caespitosa, 16
Distichlis, 94
Distichlis spicata, 16, 24, 30, 42, 70, 85, 99, 103, 111, 118, 123, 149, 154, 162, 176, 193, 208
Echinochloa, 38, 73
Echinochloa crusgalli, 86, 154
Echinochloa walteri, 86
Egretta thula, 4
Eleocharis, 38, 86
Eleocharis palustris, 87
Eleocharis quadrangulata, 73
Endomycopsis lipolytica, 209

Enhydrosoma woodini, 211
Enteromorpha, 28
Erechtites heiracifolia, 71
Erianthus, 86
Esox americanus, 91

Festuca, 8
Festuca rebra, 16, 22, 24, 25, 28, 85, 191, 196, 231
Fringilla coelebs, 34
Fulica americana, 100
Fundulus, 234
Fundulus diaphanus, 89, 91, 113
Fundulus grandis, 216, 225
Fundulus heteroclitus, 4, 89, 98, 103, 113, 167, 180, 223, 226
Fundulus luciae, 91, 113
Fundulus similis, 225, 229

Galium palustre, 84
Gallinago gallinago, 34
Gambusia affinis, 89, 112, 113
Gammarus, 90
Gammarus oceanicus, 212, 233
Geukensia, 234
Geukensia demissa, 3, 112, 132, 171, 175, 211, 215, 218, 223
Glaux maritima, 18, 191, 199

Halimione portulacoides, 16, 24, 54, 191, 197, 200, 232
Hibiscus, 121
Hibiscus moscheutos, 42, 84, 87, 96
Holcus lanatus, 23, 28
Hordeum secalinum, 24, 25, 27
Hydrobia minuta, 90

Ictalurus nebulosus, 91
Ilyanassa obsoleta, 211
Impatiens capensis, 46, 154
Iva, 85, 110
Iva frutescens, 3, 42, 71, 96, 154, 160, 162, 176

Juncus, 231
Juncus effusus, 85
Juncus gerardi, 25, 28, 70, 103, 118
Juncus maritimus, 191, 199, 232
Juncus roemerianus, 38, 97, 154, 159, 162, 176, 193, 196, 203, 208

Kluyveromyces drosophilarum, 210
Kosteletzkya virginica, 96

Lachnanthes caroliniana, 93
Laeonereis culveri, 169, 173
Larus argentatus, 114

Leersia oryzoides, 87, 154
Leisostomus xanthurus, 92
Lemna minor, 84, 85
Lepidactylus dytiscus, 171, 173
Lepomis gibbosus, 91, 113
Leptochloa fascicularis, 87
Limnodrilus, 173
Limonium, 111, 193
Limonium humile, 16, 24
Limonium vulgare, 16, 24
Littorina, 132
Littorina irrorata, 211, 216
Littorina littorea, 212
Littorina obtusata, 212, 233
Littorina saxatilis, 212, 233
Littorina vincta, 212, 233
Lolium perenne, 16, 25
Lucania parva, 91, 113

Malaclemys terrapin, 4, 5
Melampus, 98
Melampus bidentatus, 3, 112, 214
Menidia beryllina, 91, 229
Menidia menidia, 4
Mercenaria mercenaria, 132
Microtus pennsylvanicus, 90
Motacilla flava, 34
Mugil cephalus, 92
Mya arenaria, 212
Mysidopsis almyra, 229
Mytilus edulis, 212, 223, 233

Najas, 86
Nelumbo pentapetala, 42
Nereis succinea, 171, 173
Nitzschi gandersheimiensis, 133
Nitzschi perversa, 133
Notemigonus chrysoleucas, 91, 113
Nuphar advena, 42

Oenanthe lachenalii, 199, 232
Ondatra zibethica, 4, 16, 33

Palaemonetes, 216
Palaemonetes pugio, 167, 180, 229, 230
Panaeus aztecus, 229
Panicum, 121, 149, 156
Panicum amarulum, 154
Panicum dichotomiflorum, 87, 93
Panicum hemitomum, 40
Panicum virgatum, 42, 70, 84, 154
Paspalum lividum, 16
Paspalum vaginatum, 16
Peltandra virginica, 42, 46
Philomachus pugnax, 34
Phleum pratense, 84
Phragmites, 87, 110, 127

Phragmites australis, 8, 16, 22, 27, 29, 37, 42, 71, 74, 85, 167
Phytolacca americana, 85
Pichia ohmeri, 209, 210
Pichia saitoi, 210
Pichia spartinae, 209, 210
Plantago maritima, 24, 27, 191, 199, 231

Pluchea purpurascens, 42, 96, 106, 149
Podilymbus podiceps, 100
Polygonum hydropiperoides, 46
Polygonum natans, 84
Polygonum pennsylvanicum, 46
Polygonum punctatum, 93, 154
Polygonum sagittatum, 85
Pontederia, 165
Pontederia cordata, 121, 154
Populus deltoides, 154
Potamogeton, 86
Potamogeton berchtoldi, 83
Potamogeton bupleuroides, 42
Potamogeton pectinatus, 42, 83, 93
Potamogeton pusillus, 84
Potentilla palustris, 84
Puccinellia maritima, 15, 18, 23, 28, 75, 190, 196, 200
Puccinellia phryganodes, 15

Rallus limicola, 100
Rallus longirostris, 4, 69, 93, 100, 115
Rana catesbiana, 91
Ranunculus repens, 24
Rhithropanopeus harrisii, 221, 228
Rhizoclonium, 83
Rhodotorula, 210
Rubus ulmifolius, 23
Rumex orbiculatus, 85
Rumex verticillatus, 42
Ruppia maritima, 42, 75, 83, 93, 97, 111

Sagittaria, 73
Sagittaria falcata, 120, 127, 154
Sagittaria lancifolia, 121
Sagittaria latifolia, 84
Salicornia, 111, 191, 197, 199, 232
Salicornia pacifica, 156, 163
Salicornia stricta, 18, 61
Salicornia virginica, 30
Salix nigra, 154
Scirpus americanus, 16, 32, 84
Scirpus californicus, 32
Scirpus maritimus, 16, 18, 22, 28
Scirpus olneyi, 16, 32, 37, 73, 87, 97
Scirpus robustus, 16, 32, 37, 86, 93, 99
Scirpus validus, 73, 87, 120, 125

Senecio jacobaea, 23
Setaria faberii, 85
Setaria magna, 85
Solidago mexicana, 74
Solidago sempervirens, 71, 96
Sparganium eurycarpum, 85
Spartina alterniflora 3, 16, 24, 30, 49, 54, 69, 70, 75, 83, 87, 96, 99, 103, 107, 111, 114, 118, 122, 135, 147, 152, 155, 160, 163, 166, 176, 192, 196, 208, 231, 258
Spartina anglica, 15, 44, 60, 191, 199, 231
Spartina cynosuroides, 16, 32, 38, 40, 110, 154, 162, 176
Spartina foliosa, 149, 152, 156, 159, 163
Spartina patens, 3, 16, 24, 37, 68, 75, 83, 95, 99, 103, 111, 118, 120, 125, 127, 149, 153, 159, 162, 167, 176, 193, 208
Spartina pectinata, 84, 90
Spartina townsendii, 15, 60
Spergularia marginata, 18
Spergularia media, 191, 199
Spiraea latifloia, 85, 90
Sporobolomyces, 210
Sporobolus virginicus, 16
Suaeda maritima, 16, 24, 191, 197, 232

Tabanus nigrovittatus, 98, 132
Telematodytes palustris, 94
Thais lapillus, 212
Trichosporon, 210
Trifolium repens, 24
Troglochin maritima, 24, 27, 191, 199, 232
Tringa totanus, 34
Typha, 38, 70, 84, 87
Typha angustifolia, 153
Typha glauca, 84

Uca, 93
Uca pugnax, 211, 222
Uranotaenia sapphirina, 88
Utricularia vulgaris, 84

Vaccinium uliginosum, 16

Xanthium, 154

Zannichellia palustris, 85
Zizania aquatica, 73, 84, 87
Zizaniopsis miliacea, 86
Zostera marina, 28, 84

Subject Index

Abate, 180, 187
Aboiteau, 58
Acadians, 7, 14, 61
Accretion, 2, 60, 67, 75, 117, 164, 254
Adulticides, 179
Agriculture, 11
Algae, 28, 208
Ammonium chloride, 118
Amphipods, 132, 214
Anchovy, 4
Animal populations, 132
Annuals, 192
Arrow arum, 46
Arrowhead, 154
Aster, 16, 96, 191, 197
Avian fauna, 69

Bacteria, 188, 205, 207, 233
Bank, 59
Baytex, 180
Beggar-ticks, 86, 154
Benthic fauna, 175
Biodegradation, 210
Biological control, 101
Biomass, 29, 39, 43, 49, 52, 53, 97, 118,
    123, 133, 144, 155, 156, 160, 170,
    194, 205, 207, 211, 233
Biting flies, 5, 88, 115, 132, 186
Bittern, 100
Black duck, 69, 93, 100
Blind ditches, 105
Boundary question, 252
BTI, 188
Bullfrog, 91
Bullhead, 91
Bulrush, 16, 33, 37, 73, 84, 86, 87, 93, 99
Bunker C oil, 212, 230
Bunting, 70
Bur-marigold, 85
Bur-reed, 85
Burns, 36
    cover, 37
    deep peat, 37
    root, 37
    timing, 41
    wet, 37, 43

Cadmium, 129
Canals, 115
Carbon, 82, 111, 132, 205
Carex, 15, 84

Cattail, 38, 84, 154
Cattle, 16, 27, 35
Chaffinch, 34
Champagne pool, 79
Chemical control, 45
Civil law, 239
Clam, soft-shell, 212
Clipping, 133
Coastal Zone Management Act, 250,
    269, 280
Coliform count, 136
Common law, 239, 254
Commons, 238
Communities, 133
    faunal, 168
    microbial, 168
Conservation, 239, 262, 268
Construction, 8
Contaminents, 117
Control, 115
    biological, 101
    biting fly, 186
    chemical, 178
    mosquito, 68, 76, 78, 104, 181, 186,
        188
    permanent, 104, 187
Coot, 100
Crab
    blue, 180
    fiddler, 3, 76, 93, 98, 115, 131, 166,
        211, 221, 234
    mud, 221, 228
Crevey, 34
Crops, 68
Crude oil, 191, 193, 196, 206,
    209, 214
    susceptibility, 199
Cultural values, 263
Cutgrass, 86

Dalapon, 45
DDT, 178, 184, 186
Deer flies, 188
Degradation, 267
Delaware plan, 106
Destruction, 8, 261
Detoxification, 184
Detritus, 4, 36, 130, 134
Diamondback, 4
Diatoms, 24, 118, 133
Dikes, 57, 64

Disequilibrium, 276
Ditches, blind, 77
Ditching, 95
Diuron, 45
Diversity, 35, 211
Drawdown, 87, 90
Dredge material, 140, 142, 166
Dredging guidelines, 141
Duck food, 87, 92
Duck potato, 73, 84
Dunlin, 34
Dursban, 187

Eat-outs, 33
Ecosystem, 227
Ecotone, 3
Edge effect, 281
Egret, 4
Embankment, 56
Emulsifiers, 231
Enforcement, 279
Enrichment, 122
Erosion, 254

Federal Water Pollution Control Act
    (FWPCA), 250, 251
Feeding, mummichog, 114
Fenuron, 45
Fertilization, 161
Field studies, 12
Fire, 36
    effect, 38
    winter, 38
Fireweed, 71
Fish, 112, 223
    cyprinodontiform, 91
    estuarine, 91
    fresh water, 91
    mosquito eating, 77, 91
Flaedimyri, 15
Fleabane, 149
Flies
    deer, 98
    green head, 98
Flooding, 42, 43
Food chains, 226
Food production, 86
Foraminifera, 3
Gadwalls, 92
Game birds, 96
Geese, 16, 33
    barnacle, 28
    brent, 28
    Canada, 32, 41
    snow, 16, 32, 38, 41
    white-fronted, 22, 27
Glasswort, 30, 61, 191, 197
Glyphosate, 46

Godwit, 34
Golden shiner, 113
Goldenrod, 71, 74, 96
Governmental involvement, 280
Gradients, 2
Grass
    alkali, 8, 15, 22, 28, 75, 190, 200
    big cord, 32, 38, 40, 110
    cord, 5, 15, 24, 30, 32, 45, 49, 52, 60,
        71, 75, 83, 87, 96, 99, 103, 111, 115,
        118, 123, 135, 147, 149, 152, 155,
        160, 167, 192, 193, 208, 231, 258
    eel, 84, 87
    fox tail, 85, 86
    gama, 52
    maidencane, 40
    plume, 86, 93, 149, 154
    reed, 8, 16, 27, 37, 42, 46, 71, 74, 84,
        87, 110, 120, 127, 167
    salt, 30, 33, 85, 87, 94, 99, 103, 111,
        118, 123, 149, 155, 193, 208
    saw, 127, 135
    switch, 84
    wigeon, 42, 75, 83, 93, 97, 111
Grazing, 17, 22, 43
    intensity, 27
Grazing site, 14
Grebe, 100
Groundsel bush, 74

Habitat development, 142, 146
    cost, 150
    methodology, 147
Habitat Evaluation Procedures, 266
Hard clam, 132
Heavy metals, 129, 134
Hemicryptophytes, 23
Herbicides, 44
Heritage, 6
Herons, 100
Herring gulls, 114
High-tide line, 252
High-water mark, 255
Holistic perspective, 275
Horses, 17
Human consumption, 14
Human involvement, 6
Husbandry, 7, 11
Hydrocarbons, 205, 207, 211, 216, 222,
    225, 227, 233, 234

Impoundments, 56, 85, 91, 94
    age, 90
    effects, 78, 88
    high-level, 76, 79
    low-level, 76, 79, 85
    manipulation, 86
Incorporeal hereditament, 255

Insecticides, 178
Insects, 5
Invasion, 154
Invertebrates, 90
Invisible boundary, 256
Iron, 130
Isopod, 173

Jurisdictions, 253, 255
Jus privatum, 240
Jus publicum, 240
Just compensation, 244

Killifish, 216, 229, 234

Larvicides, 104, 179, 187
Law
    civil, 239
    common, 239
Lawsuits, 283
Lead, 129
Licenses, 284
Loading, 135

Macrofauna, 168, 170
Macroinvertebrates, 90
Malathion, 180
Mallows, 96
Mammals, 94
Management, 12, 36, 42, 47, 73, 76, 87,
    92, 239, 254, 262
    aims, 270
    government, 254
    "natural methods," 275
    needs, 277
    objectives, 270
    opinions, 272
    structures, 278
    tidal marsh, 262, 270
    water level, 275
    wildlife, 262
Management flooding, 42
Manganese, 131
Maps, 51
Maritime Marsh Rehabilitation Act
    (MMRA), 65
Mean high tide, 252
Meiofauna, 210, 211
Menhaden, 92, 166, 223
Mercury, 129
Milkweed, 97
Millet, 38, 73
Mining, 11
Mitigation, 176, 252, 285
Mosquito fish, 112
Mosquitoes, 5, 33, 76, 88, 94, 98, 101
    breeding, 103
    control, 77, 104

Mowing, 22
MSS bands, 51
Mulch, 104
Mullet, 92, 166
Mummichog, 4, 33, 98, 103, 113, 167,
    180, 223
Muskrat food, 87, 94
Muskrats, 4, 16, 33, 36, 94, 101
    management of, 87
Mussel
    blue, 223
    ribbed, 3, 112, 132, 175, 211, 215, 223,
        234

NAPP, 54
National Environmental Policy Act
    (NEPA), 250
Natural enemies, 184
Natural invasion, 144
Natural values, 6
Needle rush, 38, 39, 97, 103, 118, 191,
    203, 208, 231
Nitrate, 79
Nitrogen, 120, 127, 132, 135, 161, 208
No. 2 fuel oil, 193, 214, 218, 230
No. 6 fuel oil, 192
Nursery, 5, 97, 100
Nutrient removal, 117, 135
Nutrients, 4, 82, 83, 111, 118

Objectives, 83
Oil
    crude, 193, 196, 206, 210, 214
    weathered, 210
Oil pollution, 190
    chronic, 196, 200, 216, 221
    effects, 203, 220
    meiofaunal population, 203
    microbial population, 203
    mode of action, 201
Oil spills, 190, 202, 220, 230
    experimental, 200, 218
Oilings, 193, 197, 208, 218, 231
Oligochaete, 173
Open marsh water management
    (OMWM), 101, 112, 186
    concept, 102
    construction, 102
Ordinary high water mark, 256
Ordinary low-water mark, 253, 255
Organochlorides, 181
Organophosphates, 179, 187
Ownership
    private, 240, 242, 256
    public, 242
    state, 240
Oysters, 4, 132, 180, 211, 216, 218

Parathion, 180
Paris Green, 187
Pasture, 16, 68
Pathogens, 134
Perennials, 192
Periwinkle, 211, 216
Permit program, 249, 251, 282
Pest-control, 179
Pesticide
 ecological impact, 184
 non-selective, 184
Phosphorus, 82, 121, 133, 161
Photography, 48
 aerial, 49
Pickerel, 91
Pickerelweed, 154
Pintails, 93
Pioneer, 22
Pipit, 70
Pixels, 51
Plantain, 27, 85, 231
Police powers, 244, 248
Pollution, 12
Polychaetes, 169, 171, 214
Pond radials, 104
Pond vegetation, 42, 86
Ponding, 95
Ponds, 33
Pondweed, 84
Potholes, 76
Preservation, 262, 268
Preservation areas, 269
Primary functions, 263
Priorities, 263
Production, 121
 algal, 121
 cord grass, 122
 litter, 121
 macrophyte, 121
 rhizome, 125
 root, 123
Productivity, 4, 29, 38, 54, 111, 134, 141,
 158, 194, 276
Propagation, 147
 alternatives, 147
 maintenance, 150
 spacing, 152
 timing, 149
Property
 private, 253
 public, 253
Public awareness, 278
Public rights, 245, 246
Public trust, 239, 242
Puddling, 32
Pumpkinseed, 113
Purslane, 191, 197, 200
Pyrethrum, 187

Radiometers, 53
Rail
 Clapper, 4, 69, 93, 100, 115
 Virginia, 100
Reclaimed land, definition, 56
Reclamation, 11
 decline, 66, 73
 history, 59
 problems, 67
 process, 58
 requirement, 57
 reversion, 73, 75
 sluices, 72
 success, 58
 trunks, 72
 value, 63
Recreation, 12
Redroot, 93
Redshank, 34
Rehabilitation, 12
Remote sensing, 48
 satellite, 51
Resistance, 181
Rice culture, 72
Riparian landowner, 243
Riparian rights, 255
River and Harbor Act, 251
Role of public, 278
Rose mallow, 84

Salinity, 2, 144
Salt hay, 16, 24, 33, 37, 68, 83, 95, 99,
 103, 111, 118, 149, 153, 160, 167,
 208
 uses, 68
Sand flies, 89
Scaups, 93
Sea-blite, 191, 197
Sea lavender, 111, 193
Sea pink, 191
Seabanks, 61
Sedimentation, 60, 164
Selectivity, 25, 29
Sewage, 57, 118, 132, 136
Sheep, 17, 22, 25
Sheepshead minnow, 33, 113, 229, 230
Shrimp, 166, 180, 216, 229
Sill, 104
Silverside, 4, 229
Skylark, 70
Smartweed, 84, 93, 154
Snail
 mud, 211
 salt marsh, 3, 98, 112
Snipe, 34
Sociocultural values, 264
Soil maturity, 2
Soil types, 165

Sparrow
    seaside, 94
    sharp-tailed, 4, 94
    song, 4, 94
Spawning cycle, 114
Species, 3
    opportunistic, 169, 175
    palatable, 23
    rabbit-avoided, 23
    rabbit resistant, 23
    weed, 41
Species diversity, 233
Spectral reflectance, 52
Spider, 132
Spikerush, 38, 73, 87
Spills, 190, 202, 212
Spoil piles, 104
Spot, 92
State ownership, 240
Submerged lands, 241, 254
Sun angle, 51
Surfactants, 228, 234

Tabanid trap, 189
Tabanidae, 132, 188
Taking, 243
Tax assessment, 248
Tax incentives, 284
Taxa, 171
Teal, 93
Tearthumb, 46, 85
Terrapin, 4
Tidal
    flushing, 71, 83
    restrictions, 70
Tidal boundaries, 256, 259
Tidal marsh management, 239, 262, 270
Tidelands, 241, 254
Tides, 3
Tillering, 22
Tintamarre, 62, 75
Toxaphene, 166
Toxic effects, 228, 231
Toxic materials, 166

Toxicants, 178
Transplants, 147, 152, 156
Turtle, 91

Urban sites, 12
User fees, 285
Utilization, 269

Value determination, 264
Values, 263
    aesthetic, 265
    assessment, 266
    cultural, 263
    monetary, 268
    non-monetary, 268
    socio-cultural, 264
Vegetation boundary, 258
Vegetative cover, 199

Wagtail, 34, 70
Warblers, 34
Warpin, 67
Waste disposal, 12
Waste materials, 10
Waste water, 117, 134
Water hemp, 46, 73, 87, 149, 154
Water table, 95, 105
Waterfowl, 73, 76, 86, 93, 96
Waterfowl management, 92
Weathered oil, 201
Weirs, 76, 91
Wetland characteristics, 263
Wetland restoration, 140
Wetland values, 263, 267
Wigeon, 22, 25, 28, 92
Wild rice, 73, 84
Wildlife, 94, 142, 144
Wildlife management, 76, 262
Willet, 4, 100, 114

Yeast, 209

Zinc, 129
Zonation, 3, 25, 153